Change and Transformation

Change and Transformation

Essays in Anglican History

Edited by
THOMAS P. POWER

Foreword by
GEORGE R. SUMNER

☙PICKWICK *Publications* · Eugene, Oregon

CHANGE AND TRANSFORMATION
Essays in Anglican History

Copyright © 2013 Wipf and Stock Publishers. All rights reserved. Except for brief quotations in critical publications or reviews, no part of this book may be reproduced in any manner without prior written permission from the publisher. Write: Permissions. Wipf and Stock Publishers, 199 W. 8th Ave., Suite 3, Eugene, OR 97401.

Cover image from John Wycliffe sends forth his preachers (Stained Glass, Founders' Chapel, Wycliffe College, Toronto).

Pickwick Publications
An Imprint of Wipf and Stock Publishers
199 W. 8th Ave., Suite 3
Eugene, OR 97401

www.wipfandstock.com

ISBN 13: 978-1-62032-086-0

Cataloguing-in-Publication data:

Change and transformation : essays in Anglican history / edited by Thomas P. Power.

xviii + 268 p. ; 23 cm. Includes bibliographical references and index.

ISBN 13: 978-1-62032-086-0

1. Anglican Communion—History. 2. Anglican Communion—Doctrines. 3. Spirituality—Anglican Communion. I. Power, Thomas P. II. Sumner, George R.

BX5005 C34 2013

Manufactured in the USA

Contents

Contributors | vii
Foreword by George R. Sumner | ix
Preface | xi
Abbreviations | xii
Introduction | xiii

1 John Wyclif and Thomas Cranmer on Penance | 1
—Sean A. Otto

2 The King James Version, Dispersed Authority, and Anglican Identity | 24
—Alan L. Hayes

3 The Reformed Consensus on the Doctrine of the Eucharist: Daniel Brevint's *The Christian Sacrament and Sacrifice* (1673) | 48
—Eric R. Griffin

4 Reconciling the Old and New Testaments in the Eighteenth-Century Debate over Prophecy | 85
—David Ney

5 Spiritual Transformation in Sarah Trimmer's *Essay on Christian Education* | 113
—Heather E. Weir

6 "Of No Small Importance" Curricular Change in the School of Divinity, Trinity College Dublin, 1790–1850 | 140
—Thomas P. Power

7 The Waning of Protestantism in the Anglican Historical Imagination, 1874–1916 | 184
—Nathan Wolfe

8 Reforming Ecclesiastical Self-Government Within the Establishment: The Enabling Act, 1919 | 212
—Gary W. Graber

9 Anglicanism and the Search for Christian Concord | 246
—Ephraim Radner

Index | 267

Contributors

Gary W. Graber is acting Principal, James Settee College for Ministry, Prince Albert, SK, and is on the faculty of Thorneloe College School of Theology (Laurentian University), and an adjunct faculty, Wycliffe College. He is the author of *Ritual Legislation in the Victorian Church of England: Antecedents and Passage of the Public Worship Regulation Act, 1874* (1993).

Eric Griffin is honorary assistant, Christ's Church Cathedral, Hamilton ON, Canada. He has edited a new edition of Daniel Bevint's, *The Christian Sacrament and Sacrifice* from the first Oxford edition 1673 (2000), and published, "Daniel Brevint: French Preacher to the King in Exile," in *Anglican and Episcopal History* (2000).

Alan L. Hayes is Bishop Heber and Wilkinson Professor of Church History, Wycliffe College, and Director of the Toronto School of Theology. Among his publications are *Anglicans in Canada: Controversies and Identity in Historical Perspective* (2004), and *Church and Society in Documents, 100–600 AD* (1998). He has edited *By Grace Co-workers: Building the Anglican Diocese of Toronto, 1780–1989* (1989).

David Ney is currently a Th.D. candidate at Wycliffe College. His dissertation topic is Newtonianism and eighteenth-century biblical hermeneutics.

Sean A. Otto recently completed his dissertation on John Wyclif's Latin sermons. His most recent publications are "*Felix Culpa*: The Doctrine of Original Sin as Doctrine of Hope in Aquinas' *Summa Contra Gentiles*," *Heythrop Journal* 50:5 (2009); "The Authority of the Preacher in a Sermon of John Wyclif," *Mirator* 12 (2011); and "Predestination and the Two Cities: The Authority of Augustine and the Nature of the Church in Giles of Rome and John Wyclif," in *Authorities in the Middle Ages* (forthcoming).

Contributors

Thomas P. Power is theological librarian and instructor in church history, Wycliffe College. His recent publications include: *Guide for the Christian Perplexed* (ed.) (2012); *Forcibly without Her Consent: Abductions in Ireland, 1700–1850* (2010); *Converts and Conversion in Ireland, 1650–1850* (co-editor) (2005), and "Publishing and Sectarian Tension in South Munster in the 1760s," *Eighteenth-Century Ireland* 18 (2004). He is currently working on a new book titled, *Ministers and Mines: Religious Controversy in an Irish Mining Community, 1847–1858*.

Ephraim Radner is professor of Historical Theology, Wycliffe College. He has published: *Hope among the Fragments: The Broken Church and Its Engagement of Scripture* (2004), *The Fate of Communion: The Agony of Anglicanism and the Future of a Global Church* (2006), *Leviticus* (2008), and *Spirit and Nature: The Saint-Médard Miracles in 18th-century Jansenism* (2002). His book, *A Brutal Unity: The Spiritual Politics of the Christian Church* appeared in 2012.

George R. Sumner is Principal and Helliwell Professor of World Mission, Wycliffe College. He is the author of *Being Salt: A Theology of an Ordered Church* (2007), and *The First and the Last: The Claim of Jesus Christ and the Claims of Other Religious Traditions* (2004). He has co-edited and contributed to *In Spirit and in Truth: The Challenge of Discernment for Canadian Anglicans Today* (2009), and *Unwearied Praises: Exploring Christian Faith through Classic Hymns* (2004). His theological commentary on the *Book of Daniel* was recently published by Brazos Press.

Heather E. Weir has co-edited *Let Her Speak for Herself: Nineteenth-century Women Writing on the Women of Genesis* (2006), *Breaking Boundaries: Female Biblical Interpreters Who Challenged the Status Quo* (2010, 2013), and *Strangely Familiar: Protofeminist Interpretations of Patriarchal Biblical Texts* (2009). Most recently she is a contributor to *Handbook of Women Biblical Interpreters: A Historical and Biographical Guide* (2012). She is an instructor at Wycliffe College.

Nathan D. Wolfe defended his doctoral dissertation, *Mobilizing Historiography: The English High Church Historians, 1888–1906*, in 2010. A research grant from the Historical Society of the Episcopal Church, allowed him to do further archival research in England relating to Archbishops Benson and Davidson and their relationship to publishing companies. He is employed as an assistant archivist in the Wycliffe College Archives, and teaches sessionally at Lakehead University.

Foreword

I WANT TO COMMEND Tom Power's edited volume on change and transformation in Anglicanism. I am sure there is much of interest to be found here for historians, social scientists, and others related to the various questions addressed in the volume. But I come to the work as an Anglican cleric my whole adult life, a student of the vexed question of Anglican identity, a worried watcher of Anglican prospects for the future. I am told that the example loved by many a preacher that the Chinese ideogram for "crisis" may or may not mean the conjunction of danger and opportunity, but the wisdom of the idea remains. This volume has much to offer on such a question, and I want to say how.

We live in a time of confusion in the Communion, a time of projected demographic doom, or signs of life as young evangelicals continue to find the Canterbury way attractive. How does one bind all that into a theory about Anglicanism's prospects? Don't know. Is this dawn or dusk? I suspect both. Modernity has not been kind to Anglicanism, and yet some argue that the dispersedness and the fondness for symbol of postmodernism may be an opening for our tradition. Others argue that the great adaptation to the modern era has in fact been evangelicalism. My own prejudice is that Anglicanism is only coherent as a way to be an evangelical.

But grand theories of this or anything else in our tradition have passed their shelf-life. We are left with some tendencies at the grassroots. Christianity which, with its Reformation forebears, is insistently lay-oriented, which turns back earnestly to the catechetical task, which is solemn in its worship without undue romanticism, which seizes the moment's global opportunities, which finds the shape of its life in the Biblical story, which can move easily in its decentered location in society, which is nimble in how it thinks about leadership preparation—this form of the faith can flourish, and evangelical Anglicanism is a goodly heritage for it.

Foreword

This book offers no grand theory for this as "true" Anglicanism, nor a blueprint for its rise. It offers only hints, leadings, examples, precedents, warnings, and advice borne of occasions. To this we say "Amen." The way of discerning who we are, and where we are called to go, suits our time and it suits the occasional nature of our tradition as well. For all these reasons I commend these essays to many readers, but in particular to my Anglican brothers and sisters.

    Rev. Dr. Canon George Sumner
    Principal
    Wycliffe College

Preface

IN PART THIS COLLECTION of essays showcases the research interests of graduates, current faculty members, and current doctoral students in history and historical theology at Wycliffe College, which is part of the Toronto School of Theology, affiliated with the University of Toronto.

I would like to thank my fellow contributors for their individual essays. I would also like to acknowledge a grant in aid of publication from the Leonard Foundation and to Rob Henderson of the Development Office, Wycliffe College for his good offices in respect of the same.

Spelling, punctuation, capitalization, abbreviations of scriptural books and passages in quotations from original sources are unaltered.

Thomas P. Power
Wycliffe College

Abbreviations

ARCIC   Anglican Roman Catholic International Commission

BCP   *Book of Common Prayer*

DUC (E)   *Dublin University Commission: report . . .together with appendices, containing evidence, suggestions and correspondence.* HC 1852–3 (1637, 1017), xlv.

DUC (R)   *Dublin University Commission: report . . .* HC 1852 (1637, 1017), xiv.

DUM   *Dublin University Magazine*

HC   House of Commons

KJV   King James Version

LACT   Library of Anglo-Catholic Theology

n.p.   No place of publication

RCB   Representative Church Body Library, Dublin

STC   A. W. Pollard & G. R. Redgrave. *A short-title catalogue of books printed in England, Scotland, & Ireland and of English books printed abroad, 1475–1640.* London: Bibliographical Society, 1976–1991.

TCD   Trinity College Dublin

Introduction

THE INTEGRATIVE THEME OF this collection of essays is change and transformation explored in the context of its diverse expressions within the context of Anglican Church history from the medieval period to the twenty-first century. It addresses some central themes that have concerned Anglicans over the centuries, notably the sacraments, liturgy, biblical interpretation, theological education, the relationship of church and state, governance and authority, and Christian education.

First off, Sean Otto guides us in a comparative study of changing attitudes to penance in England as exemplified in the thought of John Wyclif and Thomas Cranmer. Normative penitential practice in late medieval England centered on contrition, confession, and satisfaction. These elements were influenced in their implementation by the practice of indulgences and through the exercise of papal authority.

Wyclif's position on penance changed from one where he affirmed the conventional view to one where he challenged both the papal position and indulgences. This change was dictated by his critique of abuses in the administration of the sacrament rather than over doctrinal considerations. In later life he stressed more the need for inward confession to God and rejected the necessity of confession to a priest. For Wyclif the priest should act as a guide in inducing contrition and confession but not as one who possessed spiritual power. This view was a departure from his earlier one whereby he held that the priest had the power to absolve sins.

Wyclif's rejection of the necessity of confession to anyone other than God coupled with his critique of abuses in penitential practice, were also prominent in Cranmer's thought. Both concurred that confession to a priest was an innovation and unnecessary, and the sacrament itself, while it had specific benefits, was not necessary for salvation. Cranmer's final position on penance was influenced by the Lutheran doctrine of justification especially that good works cannot precede justification but follow from the

Introduction

sinner being justified by faith alone. For Wyclif, rejection of penance was based less on predestination than on the incidence of abuses; whereas for Cranmer abuses were a doctrinal not a practical issue. Indulgences were rejected by both Wyclif and Cranmer. While some shift in his position is discernible, on the whole Wyclif was more medieval in his attitude to penance than sixteenth-century reformers maintained.

Cranmer, of course, was a key figure in the advancement of the Reformation in England. However, the process whereby the Reformation took hold in England was a long drawn-out one, and there has been little consensus among historians as to how it actually came to be embraced in the localities. In his contribution to this debate, Alan Hayes suggests the laicization of church authority at the spiritual level as a major contributing factor. With the sweeping away of the medieval sacramental system, the spiritual demotion of the priesthood occurred, resulting in the teaching authority of priests being dispersed among lay people. A second element in this process of laicization was that the English Bible was central to the Anglican ethos. Although the process whereby it occurred continues to be debated, the fact of putting the Bible in the hands of lay people meant that they could now decide on its meaning for themselves. This was a significant change and while it emanated in controversy regarding religious issues, the freedom to read and interpret the Bible for oneself became an essential feature and strength of Anglican identity.

Concurrently, the *Book of Common Prayer* had a basic purpose to make people familiar with the English Bible, because it integrated Scripture into its text. Under royal initiative, the goal of the translators who produced the King James Bible (KJV) was to strengthen the liturgy, and it powerfully shaped Anglicanism thereafter. In this regard, what made the publication of the KJV in 1611 significant was that Scripture and liturgical text became more fully fused together into a distinctive Anglican identity: the Book of Common Prayer and the KJV became mutually reinforcing authoritative and unifying texts.

An unappreciated area in which the *Book of Common Prayer* had a role was in Christian education. That role was well articulated by Sarah Trimmer (d. 1810) in her *An Essay on Christian Education* (1812). In it she details the content and methods appropriate for parents to adopt for the instruction and mentoring of their children at different stages so that spiritual growth was nurtured. Based on her own experience as the mother of a large family, Trimmer early on developed a passion for the education of her children and the conduct of Sunday schools. As a result her advice was sought by others, leading eventually to the development of curriculum resources.

Introduction

Heather E. Weir examines the educational vision outlined in the *Essay* centered round the baptismal rite in the *Book of Common Prayer* and the catechism of the Church of England. For Trimmer baptism was not only a means of grace but was foundational for Christian education. To inculcate the theology of baptism she provided a commentary on every aspect of the rite. This prescriptive and structured system of Christian education was based on the spiritual transformation resulting from baptism and nurtured thereafter by parents. Parenting, under the guidance of the Holy Spirit, Trimmer stressed, was an essential part of Christian education.

Anglican worship centered on the celebration of the eucharist. On the subject of the liturgy, Daniel Brevint's, *The Christian Sacrament and Sacrifice* (1673), is representative of the Calvinist sacramental consensus of the Church of England in the seventeenth century. While pointing to the theological uniformity found in eucharistic manuals of the period, Eric Griffin highlights how Brevint's work differentiates itself in the genre by its primary focus on the sacrament, rather than on the spiritual state of the recipient or the manner of communication. The theme of the book is that the eucharist is both sacrament and sacrifice, dual themes reflected in the division of the book. The first section treats of the sacrament as a memorial of Christ, as a sign of present grace, as a means of grace, and as a pledge of future glory. As sacrament, therefore, the eucharist unites together past, present, and future. The second section treats of the eucharist as commemorative sacrifice, and the sacrifice of our own persons, our goods and offerings. In this way the eucharist as sacrifice is seen in the peace offering, almsgiving, and in the commemoration. Overall, the work presents a consensus view being both Christocentric and biblical in its perspective of sacramentalism. Brevint's devotional work remained in print until the mid-nineteenth century, it influenced the eucharistic theology of the Wesleys (notably expressed in their hymns), and it was admired by Daniel Waterland in the eighteenth and by Pusey in the nineteenth.

The field of biblical interpretation, in particular the literal meaning of Scripture, became a preoccupation of scholars in the late seventeenth and early eighteenth centuries. The period witnessed the rise of Latitudinarian thinking, which affirmed reason and the primacy of the literal sense. The implication for biblical interpretation was a shift away from allegory towards the plain sense of Scripture. While allegory was marginalized, typology retained its position as a tool of interpretation even among the Latitudinarians but only in so far as it conformed to the plain sense of Scripture.

For the dual elements of external reality and authorial intention as considerations within the literal sense of Scripture, David Ney traces their origin back to William Whiston (d. 1752) and Edward Chandler (d. 1750)

Introduction

respectively. For Whiston, the interpretation of biblical prophecy should be in accord with the literal meaning. Eschewing typology, Whiston saw Old Testament prophecies as referring to Jesus, and this was a proof of the truth of Christianity. The most strident response to Whiston came with Anthony Collins' *Discourse* (1724), wherein he maintained that Old Testament prophecies were applicable only to their immediate contexts, and that the New Testament only contains the allegorical fulfillments of Old Testament prophecies. On this basis Collins argued that Jesus was not the Messiah, thereby undermining Christian revelation. The main respondent to Collins was Edward Chandler who in his *Defence of Christianity* (1725) emphasized Jewish anticipation of the Messiah as central, upheld prophecy, and on that basis justified New Testament applications of Old Testament texts. As a result Chandler came to be viewed in the eighteenth century as the defender of biblical prophecy, and influenced among others William Paley in his *Evidences of Christianity* (1794).

Indicative of the status of Paley's work is the fact that it was for long a standard text for those studying for holy orders in the Anglican Church. At the outset of the nineteenth century, formal theological education for Anglicans was centered on the universities of Oxford, Cambridge, and Dublin, and the Scottish universities to some extent. As matters stood, for those wishing to enter holy orders there was no more theological education available than what was obtained in their undergraduate studies. Thus the universities placed an important emphasis on the formation gained through the study of mathematics, moral and natural philosophy, and the ancient languages. In a case study of developments at Trinity College, Dublin, Thomas Power traces the transition from such a program to one dedicated to divinity studies.

In part the opportunity to implement radical change was induced in the early 1830s by the altered political and religious environment in Ireland that seemed to require a strengthening of the church from within. One expression of this was improving the quality and training of its clergy, something that already had its own internal rationale from an administrative perspective. In 1833 the period of study of divinity was extended, the course of study was expanded, and the means whereby it was conducted was changed. Henceforth aspirants to a career in the church had to commit to a program of studies in the arts (in which there was a strong biblical and catechetical content), two years in divinity, compulsory attendance, and pass a yearly examination. The academic standard was raised and the program of study proved to be more rigorous than what preceded it. In effect the changes represented a modernization of theological instruction and placed Trinity ahead of Oxford and Cambridge in terms of governance,

Introduction

curriculum revision, student requirements, and additional courses offered. Trinity graduates had an impact on the church locally and internationally, way out of proportion to the size of the Church of Ireland.

The internal and external forces inducing change in theological education had an impact on other areas of the church's intellectual life. In the late nineteenth century, high church historians turned to the study of general English history. Their goal was to prove the catholicity and continuity of the Church of England by minimizing doctrinal and ecclesiological change. William Stubbs, *Constitutional History of England* (1874), was the springboard upon which high church historians constructed this metanarrative of continuity. At the core of the continuity theory was a desire to minimize the changes wrought by the Reformation and to present it as the final assertion of Church of England independence against papal claims.

Although the continuity narrative was attacked by a variety of historians and polemicists, as Nathan Wolfe demonstrates it remained intact and was promoted with great success at a popular level. However, high church emphasis on the Church of England began to give way in the 1920s to a broader emphasis on Anglicanism. Contemporaneously, non-high church historians came to the fore in the profession, ending the position of precedence heretofore occupied by the likes of Stubbs.

The relationship between church and state, in part highlighted by the continuity theory debate, expressed itself more particularly in the role of parliament as guardian of the church. This meant that the church could not alter its doctrine, worship, or modes of operation without parliamentary approval. In a thorough treatment of the issue, Gary Graber shows how this changed with the passing of the Enabling Act (1919). The immediate need precipitating the legislation was in the late nineteenth century, when Anglo-Catholic ceremonial and liturgical innovations were proving difficult to regulate. The report of a royal commission in 1906 recommended greater flexibility in the law governing public worship, and as a result convocation (rather than parliament) was designated with the task of revising the rubrics for worship. The report was an important benchmark in establishing the general principle that the church should have more authority to govern its own affairs. Further modifications that allowed the church to regulate its own affairs within the parameters of the church and state status quo and without challenging the legal position of parliament, ensued. All this was a step towards increased self-government and efficiency of the church, which was formalized with the passage of the Enabling Act. The act gave the church a new measure of self-government (including the right to debate prayer book revision), and at the same time preserved the equilibrium of the church and state.

Introduction

Issues of governance have never been far from the concerns of the Anglican polity. While the Enabling Act freed the church to conduct its own affairs, the issue of what form of governance the church should embrace remained unresolved. Addressing the issue of ecclesial decision-making, Ephraim Radner focuses on conciliar engagement as a particular calling of Christians. Distinguishing between conciliarity (a form of ecclesial life ordered by church councils) and conciliarism (a late medieval movement that sought to bring the church to a conciliar model), he poses the question as to how the church's conciliar life should function. Central to the answer is the church's engagement with Scripture as a formative discipline that becomes transformative for the participants in conciliar contexts.

It is not that the conciliar approach is something new in Anglicanism for it has a long progeny. The reformers of the sixteenth century, Radner notes, accepted the model as long as councils were subject to the authority of Scripture. This position was continued with Richard Hooker, who in his *Ecclesiastical Laws*—with its focus on law and consent—favored retention of the conciliar ideal as the best means of dealing with controversial matters. However, conciliarism was in abeyance from the mid-eighteenth until the mid-nineteenth century. Its revival dates to the first Lambeth Conference in 1867, which was the first step to a larger conciliar self-understanding. With the emergence of newly independent churches in Africa in the mid-twentieth century, Anglicanism had the opportunity to achieve the conciliar ideal in its Communion, with its core principle of allowing Scripture to form the people of God. But the promise was never more than a hope and an ideal. The Lambeth Conference of 1998 showed how fragile the conciliar ideal was. More recently, the reception of the Anglican Covenant illustrates the incomplete acceptance of the conciliar vision among Anglicans globally, pointing to the continuing need for a revival of conciliarism.

This collection contains essays that illustrate aspects of change and transformation over the broad expanse of Anglican history. However, it is not its premise that change was normative or pervasive, perpetual or constant, within Anglicanism. Nevertheless it is my hope that these essays raise some new lines of inquiry, make some suggestive interpretations, or propose revision of accepted views.

1

John Wyclif and Thomas Cranmer on Penance

SEAN A. OTTO

THE MEDIEVAL SACRAMENT OF penance became a matter of controversy in the second half of the fourteenth century. John Wyclif (c. 1330–84), came to reject the understanding of confession and penance put forward by most of his contemporaries. Likewise, Thomas Cranmer, Archbishop of Canterbury in the early sixteenth century, came to reject the practices associated with penance advocated by those of his contemporaries still loyal to Roman theology. A number of arguments that the two men made were strikingly similar, as were their bases for rejecting contemporary practices. However, there were also a number of pointed differences in their understandings of penance. On balance, it seems that Wyclif was much more medieval than his Reformed admirers would have us believe, at least in the matter of penance.

PENANCE IN LATE MEDIEVAL ENGLAND

By the late Middle Ages, with the increasing division of the various disciplines into compartmentalized and competing faculties, along with the development of opposing schools of thought in the medieval universities, controversies over the proper understanding of penance became common. It is not the case that there was a wholesale consensus on the issue; rather, the variety of opinions and practice was more appreciated and less antagonistic. Gratian's *Decretum* and Peter Lombard's *Sentences*, the standard textbooks of canon law and theology, respectively, had given generations of students a broad sampling of the various authorities on the issues involved, but had not set out so much to define doctrine by reconciling these authorities as to master them and present them to new generations of scholars.[1]

Nevertheless, despite the variety of interpretations, there was consistency in key areas of the Church's understanding of penance. In particular, the three elements that made up penance, contrition of heart (*cordis contritio*), confession of the mouth (*oris confessio*) and work of satisfaction (*operis satisfactio*), were generally seen as the constitutive elements of the sacrament. However, there had never truly been a consensus regarding the exact role and function of these elements. All three were seen as necessary, but at different times and in different schools of thought emphasis was laid on one or the other. Changes occurred in four particular areas: penances became lighter and arbitrary, contrition came to take on a more important role, private confession became obligatory by church law, and the role of the priest became more defined and important.[2]

The lessening of penances and the move away from so-called tariff penances came about for several reasons, with the main one being that theorists argued that as the Church grew in numbers, discipline needed to be slackened in order to keep members from falling away.[3] If penances were too strict, the penitent, who might be truly sorry for their sins, might despair of ever being forgiven. For this reason, it was left up to the individual priest to decide the penance, rather than having the penance imposed according to a penitential.[4]

---

1. Joseph Goering, "The Scholastic Turn (1100–1500): Penitential Theology and Law in the Schools," in Abigail Firey, ed., *A New History of Penance*, Leiden, 2008, 219–37. See also William H. Campbell, "Theologies of Reconciliation in Thirteenth-Century England," in *Studies in Church History 40: Retribution, Repentance, and Reconciliation*, Woodbridge, UK, 2004, 84–94.

2. On these changes, there is a convenient summary in Thomas N. Tentler, *Sin and Confession on the Eve of the Reformation*, Princeton, 1977, 16–27. For a fuller discussion, see Bernhard Poschmann, *Penance and the Anointing of the Sick*, trans. Francis Courtenay, S.J., Montreal, 1964, 81–193.

3. Tentler, *Sin and Confession*, 12–19.

4. Ibid., 16–18. Penitentials were manuals for confessors, providing details on how to assign penances for different sins.

Contrition is the sorrow that a penitent feels for his or her sins. It can be distinguished from attrition, which is a lesser, imperfect sorrow over sin. As early as the tenth century theologians argued that contrition was the central element in penance, superior to satisfaction, which was seen as more important in earlier theologies of penance. Contrition's centrality to sacramental penance was secure by the thirteenth century, having been espoused by the likes of Peter Abelard and Hugh of St. Victor, although they disagreed about other aspects of the sacrament.[5] Most importantly, the centrality of contrition was affirmed by both Gratian and Peter Lombard, whose popular textbooks spread the teaching on the subject to the universities.[6]

Obligatory, once-a-year confession was made universal church law in the West at the Fourth Lateran Council of 1215 in the famous decree *Omnis utriusque sexus*.[7] This decree was not the first piece of legislation to require confession, but it, along with the other decrees of the council, did provide a framework for such an enterprise on a church-wide scale and it influenced other, local legislation, such as the pastoral syllabi of Robert Grosseteste of Lincoln and Archbishop Peckham of Canterbury.[8] These, in turn, led to large-scale educational efforts, since penitents and priests needed to understand their roles in this system of private confession.

Nonetheless, the priest's role in the sacrament of penance was difficult to define given the various practices that the Church had adopted.[9] There came to be three basic responses to this problem. The first arose out of Peter Lombard's exposition and suggested that the priest's role was to declare the sinner absolved after God had already removed the guilt of sin. This did not, however, remove the punishment of sin, which was thought to take place in purgatory, or to be reduced or eliminated through the work of satisfaction

---

5. Poschmann *Penance and the Anointing of the Sick*, 158–62. See also, Constant J. Mews, *Abelard and Heloise*, Oxford, 2005, 204–25, esp. 216–25, and Paul Rorem, *Hugh of Saint Victor*, Oxford, 2009, 109–10.

6. Tentler, *Sin and Confession*, 18–19; Poschmann, *Penance and the Anointing of the Sick*, 156–67, and Goering, "Scholastic Turn."

7. The decree is available, inter alia, in Norman P. Tanner, ed., *Decrees of the Ecumenical Councils*, 2 vols. London, 1990, i, 245.

8. Both of these pieces of legislation are available in F. M. Powicke and C. R. Cheney, eds., *Councils and Synods, with Other Documents Relating to the English Church*, Oxford, 1964, i, 265–78 and ii, 900–5. See Leonard E. Boyle, "Robert Grosseteste and the Pastoral Care," in *Medieval and Renaissance 8: Proceedings of the Southeastern Institute of Medieval and Renaissance Studies, Summer 1976*, edited by Dale B. J. Randall, Durham, NC, 1979, 3–51, reprinted as Item I in Leonard E. Boyle, *Pastoral Care, Clerical Education and Canon Law, 1200–1400*, London, 1981.

9. These questions were handled by both Gratian and Peter Lombard in a way that presented a variety of interpretations: Goering, "Scholastic Turn," 221–32.

enjoined by the priest in the sacrament of penance. This first option placed a heavy emphasis on contrition to the detriment of the priest's role in absolution. The second option was that argued by Thomas Aquinas, who taught that the words of the priest, "I absolve you," constituted the form of the sacrament: "Pronounced in the indicative mood, the absolution works to cause grace just as the words of the baptismal formula produce grace in connection with water. Only the absolution of the priest, St. Thomas argued, can apply the passion of Christ to the forgiveness of the guilt of sins."[10] The sacrament of penance, in this understanding, can change the imperfect sorrow of attrition into the perfect sorrow of contrition, and this sacrament becomes integrated into the means of justification.[11] This means that the sacrament works by the working of the work itself (*ex opere operato*) and not by the working of the one performing the sacrament (*ex opere operantis*) as would be the case if contrition were the formal element of the sacrament, and can be seen as a protection against pelagianism.

The third option went farther than that of Aquinas and made the priest even more central. This school of thought began with Duns Scotus, who taught that there were two ways to justification: through perfect contrition, which includes the intention to confess to a priest and is the exceptional route to justification, and through the sacrament of penance, which required only the imperfect sorrow of attrition, and is the easier and more common route. The absolution of the priest is central to this conception of penance, forming the essence of the sacrament.[12]

Indulgences were a common practice in the medieval church, a practice that is often misunderstood because of later controversy, associated with Luther.[13] The theology of indulgences followed on from the practice. The Church declared that certain actions were meritorious and relieved the negative effects of sin, sometimes the punishment (*poena*) due on account of sin and sometimes also the guilt (*culpa*) associated with sin. Indulgences were given not only for charitable donations, which many critics saw as the sale of forgiveness of sins, but for attending sermons,[14] for pilgrimages, for

---

10. Tentler, *Sin and Confession*, 24.
11. Poschmann, *Penance and the Anointing of the Sick*, 178.
12. Tentler, *Sin and Confession*, 26–27.
13. For what follows see Robert W. Shaffern, "The Theology of Indulgences," in R. N. Swanson, ed., *Promissory Notes on the Treasury of Merits: Indulgences in Late Medieval Europe*, Leiden, 2006, 11–36; R. N. Swanson, *Indulgences in Later Medieval England: Passports to Paradise?*, Cambridge, 2007, 8–22.
14. G. R. Owst, *Preaching in Medieval England: An Introduction to Sermon Manuscripts of the Period c.1350–1450*, New York, 1965, 101–10, 357–58.

saying prayers,[15] and sometimes for military enterprises like crusading, which were seen as another kind of pilgrimage.[16]

Various attempts were made to understand how indulgences worked theologically. Since the Church declared them efficacious, they must in some way be so, but it was not always clear how. The predominant understanding of indulgences involved the conception of a treasury of merit. This treasury was conceived as a store of the merit earned by Christ in the first instance, but also the saints and martyrs, especially the Blessed Virgin, in excess of their own spiritual needs. In other words, Christ and the saints did more than needed to secure their own salvation. Indeed, the sacrifice of Christ on the cross was thought to have earned enough merit to cover the sins of the whole of humanity throughout all time. The collective merit of Christ and his saints formed an inexhaustible store on which the Church Militant could draw and distribute for certain acts.[17] Important to this understanding of indulgences was that they worked on the basis of the power of the keys. That is, drawing on the power of the popes to forgive sins based on their Petrine office. Indulgences duly authorized by the popes, were efficacious through this jurisdictional power. Bishops likewise shared in this jurisdictional authority, but their power was derived from the pope's.[18]

Also important to the theology of indulgences was that they were only considered efficacious if the penitent seeking them had properly undergone confession, which would include proper contrition. Nothing in the medieval understanding of indulgences indicated that they were somehow a replacement for the sacrament of penance.[19] Thus, under this understanding, an indulgence would only be efficacious if three conditions were met. The first was the basis for all indulgences, that the merits of Christ and his saints might be distributed to the members of the Church Militant or those members of the Church in purgatory. Secondly, the proper authority of the Church distributed this merit, without which an indulgence could not be effective. Thirdly, it was necessary that penitents properly confess their sins and participate in sacramental penance for the indulgence to have any effect. This understanding of indulgences was rejected by both Wyclif and Cranmer.

15. R. N. Swanson, "Praying for Pardon: Devotional Indulgences in Late Medieval England," in Swanson, *Promissory Notes*, 215–40.

16. On these and the immense variety of indulgences, see Swanson, *Indulgences*, 23–76.

17. Shaffern, "Theology of Indulgences," 19–28.

18. Shaffern, 28–36. See also Joseph Goering, "The Internal Forum and the Literature of Penance," *Traditio* 59 (2004) 175–227, esp. 178–79.

19. Shaffern, "Theology of Indulgences," 14–19.

JOHN WYCLIF ON PENANCE: THE EARLY PHASE

Wyclif's teaching on penance changed over his career. Initially he was content to teach the conventional division of penance into contrition, confession, and satisfaction, and to state that auricular confession could be useful. From at least 1380 he made a point of denouncing Pope Innocent III, the famous decree *Omnis utriusque sexus* of the Fourth Lateran Council, the friars who often acted as confessors, and indulgences. Wyclif's concern regarding the contemporary understanding of confession and penance centered on the problem of corruption in the practice of the sacrament, rather than theoretical issues.[20] The development of Wyclif's position can be gauged from his early sermons, culminating in his later works where a mature view is evident.

In the first sermon, dating to 1376, Wyclif is very conventional in his teaching on penance.[21] Using medical terminology, he enumerates three things necessary for healing: first, the cause of the sickness must be removed; second, bandages must be applied; and third, a healthy regimen must be followed.[22] He equates sin with disease and penance with the cure: "Whence, since the cause of all spiritual sickness is sin, I may have said to your fraternity, therefore, how the sacrament of penance will purge you of sin."[23] Following this, Wyclif gives the traditional division of penance into contrition of heart, confession of mouth, and work of satisfaction, "because one has sinned against God in these three ways," a reference to sin in thought, word, and deed, which forms a neat parallel between sin's nature and removal.[24] This in turn leads Wyclif to a general exhortation to penitence, a suitable exhortation for the penitential season of Lent:

> Let us consider therefore the goodwill of our God in creation, in bestowal of goods and gracious preservation, [from] how many and more dangers, from fire, water, theft, sickness and other events that have occurred from all of which God has graciously preserved us. And then, attending to our ingratitude and contempt for our God, let us deservedly burst forth in tears of

---

20. Stephen Penn, "Wyclif and the Sacraments," in Ian Christopher Levy, editor, *A Companion to John Wyclif: Late Medieval Theologian*, Leiden, 2006, 283–89.

21. John Wyclif, *Sermones*, edited by Johann Loserth, 4 vols., London, 1896, iv, 35, 296–304.

22. *Sermones* iv, 35, 299/21–6.

23. Ibid., 299/27–30.

24. Ibid., 299/31–33.

sorrow, avoiding the chasm of sin and detesting the horrors of vice, humbly asking the immense clemancy and mercy of our God.[25]

A further point that Wyclif wishes to emphasize is the ability of priests, as successors to the apostles, to forgive sins, which he associates with the power of binding and loosing.[26] In the rest of the sermon, he turns from the theoretical to the practical, bringing forward and solving three problems which keep people from confessing their sins: shame, fear of the penance to be imposed, and excessive hope, presumption, or despair. Three answers to each of these are given, but the most space is devoted to answering the problems of excessive hope, presumption and despair.[27] Wyclif is insistent "that God redeems no one to the kingdom unless he truly repents after sin."[28] Repenting in the context of this sermon means the sacrament of penance: contrition of heart, confession of mouth, and work of satisfaction. In fact, the last thirty-five lines of the sermon deal with the particulars of auricular confession and the need for works of satisfaction.[29] Once again Wyclif uses the analogy of medicine: "as the sick in body tells the doctor with great diligence the circumstances of their head cold; how much more ought the sick in spirit, where the danger is more serious?"[30] At this stage in the development of his thought on the matter, Wyclif thinks that the work of satisfaction is necessary "because without that, confession with a harp is not complete."[31] However, Wyclif's teaching on confession was to change significantly thereafter.

Wyclif's second early sermon, dated to February 15, 1377, does not contain nearly as extensive a discussion of penance as the previous sermon, but still speaks of it in traditional terms. Here the focus is on the religion of Christ, of which penance forms an important part. It was not that Christ needed to do penance, but that "it would be just that the humility of the redeemer correspond to the pride of the men to be redeemed."[32] The reason

---

25. Ibid., 300/5–10.
26. Ibid., 300/31–301/3.
27. Ibid., 301/9–303/32.
28. Ibid., 302/20–1.
29. Ibid., 303/33–304/27.
30. Ibid., 303/35–8.
31. Ibid., 304/18. This is an allusion to a recurring theme of the Psalter, confession, usually translated as praise in the Douay-Rheims, with or on the harp: see Pss 32:2; 42:4; 70:22; and 146:7.
32. *Sermones* iv, 33, 284/27–8.

that Christ went into the desert to fast was, much like the reason he was baptized by John, not because he needed to for his own sake, but for ours:

> Since, however, every action of Christ is our instruction, it appears how by this we are taught about the time when, having been washed with a baptism of flame, our penance and every work of our merit is perfected, since he who cannot sin teaches us that by doing penance after his baptism.[33]

Wyclif stresses the need for Christians to confess, humbly and obediently, and to do penance.[34] For each of the three kinds of sin, the three enemies of man, the devil, the world, and the flesh, a different type of penance, prayer, alms, and fasting, is given.[35] The priests of the church are given the power of the keys in order to heal the spiritually infirm. Three things are needed for this healing: to feel the pain of the sickness, to reveal the sickness and its accidents to a spiritual doctor, and to complete the imposed diet or regimen.[36] So also are there three ways in which people can be led by the hand to believe this article of faith: first that it is rational to lighten a load, especially if taking a long journey, and, since sin is a most heavy weight, who would not want it lightened? Second, the wounds caused by arrows fester and sicken the whole body, and, since sins are arrows damaging the soul, these wounds ought to be healed before they endanger the soul. Third, in the same way that the root cause of a sickness must be purged from the body before medicines can do any good, so it is with sin, which is driven out by prayer, spiritual works of mercy, and alms.[37] The final note on penitence in this sermon is that there are three reasons for a forty day fast: in imitation of Christ and as a tithe of our life;[38] in recollection of the Israelite wanderings in the desert;[39] and because of the mystical implications of the number forty.[40] Taken together, these two early sermons demonstrate quite clearly that Wyclif's initial teaching on confession and penance was traditional and inoffensive.

There was an intimate connection between the sacraments of penance and eucharist in the Middle Ages, and Wyclif maintained this connection as

---

33. Ibid., 284/34–285/3.
34. Ibid., 285/12–25.
35. Ibid., 285/27–32.
36. Ibid., 286/11–21.
37. Ibid., 286/21–287/20.
38. Ibid., 289/22–31.
39. Ibid., 289/32–38.
40. Ibid., 290/1–14.

well. His most extensive treatment of penance is in a work entitled *De eucharistia et poenitentia sive de confessione*.[41] In a third sermon, Wyclif explicitly states the need for a communicant to purge him or herself of sin before receiving the Eucharist, although he does not expressly state that this need be done by confessing to a priest.[42] He develops the point in two digressions from the main theme of the sermon. The first of these digressions is a short discussion on the necessity of peace. This follows on from the necessity of loving all, and from the Church's practice of the priest giving peace before communion. Three types of peace are mentioned: between God and man, man and man, and man and himself. The latter two are dependent on the first, and the first is only lost through sin, so the communicant must be sure to purge him or herself of sin before receiving the Eucharist.[43] This purgation is elaborated in another digression following an explanation of justice. Here Wyclif tells his audience that "we, therefore [on account of love of justice], for the debt of sin, ought to give back to God contrition and the prevention of recidivism."[44] The emphasis is laid on contrition as a necessary component of forgiveness, "for without contrition, God does not remit [sin] and since he does not remit, the absolution of the priest does not work. And therefore first of all, the sinner is required to make satisfaction for himself by contrition."[45]

This emphasis on contrition is important to Wyclif's later teaching on penance. In the *Trialogus* (1382), for example, Wyclif discusses the difficulties inherent in the definition of the sacrament.[46] The three components of contrition, confession, and satisfaction taken together as the sacrament had been the traditional definition of penance for some time, but Wyclif suggests that these cannot form a single entity, because they are distinct types (*genera*). Rather, Wyclif claims that these are the accidents and the substance of the sacrament is an internal act of confession to God.[47] This is not so far removed from the understanding of penance as espoused by Thomists and Scotists, who likewise placed the emphasis of the sacrament's efficacy on contrition. Wyclif has taken this position much further, making contrition and inward confession to God the only necessary element

---

41. *De eucharistia et poenitentia sive de confessione* in *De Eucharistia*, edited by Johann Loserth, London, 1892, 328–43.

42. *Sermones*, iv, 42.

43. Ibid., 345/19–346/3, esp. 345/35–37.

44. Ibid., 346/36–347/2.

45. Ibid., 347/4–7.

46. John Wyclif, *Trialogus*, edited by Gotthard Lechler, Oxford, 1869, 326–30.

47. Penn, "Wyclif and the Sacraments," 284. See *Trialogus*, 326.

of penance, whereas Thomistic and Scotistic teaching, as we have seen, still made the priest's role vitally important to the sacrament.

JOHN WYCLIF ON PENANCE: THE LATE PHASE

In the last years of his life, Wyclif's complaints about contemporary penitential practices became frequent and repetitious: Innocent III instituted an unlawful obligation on the laity by compelling them to confess to a priest once a year; the friars are guilty of using the penitential system for their own financial and lascivious gain; indulgences are dangerous fictions foisted upon the laity by corrupt ecclesiastics and reek of simony. Often, these complaints are accompanied by others about the Eucharist or about Robert of Geneva, the Avignonese Pope, whose election precipitated the Great Western Schism.

Rejection of Pope Innocent's Decree

Wyclif rejects Innocent III's decree *Omnis utriusque sexus* on two main grounds.[48] First, while it is necessary for a sinner to repent with a contrite heart in order to be forgiven, this does not include of necessity confession to a priest.[49] Second, Wyclif questions the authority of the pope to introduce obligatory confession; the Church should found its practices in scripture, and there is no scriptural warrant for Innocent's innovation.[50] As to the first of these reasons, we have noted that Wyclif places the emphasis in penance on inward confession to God, but he wants to go farther than that to reject the necessity of confession to anyone else at all. He makes a distinction between these two types of confession: one to God, and the other "by the institution of Innocent III made to individual priests."[51] The first of these is "more worthy, more established, and more necessary than the second, because scripture speaks generally about the first confession and penance and on no occasion about the second. Therefore it seems to many, since the Church fought better for a thousand years and more without this second, that it would still fight better without it."[52] Secondly, while Wyclif does not

---

48. Penn, "Wyclif and the Sacraments," 285–6.
49. *De eucharistia et poenitentia*, 322–23.
50. Ibid., 334. Compare this to *Trialogus*, 327 and *Sermones* iii, 9, 67–9 and iv, 6, 49–57.
51. *Sermones* iv, 6, 56/10–3. See also *Sermones* iii, 9, 67–9.
52. *Sermones* iv, 6, 56/13–8.

make it clear who these "many" are, he does emphasize the necessity for a scriptural foundation for church practice. Wyclif argues that the Church should not be weighed down with new rites and sacraments that are not founded in the law of the Lord, and that papal laws will destroy the freedom of the Church and weigh it down with more ceremonies than were present in the Old Testament. It is on these grounds that the introduction of *Omnis utriusque sexus* is suspect.[53]

In all of this there is some ambiguity concerning the role of the priest, for if confession to a priest is not necessary, then it would seem that they have no part in the sacrament. Wyclif does not want, however, to deny the priest a role in penance. While he says, for instance, that confession to God is sufficient for the removal of sin and confession to a priest without confession to God is useless, at the same time, "since error is often useful by accident, and specifically contrition and confession, I therefore suppose that such confession might be useful for *viators*."[54] If the priest elicits the proper contrition and confession to God from the penitent, then he has done something useful and good.[55] Still, Wyclif denies that the priest as confessor has any spiritual power since the power of forgiveness of sins lies with God alone, although the priest, or some other guide, might lead the repentant sinner to this forgiveness.[56]

The priest's role becomes even more ambiguous in light of Wyclif's doctrine of predestination, which has a role to play in his understanding of the forgiveness of sins. Central to his formulation of the relationship between predestination and penance is his interpretation of the power of the keys. For Wyclif, the keys are the power of knowledge and teaching. Binding and loosing are the basis for priestly absolution and are powers held by God alone, since they are his simply, and so the gospel says that "'what is bound on earth will be bound in heaven,' but does not say that it is bound in heaven after and not before."[57] Moreover, the power to bind and loose does not effect someone's eternally foreknown status. If one were to proclaim a

---

53. Ibid., 56/19–26.

54. The term *viator* was used in the Middle Ages to describe the paradoxical situation of living in a world created by God, but in which humanity is separated from God by Adam's sin. The basic idea was that each human being is a traveler (*viator*), making his or her way through this life towards God. See Michael W. Twomey, "Homo Viator," in *Encyclopedia of Medieval Pilgrimage*, edited by Larissa J. Taylor et al., Leiden, 2010, 265–67; Gerhart B. Ladner, "*Homo Viator*: Medieval Ideas on Alienation and Order," *Speculum* 42. 2 (1967) 233–59.

55. *Sermones* iv, 6, 56/34–57/10.

56. Penn, "Wyclif and the Sacraments," 286–88. See *De eucharistia et poenitentia*, 334–38.

57. *Sermones* ii, 9, 62/3–63/9 and 62/36–63/2.

prescitus, that is, someone foreknown to damnation, loosed from his sins by the power of the keys, "he does not have those keys from God."[58] All of this is a move away from his earlier teaching on the power of the keys, which taught that priests had the power to absolve from sin. By the last years of his life, however, Wyclif taught that "a priest's role was purely declarative at best; at worst, when the priest's decision was at odds with the knowledge of God, it was of no force and was a misleading and blasphemous arrogation of divine power."[59]

Prelates and Friars as Confessors

The conduct of prelates and friars in their capacity as confessors is the target of Wyclif's contempt in numerous places. Wyclif repeatedly emphasizes that God alone can truly know what is in someone's heart, how much they sin, and whether or not they are truly contrite, and thus confessors can neither assign proper penance nor absolve from sin. Moreover, they often say that they can so absolve, simply to reap the material benefits of such lies.[60] Two more particular complaints are that the friars use French in confession, and thus demonstrate their allegiance to the group Wyclif refers to as Robertines, that is, those who support Robert of Geneva as pope,[61] and that it smacks of blasphemy to confess to a friar.[62] These complaints fit into a wider anti-mendicancy that is rampant in Wyclif's later works.[63]

Indulgences

Wyclif's teaching on indulgences, likewise, became harsher in the last years of his life, and his preaching from this later period is especially rich in

---

58. Ibid., 62/17–20.

59. Anne Hudson, *The Premature Reformation: Wycliffite Texts and Lollard History*, Oxford, 1988, 294.

60. *Sermones* i, 42, 283/1–8; i, 46, 309/14–23; ii, 18, 136/5–9, 138/24–7; iii, 4, 27/9–28/8; iii, 9, 66/30–67/9; iii, 16, 128/5–8; iii, 23, 182/26–41; iii, 32, 260/31–261/15; iv, 12, 103/8–22; iv, 17, 145/19–146/10.

61. *Sermones*, iii, 28, 222/22–31.

62. *Sermones*, iii, 42, 358/16–20, where the point arises in a discussion of the illegitimacy of letters of fraternity. The point being that only God can distribute merit, ibid., 358/20–359/33, cf *Sermones* ii, 18, 139/21–27, where Wyclif calls blasphemous the teaching that entering a fraternity absolves from sin.

63. Penn R. Szittya, *The Antifraternal Tradition in Medieval Literature*, New Haven, 1986, 152–82.

condemnations of the practices surrounding indulgences.[64] In one sermon, for instance, Wyclif accuses prelates of selling indulgences: "prelates often say, in effect, that if you wish to give me much money, I will absolve you from much sin, by giving the desired indulgence."[65] This is straightforward simony, because forgiveness cannot be sold, but only given by God. Indulgences like these are innovations in the Church brought in to supplement the religion of Christ.[66] Elsewhere, indulgences are said to be dangerous because they can induce pride: "for thus certain people exalt themselves because they have above twenty thousand years of indulgences, and since they are certain that the day of judgement will not tarry so long and again they are certain that they will not be punished for sin in purgatory after the day of judgement, they seem to be certain that they will not be punished after death on account of sin."[67] Indulgences are also dangerous for those granting them as it is blasphemous for anyone to believe that they grant these pretended indulgences, since neither they nor God can grant them.[68] Moreover, the pope certainly does not absolve from pain as some would believe, since all—this is especially true of crusaders and their indulgences—still incur the pain of death.[69] The treasury of merit is likewise a lie: "the most subtle trick invented by his [the devil's] especial disciples the friars, rests in the deceitful fiction of the infinite treasury of the supererogatory merit of the Church Triumphant which God places in the distributive power of whatever caesarian pope."[70] This fiction is based on heretical interpretations of Scripture, which would lead one to believe that Peter and his successors alone have the power of binding and loosing. Wyclif contrasts these heretical interpretations with his own, which demonstrates that only in so much as prelates and popes follow Christ, who is the exemplar for all Christians, can they be followed and believed.[71]

64. On Wyclif and indulgences, see Anne Hudson, "Dangerous Fictions: Indulgences in the Thought of Wyclif and his Followers," in Swanson, *Promissory Notes*, Leiden, 2006, 197–214; Swanson, *Indulgences*, 294–315. Wyclif discusses indulgences in milder tones in *De ecclesia*, chapter 23, and in harsher tones in *Trialogus*, 432.

65. *Sermones*, ii,18, 139/28–30.

66. Ibid., 139/36–38.

67. *Sermones*, ii, 34, 250/4–11.

68. Ibid., 252/18–21.

69. *Sermones*, iv, 15, 122/33–123/4. Such sentiments, occassioned by Bishop Despenser's Crusade to Flanders, are echoed elsewhere in this series of sermons, see iv, 4–5, 13–15, 39/3–26, 110/36–112/35, 117/24–121/40. On these, see Hudson, "Dangerous Fictions," 202–203.

70. *Sermones*, iv, 20, 174/28–32.

71. The disputed passages are the *loci classici* concerning the power of the keys: Matt 16:18–19; 18:18; and John 22:21–23. Wyclif counters that these passages must be

Change and Transformation

Teachings on indulgences exist in Wyclif's other works, which attack the theology of indulgence more than the practice. In *De ecclesia* (1378/9), he gives a cumbersome definition of indulgences: "all indulgence is the act of the indulger, so that there would be no indulgence without having the power to indulge; and to indulge is freely to concede, to give effect, or to remit ... as it is with the consigning to oblivion of things committed with regard to the performance of vengeance."[72] For Wyclif this definition means that only God can grant indulgences for sin since, according to the scriptures, only God can do this. Wyclif believed that the canonists, however, had given indulgence another sense, that is, indulgence as the remission of the penalty of sin (*poena*), and so they had distorted the clear sense of scripture.[73] Especially under attack in the *De ecclesia* is the treasury of merits. He sets out in good scholastic fashion to describe both sides of the argument, first setting out evidence supporting the treasury; that God in his absolute power can commit to his vicar the power to remit sin, that the Petrine commission empowers Peter and his successors to bind and loose, and following from this commission, the pope had declared indulgences legal.[74] Wyclif attacks these positions, arguing that the sale of pardon is blasphemy, that God cannot remit sin without satisfaction, nor grant His vicar the power to remit sins.[75] This does not mean that Wyclif rejects the concept of a treasury of merit. He simply rejects the papal understanding; there is a treasury of merit, but as the merits of Christ and the saints are in the past, they are beyond our power, so the treasury is opened and closed by God alone, and is not in the power of the pope.[76] As summarized by Swanson, Wyclif's own opinion in the *De ecclesia* is negative:

> No one can receive indulgence unless deemed worthy or disposed thereto by divine grace; therefore only God actually grants indulgence. God alone determines the amount of pardon, according to the worthiness of the recipient ... Clerics (including the pope) have no power to grant indulgences for specific time periods, unless by divine revelation; and the papal power to indulge is not founded in scripture ... For Wyclif, ultimately, there is only sin, punishment, and divine mercy. Those in

understood in light of 1 Cor 11:1: "Be ye followers of me, as I also am of Christ." See *Sermones*, iv, 20, 174–6, esp. 175/24–26.

72. *De ecclesia*, edited by J. Loserth, London, 1886, 549/6–12, quoted and translated by Swanson, *Indulgences*, 297.

73. Ibid., 549/12–550/3.

74. Ibid., 556–57; see Swanson, *Indulgences*, 298.

75. Ibid., 561; Swanson, *Indulgences*, 298.

76. Ibid., 564–66; Swanson, *Indulgences*, 298–99.

Purgatory must rely on grace, but will eventually win through to beatitude.[77]

The main point behind all of these attacks on the practice of penance was that, for Wyclif, there was no foundation for such practice in the Bible, which is the only sure guide in doubtful matters such as indulgences.[78] This can be seen in his interpretation of the treasury of merit and the passages from Matthew and John, but one last example will clearly demonstrate the problem. Wyclif identifies Luke 17:11–19 as the basis for the contemporary practice of penance. This is the story of ten lepers who are healed by Christ and told to present themselves to the priests at the temple. While Wyclif interprets the lepers allegorically as sinners seeking forgiveness of their sins, he rejects the use of this passage to support the practice of confession to a priest.[79] There are three reasons that he gives for rejecting this interpretation: first, the priests to whom Christ sent the cleansed lepers were priests of the old law; second, the legalities under the old law are not taken over into the new; and third, the lepers did not fulfill the commandment of Christ, since he would have cleansed them while they were walking if he wanted to do away with the legalities.[80] Moreover, only the one leper, the Samaritan, is truly an example of proper confession, since he turned back, glorified God, and fell humbly at the feet of Christ. Importantly, the Samaritan did not make private confession, but was properly contrite.[81]

Wyclif, therefore, moved from a traditional position on penance to a more radical position that did away entirely with the necessity of confession to anyone other than God. He also rejected completely the granting of indulgences, which he saw as dangerous and predatory. The changes in Wyclif's understanding of penance came about as a result of two factors: his interpretation of scripture, and his intolerance for the abuses that he saw in contemporary penitential practices. Both came to figure prominently in the position Thomas Cranmer adopted on penance.

THOMAS CRANMER AND PENANCE

Cranmer, like Wyclif, altered his position on penance over time. In his earlier days at Cambridge, he was exposed to the Scotistic teachings, with an

---

77. Swanson, *Indulgences*, 300.
78. *De ecclesia*, 563/2–14.
79. *Sermones*, i, 42, 304–306.
80. Ibid., 306/15–25.
81. Ibid., 306/35–307/12.

emphasis on biblical humanism and scholasticism, through the likes of John Alcock and Robert Ridley, the latter of whom was his tutor. Such teaching would have involved an immersion in voluntarism which held that the human will retained its freedom in a postlapsarian world; the will no longer moved as easily toward the good, but it was still free to do so. Yet God's grace was still needed, in this view, in order to be saved, and the instruments of grace, such as the sacraments and good works, existed because God chose them. Biblical humanism—the other aspect of his scholarly training—emphasized looking to the Bible and the church fathers to justify current practices of penance, as had the Cambridge theologian John Fisher. Eventually Cranmer rejected the idea that any human act could confer grace and he turned away from the Scotist-humanist training that he had received at Cambridge.[82]

In place of the Scotist understanding of penance that lasted through his Cambridge days, Cranmer turned toward an Erasmian approach. Erasmus attacked the traditional doctrine of penance on philological grounds, translating *metanoeite* (Matthew 3:2, 4:17) as "return to one's senses" (*resipiscite*) rather than "do penance" (*poentitentiam agite*) as the Vulgate had done; the difference stressed contrition over satisfaction. He also attacked it on historical grounds, arguing that the practice of auricular confession developed quite late: "There was of old some form of confessing a life of evil-doing, but it was a public confession in my opinion, and a general one, and we do not read that it was compulsory. The secret, aural form of confession practiced now seems to have originated in consultations with bishops, if some scruple burdened the soul."[83] Erasmus had come to much the same opinion Wyclif had held: confession was an innovation in the Church, and so not strictly necessary. Contrition, as it had been for Wyclif, was crucial to Erasmus's conception of the forgiveness of sins, contrition given by God to the penitent who continually sought to have servile fear turned into filial fear. Again like Wyclif, Erasmus still thought that auricular confession had benefits: it instilled humility and meekness in the penitent; the shame induced by confession would help to prevent recidivism; the confessor could guide the penitent; and it reconciled the penitent to the Church. For these reasons, Erasmus thought that auricular confession should be retained in the Church, although it was not necessary to salvation. In the end, his view was that works and the gift of contrition were necessary to the forgiveness of sins. Cranmer followed this line of thought at one point, annotating a

82. Ashley Null, *Thomas Cranmer's Doctrine of Repentance: Renewing the Power of Love*, Oxford, 2000, 70–81.

83. Erasmus, *Annotations*, trans. Rummell, 154; quoted by Null, *Cranmer's Doctrine of Repentance*, 88.

passage from Erasmus's *De libero arbitrio* which stated the usefulness of penance, where the human will would be aided by God, with the words "The standard for the Christian mind on free will."[84]

This was not, however, Cranmer's final position on penance. Over time, Cranmer eventually came to side with a Lutheran anthropology and doctrine of justification, including the crucial understanding of the Christian as *simul justus et peccator* (at once just and sinner), as well as the teaching that good works cannot precede justification, but come only after the sinner has been justified by faith alone. Ashley Null suggests that this conversion likely happened at Nuremberg during Cranmer's time there in 1532, pointing to Cranmer's decision to marry Andreas Osiander's niece, and Osiander's approval of the match as likely evidence that Cranmer had converted to Lutheranism.[85] However, because of the political pressures of Henry VIII's court, Cranmer was only able to advance this sort of theology by "redefining in Lutheran terms the official description of the traditional forum of post-baptismal justification—the sacrament of penance."[86] In this way, Cranmer was able to reject medieval understandings of penance and focus on a Reformed Augustinianism that rejected the role of human merit in justification, emphasizing the correspondence between the justified and the elect. The elect could be certain of their election "if they simply trusted God's promise to forgive their sins freely because of Christ's passion."[87]

Wyclif had also held a doctrine of strict predestination, but unlike Cranmer, he did not think that it led to any certainty about who was and who was not saved, and it was less on the basis of his predestinarianism that Wyclif rejected contemporary teachings on penance, than on account of abuses inherent in the system of private confession and their lack of scriptural foundation. Certainly, Cranmer also found that there were abuses in confession, but these were abuses of doctrine, not practice. Confession had its possible uses, for instance, in determining whether someone about to receive communion had saving faith, and to instruct those that were found lacking, but its chief use was to offer the comfort of absolution. Abuses were numerous, including the listing of all sins, which were unknown among the fathers except for those excommunicate. Nor was it necessary for the priest to know all sins in order to judge them, since, according to Chrysostom, penance is a place for healing rather than judgment. The idea that power of

---

84. Null, *Cranmer's Doctrine of Repentance*, 85–93; Diarmaid MacCulloch, *Thomas Cranmer: A Life,* New Haven, 1996, 30.

85. Null, *Cranmer's Doctrine of Repentance*, 98–115.

86. Ibid., 118. On the politics of Henry's court and its general theological conservatism along with Cranmer's slow progress in reform see MacCulloch, *Cranmer*, 79–348.

87. Null, *Cranmer's Doctrine of Repentance*, 120–33.

the keys changed eternal punishment into the punishment of purgatory was also rejected as erroneous. Indulgences were to be rejected as well; God forgives out of mercy, and it is the Church and those injured by the sin who are the ones needing to be satisfied, not God.[88] Wyclif, as we have seen, made many of these same claims, but he did so on a practical basis. Indulgences, according to Wyclif, are dangerous not only because they lack scriptural foundation, but because they lead to sin and damage the poor of Christ.

Cranmer's theology grew ever more Reformed as time went on, and by 1540 he had adopted a more Reformed than Lutheran position. Separating justification completely from sacramental penance, he wrote:

> Of penance also I find in the Scripture, whereby sinners after baptism returning wholly unto God, be accepted again unto God's favour and mercy. But the Scripture speaketh not of Penance, as we call it a sacrament, consisting in three parts, contrition, confession, and satisfaction; but the Scripture taketh Penance for a pure conversion of a sinner in heart and mind from his sins unto God, making no mention of private confession of all deadly sins to a priest, nor of ecclesiastical satisfaction to be enjoined by him.[89]

All of the trappings of medieval penance are done away with here; there is no need for confession to a priest, there is no need for works of satisfaction, there is only need for true contrition. This is the logical extreme of a true contritionist position, but underlying this rejection of sacramental penance is the doctrine of predestination and the identification of the elect and the just as much as biblicism. Wyclif and Cranmer diverge slightly here.

CRANMER AND WYCLIF COMPARED

Cranmer rejects the need for satisfaction, a step that Wyclif did not take. In fact, as we have seen, Wyclif was keen to keep satisfaction as part of penance, and this was one of his arguments against indulgences. Yet both held to a strict predestination, and both argued on this basis against an understanding of penance which included confession to a priest as a necessary element. Both also held that contrition was the *sine qua non* of forgiveness of sins. But there was still room in Wyclif's view for some form of sacramental penance.

---

88. Ibid., 135–39.

89. Thomas Cranmer, "Questions and Answers on the Sacraments," in *The Works of Thomas Cranmer*, edited by G. E. Duffield, Appleford, Berkshire, 1964, 26–27.

Penance And Authority

There are further similarities in their understanding of the relationship between penance and authority. As already noted, Wyclif rejected the authority of the pope in this matter, and Cranmer did likewise, writing in 1550:

> But the Romish antichrist, to deface the great benefit of Christ, hath that the sacrifice upon the cross is not sufficient hereunto, without any other sacrifice devised by him, and made by the priest, or else without indulgences, beads, pardons, pilgrimages, and such other pelfray [rubbish], to supply Christ's imperfection: and that christian people cannot apply to themselves the benefits of Christ's passion, but that the same is in the distribution of the bishop of Rome; or else that by Christ we have no full remission, but be delivered only from sin, and yet remaineth temporal pain in purgatory due for the same, to be remitted after this life by the Romish antichrist and his ministers, who take upon them to do that thing, which Christ either would not or could not do.[90]

There are several issues at hand here. First and foremost, Cranmer understands the Roman doctrine of penance to imply an insufficiency in Christ's sacrifice, which of course runs quite contrary to Cranmer's own understanding of the work on the cross.[91] One might accuse the archbishop of misunderstanding here, as the Roman teaching on penance was in fact based on the sufficiency of Christ's sacrifice, more correctly in its overflowing abundance of merit. Second, Cranmer is concerned to do away with unnecessary accretions, notably indulgences, beads, pardons, and pilgrimages, all of which he calls rubbish. Third, Cranmer takes issue with the authority assumed by Rome in this matter. There are two points to be made in this regard. First, the intercessory role of the priesthood is called into question, as Cranmer says the "Romish antichrist" asserts falsely that the "christian people cannot apply to themselves the benefits of Christ's passion." The individual Christian does not need priestly intercession to ask for forgiveness and obtain God's mercy. Following from this, Cranmer undercuts the pope's authority in this matter, perhaps in reference to the papacy's claims to have

---

90. J. E. Cox, ed., *Writings and Disputations of Thomas Cranmer . . . relative to the Sacrament of the Lord's Supper*, Cambridge, 1845, 5.

91. See, for instance, the Eucharistic prayer of the *Book of Common Prayer*, both the 1549 and the 1552 versions, which speaks of Christ, "who made there (by his one oblacion once offered) a full, perfect, and sufficient sacrifyce, oblacion, and satysfaccyon, for the sinnes of the whole worlde." *The First and Second Prayer Books of Edward VI*, London, 1910, 222 and 389.

the power to remit some sins that other, lesser clergy, including bishops, could not.[92] Cranmer, much like Wyclif before him, speaks in terms of pride and blasphemy: "O heinous blasphemy and most detestable injury against Christ! O wicked abomination of the temple of God! O pride intolerable of antichrist, and most manifest token of the son of perdition, extolling himself above God, and with Lucifer exalting his seat and power above the throne of God!"[93] A significant difference, however, is the understanding of purgatory, for Cranmer here implicitly rejects the idea of purgatory, which is a thing that Wyclif never did. It seems, as with most of Cranmer's positions, that he has gone a step beyond Wyclif.

Indulgences

The vibrancy of late medieval English devotion to indulgences has been well documented by R. N. Swanson, who notes that although they were eventually done away with during the reign of Henry VIII, the process was slow and it is debatable whether or not the practice of indulgences was ever formally abolished.[94] Cranmer had, of course, his role to play in this, by accepting solifidianism (the belief that one is saved by faith rather than works) and rejecting purgatory, it followed that he would reject indulgences. Cranmer differs from Wyclif as to the basis of his rejection of this late medieval practice. For Wyclif, indulgences were unfounded, dangerous fictions, and so they were also for Cranmer, but Cranmer's rejection is based first and foremost on his acceptance of justification by faith alone. It is for these reasons that Cranmer, or any other English Reformer for that matter, hardly speaks about indulgences or pardons; if the underlying doctrines of purgatory and justification were at the heart of theological debate in the Reformation, indulgences were merely an afterthought, a problem resolved by the resolution of the underlying issues. This is in sharp contrast to Wyclif, who speaks often and pointedly about indulgences, which were a very lively issue in his day.[95]

Cranmer was not entirely consistent in this rejection of pardons, or at least his teaching admits of some confusion. An exhortation for the

92. On papal reservation of sins, see Jacques Longère, "Les évêques et l'administration du sacrament de pénitence au XIIIe siècle: les cas reservés," in P. Guichaud et al., eds., *Paupaté, monachisme et théories politiques: études d'histoire médiévale offertes à Marcel Pacaut*, 2 vols., Lyon, 1994, ii, 537-50; Cyril Vogel, "Le pélérinage pénitentiel," *Revue des Sciences religieuses* 38 (1964) 113-53 esp. 140-47, reprinted as item VII in *En rémission des péchés*, Aldershot, VT, 1999.

93. Cox, *Writings and Disputations*, 5.

94. Swanson, *Indulgences*, 469-515.

95. Ibid., 470-71.

collection of funds for the relief of Christians against the Turks made in the Diocese of Canterbury in 1543, read, in part:

> for that ye shall of charytye and good will give to this relief, ye shall be rewarded with the true pardon of remyssion of synnes, graunted by Hym that hathe purchased pardon for all penytent synners, our Savyor and Redeamer Jesus Christ; who hathe promysed for relief doon to oure breathern here in earthe relief in heavyn, and for mercye done shewed here mercye theire, and for succor here succor there, and by what measure wee mynystre to other here, by the same yt shalbe measured to us agayne there.[96]

This is the language of indulgences, yet it also warned its readers against such, telling them "ye were wonte to be abused with vayne tales, and for counterfaite pardons departyd with your monye." Paul Ayris argues that "as far as the author of the exhortation is concerned, the abolition of indulgences is a *fait accompli*" because it "speaks of them in the past tense."[97] Ayris points to a passage in which, he argues, Cranmer "tries to maintain a theology of works, as embodied in the *King's book*, with a commitment to an evangelical doctrine of the atonement rooted in Christ's passion on the cross."[98] The *King's book or A necessary doctrine and erudition for any Christian man* was a conservative theological work published by the royal printer in 1543.[99] It emphasized both God as the principal of human salvation, but also the necessity of human cooperation. It also denounced papal abuses connected with purgatory, and wanted that name dropped. It is against this background that Ayris reads Cranmer's exhortation. The passage in question reads:

> with realevinge theyre [the Christians of Hungary and Germany] calamyties to redeame oure [the contributors'] owne synnes, as the Scrypture speaketh yt; whiche speache implyeth not that wee be oure owne redeamers, to the preiudyce or derogation of the effecte of Chrysty's passion, whiche ys the very purgation and redemption of all synne, but that wee, workynge accordyng to the grace purchased for us by that redemption, may please

---

96. Quoted in Swanson, *Indulgences*, 507 and appended in Paul Ayris, "Preaching the Last Crusade: Thomas Cranmer and the 'Devotion' Money of 1543," *Journal of Ecclesiastical History* 49 (1998) 699–700.

97. Ayris, "Preaching the Last Crusade," 693.

98. Ibid., 695.

99. *The King's Book or A Necessary Doctrine and Erudition for Any Christian Man*, edited by C. Lloyd, London, 1932. See also MacCulloch, *Cranmer*, 344–46.

Godd and be partakers of the same, whiche ys callid in us rede-amynge of synne.[100]

Cranmer, according to Ayris, "sounds like a reforming prelate who is finding it hard to win battles in the face of opposition."[101] While Cranmer exhibits some confusion here perhaps, he does not sound at all like a reforming prelate facing stiff opposition. Rather, this passage is in line with the accepted late medieval understanding of indulgences. No theologian had ever claimed that the work of indulgences somehow replaced the work of the cross. They claimed, in fact, the exact opposite; indulgences could only work because of the surfeit of merit produced by the willing sacrifice of Christ. The only real difference, as Swanson has pointed out, between this exhortation and previous indulgences "is the seeming insistence that the merit quantifiably reflected the scale of donation, a linkage assiduously avoided in the earlier doctrine of pardons."[102] Since the *King's book* had denounced the abuses of Rome connected with purgatory, and indulgences fit neatly in that category, Cranmer was not attacking indulgences or pardons as such. When he wrote "ye were wonte to be abused with vayne tales, and for counterfaite pardons departyd with your monye," it is likely that he was attacking specifically papal pardons, which he considered "counterfaite" but not the effect of the good work of giving money for defense against the Turks. The Henrician attack on papal authority had been ongoing since the 1530s, and this included attacks on papal pardons, but practice did not change as quickly as legislation, and there are other instances of pardons from after the imposition of the royal supremacy.[103] Furthermore, the exhortation explicitly states that the funds will only be used for the intended purpose: "ye may be assured that suche money, as ye shall gyve of youre devocion, shall withoute embeselinge be holy presented to the kinge's maiestye, to be by his highnes imployed accordynge to youre devocions."[104] The use of this money is therefore in contrast to the "vayne tales" and "counterfaite pardons" of the old system. Yet, just a few short years later, Cranmer's visitation articles (1548) sought to expose and remove from books "prayers having rubrics containing pardons or indulgences, and all other superstitious legends and prayers."[105] Whatever the case, Cranmer demonstrates some ambiguity in regard to pardons, but it would seem that he was, at least in this instance,

---

100. Quoted by Ayris, "Preaching the Last Crusade," 695.
101. Ibid., 696.
102. Swanson, *Indulgences*, 507.
103. Ibid., 489–97.
104. Ayris, "Preaching the Last Crusade," 700.
105. Quoted in Swanson, *Indulgences*, 503.

willing to concede that giving money to a worthy cause can pardon sin, even if indulgences themselves had faded from use in England along with the doctrine of purgatory and papal authority.

CONCLUSIONS

There are a number of similarities between Wyclif and Cranmer on penance. Each changed his position throughout the course of his career, in both cases hardening in their positions opposing contemporary penitential practices, including the necessity of confession to a priest and the practice of indulgences, both important aspects of Catholic understandings of penance and the forgiveness of sins. Both likewise held to a doctrine of strict predestination which underlay their teaching on repentance. Both turned first and foremost to the Bible as the unquestioned authority on which to rest their teaching.

Yet their respective positions demonstrate real, profound differences. Wyclif was ready to accept the reality of a treasury of merit, although one only opened and closed by God, and he was likewise ready to accept the existence of purgatory. Furthermore, his rejection of the papacy was not a rejection of the office itself, but rather of the occupants of that office in his day. In all of these areas, Cranmer went much further than Wyclif, for he rejected outright the treasury of merit, the existence of purgatory, and the office of pope. He was also convinced that one predestinate could know whether he or she was saved, something Wyclif was never convinced of. Nor can Wyclif truly be said to be a solefideist in the same mold as Cranmer; while he was convinced of the truth of predestination, Wyclif was unconvinced that there was no merit in works of satisfaction, in fact he argued that God could not forgive sins without them.

Another major difference was the concern with indulgences; they were hardly an afterthought for Cranmer and other sixteenth-century Reformers, who undermined them by rejecting purgatory. Wyclif, for his part, railed against indulgences, which he saw as dangerous and exploitive blasphemies. This last difference, of course, arises out of the different historical contexts of the two theologians, and reflects the differing concerns of their respective times. In the end, while it is relatively easy to see why Reformers found a kindred spirit in the sometime rector of Lutterworth, there were certainly a number of pointed differences, some of which can be accounted for by differences in historical context, and others that arise from differing theological points of view. In most cases, the proto-reformer was not nearly as reformed as Archbishop Cranmer.

2

The King James Version, Dispersed Authority, and Anglican Identity

ALAN L. HAYES

IN THE CENTURY BEFORE the publication of the King James Version of the Bible in 1611, two systemic changes are particularly striking in the Church of England. One is the profound laicization of church authority, both institutionally and spiritually. Institutionally, the reins of ecclesiastical power and wealth were transferred from papal legates, bishops, and abbots to monarch, Privy Council, parliament, and the lay patrons who profited from the dissolution of the monasteries. Accompanying that development was the laicization of spiritual authority which, for our present purpose, is more important. The medieval sacramental system (though, of course, not the sacraments) was swept away with the teaching of the Reformation. Thus the sacrament of penance was no longer necessary if we received God's forgiveness through repentance, not priestly absolution; masses did not need to be said for our soul if we were justified by faith alone; and the ordained priesthood was not required to mediate our relationship to God if each of us was, in a spiritual sense, a priest. With the spiritual demotion of the priesthood, the teaching authority of the clergy was dispersed into the whole people of God. People could seek their own Christian teaching

Alan L. Hayes *King James Version, Dispersed Authority, Anglican Identity*

in a religious marketplace of tracts, tavern conversations, lecturerships, sermons, "exercises" or "prophesyings,"[1] and other religious media. The other great change was the planting of the English Bible, in its canonical form, at the very heart of the Anglican ethos. As a simple quantitative measure of the significance of this change, in 1520 it was still illegal for most people in England to have English bibles (under Archbishop Thomas Arundel's Constitutions of 1408), but over the next century, three versions of the English Bible were mandated under royal authority, and several other partial and complete versions were printed privately, for a total of perhaps two million copies, enough for every household in the country.[2]

These two changes were closely linked. The collect in the *Book of Common Prayer*[3] for the second Sunday in Advent, which "every person ... inhabiting within this realm"[4] was supposed to hear at least once a year, made the linkage clear. The collect affirmed the people's authority, duty, and privilege to "read, mark, learn, and inwardly digest" the scriptures, as a means of embracing the hope of everlasting life. To learn Christ, to interpret the Word of God, to receive the assurance of the gospel directly and without priestly or sacramental mediation, to embrace the hope of eternity, was now within the authority of every believer, because every believer now had access to the Holy Scriptures. Now, the silent implication of this affirmation was that the Holy Scriptures to which each believer had access should be based on accurate sources and translated properly and effectively. Mistaken translations in the past, like "do penance" for "repent," had led believers astray. Nor was the study of the scriptures a solitary occupation. The word "we" in the collect, and the congregational setting in which the collect was

---

1. "Gatherings, at first of clergy, but soon also open virtually to all comers, for the purpose of biblical exposition, discussion, and mutual edification; ... a most effective instrument for the spread of the Reformed faith in Elizabethan England." Philip Edgcumbe Hughes, "Preaching, Homilies, and Prophesyings in Sixteenth Century England," *Churchman* 89 (1975); online: http://www.churchsociety.org/churchman/documents/Cman_089_1_Hughes.pdf.

2. David Daniell, *The Bible in English: Its History and Influence*, New Haven, 2003, 462.

3. Texts of the various historical editions of the *Book of Common Prayer* are conveniently available online at http://justus.anglican.org/resources/bcp/england.htm. Page-by-page text images of early English books can be found at Early English Books Online (www. eebo.chadwyck.com), which however has to be accessed through participating institutions such as research libraries. The standard reference for early English books from the period covered here is A. W. Pollard and G. R. Redgrave, eds., *A Short-title Catalogue of Books Printed in England, Scotland and Ireland, and of English Books Printed Abroad 1475–1640*, 2nd ed., rev., W. A. Jackson, F. S. Ferguson, K. F. Pantzer, 3 vols., London, 1976–1991, abbreviated hereafter as STC.

4. Act of Uniformity, 1558, 1 Eliz. I, c. 2.

prayed, are significant. The individual who read Scripture was part of the whole people of God that read Scripture. Learning the scriptures rightly involved conversation, mutuality, common commitment, and the support of the church. This vision of the vocation of the church came to be an essential property of what might be called Anglicanism. The publication of the King James Version (KJV) of the Bible in 1611 represents the culmination of the process by which the English Bible and a Protestant conviction of Christian freedom, authority, godly conversation, and discipleship were fused into a distinctive Anglican identity.

To speak of "Anglican identity" in the singular may raise the question whether Anglicanism is a single thing with its own identity, or a bin of approaches to Christianity that includes liberal and conservative, communitarian and individualist, traditional and anti-traditional, liturgical, charismatic, evangelical, and so on. Over thirty years ago Stephen W. Sykes raised this question in a compelling way, generating some fresh thinking about Anglican identity. His *The Integrity of Anglicanism*, after offering severe critiques of existing explanations of the problem, made a constructive proposal: diversity within Anglicanism, Sykes argued, does indeed have a common theological substratum. The integrating principle is an ethos of dispersed authority where "the means of judging matters concerning the faith are in the hands of the whole people of God by reason of their access to the Scriptures," and where the liturgy, backed by canon law, establishes these means.[5] In no other branch of Christianity, Sykes maintained, are these characteristics so intricately joined. Other communions publish confessions of faith, or identify persons or councils exercising a magisterium, or place special doctrinal restrictions on church membership. That is not the Anglican practice. Anglicans do, however, regulate public worship very carefully, and Anglican worship gives a considerable place, perhaps a central place, to Scripture. So Sykes concluded that what distinguishes Anglican life is that the people of God participate in a liturgy that gives them the unadorned, unfiltered scriptures, so that they can learn and inwardly digest them.

Sykes' explanation of Anglican identity is a very helpful one, and it nicely summarizes the achievement of the Reformation in England. Sykes' statement would not describe the Church of England as it was in 1520, but it does describe it perfectly as it was in 1611. Between these dates, the English Bible merged into the English liturgy, was published in a succession of versions, and at the end took the form of the KJV, which later became the standard biblical text for use in the English liturgy. Its liturgical use made the KJV the primary, perhaps the only, shared authoritative text of

---

5. Stephen W. Sykes, *The Integrity of Anglicanism*, London, 1978, 93.

Anglicanism, and from the liturgy the KJV was presented to the laity in the hope and expectation that they would appropriate it as the foundation and hope of their whole lives.

THE RISE OF THE ENGLISH BIBLE

Before the Reformation, Christians were well acquainted with some of the contents of the Bible through liturgy, homilies, stories, stained glass and other visual arts, drama, music, and devotional books. But the Bible in its canonical form, as a collection of sacred texts of different genres and recurrent themes organized in a certain way, was not widely available. As a result, some stories, doctrines, and commandments without a biblical basis posed as canonical, while others that really were biblical were known to few. If unwritten tradition carried authority as well as the Bible, perhaps the boundary between Bible and non-Bible was not so very important, but the people had no means, and indeed no right, to make that judgment for themselves.

There seems to be no doubt among historians that during the Reformation the Bible in its canonical form moved to a central place in English religion. But how and why that process happened has been much disputed. For convenience, we might organize the historiographical landscape into four categories.

Older Mainstream View

The first is the view that the Reformation, including its gift of the English Bible, brought about religious, political, and cultural progress in England. This could be called the older mainstream view, and it is associated with Protestant and whiggish historians, as well as many post-Christian, post-whig scholars such as G.R. Elton, the one-time doyen of Tudor historians. A distinguished representative of this group is A.G. Dickens, whose *The English Reformation* (1964) was warmly sympathetic to the spiritual and political fruits of the Reformation. He was, accordingly, frankly critical of late medieval religion, which he thought was encapsulated by the story of a certain friar who held forth that sinners could escape damnation by reciting their rosaries every day. In Dickens' narrative, the Reformation took aim at an empty-calorie diet of "devout observances," characterized particularly by a "fantastic emphasis on saints, relics, and pilgrimages," and a repressive, clericalist church establishment. By 1520, in his view, the laity were a tinderbox ready to be ignited by Protestant preaching, treatises, and bibles. The English Reformation was not primarily a political process and, instead,

Change and Transformation

it "arose and grew largely in opposition to the will of Henry VIII." It gained traction because "for his own reasons the King soon initiated a second Reformation" by wresting the control of the English Church from the papacy, and then appointing a number of reforming church leaders.[6]

For Dickens, the English Bible was a means of evangelism. As a favourite example of his, English Lutherans made effective inroads in the early years of the Reformation by marketing the new, improved, and illegal Bible translation by William Tyndale to religious consumers who already owned the archaic, hard to understand illegal Bible version connected with the fourteenth-century Oxford scholar John Wyclif. It was a victory for the Protestant cause when in 1538 King Henry VIII's chief ecclesiastical administrator, Thomas Cromwell, published injunctions requiring an English Bible in every parish church in England. His motivation, said Dickens, was a "positive desire to establish a religion based upon the Bible."[7] Cromwell then made sure that an officially mandated English Bible—the "Great Bible," so called because of its size—was brought through the press the following April.

Revisionist View

Against this once mainstream view, a challenge was raised by a generation of revisionists, notably J.J. Scarisbrick, Christopher Haigh, John Bossy, and Eamon Duffy, all of them Roman Catholic. In particular, Duffy's mammoth *The Stripping of the Altars* (1992) vindicated late medieval religion in England as lively, engaged, rich, communal, and well informed. From contemporary devotional texts, pastoral manuals, wills, church buildings and decorations, parish and guild records, and other evidence, he exploded Protestant stereotypes of late medieval religion as privatized, anxious, clericalized, and sub-Christian. Celebrations of the Mass, both on Sundays and weekdays, involved meaningful lay participation in a number of ways. The saints, whose stories could be a source of "pious wonder and simple entertainment value," gave assurance of God's protection and love, and, Protestant calumnies notwithstanding, pointed people to Christ, not paganism. English Christians would not have willingly repudiated this most attractive spirituality. They were deprived of it by radical preachers, powerful reforming bishops, and well-placed Tudor officials who applied force and

---

6. A. G. Dickens, *The English Reformation*, 3rd printing, New York, 1971, 4–5, 83.
7. Ibid., 135.

fear. Finally, under the Protestant governments of Edward VI and Elizabeth, traditional religion was practically obliterated.[8]

Duffy does not discuss the attractions of bible-reading, but sympathetically explains the position of those who opposed it. The Bible had been used in traditional religion to support true teaching, effective prayer, and healthy community, but on its own, divorced from the church's guidance, it was dangerous. Duffy quotes Reginald Cardinal Pole, the pope's legate to England during the reign of Queen Mary (1553–1558), to the effect that "indiscriminate Bible-reading by laypeople" bred "religious argument and the spirit of self-sufficiency." Pole stated the precept, "They are more apt to receive light, that are more obedient to follow ceremonies, than to read." In the end, Duffy says with what appears to be a note of regret, the Bible came to be at the centre of "new pieties;" and "something of the old sense of the sacred was transferring itself from the sacramentals to the scriptures."[9]

Status Quo View

If the once mainstream view saw the Reformation as an improvement, and if the revisionists saw it as a deterioration, a third group saw it as basically just more of the same. Writing in 1912, Ernst Troeltsch, a sociologist and liberal theologian, presented the Reformation as a medieval event. In his view, the great interests of the Reformation, such as seeking an assurance of salvation and explaining Christian truth in scholastic categories like justification and sanctification, were medieval activities. The Reformation's ideals of "the universal dominion of the only saving truth over society, the absolute objective conception of truth, and the universal idea of a Christian society supported by it" were medieval ideals. For Troeltsch it was the Enlightenment that inaugurated modernity, rather than the Reformation.[10] A later writer who pictured the Reformation as a medieval event was Joseph Lortz, a Roman Catholic historian, in his *Die Reformation in Deutschland* (1939).[11] Like Troeltsch, he had nothing good to say about the late Middle Ages, and like Troeltsch he thought that Luther was thoroughly medieval, but, unexpectedly, he thoroughly admired Luther for recognizing and bat-

---

8. Eamon Duffy, *The Stripping of the Altars: Traditional Religion in England 1400–1580*, New Haven, 1992, 174.

9. Ibid., 531, 586.

10. Ernst Troeltsch, *The Social Teaching of the Christian Churches*, 2 vols., trans. Olive Wyon, New York, 1960, ii, 485, 487, 493–94.

11. Joseph Lortz, *The Reformation in Germany*, trans. Ronald Walls, New York, 1968.

tling the religious defects of the age. In the next generation after Lortz, in the decades surrounding the Second Vatican Council, the writers who, as a group, most passionately embraced the medieval picture of the Reformation were the Protestant, Catholic, and Anglican advocates of liturgical change. One among many was James White, an influential and well published Methodist liturgist, who wrote: "In many cases, the Reformers took medieval beliefs to their full and logical conclusion. In this they were simply the most consistent of late medieval thinkers."[12] Much of the thought of the liturgical movement of the period was founded on the following syllogism:

- Medieval liturgy and piety were bad;
- Reformation liturgies and piety were medieval;
- Therefore, Reformation liturgies and piety should be replaced.

As a result, in the 1960s the Tridentine Mass, the mid-Tudor Prayer Books, and some mainstream Protestant worship traditions were sidelined.

For those who periodized the Reformation in the Middle Ages, the vernacular Bible did not represent a truly new era. Troeltsch maintained that Protestants had simply substituted Scripture for priestly hierarchy as the authoritative extension of the Incarnation: "The authority and saving power of the Bible alone were held capable of accomplishing what had been unattainable by the bishops and the Pope."[13] But in this respect Protestants were loading Scripture with a medieval function, which would not be needed in modernity.

Post-Revisionist View

A fourth historiographical explanation of the place of the Bible in the Reformation has sometimes been called post-revisionist. Diarmaid MacCulloch has tried to avoid a master narrative with massive generalizations, and instead has described a dynamic situation marked by a diversity that defies simplification. Like the revisionists, MacCulloch celebrates the "rich devotional world" of the late Middle Ages, with its lay-run guilds, its commitment to prayer, and its liturgy that was "not only good for the soul, it was fun."[14] But "devotional life was far from uniform," he warns.[15] Some in the

---

12. James F. White, "Where the Reformation Was Wrong on Worship," *Christian Century* 27 (1982) 1074.

13. Ernst Troeltsch, *A Historical Study of the Relation of Protestantism to the Modern World*, trans. W. Montgomery, New York, 1912, 47–48.

14. Diarmaid MacCulloch, *The Reformation: A History*, New York, 2004, 24.

15. Ibid., 15.

Tudor age may have liked the status quo; some may have preferred reform; but no one was herding them like sheep, because laypeople "were perfectly capable of thinking for themselves."[16] Like the revisionists, MacCulloch recognizes the brutal fist of the government in enforcing its religious policies in England, but like the old mainstream, he affirms that evangelical enthusiasm arose independently of government policy, and in some ways in opposition to it—but not uniformly across the country. One generalization that he does offer tentatively, in apparent disagreement with the revisionists, is that "ordinary people" were probably more affected by evangelicalism "than clergy and the landed elite, who had more emotional and financial investment in the old system."

MacCulloch sees the vernacular Bible as a powerful instrument of protestantization, or perhaps more accurately, he sees protestantization as a powerful instrument of the vernacular Bible. He appears to sympathize with the view that "the increase in Bibles created the Reformation rather than being created by it."[17] English bibles were in considerable part the result of technological and cultural change, including printing presses and the economics of the new book industry, increased literacy and broadening readerships, improvements in the study of Greek and Hebrew, and the humanist spirit of returning to original texts. That is, vernacular bibles can be seen as the fruit of cultural changes that pre-dated Protestantism. As people discovered how little the Bible had to say about the papacy, the Mass, auricular confession, liturgical ceremonies, and the Christian priesthood, some were moved to doubt received religious traditions.

Conspectus View

We can draw value from each of these views. From the work of the Roman Catholic revisionists we can see that biblical stories, drama, art, and music promoted a deep and widespread Bible-based spirituality that attracted many to the English Bible when this became available in its canonical form. With Troeltsch we can recognize that Bible-reading did not represent a new religious quest but a surer authority for an old one. With the older mainstream historians we can appreciate that the successful economics of the English Bible industry, among other things, demonstrates that Bible-reading was at the base a popular movement, not a government project. Finally, we can agree with MacCulloch's hint that the vernacular Bible was

---

16. Ibid., 204.
17. Ibid., 73.

not so much the consequence of a prior religious movement as the grounding for a new one.

In a longer study we might show in some detail how the English Bible changed the religious practice and culture of England. It changed how preachers preached, how Elizabethan and early Stuart playwrights, poets, and musical lyricists wrote, how craftspeople decorated churches and designed religious items, and how visual artists represented the world. It changed how English was spoken and how people thought.[18]

But Cardinal Pole was right, too, when he warned that popular Bible-reading would foment argument and subvert the authority of the Church. A year after Cromwell's injunctions of 1538, a draft royal proclamation decried the "murmur, malice, and malignity" arising from arguments about Scripture in alehouses and taverns.[19] A statute of 1543 attempted to limit the reading of the English Bible to the upper classes.[20] Early Reformers were mistaken if they thought that releasing the Word of God to ordinary people would teach them clear lessons on the essentials of the faith, and help build a peaceful commonwealth. On the contrary, giving them the scriptures in their canonical form generated endless Bible-based disagreements.[21]

In Sykes' language, putting the English Bible in the hands of the whole people of God created "a dispersed authority" of interpretation and theological judgment. Without the approval of priests or scholars or government officials, people could decide for themselves what the Bible intended. True, if people contumaciously defied the laws of uniformity in respect of public religious observance, or disturbed the peace, they could face serious penalties; but in regard to weighing and approving interpretations of the Christian faith, they gave their account to God. Dispersed authority guaranteed argument about the interpretation of Scripture because there existed no authority higher than Scripture this side of the eschatological veil that could end debate. The result in England was a culture of religious critique, a testing of received ideas, a suspicion of human religious authority, and a refusal to identify the gospel with any existing historical institution or statement, which Paul Tillich has called the Protestant principle.[22]

---

18. For general discussions, see Daniell, *The Bible in English*; Christopher Hill, *The English Bible and the seventeenth-century revolution*, London, 1994, ch. 1.

19. Duffy, *Stripping of the Altars*, 422.

20. The Act for the Advancement of True Religion, 34 & 35 Henry VIII, c. 1.

21. This religious diversity percolating from below is a problem for any theory that the English Reformation was imposed from above.

22. Paul Tillich, *The Protestant Era*, trans. James Luther Adams, Chicago, 1948, ch. 11.

In another period, the impossibility of theological finality might lead to relativism or indifference, but in these decades the general result was a perpetual social unsettlement concerning religious issues. This unsettlement registered in numerous ways. The official homilies of the Church of England, published in 1547 under Edward VI and re-issued under Elizabeth, and supplemented by new homilies in 1562, written by people of notably different theological outlooks, presented a variety of un-reconciled religious opinions. Elizabethan officials, including the bishops, who now functioned as agents of the Crown, tried to develop ground rules and broad limits for disagreement, and sometimes applied a heavy hand with unhappy consequences. John Jewel in his *Apology for the Church of England* traced the Anglican culture of biblical debate to the practice of the early Church where "the old fathers Origen and Chrysostom, exhort the people to read the scriptures, to buy them books, to reason at home betwixt themselves of divine matters—wives with their husbands, and parents with their children."[23] Richard Hooker, remembered today as the classic theologian of the Elizabethan settlement of religion, was only one writer in an active and sharp theological controversy. "The long Anglican history of the experience of conflict," Sykes writes, is not an embarrassment, a shame, or a problem; in fact, he says, it is "of potentially great service" to the wider Christian community. He contrasts this essential feature of Anglican identity with Roman Catholicism, where the documents of the Second Vatican Council conspicuously failed to expect conflict in the Church, and where many Roman Catholic leaders seemed surprised and distressed when disagreements did arise.[24]

THE ANGLICAN LITURGY AND THE ENGLISH BIBLE

Ten years after copies of the Great Bible were placed in all the churches of England, the government published the *Book of Common Prayer* (1549), a set of English-language liturgical texts to replace the old Latin services. A second edition in 1552 moved the liturgy further in a Protestant direction. Both editions, and subsequent editions, were established by parliamentary statute. A principal purpose of the BCP was to make people familiar with the English Bible in its canonical form. The main author of the BCP, as historians agree, was Archbishop Thomas Cranmer, a committed advocate of

---

23. John Jewel, *The Apology of the Church of England*, ed. Henry Morley, London, 1888, 117. Jewel knew that in his own day such "reasoning" was not confined to families and households.

24. Sykes, *The Integrity of Anglicanism*, 88–89.

the Protestant Reformation, who had also written the preface to an early edition of the Great Bible. The preface to the BCP explained the intimate connection between the BCP and the English Bible. "The first original and ground" of common prayers (meaning the daily offices), Cranmer asserted in the first sentence of the preface, was to ensure "that all the whole Bible (or the greatest part thereof) should be read over once in the year." Cranmer took evident pride, therefore, in presenting "an order for prayer (as touching the reading of holy scripture)" that would bring English Christians almost the entire Old Testament once in a year, the New Testament three times in a year, and the book of Psalms twelve times in a year.

In the 1552 edition of the BCP, Cranmer inserted an "exhortation" near the beginning of the daily offices, which offered a liturgical rationale for these services. It was to render thanks to God, to give God praise, "to hear his most holy word," and to offer prayer. Cranmer's lectionary ("Kalendar") for the daily offices was a simple, systematic schedule of Scripture-reading according to the form of the canon. Thus the Old Testament began with Genesis 1 and 2 on January 2, followed by Genesis 3 and 4 on January 3, and so forth. The New Testament began with Matthew 1 and Romans 1 on January 2, followed by Matthew 2 and Romans on January 3, and so forth. The exceptions to this canonical pattern were few.[25]

The Scripture readings for Holy Communion for Sundays and feast days—from the psalms, epistles, and gospels—were written out in full in Cranmer's BCP, as they continued to be in all prayer books until the era of alternative services in the 1960s. In 1549 and 1552 the translations were those of the Great Bible, which was still novel and, as we can suppose, exciting to hear. Reading Archbishop Cranmer's preface, we can sense his passion and enthusiasm in this invitation to his reader: "Take the books into thine hands, read the whole story, and that thou understandest, keep it well in memory; that thou understandest not, read it again, and again." In 1662 the KJV would replace the Great Bible as the appointed translation for the epistles and gospels, but the Great Bible continued to be used for the psalms.

English Christians and, as the British Empire moved overseas, Anglican Christians all over the world, heard a great deal of Scripture in their liturgy. Until the twentieth century, the most common form of Anglican Sunday service was Morning Prayer (or Evening Prayer) followed by the first part of the service of Holy Communion ("antecommunion"). Since

---

25. Cranmer would have been surprised at modern Anglican daily office lectionaries, with their very short selections, frequent bowdlerisations to avoid offensive or controversial material, apparently random ordering, and generous lacunae, ensuring that no one would hear the entirety of Scripture even if they attended Anglican services twice a day for their entire lives.

the service of Morning Prayer included two readings from Scripture plus Psalms, and antecommunion included another two readings, worshippers heard at least five Scripture passages every Sunday.

Not only did the liturgy showcase Scripture, but it was itself scriptural. It is commonly said that about 80 percent of the text of the BCP comprises quotation or direct paraphrase from Scripture. In other words, the BCP surrounded the reading of Scripture with a liturgical structure that was composed of the words of Scripture. The Morning Prayer of 1552, for example, included opening scriptural sentences, the Lord's Prayer (twice), the invitatory psalm (Psalm 95), a choice of the Benedictus (Luke 1:68–79) or Psalm 100, and the preces (a set of short responsory petitions, all drawn from verses of Scripture). The proper collects, too, drew generously on the wording of Scripture, most frequently borrowing the language of the epistle for the Sunday. Thus the epistle for Advent Sunday, from Romans 13, spoke of casting away the works of darkness and putting on the armour of light; so did the collect. The epistle for Advent 2, from Romans 15, spoke of the patience and comfort that was to be derived from the scriptures, "written aforetime for our learning"; so did the collect.[26]

Sykes is accordingly quite right to say that the Anglican liturgy established the means of the laity's access to Scripture. Immersing English Christians directly in Scripture, with a minimum of commentary, was its major purpose in the daily offices, and arguably its single greatest purpose overall. Since all persons were legally required to attend the public worship of the Church of England on the Lord's Day, the parish church became the instrument of a universal compulsory education in the English Bible.

As Anglicanism migrated overseas, the liturgy was no longer established by the laws of any local authority, but custom, common commitment, and canon law maintained the rights of Anglicans to participate in the same liturgy (or almost the same liturgy) that other Anglicans did, as well as their access to Scripture.

THE KING JAMES VERSION

The KJV was the culmination of the Reformation project of "en-Scripturing" England. Not immediately but in the long run, it provided a respected scholarly translation on which most church people could agree, across their

---

26. The scriptural inspiration of Cranmer's artistry seems to have apparently eluded modern liturgical revisers. "Scholars speculate on the secret of Cranmer's style," says the Canadian *Book of Alternative Services*, Toronto, 1985; "some attribute it to his proximity in time to the period of Middle English ..." (12).

Change and Transformation

many theological divisions. It could, therefore, serve as a common ground for conversation and debate in the Church of England.

The story of the KJV begins almost as early as King James' accession to the English throne in 1603. By then there was no question that the English Bible had a vital part to play in the liturgy and theological conversation of the church, the devotional life of Christians, and the culture of the nation. But no English version of the Bible suited all parties. If England were to worship together and discuss theology together, a common agreed text would be necessary.

It is easy to see why all the existing versions were defective in one way or another.[27] William Tyndale's editions (beginning in 1526) were excellent, but they did not include the entire Bible, and he was executed in 1536 while his work was in progress. Miles Coverdale, who published a translation in 1535, had little Greek and no Hebrew, and depended largely on the Vulgate and German translations, in addition to Tyndale. The Matthew Bible (1537) and the Great Bible (1539) depended heavily on Coverdale. The Geneva Bible (1560), an accurate and accessible translation, won a popular following, but some of its vocabulary choices were contentious, and it came with some very provocative and sometimes erroneous marginal comments in a Calvinist direction. King James was particularly aggrieved with its frequent use of the word "tyrant" for the word usually translated "king," and the many marginal comments that a real king like himself would find highly incendiary,[28] as at Judges 9:54: "Thus God by such miserable death taketh vengeance on tyrants even in this life." The Bishops Bible (1568, revised in 1572), used stilted language, and its principles of translation and style varied from book to book. There was also a Roman Catholic translation (New Testament 1582, Old Testament 1609–10), usually called the Douai-Rheims, but it was intended for clergy, not laypeople. It was so Latinate as to be sometimes unintelligible (its translations included "odible," "promerited," and "exinanited"), and it also included provocative commentary.

The king's decision to mandate a new English version came out of a conference that he convened at Hampton Court in January 1604. Sixty-six persons are known to have participated, including privy councillors, bishops, and "other learned men," of whom at least four were moderate Puritan ministers. Despite all that has been written about this conference and about the KJV, no one knows for sure what the conference was originally intended

---

27. The texts and marginalia of sixteenth-century Bibles can be read online at http://www.biblesofthepast.com.

28. Alister E. McGrath, *In the Beginning: The Story of the King James Bible and How It Changed a Nation, a Language, and a Culture*, New York, 2001, 143.

to accomplish or how the proposal for the new English Bible was raised and processed there.

As for the purpose and agenda of the Hampton Court Conference, no document has survived. Half a century later, in 1655, one of the earliest historians of King James' reign, Thomas Fuller, neatly summarized the theories about its origins: "It is left uncertain, whether this Conference was by the king's favour graciously tendered; or by the mediation of the lords of his Council, powerfully procured; or by the bishops, as confident of their cause, voluntarily proffered, or by the [Puritan] ministers' importunity, effectually obtained. Each opinion pretends to probability ... "[29] A frequently stated theory is that, on King James' accession, Puritans who had been frustrated with Queen Elizabeth's antagonisms towards them conceived a hope for better things from the new king, and successfully requested a meeting. But it is also possible that the king took the initiative, since he was well experienced in church affairs from his years of rule in Scotland.

If for the purpose of the conference we are lacking documentation, for the processes and dynamics of the conference we have the opposite problem: a multitude of reports were written, but they differ among themselves. William Craig, in his careful study of the Hampton Court Conference, identified sixteen contemporary documents containing reports about it: nine were written by persons that we know attended at least part of the time, and seven were written anonymously.[30] Craig believes that a fairly lengthy official account commissioned by the Archbishop of Canterbury and written by William Barlow, dean of Chester, deserved most credit.[31] However, Mark H. Curtis has warned that this narrative is "a skilful piece of party propaganda," designed to show the bishops to be more united than they were, and the king to be more disaffected from the Puritans than he was.[32] According to Barlow, the proposal for a new translation of the Bible came on the second day of the conference from John Rainolds, a Puritan who was president of Corpus Christi College, Oxford. Rainolds identified several defects with the Great Bible, the translation used for the *Book of Common*

---

29. Thomas Fuller, *Church History of Great Britain*, 3 vols., London, 1868, iii, 192–93.

30. William Leonard Craig, "The King's Own Conference: A Reassessment of Hampton Court 1604," ThD thesis, Trinity College, University of Toronto, 2006.

31. William Barlow, *The Summe and Substance of the Conference which It Pleased His Excellent Majesty to Have* ... 2nd ed., London, 1605, in STC 1457, 45–48.

32. Mark H. Curtis, "Hampton Court Conference and its Aftermath," *History* 46 (1961) 1–16, quotation at 3. For a response, see Frederick Shriver, "Hampton Court Re-Visited: James I and the Puritans," *Journal of Ecclesiastical History* 33 (1982) 48–71.

Change and Transformation

Prayer,[33] and his main argument for a new translation was that Anglican worship deserved better. That this was the Puritans' main argument was affirmed by the preface ("The Translators to the Reader") to the KJV when it appeared in 1611. The king entirely agreed with Rainolds that there was no fully satisfactory English version of the Bible, but the king's least favourite was the Geneva Bible (which was also used in Scotland), and he identified several defects in it.[34]

Did the Puritans know that King James had already gone on record in favour of a new translation of Scripture when, as King James VI of Scotland, he had met with the General Assembly of the Kirk of Scotland at Burntisland in May 1601?[35] None of the reports of the Hampton Court Conference mentions that fact. But in retrospect we can see that both the king and the Puritan ministers arrived at Hampton Court with the same purpose of a new English Bible. The bishops were happy to agree once they knew the king's position on the matter, although in the moment between Rainolds' proposal and the king's assent the bishop of London, Richard Bancroft, interjected sarcastically: "If every man's humour should be followed, there would be no end of translating."[36] The king's conclusion was that a new uniform translation of the Bible, without marginal notes, should be prepared by the best scholars of both universities, then reviewed by the bishops and other learned people, then submitted to the Privy Council, and then finally

---

33. According to Barlow, Rainolds identified the following mistakes: Gal 4.25 of the Great Bible said, "For Mt. Sinai is Hagar in Arabia and *bordereth* upon the city"; Ps 105:28 said, "They were not *obedient* unto his word"; Ps 106:30 said, "Then stood up Phineas and *prayed*." Rainolds objected to "bordereth" (NRSV: "corresponds to"), "obedient" (Rainolds preferred "disobedient"; NRSV: "they rebelled against his words"); "prayed" (Rainolds preferred "executed judgment"; NRSV: "interceded."). By modern scholarship, Rainolds was right on only one of his three objections. If Rainolds identified only three problems in the entire Great Bible, we can see why the king said at the end of the discussion: "If these be the greatest matters you be grieved with, I need not have been troubled . . ."

34. The king objected to the note on Exod 1:19, where the midwives disobey Pharaoh's orders to kill the boy babies: "Their disobedience herein was lawful, but their dissembling evil." The king did not think that disobedience to a king should be justified. He also objected to the note on 2 Chr 15:16, where King Asa of Judah deposes the Queen Mother for idolatry: "Herein he showed that he lacked zeal: for she ought to have died both by the covenant, as verse 13, and by the Law of God: but he gave place to foolish pity." It has been noted that this verse had been used by those advocating the execution of Mary Queen of Scots, King James' mother. The king said that the comments of the Geneva Bible were sometimes seditious, "savouring too much of dangerous and traitorous conceits."

35. Craig, "The King's Own Conference," 221–22.

36. Barlow, *Summe and substance*, in STC 1456.5. 45–48.

ratified by himself "and so this whole Church to be bound unto it, and none other."

The forty-seven (or so) translators were chosen in an inclusive spirit. They were drawn from different theological sections of the Church of England, and they included both ordained and lay. Whereas bishops in the reigns of Henry VIII and Elizabeth had wanted Bible translations to be controlled by bishops, King James recruited his translators more widely.[37] The universities at Oxford and Cambridge, which by then had achieved international reputations for Greek and Hebrew studies and textual criticism, were well represented. The translators were divided into teams to focus on different parts of Scripture, but they made sure to check each other's work for the sake of consistency in their principles of translation as well as English style. They would work from the best manuscripts in the original languages. It is said that the king himself gave them fourteen instructions, although they were distributed by Bancroft. The translators must also have reached many specific agreements of their own. They aimed to apply the best Greek and Hebrew scholarship of the day. They were to build on the best previous English translations, correcting for errors (the Bishops Bible was named as the main model, but many think that the Geneva Bible proved more influential). They wrote no theological or devotional commentary, since that would have narrowed the appeal of the work and defeated the purpose of a commonly acceptable translation. But they explicitly noted significant variants and doubtful meanings. Where they supplied words without equivalent in the original in order to make the translation read well, they had those words printed in a distinctive font. The apparatus served as a reminder to all readers that only the original text of the Bible, and not any translation, could be definitive.

Not since the Septuagint, perhaps, had there been such a project of Bible translation. A team of first-rate scholars was appointed by a theologian-king, the supreme governor of the church. They assembled some of the best sources known at the time. They worked together in a cooperative spirit, notwithstanding the theological and other differences among them. They brought to their study a combination of piety, industry, and deep learning. They included textual notes to remind readers of the limited dependability of even the best scholarship, but they excluded theological commentary to remind readers of the sufficiency and supremacy of the pure Word of God. Their goal was to strengthen the liturgy, and to support scriptural learning,

---

37. When Thomas Cranmer proposed having the Great Bible revised by scholars, all but two bishops "vigorously objected, . . . saying that biblical translation was a more suitable task for a clerical assembly than for the universities," Diarmaid MacCulloch, *Thomas Cranmer: A Life*, New Haven, 1996, 291.

Change and Transformation

conversation, challenge, and debate as broadly as possible in the English Church, across theological boundaries. In all these things, the KJV nicely reaffirmed and shaped the ideals of the Reformation Church of England.

The experience was characteristically Anglican in one more way: the completed work was greeted by some with sharp criticism, and by others with what Alistair McGrath has called "polite disinterest."[38] One of the sharpest critics was a noted Hebraist named Hugh Broughton, who had felt slighted by not being chosen for the KJV translation team, and who immediately published an eight-page diatribe against it. "Tell his Majesty," he says in the pamphlet, "that I had rather be rent in pieces with wild horses, than any such translation by my consent should be urged upon poor Churches."[39] The polite disinterest is demonstrated by the continued popularity of the Geneva Bible for at least another half a century, and probably much longer than that. There have continued to be conflicting evaluations of the KJV in modern times. One modern scholar agrees with those in the seventeenth century who preferred the Geneva Bible over "the backward-looking, increasingly Latinist, often baldly unhelpful KJV."[40] Some say that the KJV is a poor study bible because it often translates the same Hebrew or Greek word in different ways in different places, although others say that it generally translates the most common words in the same way. Some say that its "normalizing" of voice disguises the great diversity of genres and styles of biblical literature, while others say that the consistency of style is liturgically useful and that it also conveys the canonical integrity of the entire text. Some say that its principle of "formal equivalence" or word-for-word translation pointlessly retains obscure Hebrew and Greek idioms instead of ensuring that the real English sense shines through. For instance, the phrase translated in the KJV "him that pisseth against the wall," which appears five times in the historical books of the Old Testament, receives a much more genteel rendering in modern translations.[41] On the other hand, there is general agreement today that the sixteenth-century *textus receptus* on which the KJV relies can no longer be regarded as dependable, and we also now have a better knowledge of ancient Semitic languages than any of the KJV translators had.

Nevertheless, the style, melodics, and language of the KJV are quite delicious, and they powerfully shaped Anglican Christianity, and indeed the English-speaking world. The KJV translators do not deserve all the credit

38. McGrath, *In the Beginning*, 278.

39. Hugh Broughton, *A Censure of the late translation for our Churches, 1611?*, in STC 3847, [p. 1].

40. Daniell, *The Bible in English*, 347.

41 Gerald Hammond, "English Translations of the Bible," in Robert Alter and Frank Kermode, eds., *A Literary Guide to the Bible*, Cambridge, MA, 1990, 647–667.

for this success: as we noted earlier, they were instructed to build on existing translations, and for the New Testament and much of the Old Testament, it has been estimated that they drew between 80 percent and 90 percent of the KJV from William Tyndale's translations. With a keen appreciation of the Anglo-Saxon spirit of English, Tyndale had a genius for poetic phrasing, an inspired skill at creating new English words like "Passover" and "scapegoat" instead of anglicizing Latin words, and a fine sensibility for the well-turned phrase ("live and move and have our being," "gave up the ghost," "twinkling of an eye," "my brother's keeper"). The principle of respecting continuities and familiarities in translation was followed also in the New Revised Standard Version, which in its preface promises to continue in "the tradition of the King James Version," except where change is required for "accuracy, clarity, euphony, and current English usage."

The KJV was intended to be read publicly in church, and perhaps its main strength is its liturgical character. In this, indeed, we are left to argue in a circle, since we have said that the main appeal of the *Book of Common Prayer* was its biblical character. But that is to say that the synergies between English liturgy and English Bible were profound. Adam Nicolson, drawing on notes by one of the KJV translators, John Bois, and a remark sometime later by John Selden, a legal scholar, says that the procedure of translation included listening. One translator would read the draft of a section out loud, while the others would read silently along from bibles in other languages.[42] Cecily Raysor agrees: the KJV met "habitual expectations established by liturgical language," partly because its archaic vocabulary and syntax were consistent with liturgical language that was familiar, traditional, and resistant to change. Language venerable for its age, but entirely intelligible, can be effective for liturgy because it reminds us that the worship in which we participate is raised not with our voices alone but with all the saints throughout the ages. Raysor identifies numerous phrases in the KJV that already sounded archaic in 1611: "these my brethren," "when saw we thee," "a far country," "go ye out to meet him," "I know you not."[43] Not only did the KJV evoke liturgical resonances in its vocabulary and syntax, it did so as well in its rhythms and melody. Bruce McLeod, a former moderator of the United Church of Canada, invites the reader: "Try it yourself with Proverbs 3:17. Say it aloud: 'Her ways are ways of pleasantness, and all her paths are peace.' You can conduct that rhythm, like music. Now read the New English Bible

---

42. Adam Nicolson, *God's Secretaries: The Making of the English Bible*, New York, 2003, 209.

43. Cecily Raysor, "A Comparison of the Style of Four Recent Translations of the New Testament with That of the King James Version," *Journal of Religion* 41 (1961) 73–90.

version: 'Her ways are pleasant ways, and all her paths lead to prosperity.' It's school-perfect—even reaching back for a good word from a KJV precursor, the Geneva Bible of 1560—but it doesn't sing."[44]

THE KING JAMES VERSION AND ANGLICANISM

Increasingly after 1611, the KJV was read out in the lections for the liturgy Sunday by Sunday to all of England, and studied by groups of Christians, and used for family devotions, and absorbed privately by individuals. Accurate in scholarship (by contemporary standards), attractive in language, as free as could be of partisan linkages, it stood for three centuries as the culmination of a process by which the Church of England gave the people of God, as Sykes says, "the means of judging matters concerning the faith." In the context of Anglican Christianity, it promoted religious conversation and guided theological argument. It functioned as an instrument of dispersed interpretive authority.

But can we go farther than this? Could it be that dispersed interpretive authority was not merely a function of the KJV, but its deliberate intent? For even if we agreed that the KJV gave the people of England the resource they needed to draw their own conclusions about the Christian faith, that might have been an unforeseen and unwelcome outcome. Can we assert that the KJV was intended for the very purpose of giving the people of God the means and the authority to understand Scripture for themselves?

Our answer will depend in large part on our view of King James I. He was the supreme governor of a quasi-Erastian church. He wielded enormous authority over its policies and character. He claimed the authority and responsibility of a Christian prince, following the model of Christian princes dating back to Constantine, who in turn claimed the authority of the faithful kings of Judah and Israel, to promote the spiritual welfare of his people. Moreover, he took a deep personal interest in the churches and in things theological; he was a published theologian of some international profile, endorsed by no less an authority than Theodore Beza, Calvin's successor at Geneva. Did King James want the laity to use his Bible version to form their own judgments about the Christian faith?

According to older views of King James, such a motive would have been very far from his mind. He was long seen by historians as an authoritarian monarch who brooked no dissent. He was an early and forceful proponent

---

44. Pearce J. Carefoot, *Great and Manifold: A Celebration of the Bible in English: Commemorating the Four-hundredth Anniversary of the First Printing of the King James Bible*, Toronto, 2011, 66.

of the divine right of kings. He was ruled by profoundly anti-Puritan and anti-Catholic prejudices. His regime jailed Puritans, executed Catholics, and burned heretics.

Since the 1970s, however, a revised historiography has emerged. The king has more recently been recognized as a wise and politically astute ruler, who, having received a divided and demoralized church from his predecessor Queen Elizabeth, steered it into relative peace and strengthened its pastoral effectiveness. This point of view is encapsulated in the title of Maurice Lee's biography of King James, *England's Solomon*,[45] a reference to the fact that even in the king's own day contemporaries compared him to the wise, practical, and faithful king of Israel.

Four dimensions of James' ecclesiastical policy are especially pertinent. First, he practiced a wide toleration of religious opinion, particularly after about 1611. True, he found religious "extremism" personally distasteful, and he was by no means indulgent of persons who were potentially dangerous or defiant. But his preference, which became clear after the first few years of his reign, was to leave both Roman Catholics and Puritans. "James had none of Elizabeth's fearful paranoia about Catholics and Puritans," writes Jenny Wormald; "theological debate, not the imposition of conformity, was what interested him." She concludes with forgivable overstatement: "He was never afraid of differences of religious opinion."[46] Another historian declares that he had "the most advanced royal ideas on toleration that the seventeenth century would see."[47] Perhaps the word "toleration" does not do justice to the king's positive appreciation of theological argument. At the beginning of his reign, his more rigid approach to religion was understandable. He had some justification to worry about Roman Catholicism after the Gunpowder Plot of 1605, the third unsuccessful Roman Catholic conspiracy against his life in three years, and after the assassination of the Protestant King Henri IV of France by a Roman Catholic in 1610. But increasingly he was pleased to overlook Roman Catholic activity in the country and even at court. In regard to Puritanism, he was provoked by clergy early in his reign who refused to conform to the legal requirements of liturgical leadership; about eighty of them were deprived of their church livings before 1611. But after that, only two Puritan clergy were deprived in the rest of his reign. Outright separatists and heretics remained outside the pale, and Edward Wightman was painfully executed in 1611 for anti-Trinitarian teaching. But

---

45. Maurice Lee, *England's Solomon: James VI and I in his Three Kingdoms*, Urbana, IL, 1990.

46. Jenny Wormald, "James VI and I," *History Today* 52/6 (2002) 27–33.

47. Dorothy Boyd Rush, "The Religious Toleration of James I," *History Today* 29/2 (1979) 106–12.

his heterodoxy seems to have been overlooked until he began disrupting meetings, confronting citizens, and breaking the peace, and as it turned out he was the last person to be burned for heresy in England. In these first years of his reign, the king's strong hostility to dissent may have been influenced by his advisers: Sir Robert Cecil, his leading minister, who was obsessed by state security; John Whitgift, the archbishop of Canterbury whom he inherited from Queen Elizabeth, who was virulently anti-Puritan; and Richard Bancroft, whom he appointed to follow Whitgift, and who was equally hostile to Puritans. But his next and last appointment to Canterbury was George Abbot, who took a very lenient approach to Puritan nonconformists. Throughout his reign the king appointed bishops of a variety of theological beliefs, ensuring that no one school of thought would dominate, and that theological discussion would be fertile. "Since the Church of England claimed to embrace the entire population," Roger Lockyer writes, "it was appropriate that its hierarchy should be similarly all-embracing."[48]

Second, King James aspired to strengthen the intellectual and theological quality of the Church of England. Unlike Elizabeth, who suppressed the Bible studies called "prophesyings" in the province of Canterbury, James proclaimed the Canons of 1604, which specifically protected them. The practice appears to have become widespread. Also, unlike Elizabeth, who was always anxious about unsupervised preachers, James supported Abbot's efforts "to promote a learned and diligent preaching ministry." The reason Archbishop Abbot was lenient with Puritans, according to one of his biographers, was his sense that "the church could ill afford to lose some of its most committed preachers by a close scrutiny of their adherence to ecclesiastical discipline,"[49] and the king seems to have agreed. Near the end of James' reign one of the bishops memorably declared in a sermon to the Convocation of Canterbury in 1624, "*Stupor mundi clerus britannicus*"—the British clergy were the wonder of the world.[50]

Third, King James was committed to the doctrine called adiaphorism—the view that beliefs and practices neither prescribed nor prohibited in Scripture could not bind conscience one way or the other. Adiaphorism had found its way into the Thirty-Nine Articles of Religion of the Church of England in Article XXXIV: "It is not necessary that traditions and ceremonies be in all places one or utterly alike." For James religious extremism

---

48. Roger Lockyer, *The Early Stuarts*, 2nd ed., London, 1989, 70.

49. Kenneth Fincham, "Abbot, George (1562–1633)," in *Oxford Dictionary of National Biography*, ed. H. C. G. Matthew and Brian Harrison, Oxford, 2004; online ed., ed. Lawrence Goldman, January 2011, http://www.oxforddnb.com.myaccess.library.utoronto.ca/view/article/4.

50. Joseph Hall, *Works,* ed. Philip. Wynter, 10 vols., Oxford, 1863, x, 29.

meant "making for every particular question of the policy of the Church, as great commotion, as if the article of the Trinity were called in very controversy."[51] Fourth, King James had a personal passion and vision for international ecumenism. He wanted to improve understanding between the churches of his two realms, the Church of England and the Church of Scotland. He wanted to see cooperation throughout the wider Reformed world, and he had a broader ecumenical vision that encompassed Lutherans, Roman Catholics, and Greek Orthodox. He announced to his first parliament in March 1604 that he intended to organize an ecumenical church council with the purpose of reuniting Christendom. In 1618 he saw an opportunity to further that aim when Dutch Reformed clergy met at the Synod of Dort. He sent representatives there with a proposal for church unity. He invited foreign theologians to teach in England, including an Italian scholar and archbishop, Marco Antonio de Dominis, whose *De Republica Ecclesiastica* articulated an ecumenical theology.[52]

All these dimensions of the King's ecclesiastical policy—accepting or even welcoming a circumscribed range of religious difference, strengthening the theological and pastoral quality of the church, distinguishing the essentials of faith from things indifferent, promoting international Christian ecumenism—were related to each other and were all related to improving the knowledge of Scripture among the people of God. In his *Basilikon Doron*, which was addressed to his son but published to the world, James echoed Cranmer's advice on Bible-reading in the preface to the Great Bible: "Read with delight the plain places, and study carefully to understand those that are somewhat difficult."[53] Scripture alone was authoritative, not the church and not individual opinion. "Beware therefore in this case with two extremities," he wrote, "the one, to believe with the Papists, the Church's authority better than your own knowledge; the other, to lean with the Anabaptists, to your own conceits and dreamed revelations."[54] Educating his kingdom in Scripture so that people could distinguish essentials from adiaphora, discuss their disagreements, strengthen the church, and help lead Europe towards Christian reunion was King James' vision for the Church of England.

The king seems to have assumed that Scripture would ultimately lead everyone except extremists in one direction to the fundamental truths of the

51. James I, *Basilikon Doron*, in *Political Works*, ed. C.H. McIlwain, Cambridge, MA, 1918, 7.

52. W. B. Patterson, *King James VI and I and the Reunion of Christendom*, Cambridge, 1996; Rush, "The Religious Toleration of James I," 106.

53. *Basilikon Doron*, 14.

54. Ibid., 17.

Change and Transformation

Christian faith, such as the doctrine of the Trinity. From our post-modern vantage point, we may suppose that this was naive. There were probably those in his own day who were skeptical on this point, too. Shakespeare's Richard III knew that psychology was at play in the interpretation of Scripture, and he notoriously exploited that in his scheming:

> But then I sigh; and, with a piece of scripture,
> Tell them that God bids us do good for evil:
> And thus I clothe my naked villainy
> With old odd ends stolen out of holy writ. (Act I, Scene III)

Of course the real Richard III, who lived a century before any English Bible was legal, could not have used it to fool people. Shakespeare was writing to an audience that was accustomed to study Scripture to answer questions on which people could disagree. The KJV stands as evidence that in King James' mind the antidote to the misinterpretation of Scripture was not less Bible study by the whole people of God, but more. To be peaceful, strong, merry, and holy, England needed to agree on a version of the English Bible, esteem it highly, read it diligently, and understand it well.

AFTERMATH

After the reign of King James, the murderous power of religious division became acutely obvious in the Civil War and, across the channel, in the bloody Thirty Years War. As a result there came a widespread revulsion against what was called revealed religion. Like new plants in a disturbed soil, Enlightenment science and latitudinarian Christianity took root in England, teaching that religion should be reasonable, that is, demonstrable to universal human reason. Revelations divided; reason united. Meanwhile, views of the role of the state were changing, too. King James had assumed that a Christian prince should promote the people's spiritual well-being and that the state should enforce a good religious order. That premise came under attack from both left and right. From an Enlightenment direction, John Locke removed religion from civil oversight in the *Fundamental Constitutions* (1669) for Carolina. From a religious direction, Roger Williams, who wanted people to be Christian in obedience to God and not in obedience to the state, erected a "wall of separation" between citizenship and religion in Rhode Island (1637). By the end of the century, the prospect of religious unity had become so distant in England that parliament began to allow citizens to exit the Church of England and start their own churches under licence. King James' dream of a religiously united England, a religiously united Great Britain, and a religiously united Christendom, all joined on the basis of the pure word of God, was no more.

Nevertheless, the king's vision did take root in the Church of England. With Scripture and liturgy at its centre, and interpretive authority dispersed among the people of God, the church could realize the fellowship of the Holy Spirit. A common Bible and a common Prayer Book were necessary. The KJV and *Book of Common Prayer* in close partnership held sway for three centuries as the hallmarks of Anglicanism, although the Prayer Book began to undergo changes here and there in the various branches of the Anglican Communion. Even after the KJV yielded, in most twentieth-century churches, to more modern translations, and even after the mid-Tudor *Book of Common Prayer* yielded, in many Anglican congregations, to the modern products of the liturgical movement, the fundamental elements of Anglican identity endured. The means of judging matters concerning the faith remained in the hands of the whole people of God by reason of their access to the scriptures, as established by the liturgy, backed by canon law.

3

The Reformed Consensus on the Doctrine of the Eucharist

Daniel Brevint's *The Christian Sacrament and Sacrifice* (1673)

ERIC R. GRIFFIN

> He stood upon the *ancient* ground, looked upon evangelical *duties* as the *true* oblations and *sacrifices*, resolved the *sacrifice* of the Eucharist, *actively* considered, solely into them. He explained the *practical* uses of that doctrine in so *clear*, so *lively*, and so *affecting* a way, that one will scarce meet with any thing on the subject that can be justly thought to exceed it, or even come up to it.
>
> Bishop Daniel Waterland on Daniel Brevint[1]

Daniel Brevint (1616–95), prebendary of Durham then dean of Lincoln, was born on Jersey in the Channel Islands and was educated at both the reformed academy at Saumur and at Oxford. He is best known for his

---

1. Daniel Waterland, "The Christian Sacrifice Explained," in William Van Mildert, ed., *The Works of the Rev.Daniel Waterland, D.D.*, 2nd ed., 6 vols., Oxford, 1843, v, 139–40.

Eric R. Griffin   *The Reformed Consensus on the Doctrine of the Eucharist*

small book *The Christian Sacrament and Sacrifice* published in 1673, which became popular, going into three editions during Brevint's own lifetime, reprinted three more times during the eighteenth century and again in 1847.[2] It strongly influenced the eucharistic theology of John and Charles Wesley, who used John's abridgement of it as the preface to their enormously popular *Hymns on the Lord's Supper*, which was itself inspired, both in form and content, by Brevint's book. Apart from two studies of John Wesley's abridgement,[3] and a very brief examination of Brevint's book itself,[4] Brevint remains largely neglected among the seventeenth-century English divines.[5]

The Nonjuring Bishop George Hickes in his *Christian Priesthood* (1707) called *The Christian Sacrament and Sacrifice* an "excellent little book," which he quoted, and added "I wish it were reprinted, for the honour of God and the benefit of the Church."[6] The eighteenth-century bishop, Daniel Waterland, admired Brevint, this book in particular, and quoted it and Brevint's *Missale Romanum or Depth and Mystery of Roman Mass*[7] many times. Waterland included him among the "best learned Protestants," placing him in the company of Cranmer, Andrewes, Buckeridge, Taylor, Montague, DuPlessis-Mornay, and Laud, among others. During the main period of the Oxford Movement, Pusey quoted *The Christian Sacrament*

---

2. Daniel Brevint, *The Christian Sacrament and Sacrifice: by way of discourse, meditation, and prayer upon the nature, parts, and blessings, of the Holy Communion. Missale romanum; or, Depth and mystery of Roman mass: laid open and explained, for the use of both reformed and un-reformed Christians*, new edition, Oxford, 1847. This is the last printing of *Missale Romanum* and is the one used in this study. All citations from *The Christian sacrament and sacrifice* are to chapter and paragraph from the 1st Oxford edition 1673. These do not correspond to the divisions of Wesley's abridgement: John and Charles Wesley, *Hymns on the Lord's Supper, with a Preface concerning The Christian Sacrament and Sacrifice, Extracted from Dr. Brevint*, 2nd ed., Bristol, 1752.

3. Ernest Rattenbury, *The Eucharist Hymns of John and Charles Wesley*, London, 1948; Henry R. McAdoo, "A Theology of the Eucharist: Brevint and the Wesleys," *Theology* 97 (1994) 245–56.

4. Kenneth Stevenson, *Covenant of Grace Renewed: A Vision of the Eucharist in the Seventeenth Century*, London, 1994.

5. For an account of Brevint's life from primary sources see Eric R. Griffin, "Daniel Brevint: French Preacher to the King in Exile," *Anglican and Episcopal History* 69/3 (2000) 295–314.

6. George Hickes, *Two Treatises on the Christian Priesthood and on the Dignity of the Episcopal Order*, 3 vols., 4th ed., Oxford, 1847, 99–100.

7. Besides the expected rant against Rome, it also contains some comments on the Reformed doctrine of the eucharist that complement *The Christian Sacrament and Sacrifice*.

and Sacrifice extensively in *Tract 81* and took a few passages from *Missale Romanum* as well.[8]

Despite the well-known divisions that existed in the Church of England between "Anglicans" and "Puritans" over issues such as episcopal polity, eternal election, sabbatarianism, predestination, liturgical conformity etc., there was little or no disagreement among them regarding the Lord's Supper.[9] This unanimity found its source in John Calvin. John Cosin wrote that regarding the eucharistic sacrifice, Calvin's " ... words in his Institutions and elsewhere are such, so comfortable to the style and mind of the ancient fathers, that no Catholic Protestant would wish to use any other."[10] This Calvinist consensus on the eucharist can be generally summarized as:

- the assertion of the real and objective presence of Christ as sacrificed, which is not dependent on the subjective condition of the recipient;
- the rejection of both transubstantiation and Lutheran consubstantiation;
- the rejection of the "bare" memorialism of Zwingli;
- the refusal to speculate on the manner of Christ's presence;
- the condemnation of the adoration of the sacrament;
- the insistence on administration of both bread and wine;
- the insistence on the vernacular;
- consecration is the setting apart of the elements for sacred use;
- the consecrated elements have no virtue in themselves apart from consumption;
- an emphasis on frequent reception;
- a real and spiritual, that is, neither imaginary nor corporeal, communication of Christ in the sacrament; the sacrament conveys what it symbolizes while nevertheless not containing it;

---

8. "Catena Patrum No. IV: Testimony of writers of the later English Church to the Doctrine of the Eucharistic Sacrifice, with an historical account of the changes made in the Liturgy as to the expression of that doctrine," in *Tracts for the Times: By Members of the University of Oxford*, 6 vols., London, 1838, iv, 190–99, 272, 369.

9. The historiographical controversy regarding the meaning of "Puritan" and "Anglican," is immense, but it seems the use of the terms themselves is unavoidable. For the purposes of this essay the word "Puritan" is restricted to those conforming "hotter sort of protestants" (a designation coined by Percival Wiburn in 1581) who remained in the Established Church.

10. John Cosin, "The History of Popish Transubstantiation," in *The Works of the Right Reverend Father in God, John Cosin, Lord Bishop of Durham. Now first collected*, 5 vols., Oxford, 1851, iv, 167.

- the faithless do not receive the Body of Christ, not because Christ is not presented to them, but without faith they are unable to receive him;
- the insistence on the reality and necessity of the eucharistic sacrifice;
- rejection that the eucharist is in any way a propitiatory sacrifice;
- the sacramental union between the sign and the thing signified is such that one may legitimately be called by the name of the other.[11]

The Puritans and Anglicans were aware of their consensus, although not everyone has believed their self-assessment. Gregory Dix wrote:

> Ever since the sixteenth century we Anglicans have been so divided over eucharistic doctrine, and are to-day so conscious of our divisions, that there is scarcely any statement that could be made about either the eucharist or one's own rite which would not seem to some of one's fellow churchmen to call for immediate contradiction on conscientious grounds.[12]

This statement is simply contrary to fact. The theology of *The Christian Sacrament and Sacrifice* typifies the Calvinist sacramental consensus of the English church, and it became so popular precisely because it comprehensively presented the best of the eucharistic writing of the time. Crockett writes: "There is nothing in his treatise that cannot be paralleled in other seventeenth-century Anglican writers. What is remarkable about the treatise is its scope and balance, and its recovery of eucharistic themes which had not achieved as clear expression in earlier Anglican tradition."[13] Brevint's book contributed little that was unique in itself; it is the breadth and clarity of Brevint's presentation rather than his originality that makes his contribution significant.

GENRE, COMPOSITION, AND SOURCES

The Christian Sacrament and Sacrifice was originally composed sometime between 1654 and 1659 in Paris as a devotional manual for the private use of "thoſe two incomparable Princeſſes" the wife of Marechal Vicomte de Turenne, Charlotte, to whom Brevint was chaplain during the Interregnum, and the Duchesse de Bouillon, the Marechal's mother.

---

11. For Calvin's doctrine of the eucharist, see Brian Garrish, *Grace and Gratitude: The Eucharistic Theology of John Calvin*, Minneapolis, 1993.
12. Gregory Dix, *The Shape of the Liturgy*, London, 1945, 613–14.
13. William R. Crockett, *Eucharist: Symbol of Transformation*, New York, 1989.

Change and Transformation

Eucharistic manuals were highly popular during the seventeenth century[14] and encyclopedic devotional manuals had extensive eucharistic sections. The best-known of these, Lewis Bayly's *The Practice of Piety*[15] and the anonymous *The Whole Duty of Man*[16] went through many reprints, and both placed high emphasis on both the correct understanding and the worthy reception of the Holy Communion. The uniform theology of the eucharist found in these devotional manuals further witnesses to the unanimity concerning the sacrament.

Brevint's presentation is very different from these manuals, however. He keeps *The Christian Sacrament and Sacrifice* firmly fixed on the sacrament and not on the state of the soul of the recipient. There are certain penitential elements in its prayers, but no specifically penitential section, no sense of morbid introspection and minute spiritual scrutiny of the worthy communicant, or the resolving of cases of tender conscience which are dominant themes in other manuals. Brevint avoids such controversies as the wearing of surplices, liturgical conformity, kneeling, the worthiness of the presiding minister or the fencing of altars against the non-elect. He never considers subjects such as ceremony, episcopal legitimacy, or (to use an anachronism) "ecumenical" hospitality. He alludes to Scripture at every opportunity, but never mentions the dependence of the sacrament upon the word or whether the communion was valid apart from preaching. *The Christian Sacrament and Sacrifice* is about the sacrament, neither the state of the soul of the communicant nor the manner of communication. *The Christian Sacrament and Sacrifice* is also very different from Brevint's other two books. It is much shorter, and apart from one barb in the preface, it contains little anti-papal polemic, and lacks the nasty, jeering tone of his others. It is primarily devotional, chapters concluded with long carefully

---

14. Some other manuals of note are: *A Weeks Preparation Toward a Worthy Receiving of the Lord's Supper*, 47th ed., London, 1738; John Gauden, *The Whole Duty of A Communicant: Being Rules and Directions for a worthy receiving the most Holy Sacrament of the Lord's Supper*, 3rd ed., London: 1687; Jeremy Taylor, *The Worthy Communicant*, London, 1671; Simon Patrick, *Mensa Mystica*, 4th ed., London, orig. 1660; Simon Patrick, *The Christian Sacrifice: A Treatise Shewing the Necessity, End, and Manner of Receiving the Holy Communion*, 8th ed., London, 1687; Christopher Sutton, *Godly Meditations upon the Most Holy Sacrament of the Lordes Supper*, n.p., 1630, which was reissued by John Henry Newman with a new preface in 1838, and became very popular with Tractarians.

15. Lewis Bayly, *The Practice of Piety*, n.p., c. 1612. It was staggeringly popular amongst Puritans running into a 58th edition by 1619, the largest section in the book being on the Lord's Supper. See C. J. Stranks, *Anglican Devotion: Studies in the Spiritual Life of the Church of England between the Reformation and the Oxford Movement*, London, 1961, 54.

16. Attributed to Richard Allestree (1657).

composed prayers, and although there are a few scattered footnotes, it is not a scholarly dissertation. *Missale Romanum* demonstrated that Brevint had a good facility with the Fathers, but in *The Christian Sacrament and Sacrifice* he makes few direct patristic references: nine scattered references to Augustine, and a single reference to each of Tertullian, Ignatius, Cyprian, Gelasius of Cyzicus, Irenaeus, and Chrysostom. He cites no classical, medieval, reformation, contemporary or Jewish writers.

THE CHRISTIAN SACRAMENT AND SACRIFICE: METHOD

The main theme of *The Christian Sacrament and Sacrifice* is that no one is to approach the altar of the Lord with empty hands, and so we must come with our hands full of sacrifices. Gregory Dix argued that ever since the Reformation there has been a deliberate effort to suppress any sense of sacrifice in the eucharist, and described Cranmer's difficulty regarding the offering of alms and the preparing of the bread and wine, so that there would be no "stink of oblation," to use Luther's term.[17] To the contrary, the eucharistic sacrifice is "indispensable" to the Lord's Supper according to Calvin,[18] and the sacrifice of the eucharist is that of praise and thanksgiving, in memory of the one and only propitiatory sacrifice of Christ on the cross. Stephen Gardiner tried to undermine Cranmer by declaring that the 1549 liturgy clearly implied the propitiatory sacrifice of the mass, yet Cranmer did not avoid sacrificial language in his response, so long as it was made clear that the eucharistic sacrifice is commemorative, not propitiatory. Launcelot Andrewes continued the argument with his now familiar statement in his dispute with Cardinal Bellarmine: "Do you take away from the Mass your transubstantiation; and there will not long be any strife with us about the sacrifice" and that "Eucharistia est simul sacrificium et sacramentum" (the eucharist is simultaneously sacrifice and sacrament).[19] In his reply to "R.F.," Brevint criticized Fuller for the long lists of authorities in which "he musters out as many places as he can find, that make any mention of *Liturgy, Oblation, Holy Victim, Incruental Sacrifice*, and *Mass* somtimes, which no Protestants dispute against."[20] In *The Christian Sacrament and Sacrifice* he

---

17. Dix, *Shape of the Liturgy*, 660–61.

18. John Calvin, *The Institutes of the Christian Religion*, ed. John T. McNeill, trans. Ford Lewis Battles, Philadelphia, 1960, IV.18.17.

19. Andrewes, *Responsio ad Apologiam Cardinalis Bellarmini*, LACT, 1841, 248–67.

20. Brevint, *Saul and Samuel at Endor, or, the new waies of salvation and service . . .*, Oxford, 1674, 408.

Change and Transformation

states concerning Christ's sacrifice at the crucifixion: "Nevertheless this sacrifice which by a real oblation was not to be offered up more than once, is by an Eucharistical and devout commemoration to be offered up every day."[21] Here Brevint succinctly asserts the reformation principle of Christ's unrepeatable sacrifice, and that the eucharist is a perpetual commemoration of that sacrifice; in fact approval of daily celebration may here be implied.[22]

As was the norm, Brevint's exegesis of the Old Testament was typological, and he discussed the eucharist in terms of the Old Testament sacrifices. The Church is the "New Israel" and heir to all of the promises of the Hebrew covenants. The Old Testament rites and sacrifices were themselves sacraments that "prefigured" and were fulfilled by the sacraments of the New Covenant. The Puritans commonly called circumcision a sacrament of the Old Covenant, parallel to, fulfilled and superseded by baptism;[23] similarly the Passover was understood to foreshadow, and contain the same grace as the eucharist. The Westminster Confession (XXIX.5) declared: "The sacraments of the Old Testament, in regard of the spiritual things thereby signified and exhibited, were, for substance, the same with those of the New."[24] An example of Brevint's typological exegesis is that of manna, which was a "type" of the sacramental nature of the eucharist, which is its fulfilling "antitype:"

> The Body of the Lord as it was offered up to God in sacrifice, is the truth represented by the *Passover*: and as represented to us at the Holy Communion, is the truth and accomplishment typified by the *manna* . . . That is to say, as bread and wine do not produce, but keep up that animal life, which another Cause hath produced: so doth our Lord Jesus by a necessary and continual *supply* of strength and grace, represented by *bread and wine*, sustain, improve, and set forward that *spiritual life* and new being, which He hath procured us by his cross. (III.6)

---

21. Brevint, *The Christian Sacrament and Sacrifice*, VI.3.

22. Brevint supported Bishop Barlow in his efforts to re-establish weekly eucharist at Lincoln, as he had similarly supported Dean Granville in Durham.

23. For example, according to Sibbes the circumcision of Abraham was such a sacrament, not only a bare sign, or a sign of faith, but also a seal of the covenant. Richard Sibbes, "The Right Receiving," *The Complete Works of Richard Sibbes, D.D*, ed. Alexander B. Grosart, 7 vols., Edinburgh, 1863, iv, 65.

24. *The Westminster Confession of Faith: With Introduction and Notes*, ed. John MacPherson, 2nd ed., Edinburgh, 155–56. See also *Missale Romanum*: "Run over all, whether sacraments or signs, in the Old and New Testament. The lamb is the passover. Circumcision, the covenant. The seven kine, seven years. The rock, Christ. Sarah and [H]Agar, two covenants." *Missale Romanum*, 297.

As Christ is the "truth" of the paschal lamb, Christ is the "truth" of the manna, but the figure is incomplete, says Brevint, because it shows only the giving, not the suffering and passion. In the eucharist alone is the representation of Christ made complete:

> Christ relates to these four figures as the *body* which fulfils them: and the Holy Communion relates to them on the other side, as an *antitype*, that is, as one image may relate to another, all to express the same object ... But this is the advantage of the Holy Communion above all the ancient figures. Adam with his open side, and all sacrifices with their blood did foretel only Christs passion: and the tree of life with all its fruit, and the Angel with all his food [manna] did foretel only, his *preserving* grace: whereas this sacrament alone represents both his passion, and *preserving*, and besides these, another great mystery, by their mutual dependency. (III.11)

Typological exegesis is by its very nature supercessionist, and Brevint says explicitly that the eucharist "replaces" the Passover. His reference to "the late Jews" presumably refers to the doctrine that the Church is now the "True Israel," while the Jews, the "former Israel" so to speak, had relinquished any claim they had of being the people of God. Brevint was no more anti-Semitic than anyone else of his age.[25] His appeal to the Hebrew sacrificial tradition, his familiarity with the Seder and the fact that his real contempt and vitriol were reserved for Roman Catholics may imply that he was rather more sympathetic than hostile. In *The Christian Sacrament and Sacrifice* VIII.8, Brevint praises the "Old" Israel, stating: "So shall the new Israel tread on the pious steps of the old, who ever from time to time reiterated ... that Covenant which the Lord had made with him in Sinai." In VIII.9, Brevint quotes Deuteronomy 16:10—11, and states that in this passage Moses "with the same power" commands both Old and New Israel to keep feasts with offered sacrifices.

THE CHRISTIAN SACRAMENT AND SACRIFICE: OUTLINE

Christian Sacrament and Sacrifice is divided into two sections, one on the eucharist as sacrament, and the other as sacrifice. It is divided into eight chapters prefaced by the epistle. The argument does not strictly follow the

---

25. Wesley further softened Brevint's comment at the beginning of ch. VI that "the Jews and the Pagans" both "slandered" the Christian Church by accusing it of lacking sacrifices: section VI.1 of the abridgement reads only "heathens."

chapter divisions, so different outlines of the book have been suggested. Although using Wesley's abridgement, Rattenbury's summary is exactly right, dividing Brevint's argument into two major parts with further subdivision by chapter. First, Chapter 1 serves as the Introduction, then Part I The Eucharist as Sacrament" consists of three sections: Chapter 2: The Sacrament as a Memorial of Christ; Chapter 3: The Sacrament as a sign of present graces, with Chapter 4: The Sacrament as a means of grace;[26] and Chapter 5: The Sacrament as a pledge of future glory. Secondly, there is "The Eucharist as Sacrifice" which is comprised of Chapter 6: The Eucharist as a Commemorative Sacrifice; Chapter 7: The Sacrifice of our own persons; and Chapter 8: The Sacrifice of our goods and offerings.[27]

But in point of fact, Brevint drew his outline from Theodore Beza's *Quaestionum et Responsionum christianarum pars altera, quae est de Sacramentis*, which states that the sacramental nature of the eucharist looks to, and unites together, the three times of past, present and future, the idea that Brevint uses for the basis of the first section of *The Christian Sacrament and Sacrifice*.[28] Beza further stated that the eucharist may be understood as a sacrifice in three ways: as a peace-offering, the sacrificial aspect of our almsgiving, and thirdly the commemoration of the death of Christ,[29] which Brevint uses as the basis of the second part. Although Beza was the immediate source for Brevint's teaching that the sacrament unites past, present and future, using the idea was by no means unique to Brevint. John Buckeridge's funeral sermon for Lancelot Andrewes, written fifty years after Beza's *Quaestionum et Responsionum*, also stated that the sacrament had a "triple signification:" a commemoration of Christ's death in the past, a means of grace in the present, and assurance of salvation in the future; but Buckeridge attributed the idea to Thomas Aquinas.[30]

---

26. Wesley combined these two chapters into a single section.

27. J. Ernest Rattenbury, *The Eucharistic Hymns of John and Charles Wesley*, London, 16.

28. Theodore Beza, *Quaestionum et Responsionum christianarum pars altera, quae est de Sacramentis*, Geneva: 1576, Pt. II, 331:12; Jill Raitt, *The Eucharistic Theology of Theodore Beza: Development of the Reformed Doctrine*, Chambersburg, PA, 1972.

29. Beza, *Quaestionum*, 351:164–5. Although this work is theologically and philosophically technical, in the form of questions and answers, and longer than *Christian Sacrament and Sacrifice*, it too is eirenic rather than polemical, which is unusual for both Brevint and Beza. It has not been translated or reprinted since the late sixteenth century.

30. John Buckeridge, "A Sermon Preached at the Funeral of the Right Reverend Father in God Lancelot, late Lord Bishop of Winchester," in Andrewes, *Ninety-six Sermons*, 5 vols., London, 1843, v, 259–60, 263. Though Buckeridge does not cite the place, it is *Summa Theologica* Part III, quaes. 73, art. 4. *Christian Sacrament and Sacrifice* and

Eric R. Griffin   *The Reformed Consensus on the Doctrine of the Eucharist*

THE EPISTLE

The epistle which prefaces the work is addressed to Brevint's sister-in-law Elizabeth Carteret. The eucharist, he writes, "is as the most generous plant in the vineyard of the Lord" and that it is as "the tree of Life" in Eden, an image he will repeat often. It is found also in Jeremy Taylor, Bayly's *Practice of Piety*,[31] and Samuel Bolton's devotional book *The Guard of the Tree of Life: or A sacramentall discourse*.[32] The sacrament has suffered, Brevint says, first because it was "despitefully treated by popery," second because Protestants were too busy defending it to "dress and improve it," and thirdly because the Anabaptists and Socinians "pretend that the best way of pruning luxuriant excrescencies, is to cut up by the roots." Brevint asserts that he has attempted to avoid both errors:

> I make it my endeavor to rescue it out of the hands of such husbandmen, and to restore all back again both to the full meaning and institution of Christ, who is the Planter as well as the Master of the vineyard, and to the practice of the Holy Fathers, who for several hundreds of years, dressed it, and made it bear excellent fruit. So here I take no more notice of either Papists or Sectaries, no nor Protestants neither ... (Epistle, par.4)

He says that anyone who reads the book will see that the sacrament is like the "Ladder of Jacob." Jacob's Ladder was commonly used in the seventeenth century as a type of Christ, always associated with the allusion to it in the conversation between Jesus and Nathaniel. For Calvin, the Ladder of Jacob represents Christ's perpetual intercession for us.[33] Andrewes refers to it in his "Nativity Sermon" of 1619 and Sibbes uses it to good effect in "The Fountain Opened."[34] Applying the image directly to the eucharist seems to be unique to Brevint.

Buckeridge's sermon have much in common, e.g. Buckeridge likens the sacrament to the "daily offering" of the Jewish Temple, as Brevint will do in chapter VII. It is not unlikely that Brevint might have known about the sermon; Andrewes was bishop of Winchester, to which diocese the Channel Islands were annexed. Brevint would have been about ten years old when he died.

31. Bayly, *Practice of Piety*, 334.

32. Samuel Bolton, *The Guard of the Tree of Life: or A sacramentall discourse ...*, London, 1644.

33. Calvin, *Institutes*, I.14.12. This perpetual intercession of Christ in heaven, in the light of Heb 7:22–28 and 9:12, 24–26, has distinct eucharistic implications, though Calvin does not himself draw eucharistic ideas out in his commentary on Hebrews, apart from condemning the mass.

34. Andrewes, "Sermons of the Nativity Preached upon Christmas-Day," *Works*, 8 vols., Oxford, i, 216–233; Sibbes "The Fountain Opened," in *Works*, v, 516–17.

Change and Transformation

Brevint states that since the sacrament is a mystery, it cannot be comprehended by bare understanding. It is not merely an intellectual problem, but also a spiritual one, and therefore his book will contain both "discours that refers to advancing the mind in knowledg" and meditations and prayers, which "are the only probable means of dealing successfully with holy things." This method of discourse and meditation was used by others such as Lewis Bayly, Richard Baxter and Jeremy Taylor.

Although *The Christian Sacrament and Sacrifice* does contain some attack on Rome, Brevint's presentation may be something of a game; some of his points are subtly made, implying the offender by naming the offence as though he knew that he did not need to state the obvious. As noted above, the first is explicit that the eucharist was "most despitefully treated by Popery," and that the Romanists "made havock of the vineyard, and laid it wast; the fatness of the ground brought forth that poisonous wild vine of the Roman-mass . . . " This is very much like Cranmer, who wrote:

> [B]ut the very body of the tree, or rather the roots of the weeds, is the popish doctrine of transubstantiation, of the real presence of Christ's flesh and blood in the sacrament of the altar (as they call it), and of the sacrifice and oblation of Christ made by the priest, for the salvation of the quick and the dead. Which roots if they be suffered to grow in the Lord's vineyard, they will overspread all the ground again with the old errors and superstitions.[35]

The comparison between Cranmer and Brevint is apt: Book V of Cranmer's *Answer unto a crafty and sophistical cavillation devised by Steven Gardiner Against the True and Godly Doctrine of the most holy sacrament* also concerns the eucharist as a sacrifice, and its relation to the Old Testament sacrificial system.[36] Brevint does not attack Catholics by name again, but his intentions are clear. For example, his allusion in VI.2 to communion in one kind uses the word "mutilated." The use of this word was common in the Caroline period for "half-communion," or the reception of the bread alone. He repeats it in VIII.4: "It is the same act of an impious wretch to mangle, and to mutilate, either the holy sacrifices which Jesus hath made to his father, or the holy Sacrament which he hath ordained to his Church . . . "

Brevint asserts in VI.2 that the sacrifice of Christ on the cross is complete and needs no repetition. Brevint is clearly condemning the Roman

---

35. From "Preface" to Thomas Cranmer, "An Answer unto a crafty and sophistical cavillation devised by Steven Gardiner Against the True and Godly Doctrine of the most holy sacrament . . .," in *The Works of Thomas Cranmer*, ed. John Edmund Cox, 2 vols., Cambridge, 1844, i, 6.

36. Ibid., 348ff.

understanding of the propitiatory sacrifice of the Mass because it implies that the sacrifice of the cross was defective:

> It is most certain also, that this great sacrifice being both of an infinit virtue to satisfy the most severe justice, and of an infinite virtue to produce at once all the effects, that can be expected of it; it were impiety to think, it should need to be don again, as weak and infirm causes must, in order to make up by degrees and at several times their full effect . . . But it were a much greater offence both against the Blood of Christ, to question its infinit worth, and against the infinitness and immensity of this worth, to charge it with som emtiness, which any reiteration should fill up. Therefore as the expiatory sacrifice, which Christ offered upon the cross, was infinitly able to do at once whatever an infinit number of other sacrifices had bin able to do, either all together at one time, or each of them severally during the succession of all ages; the offering of it must needs be one only: and the reiteration of it were not only superfluous as to its real effect, but also most injurious to Christ in the very thought and attemt. (VI.2)[37]

Brevint is careful not to confuse the understanding of the eucharist as a memorial with merely empty figures or signs (II.4), and in this context he is not afraid to use the words "venerable," "devotion," "reverence," and "adoration" regarding the consecrated elements; but then he cannot resist one more allusion to popish error by adding "as soon as I see them used in the Church to that holy purpose that Christ consecrated them to," attacking the elevations and processions of the sacrament.[38] Brevint concludes the epistle with a succinct statement regarding the purpose of the sacrament: "[T]he true end of this Sacrament, . . . [is] nothing less then a mutual communion between us and Christ, even here on earth while we seem to be absent from him."

---

37. This is more specifically and briefly stated in Brevint, *Missale Romanum*, 142: "So [the] Roman Mass is a reproach to the infinite value of Christ's oblation, being visibly grounded on this plain blasphemy, that Christ's oblation upon the cross was defective. To this Mass-priests confess, that the oblation upon the cross is all-sufficient, and so needs not to be reiterated, as far as to redeem: but they maintain withal, that this redeeming is beneficial to nobody, unless it be applied by Mass."

38. Article XXV, "The Sacraments were not ordained of Christ to be gazed upon, or to be carried about, but that we should duly use them."

SACRAMENT AND SACRIFICE

Chapter I is very brief, shorter indeed than the Epistle, and is the introduction to the book. In the first paragraph Brevint asserts that "the Lords Supper is without controversies one of the greatest mysteries of godliness, and the most solemn festival of the Christian religion," and immediately states his theme that it is both sacrament, at which we receive, and a sacrifice, at which we offer. He also used this definition in *Missale Romanum*:

> For, what we call properly Sacrament, is a Divine Ordinance, whereby Christ offers himself and his blessing to faithful people who receive them: and Sacrifice is, as it were, an opposite kind of ordinance, whereby his faithful people are to offer and give up themselves, their praises, their prayers, and all such good works as God, in his mercy, will be pleased to accept of.[39]

Beza's *Quaestionum et Responsionum* makes this precise distinction.[40] The sacrament is the "meeting place" or "tabernacle" between the people and God. Here is an instance of Brevint naming the offence in order to condemn the offender, in this case both Catholics and Zwinglians: he writes that one needs to properly understand the sacrament as being both a sacrament and a sacrifice in order to avoid the errors of making the eucharist either "a false god or an empty ceremony," resulting in superstitious idolatry (popery) or profane abuse (memorialism).

THE SACRAMENT AS MEMORIAL

Part I is organized in terms of salvation history. The sacrament, as it looks to the past, is a commemoration of Christ's death; to the present, it is a means of grace; to the future, it is a pledge and assurance of our salvation. This temporal structure is not commonly found amongst English writers, but it is expressed in very similar terms in Beza's discussion of sacraments: "But sacraments touch all three moments in time: past, present and future. While they commemorate a past saving event, they also make present and witness to that which by signifying they offer to us. By doing so, they are pledges and seals of the promise of eternal life."[41] Chapter II of *The Christian Sacrament*

---

39. Brevint, *Missale Romanum*, 125.

40. Raitt, *Beza*, 45, 51–52.

41. Raitt, *Beza*, 43. The idea originated with Aquinas, *Summa Theologica* part III, quaes. 73, art. 4: "This sacrament has a threefold significance. One with regard to the past, inasmuch as it is commemorative of our Lord's Passion, which was a true sacrifice . . . .With regard to the present it has another meaning, namely, that of Ecclesiastical

and Sacrifice concerns the sacrament as a memorial. Brevint here closely connects the idea of *anamnesis* with the eternal self-offering and heavenly intercession of Christ from Hebrews 7 and 9, and ends with a meditation on the visible sufferings of Christ.

Using the example of the Passover seder, Brevint explains that the eucharist is our participation in the present in the events of the past. The Lord's Supper as a sacrament is "a memorial, representation, and image" of the Passion of Christ. Although the actual crucifixion lasted but a few hours, the eucharist has been ordained to be a perpetual memorial of it. Brevint never actually uses the word "*anamnesis*," but he certainly means it when he says that the eucharist is for Christians as the Passover is for the Jews, "as if they had bin present" at the first one. The eucharist parallels and supersedes the solemnity of the Passover, which itself had the character of being both sacrament and sacrifice. The idea of *anamnesis* is that the sacrifices of the past continue to be effectual, and through their re-presentation in the sacraments we actively participate in them in the present: "Because especially, besides the *commemoration*, this Sacrament duly given, and faithfully received, makes the thing which it represents as really present for our use, and as really powerful in order to our salvation, as if the thing it self were newly done or in doing." (II.3) Lancelot Andrewes also made much use of the idea of *anamnesis*, using it to affirm that the sacraments "recapitulate" time, salvation history, collapsing the present and the salvific events of the past into a single event.[42] Crockett adds: "In making the memorial of Christ's death in the Eucharist the Church not only commemorates a past action, but Christians on earth are united with Christ in the eternal pleading of his completed sacrifice in heaven."[43] This is precisely what Brevint means when he writes:

> So now the ministers of our Lord Jesus Christ, having in their hands the sacraments of the Gospel . . . may both produce and give them out as evidences; that the sacrifice of their Master is

---

unity, in which men are aggregated through this Sacrament; and in this respect it is called 'Communion' or *synaxis* . . . With regard to the future it has a third meaning, inasmuch as this sacrament foreshadows the Divine fruition, which shall come to pass in heaven; and according to this it is called 'Viaticum,' because it supplies the way of winning thither. And it this respect it is also called the 'Eucharist,' that is, 'good grace.' . . ."

42. Nicolas Lossky, *Lancelot Andrewes The Preacher, 1555-1626*, Oxford, 1991, 340-43. Brevint seems to have a great deal in common with Andrewes besides *anamnesis*: the sacrifice is to be eaten by the worshippers. The eucharist is like the Passover and is both sacrifice and sacrament. See particularly his sermon for Easter 1612, which Stevenson says is Andrewes' fullest statement of eucharistic theology.

43. "Holy Communion," in *The Study of Anglicanism*, ed. Stephen Sykes and John Booty, London, 1988, 278.

> not less able to save mens souls, when it is offered to men, and sacramentally offered again to God, at the holy Communion, then when it was newly offered upon the cross. (VIII.8)

McAdoo has examined Wesley's abridgement for the concept of *anamnesis*, comparing Brevint's ideas with those of Jeremy Taylor. He concludes that because of Brevint's use of the concept of "value," his theology of the eucharist "has an anticipatory individuality worthy of note,"[44] meaning that Brevint's language is very amenable to modern discussions such as the 1938 *Doctrine Report*, the *Lima Report* (B.E.M.) and ARCIC I. McAdoo correctly points out that Brevint does not use the language of sacramental change; nevertheless, he says, Brevint is clearly stating a "belief in a real and dynamic presence of Christ."[45]

McAdoo restricted himself to Wesley's *Abridgement*, and unfortunately the word "virtue" on which he hangs his exposition of Brevint was Wesley's interpolation: "These three make up the proper sense of those words, *Take eat; this is my body*. For the consecrated bread doth not only represent his body, and bring the *virtue* of it into our souls on earth; but as to our happiness in heaven bought with that price, it is the most solemn instrument to assure our *title* to it."[46] Compare this with Brevint's original wording:

> And these three parts put together make up the proper and true sense of these words, "Take and eat this is my Body": for the consecrated bread is not said to be the Lords Body only, *because it represents the Lords Body, but because also as to our present use on Earth, it doth as good as exhibit it:* and as to our happiness in Heaven bought with the price of this Body, it is the most solemn instrument to assure our title to it. (V.6)[47]

McAdoo believes that Brevint's most significant contribution is the integration of the eucharistic *anamnesis* with the image from Hebrews of Christ's perpetual intercession on our behalf, as both priest and victim, before the heavenly altar. This idea of the communion table being a copy of the heavenly altar is also prominent in Jeremy Taylor. McAdoo quotes Wesley's abridgement of VI.4:

> So let us ever turn our eyes and our hearts toward Jesus our eternal High Priest, who is gone up into the true sanctuary, and

---

44. H. McAdoo, "A Theology of the Eucharist: Brevint and the Wesleys," *Theology* 97 (1994) 245–56.
45. Ibid., 253.
46. Ibid., 253; Wesley, "Abridgement," V.4.
47. Emphasis mine.

doth there continually present both his own body and blood before God, and (as Aaron did) all the true Israel of God in a *memorial*. In the meantime we, *beneath in the church*, present to God his body and blood in a *memorial*, that under the shadow of his cross, and figure of his Sacrifice, we may present ourselves in very deed before him.[48]

Christ the high priest offers his completed offering, and the past, present, and future merge in the *anamnesis* of the eucharist, "still new" at the heavenly altar, and we, united with him, both offer and are offered "in the eternal pleading of that perfect offering."[49] This sacrifice is eternally active, and the eucharist is not merely a memorial, but a "making effective in the present"[50] of that saving event. This *anamnesis* is both commemorative and representational.

McAdoo refers to the well-known frontispiece used in Wheatly's *Rational Illustration of the Book of Common Prayer* (1810). It depicts a celebration of the eucharist as it would have appeared in the late seventeenth century, and in a cloud of glory over the Holy Table stands Christ at the Heavenly Altar. In a nimbus is the scriptural reference Heb 7:25 and 9:11, 23:

> [T]his is the master theme in *The Christian Sacrament and Sacrifice*. Heaven and earth meet in the eucharistic action, as depicted in the Wheatly frontispiece . . . the high priest presenting his completed offering at the heavenly altar, and the Church united with him in the eternal pleading of that perfect offering.[51]

Therefore, says Brevint, "I will not fail to worship God, assoon [sic] as I perceive these sacraments . . . Here I worship neither sacraments nor tabernacle . . ." Just as the Ark of the Covenant was more than just a chest, it was not itself worshipped, but was hallowed by God to be a sign of his presence. (II.6) To be prostrate before the Lord's Table is as though to be at the very foot of the cross and find that it is as Jacob's Ladder, joining heaven and earth. (II.10)

Brevint continues that there are different degrees of memorial, from mere reminders, such as the cross, to more "venerable" ones that bear real authority, such as the king's arms, and he stresses that "figure" or "memorial" are not to be understood as "empty figure." He uses the phrase "signs and monuments" to explain that the eucharist is an "effectual and real

---

48. Wesley, "Abridgement," VI.3. This is fairly faithful to Brevint's text.
49. McAdoo, "Brevint and the Wesleys," 247.
50. See also *ARCIC: The Final Report*, 1981, 14.
51. McAdoo "Brevint and the Wesleys," 247.

presence" of Christ's "continued atonement." Furthermore, he adds that "*[s]igns* and *monuments* become more or less venerable according to the greater, or lesser worth of the objects, which they are made to represent." (II.4) The king's arms in a public place are understood by common people to be different in degree and authority from an imaginary coat of arms painted for mere decoration. He explains this difference as a sort of transfiguration: " . . . these signs and monuments, besides their ordinary use, bear withal as it were on their face the glorious character of their institution from above." (II.4) The bread and wine bear the intention of God to be a memorial of Christ's passion. Therefore the eucharist makes the sufferings of Christ visible, requiring of the "pious beholder" three degrees of devotion, and again Brevint's theme is temporal: memory of the past event, worship and adoration in the present, and that which completes the other two, an "act of faith" in the continued atonement.

The devotional postscript to chapter II is almost entirely given over to rehearsing the sufferings of Christ made visible in the elements of the eucharist, and Brevint takes the further step of comparing the actual manufacture of the bread and wine with the passion:[52]

> My Lord! and my God! I behold here in this bread made of a substance that was cut down, beaten, ground and bruised by men, all the heavy blows and plagues and pains, which my Savior did suffer from the hands of his murtherers: I behold in this bread dryed up, and baked and burnt at the fire, the fiery wrath also, which he suffered for me from above, and from the hand of his own Father. My God, my God, why hast thou thus forsaken him! the violence of wicked men first hath made him a martyr, then the fire of Heaven hath made him a burnt sacrifice: and under both these sufferings, lo he is become to me the Bread of Life! Let us then go, to take and eat it. For tho the instruments that bruised him be broken to pieces, and the direful flames that burned him be quite put out, yet this bread, which is the Body of the Lord, continues new. The spears and swords that slew, and the burnings that compleated the sacrifices, are many years since scattered and spent; but the strength and sweet smell of the oblation is still fragrant, the blood still warm, the wounds still fresh, and "the Lamb still standing as slain." . . . Rock of Salvation, Rock struck and cleft for me, let those two streams of blood, and water which once gushed out of thy side, when the curse of

---

52. See also Brevint, *Missale Romanum*, 240–41, where the image is also rehearsed, but in support of the idea that Melchizedek was a type of Christ, the bread and wine he offered foreshadowing the sufferings of Christ. Brevint continues that Melchizedek's bread and wine also had the character of being both sacrament and sacrifice.

the Law, and the Rod of Moses had opened it, bring down with them Salvation and Holiness into my soul, tho far distant from the mountain, where thou didst receive that deadly blow. And let not my soul less thirst after them at this distance, then if I stood upon Horeb, whence sprung this water, and near the very clef of that rock, the very wounds of my Savior whence gushed out this sacred blood. All the distance of times and countries, how great soever, which is between Adam and me, doth not keep his sin or his punishment any more from pursuing and reaching me, then if I had bin born in his house: and notwithstanding this distance we sin and dye after his image, as if we were immediatly sprung from his loines. Second Adam, Adam descended powerful from above, let thy blood reach as far . . .

There is a brief reiteration in III.5:

> The first I say to represent Christs [sic] sufferings. This bread and wine could neither sustain nor refresh me, had not their intrinsecal substance lost its first condition and estate: that is if the one had never fallen under the sickle, the threshing, the millstone, the fire: and the other under the hook, the trampling, and the press of husbandmen: nor doth the Son of God save me, but by emtying himself in a manner, for a while of his first glory in Heaven: and by losing that second life which he had taken in Bethlehem.

Brevint hints in II.11 that the mingled chalice is also a part of the visible passion, that blood and water both gushed out. He takes some pains over the water image, comparing Christ to the Rock of Horeb.[53] The mingled chalice is more explicitly referred to in VIII.2, in a reference to Cyprian's metaphor that Christ and his people are united together in the sacrament represented by the wine and the water united in the chalice.

SIGN AND MEANS OF PRESENT GRACES

Chapters III and IV are combined by Wesley, into a single unit on "present graces," and because the chapters are so closely related in content, they will be considered together here. Brevint affirms that the sacrament is both a sign

---

53. As with the manna, Brevint is fond of repeating this image of the rock of Horeb. The relating of manna and the rock of Horeb is found in Bourne's hymn "Lord enthroned in heavenly splendour" (1874), the fifth stanza: "Life-imparting heavenly manna, stricken rock with streaming side." Also in Calvin: "The water gushing from the rock in the desert [Ex. 17:6] was for the fathers a token and sign of the same thing as wine represents for us in the Supper." Calvin, *Institutes*, IV.17.15.

of the presence of God, and also a "moral instrument," that is, a conveyance of God's grace. In chapter III Brevint uses the conventional definition of a sacrament, that it is "a sign of an invisible grace,"[54] and makes two points. The first is the reiteration of the Calvinist statement that the eucharist is a "visible sign" that God has added to his Word to help our feeble faith; the second is that the attributes of the signs themselves provide by analogy spiritual insight into the nature of that which is signified.

Faith is strengthened, he says, by the addition of visible signs, and Brevint lists several such signs from the Old and New Testaments, such as the ark, the burning bush, the pillar of cloud, Christ's laying-on-of-hands, or breathing on the disciples. Many of these images are precisely those used by Calvin in *Institutes* IV.14.18: the rainbow, the Tree of Life in Eden, the smoking firepot, Gideon's fleece: "Since these things were done to support and confirm their feeble faith, they were also sacraments."[55] They are repeated here by Brevint as examples of sacramental signs God used to confirm his Word and strengthen faith.

Part of the nature of a sacrament is that the signs are peculiarly suited to reveal what they do. There is a correspondence between their own natures and what they are made to represent. For example, water was chosen for baptism, he says, because of its natural virtue of cleansing, refreshing, and making fruitful. In the eucharist, the making of the bread and wine themselves represents Christ's sufferings. He uses the word *kenosis* (emptying or pouring out) from Philippians 2 to amplify the theological significance of these visible sufferings of Christ represented in the eucharistic elements, that the harvest of the wheat and the crushing of the grapes is a memorial in the present of Christ's "pouring out" of himself.[56]

The eucharist is also intended to represent the blessings we receive in the present from these sufferings. Because they are also common food, they represent life-giving and sustaining nourishment.[57] A body will perish with-

---

54. From Augustine, *De catechizandis rudibus*; Calvin, *Institutes*, IV.14.1.

55. Calvin, *Institutes*, IV.14.18.

56. Richard Baxter included in his liturgy a libation offering, a liturgical sacrificial "pouring out" of the wine to parallel the fraction. He wrote that the fraction and libation are important because they effect more completely the consecration and setting apart of the bread and wine: Baxter, "Reformed Liturgy," in *The Practical Works of the Rev. Richard Baxter*, 23 vols., edited by William Orme, London, 1830, xv, 479.

57. Also Calvin, *Institutes*, IV.16.3: "These benefits are to nourish, refresh, strengthen and gladden. For if we sufficiently consider what value we have received from the giving of that most holy body and the shedding of that blood, we shall clearly perceive that those qualities of bread and wine are, according to such an analogy, excellently adapted to express those things when they are communicated to us." Also *Institutes*. IV.17.10: "Our souls are fed by the flesh and blood of Christ in the same way that bread

out food and without Christ a soul will perish; contrarily Christ is certainly and really received, as certainly and really as the bread and wine are taken. Here Brevint refers to manna and the Passover as types of the sustaining and sacrificial natures of the eucharist.

Perkins also agreed that the sacramental signs are chosen because they bear some appropriate resemblance to that which is symbolized:

> There is a certaine agreement and proportion of the externall things with the internall, and of the actions of one with the actions of the other; whereby it cometh to passe, that the signs, as if it were certaine visible words, incurring into the external senses, do by a certain proportionable resemblance draw a Christian mind to the consideration of the things signified, and to be applyed.[58]

Brevint then moves to a complicated image comparing the taking of Eve out of the side of Adam, with the Church, the second Eve, being drawn alive from the wounded side of Christ, the second Adam. (III.7) Just as humanity inherited sin and death from its first parents, forgiveness is imputed to us by the substitutionary atonement of Christ. Thus we have been given three new lives in the death of Christ, one each for the past, present and future. The first is life restored to us by the sacrifice of the cross, and the second is the sustained life in the present. The water and the blood which flowed out of Jesus' side represent washing and sanctification, restored life and sustained life, which are the first two "effluxes" from Christ. The first life is that of justification, the second of sanctification, and the third new life is that of future redemption yet to come (III.9).

Christ, Brevint says, sets up a table by his Altar at which we are fed, nourished and sustained until "the very day of eternal salvation," just as really as we receive the bread and wine. The Tree of Life in Eden was a type of Christ which sustained Adam and Eve; and corresponds also to the Passover lamb in Egypt by which God's people were redeemed, and these figures are

---

and wine keep and sustain physical life. For the analogy of the sign applies only if souls find their nourishment in Christ . . ."

58. E. Brooks Holifield, *The Covenant Sealed: The Development of Puritan Sacramental Theology in Old and New England*, New Haven, 1974, 53; William Perkins, "Golden Chaine," in Ian Breward, ed., *The Work of William Perkins*, Abingdon, Berks, 1970, 72. Interestingly, John Owen stated that the sacramental signs work precisely because they do *not* resemble what they represent, and there is an inappropriateness about them which works to sacramental advantage. Appropriate visible signs such as crucifixes do not require faith to comprehend their relation to Christ's passion, which is why the faithless adopt them. Stephen Mayor,"The Teaching of John Owen Concerning the Lord's Supper," *Scottish Journal of Theology* 18 (1965) 175.

fulfilled in him.⁵⁹ Thus the sacramental giving and the sacrificial offering are again represented, the first in the Tree of Life, and the manna, the latter by the Passover lamb and the breaking of bread and pouring of wine. Our life comes out of his death and our heavenly inheritance is, he says, *akeldamah* "bought with blood money."

Brevint uses the transfiguration again to explain the twinned ideas of receiving and offering. As Moses and Elijah, representing the Law and the Prophets, stood on either side of Jesus on the mountain, so at the holy table Jesus is flanked by Aaron and Melchizedek, one representing blood sacrifice, the other bread offering made to Abraham (III.12). Chapters VI and VII develop these associations.

Chapter IV shifts the discussion from the eucharist as a sign of grace, to the eucharist as a positive means of grace, and what it means to call the bread "Christ's body." Brevint describes the sacramental exchange of names between the sign and the signified, called by Calvin a sacred "metonymy" although Brevint cites Augustine instead. He uses as an example what is commonly called "investiture": a royal document that has the king's authority because it bears his wax seal.⁶⁰ He refers to the sacramental exchange of names in IV.1, 2 and 4, and in VIII.7, and alludes to it in V.6. As with "anamnesis," Brevint does not actually use the word "metonymy," but seems to assume that the reader will be well-enough acquainted with the concept that he need not explain it.

Brevint is deliberately agnostic about the manner of Christ's sacramental presence, declaring that because it is a mystery, it cannot be known, and again he refers to the manna in the wilderness ("meat" meaning "bread"):

> The manner of this real communication and conveyance, is the great unfathomable mystery, which the Holy Fathers have ever admired: and which therefore we neither need, nor do take upon us to explain. The shepherds think themselves happy with the message brought to them by an angel, "This day is born to you a savior," (Luke 2. 11.) tho they know nothing of the way of

---

59. The Tree of Life is also used by Beza in *Quaestionum et Responsionum*, 351: 164–5 as an example of one of four ways in which a sign is related to the signified. Raitt, *Beza*, 49.

60. The investiture image is also found in Beza's, *Confessio Christianae fidei et eiusdem collatio cum Papisticis haeresibus*, Geneva, 1560: "The principle is not unlike that which underlies the use of wax which is customarily impressed by the seal of a prince or magistrate to confirm a public document. In this case, the nature or substance of the wax differs not at all from any other wax, but in its use, it is far and away different. Further, if someone were to deface the wax impressed by the seal, he would be guilty of the crime of *lese majesté*." Quoted in Raitt, *The Eucharistic Theology of Theodore Beza*, 24. Brevint also makes much use of "investiture" in *Missale Romanum*, 283.

his most miraculous birth: and the honest Israelites ought not to receive manna less thankfully (as they do not less effectually) tho they know neither of what matter, nor by what means the heavens, the air, or the clouds can thus every morning shed about their tents this strange meat.[61] I must not wonder if the waies of the Lord be unknown to me in his miracles, since they are so very often in his most ordinary works. (IV.6)

He then continues in IV.8:

> Here then I come to Gods altar with a full perswasion that these words "This is my body," promise me more then a figure: that this holy banquet is not a representation made of outward shews without substance ... But how these mysteries become in my behalf the supernatural instruments of such blessings; it is enough for me to admire.

He specifically uses the words "real presence" and qualifies that this statement does not mean "localized":

> This victim having bin offered up both in the fulness of times, and in the midst of the habitable world, which properly is Christs great temple, and thence being carried up to Heaven, which is his proper sanctuary, thence he spreads all about us salvation, as the burnt offering did its smoke: as the golden altar did its perfumes: and as the burning candlestic its lights. And thus Christs Body and Blood have every where, but most especially at the Holy Communion a most true and *real presence*. (IV.11)

It is true that grace is not restricted to the communion, and that other forms of worship are means of grace, but the eucharist is superior to them all:

> And his ordinances in the Church, as well as his stars in heaven, differ in glory one from another. *Fasting, prayer, hearing* of the Word, public and private *services*, and all like holy duties, are all very good vessels to draw water from this well of salvation: but yet they are not all equal. The blessed Communion must exceed as much in blessings, when well used, as it exceeds in danger of a curse, when it is not ... But in those places and ordinances, which he hath in an especial manner set out to record his *Passion*, and to renew the sacrifice of his body; he will certainly come with such a fulness of blessings, as attend this sacred body, which is the proper seat of blessings: the bread which we do

---

61. In the seventeenth century, the word "meat" referred to grain products such as bread or meal.

> break, being the communion of his body: just as the eating of the *unleavened loaves* were (out of Jerusalem) the communion to the *passover*, which was the type of Christ crucified. "Christ our passover," saies the Apostle, "is sacrificed for us: therefore let us keep the feast, &c." (IV.12)

It is a "true sign, an effectual means" of grace, of the "the richest gift, that a Saint can receive on earth, the *Lord Jesus crucified*." (IV.15)

PLEDGE OF FUTURE GLORY

In chapter V Brevint addresses the subject of hope and assurance as the aspect of the eucharist that faces the future, and like Calvin, he understands assurance of salvation as the primary grace of the sacrament. As he earlier used the idea of "signs and monuments," Brevint now states that the sacrament is an "earnest and pledge" of our future glory, continuing the thematic emphasis on the twin aspects of sacramental receiving and sacrificial giving. The terms "earnest" and "pledge" mean very specific, but different things.[62] An "earnest" is a "down payment," something "allowed upon account" as Brevint says; it is itself applied against the balance of the promise when fulfilled. Brevint uses as examples the charity and holiness that we receive from God in the sacraments, and which will remain ours in heaven.

A "pledge" however, is rather like "collateral security," a token used as assurance that the promise will be fulfilled, but recalled or taken away when it is. An example is the eucharist itself, which will have no purpose when we are with Christ face to face. The Church is another such example. Although it and Christ's Kingdom certainly go together, Brevint is not terribly concerned about the Church as such: "Let them not, whom He hath invited to eat and drink at Abraham's *Table*, trouble themselves about the room where our blessed Savior will feed them . . . it is a sufficient assurance that in time He will also make them sit in that other palace." (V.3)

Referring to I Corinthians 2:26 Brevint says that Paul stated not only what the eucharist was for, but also its duration, for it is to show forth the death of Christ, until he comes. Thus the eucharist, representing the crucifixion, looks to the future when Christ will come again, keeping passion and parousia connected in the present.

Brevint in V.6–8 moves to a discussion of the meaning of "is" in the statement "this is my body,"[63] as he had in *Missale Romanum* regarding the

---

62. Cf. Calvin, "guarantees and tokens," *Institutes* IV.14.1.

63. Calvin also examines at some length the meaning of "is" regarding the sacrament: Calvin, *Institutes*, IV.17.22. Beza, like Calvin, uses the word "metonymy" in

grammatical identity of the sign and the signified. There he had said that Christ's words and action as recorded in Matthew 26 are to be taken plainly and literally: "So that the sacred Eucharistical act of receiving this holy Sacrament with faith and contrition, must not be less accounted of than the very real communion of Christ's body. All this is both said and done literally and really, without scarce so much as one figure."[64] In *The Christian Sacrament and Sacrifice* Brevint repeats the investiture image saying that deeds *are* lands and maps *are* countries, because they truly convey the reality they represent. Since one cannot actually give a whole estate into someone else's hands, they are substituted by "some ceremonies, forms, or tokens, which may visibly pass from hand to hand." (V.8). The Kingdom of God is no more moveable than an earthly estate, but it is given in "sure title" and the Body and Blood of Christ are given "in full value" at communion.

In V.9–11 Brevint explains his use of "worthy reception," but unlike his contemporaries, he does not mean spiritual preparation in prayer, repentance, self examination, pious devotions, or a holy manner of life. Brevint spends surprisingly little time on the topic, particularly when his book is compared to the vast bulk of other contemporary eucharistic manuals. He simply states that the crime of unworthy reception is "not to discern the Lord's body." In this he is again faithful to Calvin himself.[65]

Brevint had already used the term "worthy receiver" several times, first at the beginning of chapter II, and again in II.10. In III.5 the issue of the danger of unworthy reception was used as an argument for the real efficacy of the sacrament: "The real efficacy which the Holy Communion hath to convey grace and blessing on the true Christian receiver, is evidently demonstrated by the opposite efficacy it hath to convey a curse and destruction on the profane." If the sacrament was merely an empty sign, devoid of power, it would pose no threat whatever to the unworthy receiver; but since all agreed that it is mortally dangerous to receive unworthily then the sacrament must be indeed efficacious. And in the very next sentence Brevint attacks those who teach that unworthy communion leads to damnation, but even when devoutly used the sacrament has no salvific force:

> Now certainly this would be as much to think *unworthily* as to eat *unworthily* of this holy bread, to think it might be really pernicious when it is abused, but not really blissful and saving in its right use; and that this bread, which we eat of, should be an

---

Quaestionum et Responsionum; the grammatical-rhetorical discussion of the meaning of "this is my body." See Raitt, *Beza*, 55.

64. Brevint, *Missale Romanum*, 281.

65. Calvin, *Institutes*, IV.17.40.

effectual communion to procure death, but meerly *sacramental* only to shew, and not to procure salvation. (IV.5)

Nearer the beginning of chapter V, Brevint connects the idea of the eucharist as assurance with the problem of unworthy reception, again obliquely, by referring to the "wedding garment" of Matthew 22:12.[66] The wedding garment was usually interpreted to indicate adequate spiritual preparation for the reception of the sacrament so that one will not attend the feast of the King carelessly. As noted above Brevint refers to the future glory of the Kingdom of God as the wedding feast of the King's Son, of the "sufficient assurance" that we will be brought there, then states in V.3: "whosoever are admitted to the dinner of the Lamb slain (Matthew 22:4) unless they be wanting to themselves must not doubt of being admitted to the wedding supper of the same Lamb . . ."

Unworthy reception is the failure to discern Christ in the sacrament, and to treat it as common food. Brevint again turns to the "investiture" image comparing unworthy reception to "rebels who pull down their princes' statues," as an example of a "profane want of discerning." The brass or marble suffer nothing, but the outrage passes to the King himself, who alone suffers the wrongdoing. To come to the sacrament unworthily not discerning the pledges of salvation is not just to fail to discern and honour Christ, but to despise and cast him away. (V.11)

THE COMMEMORATIVE SACRIFICE

Chapter VI begins the second part of the book, as its title states: "Of the Holy Eucharist, as it implies a Sacrifice. And first of the Commemorative Sacrifice." As noted above, Beza wrote that the three sacrificial aspects to the eucharist are as commemoration of Christ's death, as "peace offering" and the offering of our alms, which Brevint dutifully reproduces. The chapter is in fact a commentary on Hebrews 6–10, and although Brevint makes no direct reference to Hebrews, the chapter's central theme is summed up in Hebrews 9:22b: "without the shedding of blood there is no forgiveness of sins." Hebrews was commonly used by writers with respect to the perfect offering of Christ as both victim and High Priest, but particularly in recalling Melchizedek's tribute of bread and wine to Abraham. The bread and wine

---

66. Compare William Bradshaw and Arthur Hildesham, *A Direction for the weaker sort of Christians, shewing in what manner they ought to fit and prepare themselues to the worthy receiuing of the Sacrament of the body and blood of Christ*, London, 1609; Andrewes, "Sermons of the Resurrection Preached on Easter Day 1612," in *Works LACT, Sermons*, ii, 290–308.

were commonly understood to prefigure the elements of the holy eucharist, and the tithe offered by Melchizedek to Abraham was understood as sacrificial.

All true religions on earth involve some sort of sacrifices, Brevint says, and it is a great lie and slander to say that Christians lack them. Just as pagans accused Jews of "adoring nothing but clouds" because they had no sacred images, Jews and pagans both accused Christians of lacking sacrifices because they did not kill and burn animals on altars. Just as an idol is not a real god, the slaughter of animals is not true sacrifice, says Brevint, and of the six kinds of Jewish "carnal sacrifices," none had any saving reality apart from their dependence on Christ. Sacrifices represent not only the forgiveness of sins, but also our service to God, and none but the eucharist brings together both of these ends "towards which all the old sacrifices never look't, but as either simple engagements, or weak shadows." (VI.2)

Only the sacrifice of Christ is sufficient for the expiation of sins, and it is completely sufficient in and of itself. Brevint alludes to Hebrews 10: 1–16 when he says "the expiatory sacrifice, which Christ offered upon the cross, was infinitly able to do at once whatever an infinit number of other sacrifices had bin able to do . . . " (VI.2). This sacrifice, which can never be reiterated, is "by an Eucharistical and devout commemoration to be offered up every day." Brevint notes St. Augustine, saying that the flesh of Christ was offered up in time three ways: prefiguring sacrifices under the law, in real deed on the cross, and by commemorative sacrament after his ascension.

Brevint sounds much like Andrewes when he asserts that what for humanity is a table at which we receive, is to God an altar[67] "whereon men mystically present to him the same sacrifice as still bleeding and still sueing for expiation and mercy." Besides implying several times in this chapter that the eucharist might well be celebrated every day, he affirms the advantages of more frequent communion, asserting as many others did, that the primitive Church observed the sacrament every Lord's Day, and he perhaps verges on irreverence when he states that the sacrament was " . . . the most powerful means the Church had to strengthen their supplications, to open the gates of Heaven, and to force in manner God and his Christ to have compassion on them." (VI.4)

---

67. Calvin, *Institutes*, IV.18.12. Calvin states clearly that the Lord has given to us a Table for feasting, not an altar for sacrificing.

THE SACRIFICE OF OUR OWN PERSONS

Chapter VII is the longest chapter in the book, and the one in which Brevint most explicitly draws the relationships among the crucifixion, the eucharist, and Old Testament sacrifices.[68] He first takes up the familiar idea of the death of Christ as an offering for sin, likening it to the Day of Atonement. He then moves to the idea that the Church is joined with Christ in his sacrifice as the grain-offering accompanied the animal sacrifice of the daily "peace-offering." In most other comparisons between the eucharist and the sacrifices of the Old Testament, Christ's death was linked typologically to the sacrifice for sin upon which God makes a feast. For example, Patrick's *Mensa Mystica* and *The Christian Sacrifice* both assert that the eucharist is a feast upon a sin offering.[69] To understand Christ's sacrifice instead as a "peace offering" is distinctive of *The Christian Sacrament and Sacrifice*.[70] Again Brevint is indebted to Beza, who stated that the Lord's Supper is correctly called a eucharist, and such giving of thanks is the main purpose of the Old Testament Peace offering.[71]

Brevint begins by asserting that there can be only one sufficient sacrifice for sin to which nothing can be added, but this does not obviate the need for other sacrifices that Christians need to offer. He states that though only Christ's sacrifice can procure salvation, nevertheless the self-sacrifice required of each Christian is "absolutely necessary to *receive* it." (VII.1) He repeats this near the end, in VII.17: "And as to their several ends, the one is made to procure and work expiation, and the other only to get some capacity to receive it." To be in communion with Christ we must be conformed to Christ, follow Christ, to live lives of holiness and, Brevint says, "bearing part of his cross and dying with him." As chapter V was about assurance, chapter VII is about discipleship.

Brevint had earlier likened Christ to Melchizedek, but now he likens him to Aaron. As Aaron entered to offer sacrifice wearing the ephod, the twelve stones of which represented all of Israel, so Christ and the Church are always associated together. Christ acted and died for the Church, and so the Church must imitate and follow him in any way it can, particularly in his sufferings: "we shall have *communion* with him in his *glory*, if we will keep *conformity* with him here in his *sufferings*." This conformity is not a matter of morals only, but to imitate Christ in all parts of his life:

68. Calvin's discussion is shorter, but has much in common: *Institutes*, IV.18.12–13.

69. Patrick, *Mensa Mystica*, 74–76; Patrick, *The Christian Sacrifice*, 32, 50.

70. Patrick mentions the peace offering of Deut 12 and 16 once in the second chapter of *Mensa Mystica*, that it is a feast upon a sacrifice. Patrick, *Mensa Mystica*, 25

71. Raitt, *Beza*, 49.

> We must be regenerated in his birth, dye on his cross, be buried in his grave, bear his shame in his tribulations; in a word, Christ and Christians are and must be continually together, 'Where I am there my servant shall be also.' (Ioh. 12. 26.) But of all these duties the most fundamental and most indispensable, is that of bearing part of his cross and dying with him in *sacrifice*. (VII.5)

Brevint moves on to discuss Christ's sacrifice in terms of the sin offering and the scapegoat of Leviticus 16 on the Day of Atonement. Because they had laid their hands on it, the death of the victim was accepted as the people's offering of themselves. In the same way Christians are not crucified as Jesus was, yet in communion with Christ, his sacrifice and theirs are "both accounted before God for one and the same" by imputation, (VII.8), as the first fruits offering represented the offering of the whole harvest. The renunciation of sin is thus a sacrifice because it is a crucifixion of the former, sinful self:

> The first is, that they endeavor to crucify their sinful members as really as Christ himself had his sinless body crucified. So that the feet, that before did run to evil, the violent hands that did injure, the greedy eyes that did covet, and all those members of the flesh, that were weapons of wickedness, may by this cross and sacrifice be most really bound, and in a good measure destroyed as to their corruption. 'I do glory in the Cross of Jesus Christ, by which the world is crucified unto me, and I unto the world.' (Galat. 6. 14.) (VII.9)

The second element of this self-sacrifice is the "serious resolution to piety, and universal consecrating both of our persons and our actions." The Church joined to Christ makes a single offering. This mystery is represented, says Brevint, by the daily sacrifice mentioned in Numbers 28 which consisted of two parts, the slaughtered animal and the grain-offering that accompanied it, what Brevint calls the "secondary oblation."

There are many sorts of sacrifices and offerings (*corban*) listed in Numbers and Leviticus: the daily sacrifice, the peace-offering (*shalomim*), and the sin offering (*chatta'ah*). Of these latter there were several types: the burnt offering or holocaust (*owlah*, offered whole); the grain, or meal offering (*mincha*);[72] and the drink offering, or libation (*nesekh*). Brevint's typological analysis makes the distinctions among these different offerings important. "Peace-offering" is an inadequate translation of the Hebrew word *shalomim*,

---

72. Implying bloodless. Although Brevint doesn't refer to the sacrifice as "unbloody" as many others had, Stevenson says he "all but" does: Stevenson, *Covenant of Grace*, 106.

Change and Transformation

"sacrifice of well-being," is closer, and "sacrifice of communion" seems to be best. This particular offering is one of reconciliation and joyful celebration between God and the faithful, in which God and the faithful share the sacred food. Eucharistic interpretations of this are obvious.

The daily sacrifice consisted of two parts. Brevint states that the lamb, and the accompanying "meat" offering, which was bread made of flour, oil, incense and wine, part of which was to be burned on the altar of sacrifice with the sacrificial lamb, constituted a single sacrifice. Brevint calls these grain offerings "supplemental" or "secondary" sacrifices, which become sacred only by imputation of the merit of the animal sacrifice. The grain offering is of itself insufficient, a "burthen" on the lamb, which imparts its own righteousness to it (VII.18).

Here Brevint has not been entirely faithful to Scripture. Grain offerings were indeed part of the regular sacrificial system, and did accompany the animal sacrifice of the peace offering (Num 15: 28). When they accompanied animal sacrifice, a drink offering of wine was added; however, they were capable of being independent offerings.[73] The Bible nowhere says that the meal offering is a "secondary" or "supplemental" oblation, that it is inadequate, subordinate to, or dependent upon the slaughtered animal. Leviticus 2 mentions the meal offering as an acceptable form of sacrifice in and of itself.

This grain offering image is used by Brevint to describe how the Church's sacrifice is added onto Christ's once-for-all sacrifice. The bread and wine of the grain offering correspond typologically to the bread and wine of the eucharist, and as they took their sanctity from the merits of the lamb offered on the altar, so too the sacrifice of the eucharist that we celebrate in the present is thrown onto the sacrifice of Christ on the cross, and thus we participate in that sacrifice, and in the eucharist offer ourselves to God in Christ. The bread of communion as sacrament signifies the natural body of Christ, the bread of communion as sacrifice represents the mystical body of Christ, the Church. (VII.10) All our works of charity, praise, alms and holiness are in themselves insufficient, and depend on the sacrifice of Christ to be consecrated to God and found acceptable: "And these are the spiritual offerings which every true Christian must join to cast upon the fundamental sacrifice of Christ Jesus." (VII.11)

Joseph Mede also connected the "meal offering" with the eucharist, working from Malachi 1:11: "For from the rising of the sun even unto the going down of the same my name shall be great among the Gentiles and in

---

73. See Exod 29:40; 46:4–7; Lev 23:13; and Num 15:1–12. Brevint is referring to the description of the daily sacrifice in Numbers rather than in Leviticus.

every place incense shall be offered unto my name, and a pure offering." The incense represents prayers, thanksgiving and commemoration; the material part of the Christian sacrifice, the pure offering of the gentiles, is the *mincha purim*, the bread and wine of the meal offering: "[T]his title of *Purity* is given to the Christian *Mincha* in respect of Christ whom it signifies and represents, who is a Sacrifice without all spot, blemish and imperfection."[74] Mede does not, however, refer to the *mincha* as "secondary" or interpret it as the church's self-offering cast upon the sacrifice of Christ.

Brevint concludes the chapter with a two-part recapitulation with each including discourse and prayer on intercession and the mortification of sin, which are the two aspects of offering, priesthood and sacrifice (VII.17–18). Curiously, considering the language of the English liturgy, the Levitical sacrifice to which Brevint did not appeal is the *todah*, or sacrifice of "praise and thanksgiving." It is also a sacrifice of reconciliation and rejoicing; the fatted calf of the parable of the prodigal son might be a good example, particularly because of this explicit connection with the teaching of Jesus. Ratzinger has written that the "do this" of the institution narrative of the eucharist relates to what Jesus is adding to the Passover, that is, interpreting the Passover as *todah* for his followers.[75]

McAdoo connects the Aaronic and the Melchizedekian images, stating that for Brevint, the Church is "united with Christ in the eternal pleading of the completed offering"[76] and this uniting makes a single offering. Rattenbury took the image even further, and his conclusion is certainly correct: Brevint's inference is that the Church's self-offering in the eucharist is in fact offering to God the Body of Christ, for the Church is that Body.[77]

Just as the supplementary sacrifice of meal and wine is identified with the main sacrifice and accepted as an integral part of it, so too the Church's self-offering is identified with Christ's sacrifice, because the Church is the Body of Christ. Christ and his people "are accounted for one oblation." (VII.17) We are his body, hence the sacrifice of ourselves is the sacrifice of Christ's body. The offering of bread and wine, *mincha* and *nesekh*, is the offering of ourselves, because in the Offertory we are identified with the

---

74. Joseph Mede, *The Christian Sacrifice*, in *The Works of the Pious and Profoundly-learned Joseph Mede*, 3rd ed., ed. John Worthington, London, 1672, 361.

75. Joseph Ratzinger, "Form and Content in the Eucharistic Celebration," in Joseph Cardinal Ratzinger, *The Feast of Faith: Approaches to a Theology of the Liturgy*, trans. Graham Harrison, San Francisco, 1986, 33–60. For an alternative opinion, see Paul F. Bradshaw, "*Zebah, Todah,* and the Origin of the Eucharist," *Ecclesia Orans* 8 (1991) 245–60.

76. McAdoo, "Brevint and the Wesleys," 249.

77. Rattenbury, *Eucharistic Hymns*, 132–33.

elements, and by consecration they are returned to us as the gift of the Body and Blood of Christ. A paragraph from the *Missale Romanum* is worth quoting at length, particularly with its note of rejoicing:

> This Sacrifice being done [the bringing up of the offertory gifts], immediately after, the primitive Church proceeded to the celebration of the Holy Sacrament: for which she constantly used some part of those offerings, that the people had presented before: thereby imitating, as near as it was possible, both the example of Jesus Christ, who, for the use of the Communion, that he instituted at his last supper, took some of that Bread and Wine, that he had sanctified before at the Paschal Oblation: and the nature of those other more ordinary Sacrifices, (whereof the Christian eucharist is a most signal antitype,) which Moses called Shelomim, that is, sacrifices of peace; ere first the Israelites did lay their offerings at God's altar, and where God having graciously accepted of them, did then with part of these, as with a banquet of his own goods, treat them liberally, and bid them to eat and drink, and to rejoice before him at his table. Deuter. 16. 11. So that we have a complete emblem of a perfect communion, where christian people declare by their small oblations, that whatsoever they have is God's: and where God, infinite in mercy, accepting of small offerings, returns and improves them into great sacraments: and here both representing, and sacramentally presenting the body and blood of his Son, declares also thereby, that whatsoever he hath, and whatsoever his Son hath purchased with that body and blood,—heaven, mercy,—and immortal happiness becomes his people's.[78]

In VII.17 Brevint refers to the vestments of the Aaronic priesthood, typologically representing the "holy dispositions, and as it were, sacerdotal ornaments," the "personal and priestly endowments" of Jesus' disciples "considered as they are priests." There is, he says, a correspondence between officiating at one altar and the other "with all the proper attire of Aaron" and "without indecency." The "holy dispositions" of the Christian disciple are analogous to the vesture of the Aaronic priesthood, representing preparedness and spiritual covering of the "secular" self before worship. This seems to be Brevint's Old Testament version of the "wedding garment" image often used by others. Brevint's discussion is strikingly similar to Herbert's poem "Aaron."[79]

---

78. Brevint, *Missale Romanum*, 129.

79. For Herbert's poem see "Aaron" in *George Herbert*, ed. Louis L. Martz, Oxford, 1994, 153–54.

SACRIFICE OF OUR GOODS AND OFFERINGS

Chapter VIII concludes the book and it may be the most important chapter of all. Brevint writes that in order to receive the sacrament, Christians must bring sacrifices:

> It is an express and often repeated Law of God by Moses, and no where repealed by Christ, that no worshipper shall presume to appear before him with emty hands. Sincere Christians must have them full at the receiving of the holy Communion, with four distinct sorts of sacrifices. 1. The Sacramental and *commemorative Sacrifice* of Christ. 2. The real and *actual sacrifice* of themselves. 3. The *free will offering* of their goods. 4. The *peace offering* of their praises.

Chapter VIII explores the "social justice" responsibilities Christians have for the poor and for one another. The freewill offering of our goods and the peace offering of our praises are the natural consequences of the sacrificial offering of ourselves,[80] just as our self and bodies become attendant sacrifices, "secondary oblations," accompanying the sacrifice of Christ. Without them our self offering is defective and "mutilated":

> And as the *lamb*, in the daily sacrifice was never offered without its *meat oblation*, nor this meat oblation without its incense, its wine, its oil: So the Eternal Son and Lamb of God, who was pleased to offer himself for me, must neither be offered without me; nor whensoever I offer up my self, both by him and with him, must I appear as a dry and unsavory meat offering without juice, without sweet smell, without all the holy dispositions of readiness and joy to obey and please my God in all good works, whereof the incense, the wine, and the oil, were under the Law sacred emblems. In a word, whensoever we offer our selves, we offer by the self same act, all that we have, all that we can: and so consequently we do engage for all, that it shall be dedicated to the Glory of God, and that it shall be surrendred into his hands, employed to such uses, upon such occasions and times, as he will be pleased to appoint. (VIII.3)

To offer the person without the attendant goods is, he says, a defective sacrifice, the "sacrifice of fools" (Ecclesiastes 5) akin to offering the bones

---

80. Cf. Calvin, *Institutes*, IV.18.17; the sacrifices of thanksgiving include "all the duties of love." and "all our prayers, praises, thanksgivings, and whatever we do in the worship of God. All these things finally depend upon the greater sacrifice, by which we are consecrated in soul and body to be a holy temple to the Lord."

without the flesh, or to communion in one kind. As in VI.2, he is not explicit in the reference to half-communion and he again uses the conventional euphemism of mutilation: "It is the same act of an impious wretch to mangle, and to mutilate, either the holy Sacrifice which Jesus hath made to his father, or the holy Sacrament which he hath ordained to his Church, or that holy Oblation, which after his Sacrifice and at his Sacrament he is pleased to require of us" (VIII.4). All we have is God's, not only because he made it and as Lord has proprietary rights over everything, but also because we have given it freely along with ourselves.

The consecration, Brevint says, "becomes a Christian *apotheosis*" because by it we become capable of Christ's grace, and we are raised to God's immortality; but if our possessions, having been offered to God, are put to a profane use, "if Levi come to serve Ashtaroth," then they invoke curses. Thus we must give up all to God, and also avoid the two most odious sins, first of withdrawing from God anything that has been consecrated to him, and secondly misspending our goods profanely, that is, apart from what God permits for our necessities.

Of all the liturgical elements Brevint might have emphasized, typically the consecration, or the fraction and libation, it is the offertory as oblation and sacrifice that has for him the greatest theological significance. He begins the discussion at VIII.10 that Christians have always offered and distributed goods in common among themselves at the eucharist, and that it is unclear in the *Apostolic History*[81] whether "breaking of bread" refers to the sacrament itself or to the offerings of the people. Brevint here mentions that some bishops in antiquity used two tables: "One of them was ἔσω τo θυσιαστηρίου καὶ περιπετάσματος i.e. within that space where the ministers did officiate at the altar, and where were curtins purposely shut to keep non-Communicants from the sight of and access to the Holy Mysteries." The other was for the offerings of the people, from which the elements of the communion were taken.[82] This offertory Brevint accepts as being of central importance to the eucharist, as "representative of all their goods," which is why the offering precedes communion. This close identification of the sacrament with the offerings "which went constantly together," is another reason that the eucharist was called by Irenaeus and others "promiscuously as Sacrament, or Sacrifice."

---

81. Brevint apparently means the *Ecclesiastical History* [of the Nicean Council] of Gelasius of Cyzicus, to which he had referred earlier in VII.14.

82. This conclusion is supported in Jungmann *Missarum Sollemnia*; but neither Brevint nor Jungmann are explicit regarding their sources. Joseph A. Jungmann, *Missarum Sollemnia*, trans. Francis A. Brunner, New York, 1955.

Eric R. Griffin *The Reformed Consensus on the Doctrine of the Eucharist*

Brevint is more expansive in the *Missale Romanum*. He affirms again that the Offertory in ancient times was called "the oblation," out of which the eucharistic elements were taken. He then specifically calls them *shelomim*, because the elements are given to God, who blesses them, and then all share in the sacred banquet with rejoicing.[83] In VIII.9, Brevint repeats this, footnoting that the "peace offerings" are שלמים, εἰρηνικὰ εὐχαριστικά.

In Dix's discussion of the 1552 BCP, he equates the offertory with the element of "taking" in the "four-fold shape," and writes that Cranmer reduced it almost to the point of non-existence. Such an accusation cannot be leveled at Brevint. The whole of chapter VIII is concerned with the offertory as a material and representative sacrifice of our goods, representing ourselves.[84] Identification of the "four-fold shape" of the liturgy was no news in the seventeenth century, especially among the Puritans. Several writers such as Ames, Perkins, Baxter, and particularly Owen, explicitly affirmed that the presiding minister was to observe four "manual acts" which were essential to a full and complete consecration: to take the bread and wine; bless it; break the bread (and pour the wine); and then distribute communion. Brevint also notes the "four-fold shape" explicitly in the *Missale Romanum*.[85]

The discussion of alms begins in VIII.12, in which Brevint states that each person must give according to his means, and the actual amount and proportion is not dictated by scripture. Brevint says that the Law prescribed for the Jews, "as fathers do with children in an age unfit to guide itself," what their offerings were to be: but for Brevint the gospel has freed Christians from such "punctual pedagogy" and each is free to give according to his conscience. Because we are free and accountable, he writes, we are obliged to do as well as, even better than, the Jews. Brevint lists several of these Old Testament obligations: a tenth of everything annually, another tenth every third year, and everything that grew of itself during the fallow of every seventh year:

---

83. Brevint, *Missale Romanum*, 128–29.

84. For further discussion of Dix on this point, as it affects the Book of Common Prayer see Stephen Reynolds, "'Sacrifices by Resemblance,' The Protestant Doctrine of Eucharistic Sacrifice in Late Elizabethan and Early Stuart Divinity," *Toronto Journal of Theology* 3 (1987) 83.

85. Brevint, *Missale Romanum*, 284. An early advocate of the "four-fold shape" was Thomas Cooper, defending Jewel's "Challenge sermon." Thomas Cooper, *Answer in Defence of the Truth Against the Apology of the Private Mass*, Cambridge, 1859, 71. Gordon Maitland, "The 'Four-Action' Shape of the Liturgy Revisited: Was Dix the First to Suggest a Four-Fold Shape?" Unpublished paper read at the annual meeting of Societas Liturgica, Dublin, 1995.

Change and Transformation

> Here then a downright Christian will do well to take notice, of what all these charges may come to, and what proportion they will bear with the estate and revenue that God blesses him with, that so he may contribute towards works of piety and charity, not only so much but more; and if not in the very same, yet in as good a kind as the Jews did. So that he may go beyond them in charity, whom the Gospel commands us to exceed in all other virtues, as we exceed them in blessings. (VIII.12)

Although this is called charity, Brevint says that the Jews called it "justice," because it was commanded by Law. Our sacrifices in this kind are best set aside daily, first to make them easier to bear, and secondly so that we may daily discipline ourselves in holiness; and especially at the time of unexpected good fortune. We have received all we have from God, and we have offered it all back to God. Some we keep for our own use and necessities, some is required of us to give up back to God. Since Christ's own time the Church has depended upon the offerings of people like Susanna and other religious women, and such goods given to the Church are received by Christ as if they had been given directly to him. Only in this same spirit can we apply the offering of pious good works as acceptable "heave offerings," i.e. the "first fruits."

Again, Brevint is not unique in his explication of alms and good works as eucharistic sacrifices. Patrick certainly takes this approach, as do Andrewes in his "Imaginations" sermon, and Perkins in *Reformed Catholic*.[86] But it is Hamon L'Estrange whose exposition is most like Brevint's, explicitly connecting the sacrifice of the eucharist with the offertory. L'Estrange says that the first of the sacrifices and oblations in the eucharist is "the bringing of our gifts to the altar." He comments that there are four species of sacrifices at the eucharist, and his comments are worth repeating at some length, for his tone is remarkably similar to Brevint's:

> The whole action of the sacred Communion is elemented of nothing but sacrifices and oblations. So in our Church, so in the Apostolic, which should be the grand exemplar to all . . . These sacrifices and oblations we may cast into four partitions, and find them all in the primitive, and in our service . . . The first is the bringing of our gifts to the Altar, that is, the species and elements of the sacred symbols, and withal some overplus, according to our abilities, for relief of the poor. And this eleemosynary offering is a sacrifice, so called, Phil.iv.18 and Heb. xii.16, and declared to be 'well pleasing to God:' pleasing to God, though

---

86. Reynolds, "Sacrifices by Resemblance," 84.

> extended to the poor: these have a warrant of attorney from God Himself to receive our alms. 'He that hath pity on the poor, lendeth to the Lord,' Prov. xix.17. So that when we come together to break bread, in the Scripture notion, that is, to communicate, we must break it to the hungry, to God Himself in his poor members, as ever we expect a share in that last Venite, 'Come ye blessed,' &c."[87]

L'Estrange writes of the specifically sacrificial character of this "eleemosynary" offering of alms and compassion for the poor. The remaining three sacrifices are the consecration of the elements, "whereby they become that Sacrament for which they are set apart and deputed," the sacrifice of praises and prayers, which are called sacrifices, the oblation of our selves, of our souls and bodies.

Brevint's discussion is very much the same, and he, like both Calvin and L'Estrange, cites Philippians 4:18. In chapter VIII.14 Brevint writes of "charitable assistances," which are the sacrifice of justice or the "acceptable sacrifice." Therefore it is clear that part of the self-offering of the Church in the eucharist is the offering of care and alms for those naked, hungry, sick or in prison, the "least of these my brethren." Part of the sacrificial element of eucharistic worship is the offering of our alms for the poor, the Sacrifice of Justice, without which our eucharistic worship is meaningless.

John Buckeridge in his funeral sermon for Lancelot Andrewes insisted that the eucharist is defective without distribution of relief for the poor:

> Now as it is not enough to feed our own souls, unless we also feed both the souls and bodies of the poor, and there is no true fast unless we distribute that to the poor which we deny to our own bellies and stomachs; and there cannot be a perfect and complete adoration to God in our devotions, unless there be also doing good and distributing to our neighbours; therefore to the sacrifice of praise and thanksgiving in the Eucharist in the Church ... we must also add beneficence and communication ... So then offer the sacrifice of praise to God daily in the church ... and distribute and communicate the sacrifice of compassion and alms to the poor out of the church.[88]

---

87. Hamon L'Estrange, *Alliance of Divine Offices*, 4th ed, Oxford, 1846, "Annotations upon Chapter IV," pt. N, the offertory, 270–1.

88. Buckeridge, "Funeral Sermon," 267. This aspect of the Sacrifice of Justice has found admirable expression in our own time. During the 1923 Anglo-Catholic Congress Bishop Frank Weston preached: "[I]f you are prepared to fight for the right of adoring Jesus in the Blessed Sacrament, then you have got to come out from behind your tabernacle, and walk, with Christ mystically present in you, out into the streets of this country, and find the same Jesus in the people of your cities and your villages. You

CONCLUSION

Daniel Brevint's thoroughly christocentric and biblical sacramentalism marks one point where "Anglicans" and "Puritans" knew they were of one mind. His *The Christian Sacrament and Sacrifice* expresses the Calvinist consensus not only among the English, but also the Huguenots and continental reformers such as Peter Martyr, Bucer, and Bullinger. It illustrates tangible theological links among John Calvin, Theodore Beza, and John Wesley. It has been very influential, though indirectly, on both Methodist devotion through Wesley, and generations of Anglican teaching via Waterland's *A Review of the Doctrine of the Eucharist*,[89] which was long a standard textbook in Anglican schools. It is not surprising that Kenneth Stevenson has concluded that Brevint is "a figure of considerable ecumenical significance."[90]

---

cannot claim to worship Jesus in the tabernacle if you do not pity Jesus in the slum . . . If you say that the Anglo-Catholic has a right to hold his peace while his fellow-citizens are living in hovels below the level of the streets, this I say to you, that you do not yet know the Lord Jesus in his sacrament . . ." A sermon preached at the Anglo-Catholic Congress 1923, quoted in Kenneth Leech, *Care and Conflict: Leaves from a Pastoral Notebook*, London, 1990, 159.

89. Daniel Waterland, *A Review of the Doctrine of the Eucharist as Laid Down in Scripture and Antiquity*, Cambridge, 1737.

90. Stevenson, *Covenant of Grace Renewed*, 7.

4

Reconciling the Old and New Testaments in the Eighteenth-Century Debate over Prophecy

DAVID NEY

> The author of Holy Scripture is God, in Whose power it is to signify His meaning, not by words only (as man also can do), but also by things themselves. So, whereas in every other science things are signified by words, this science has the property that the things signified by the words have themselves also a signification. Therefore that first signification whereby words signify things belongs to the first sense, the historical or literal. That signification whereby things signified by words have themselves also a signification is called the spiritual sense, which is based on the literal, and presupposes it.[1]
>
> Thomas Aquinas

THE TENDENCY FOR CHRISTIANS is simply to assume that when they read the Bible they are reading "literally" because they are simply reading "what

---

1. Thomas Aquinas, *Summa Theologicae: Latin Text and English Translation, Introductions, Notes, Appendices, and Glossaries*, trans. and ed., Thomas Gornall, 61 vols., Cambridge, 1964, i, 37–38.

is there." The very notion that "literal meaning" might require further definition, therefore, has a peculiar ring to it. Richard Corney, however, exposes the need for further definition and concludes that, "Through the centuries the meaning of 'literal meaning' has been understood in different ways." These include "a code which we decipher, a foundation on which we build, a door through which we walk" and, since the eighteenth century, "a one-to-one 'correspondence' with external reality on the one hand and . . . authorial intention on the other."[2]

Corney's conviction that literal meaning came to mean "correspondence with external reality" and "authorial intention" in the eighteenth century takes for granted Hans Frei's analysis of eighteenth-century hermeneutics. Frei traces the genesis of both concepts to Anthony Collins' (1676-1729) *Discourse of the Grounds and Reasons of the Christian Religion* (1724).[3] Frei is right to discern important shifts in the meaning of "literal meaning" taking place at the time of Collins' work, but his genealogy is historically inaccurate. As distinct theories regarding the nature of the literal sense, the notion that the literal meaning of a word is its one-to-one "correspondence with external reality" can be traced, at the very least, to earlier work done by Collins' opponent William Whiston (1667-1752) and his mentor, Isaac Newton, and the notion that it is synonymous with authorial intention awaits the work of Collins' opponent Edward Chandler (1668?-1750).[4]

Whiston's articulation of literal meaning as "correspondence with external reality" provoked a crisis in the interpretation of biblical prophecy because it challenged the traditional notion of typology by forcing interpreters to assign but one referent to each prophetic sign. While Anthony Collins denied the existence of messianic prophecies in the Old Testament altogether by insisting that they refer univocally to immediate Old Testament realities, his opponents, such as Arthur Ashley Sykes (c. 1684-1756), followed Whiston by insisting that they refer univocally to Jesus Christ. Although some interpreters continued to affirm Whiston's position in the aftermath of the debate, one outcome of the debate was the re-establishment

---

2. Richard W. Corney, "What Does 'Literal Meaning' Mean? Some Commentaries on the Song of Songs," *Anglican Theological Review* 80 (1998) 515-16.

3. Hans W. Frei, *The Eclipse of Biblical Narrative: A Study in Eighteenth and Nineteenth Century Hermeneutics*, New Haven, 1974, 78-85.

4. Although the quest for authorial intent continues to enjoy prominence in biblical studies, it has come to be seen as highly problematic in the field of literary theory. This development can be traced to W. K. Wimsatt Jr. and M. C. Beardsley, "The Intentional Fallacy," *Sewanee Review* 54 (1946) 468-88. For a contemporary discussion see Jonathan Culler, *Literary Theory: A Very Short Introduction*, 2nd ed., Oxford, 2011.

of the typological interpretation of messianic prophecies. In the course of the debate Herbert Crofts (b. 1691) ventured this re-establishment upon Whiston's theory of correspondence, but the implausibility of his scheme demonstrated the necessity of a reinterpretation of "literal meaning." This reinterpretation was aptly supplied by Chandler: Chandler's notion of literal meaning as authorial intent enabled him to argue that Old Testament authors *intended* their prophetic utterances to refer simultaneously to immediate realities and the coming Messiah.

THE LATITUDINARIANS AND THE MARGINALIZATION OF ALLEGORY

In his monograph of seventeenth century English typology Joseph Galdon claims, "the seventeenth-century reader invariably read the Bible typologically."[5] There can be no doubt as to the flourishing of the typological imagination in the early seventeenth century (most evident in the allegorical musings of the Caroline divines), but the tumult of mid-century dramatically altered this imagination and the status of allegory sharply decreased.[6] Thomas Luxon attributes this decrease to the religious ferment of the Civil War and Commonwealth periods when allegorical interpretation became irreversibly tied to the notion of religious "enthusiasm." Luxon focuses on an interesting exchange between William Franklin [Frankelin] (b. c. 1610) and Congregationalist minister Humphrey Ellis to illustrate this point. Franklin claimed that his outward body had been destroyed and that he had received the glorified body of Christ, and a number of followers quickly rallied to him.[7] Ellis, surprisingly, claims that Franklin's chief sin—which he regards as the chief sin of all pseudo-Christs—is the abuse of Scripture. For Ellis their abuse of Scripture is manifest in the fact that they interpret it according to their own "Allegorical fancies."[8] The conviction that religious

---

5. Joseph A. Galdon S. J., *Typology and Seventeenth-Century Literature*, The Hague, 1975, 14.

6. For an account of the societal and ideological ferment brought about by the English civil war see Christopher Hill, *The World Turned Upside Down: Radical Ideas During the English Revolution*, London, 1975.

7. Thomas H. Luxon, *Literal Figures: Puritan Allegory and the Reformation Crisis in Representation*, Chicago, 1995, 1.

8. Humphrey Ellis, *Pseudochrisus: Or, A True and Faithful Relation of the Grand Impostures, Abominable Practices, Horrid Blasphemies, Gross Deceits; Lately Spread Abroad and Acted*... London, 1650, 7; Luxon, *Literal Figures*, 21. Luxon points out that Franklin might equally be interpreted as an extreme literalist. Franklin himself claimed to be reading Scripture literally, and therefore accused Ellis of allegorizing.

"enthusiasts" interpret Scripture according to "allegorical fancies" became a mainstay in Restoration England, and was to be an important contributing factor in the Latitudinarian quest to establish a new pattern of universal scriptural reasoning. By the end of the century most biblical interpreters were no longer engaging the traditional process of allegorical reasoning, which, in the words of Aquinas, formerly allowed interpreters to explore the "signification whereby things signified by words have themselves also a signification."

The term Latitudinarian is somewhat contentious, and may have initially been used to refer to the Cambridge Platonists of mid-century.[9] The next generation of Latitudinarians—men such as Simon Patrick (1626-1707), Isaac Barrow (1630-77), John Tillotson (1630-94), Robert South (1634-1716), Edward Stillingfleet (1635-99), and Thomas Tenison (1636-1715)—continued to affirm with the Platonists that the right use of reason was the antidote to religious enthusiasm and discord.[10] They went well beyond this foundation, however, proposing the re-establishment of the English Commonwealth on the foundation of the Reformation doctrine of the primacy of the literal sense, convinced that the religious, political, and moral upheaval that had ravaged England at mid-century might well have been avoided on this basis. This vision propelled them to attempt to base every aspect of church doctrine and practice on the literal sense, an attempt that was, in Gerard Reedy's words, "extremely ambitious."[11] Their passion to uphold the primacy of the literal sense was evident in a multitude of endeavors that accompanied their ascendency after the Glorious Revolution, including a movement towards the "plain style" of preaching in opposition to their Caroline forbearers, the writing of great apologetic tomes in defense of Anglican establishment, and their endorsement of the new empirical science.

Peter Harrison observes that a decisive shift in biblical interpretation occurred during the period of Latitudinarian ascendancy—a shift that was

---

9. The term "Latitude-men" was first put in print in Simon Patrick, *A Brief Account of the New Sect of Latitude-men*, Cambridge, 1662, 3. Patrick acknowledged the difficulty of defining this new sect and admitted that the one thing that was certain about the "Latitude-men" was that they "had their rise at Cambridge." For an appraisal of the Cambridge Platonists as direct antecedents of Stillingfleet and other prominent Latitudinarians, see John Tulloch *Rational Theology and Christian Philosophy in England in the 17th century*, Hildesheim, 1966. W. M. Spellman, on the other hand, tends to downplay the relationship between the Latitudinarians and the Platonists: W. M. Spellman, *The Latitudinarians and the Church of England, 1660-1700*, Athens, GA, 1993.

10. Tulloch, *Rational Theology and Christian Philosophy in England*, 42.

11. Gerard Reedy, SJ, *The Bible and Reason: Anglicans and Scripture in the Late Seventeenth-Century*, Philadelphia, 1985, 16.

to mark the end of Aquinas' view of multivalent signification. Harrison interestingly points to the 1678 work of Cambridge naturalist John Ray (1627–1705)—*The Ornithology of Francis Willughby*—as important in this regard. Ray boasts that his work stands in opposition to what has now become an antiquated ornithological tradition in which authors focused upon "*Homonymous* and *Synonumous* words, or the divers names of Birds, *Hieroglyphics, Emblems, Morals, Fables, Presages* or ought else appertaining to *Divinity, Ethics, Grammar,* or any sort of Humane Learning" rather than the physical specimens themselves.[12] Harrison's thesis is that the Bible was subjected to the rules that governed the new approach to natural philosophy, to the effect that as emblematicism gave way to analysis of physical specimens, allegory gave way to focus upon the "plain sense" of the words of Scripture. Harrison's point, however, is not that earlier ornithologists failed to look at birds, or that earlier biblical interpreters failed to attend to the meaning of words. At issue is not *that* one looks at the object in question but *how* one looks at it. Within the traditional allegorical frame interpreters were drawn away from words "to the infinitely more eloquent things of nature to which those words referred," but in the new "scientific" orientation delineations and associations were cut short by the fact that there is a one-to-one correspondence between word and thing.[13]

The movement away from allegory was accompanied, not surprisingly, by the devaluation of practitioners of allegory, particularly the Church Fathers.[14] In the new context biblical interpreters that retained a fondness for patristic allegory, such as Henry More (1614–87), were increasingly criticized, if misunderstood.[15] Thomas Woolston (1668–1733), allegory's most vocal defender, on the other hand, was not criticized. He was simply ignored. Woolston was convinced that the ecclesial division that plagued England was attributable, not to the lack of attention to the literal sense as the Latitudinarians maintained, but to the fact that Anglicans had failed to embrace patristic allegory.[16] He preached his views on the subject to little

12. John Ray and Francis Willughby, *The Ornithology of Francis Willughby*, London, 1678, Preface.

13. Peter Harrison, *The Bible, Protestants, and the Rise of Natural Science*, Cambridge, 1998, 3.

14. Jean-Louis Quantin, *The Church of England and Christian Antiquity: The Construction of a Confessional Identity in the 17th Century*, Oxford, 2009, 203–51. Quantin traces this decline in status to elements already at work at mid-century.

15. Sarah Hutton, "Iconisms, Enthusiasm and Origen: Henry More Reads the Bible," in Ariel Hessayon and Nicholas Keene, eds., *Scripture and Scholarship in Early Modern England*, Burlington, 2006, 192–207.

16. Thomas Woolston, *A Free Gift to the Clergy . . . Challenged to a Disputation . . .*, London, 1722, 39–40.

effect, and when he published his plea for a return to allegory as an antidote to unbelief in *The Old Apology for the Truth of the Christian Religion* (1705), he was bitterly disappointed when his work was almost completely ignored.[17] After a long bout of depression and confinement, Woolston reinvented himself as an anti-clerical controversialist, desperate to find a hearing for his peculiar views.[18]

Although it can be fairly said that allegory had become marginalized by the beginning of the eighteenth century, the same cannot be said of typology. Typological exegesis is clearly evident in countless sermons and writings of the time, being clearly seen even in those of leading Latitudinarians.[19] Stillingfleet—whose scholarship was held by his contemporaries in the highest regard—continued to affirm that "Our salvation by Jesus Christ is represented to us in the Scriptures of the Old Testament, by a variety of significant images and descriptions; all which point to, and center in these great truths." This framework allows him to assert, for example, that the paschal lamb was "a type and figure to the Israelites, of Christ's propitiatory sacrifice" and that the land of Canaan was "not the rest itself but it was a figure and representation of it."[20] Isaac Newton's mentor, Isaac Barrow, likewise interprets Old Testament realities as "types and shadows" of New Testament dispensations, and the same can be said of Tillotson and South.[21]

The Latitudinarian justification of typological exegesis is clearly articulated in Stillingfleet's discussion of Matthew's use of Isaiah 53. Stillingfleet, in a learned and detailed exposition of the relationship between the Hebrew text of Isaiah 53 and the Greek text of Matthew 8, defends Matthew's conviction that Jesus Christ is Isaiah's suffering servant. In opposition to his Socinian detractors—those that claim the gospel inserts foreign signification into the words of the prophet by means of "accommodation"—Stillingfleet endeavors to demonstrate that Matthew is justified in his literal application of Isaiah's words to Christ. For Stillingfleet, Matthew is justified because the words he applies to Christ are used in their "primary and natural sense,"

---

17. William H. Trapnell, *Thomas Woolston: Madman and Deist?*, Bristol, 1994, 33–36.

18. Trapnell, *Thomas Woolston*, 41–50. See also William Whiston, *Memoirs of the Life and Writings of Mr. William Whiston*, 3 vols., London: 1753, iii, 198.

19. Reedy, *The Bible and Reason*, 15.

20. Edward Stillingfleet, *Sermons on Some of the Principal Doctrines of the Christian Religion*, York, 1794, 156.

21. Isaac Barrow, *The Sermons of the Learned Dr. Isaac Barrow, Late Master of Trinity-College, in Cambridge* Edinburgh, 1751, 379–380; John Tillotson, *The Works of the Most Reverend John Tillotson, Lord Archbishop of Canterbury. In twelve volumes*, 12 vols., London, 1757, iii, 13, 67; vi, 178; ix, 94; xii, 311; Robert South, *Five Additional Volumes of Sermons Preached upon Several Occasions*, London, 1744, vii, 29.

and therefore allow the gospel to retain the "same signification" as the Isaian text.[22]

This Latitudinarian justification of typology on the basis its conformity to the "plain sense" of the words of Scripture clarifies the nature of the shift in the typological imagination of the late seventeenth century. While the terms typology and allegory were used freely, and sometimes interchangeably, by the early eighteenth century typology gradually came to be distinguished from allegory on the basis of its agreement with the literal sense.[23] Confidence in this agreement was well established by the beginning of the eighteenth century, but—as we shall see—it was not without problems.

WILLIAM WHISTON'S PROBLEMATIC

In 1720 Woolston published *Origenis Adamantii Epistola ad doctores Whitbeium, Waterlandium, Whistonium* and an *Epistola secunda*, hoping to provoke a response from Daniel Whitby, Daniel Waterland, and William Whiston—the three men he deemed to be the leading exponents of literal biblical interpretation in England.[24] He renewed his attack against Whiston in his *Moderator between an Infidel and an Apostate*.[25] In this work Woolston complains that, "Mr Whiston is indeed so averse to allegorical Interpretations of the Scriptures," that for him "they are the most pernicious and ill-grounded Things that ever were admitted among Christians."[26]

---

22. Edward Stillingfleet, *Origines Britannicæ; or, the Antiquities of the British Churches . . .*, London, 1710, 270. Tillotson and South employ Stillingfleet's rationale when they declare that the Old Testament prophecies are "exactly" fulfilled in Christ. See John Tillotson, *Several Discourses of the Truth and the Excellency of the Christian Religion*, London, 1703, 24; Robert South, *Five Additional Volumes*, London, 1744, vol. viii, xii.

23. The necessity of distinguishing typology from allegory on the basis of its conformity with the literal sense was famously debated by patristic scholars Henri de Lubac and Jean Daniélou in the middle of the twentieth century. For a helpful review of the debate see Pater W. Martens, "Revisiting the Allegory/Typology Distinction: The Case of Origen," *Journal of Early Christian Studies* 16:3 (2007) 283–317.

24. Thomas Woolston, *Origenis Adamantii Epistola ad doctores Whitbeium, Waterlandium, Whistonium*, London, 1720; *Origenis Adamantii renati epistola (epistola secunda) . . .*, London, 1720.

25. Thomas Woolston, *The Moderator between an Infidel and an Apostate . . .*, London, 1725, 82. Although the "infidel" Woolston here speaks of is Anthony Collins and the "apostate" is Edward Chandler, Woolston seems to be largely in agreement with Collins. As the work progresses it becomes obvious that his primary opponents are not Collins and Chandler, but Whiston and Chandler.

26. Ibid., 66.

Woolston's statement offers an appropriate entry point into a discussion of Whiston's biblical hermeneutic.

As Whiston's mentor, Newton was undoubtedly the most formative influence upon Whiston's developing hermeneutic. As a biblical interpreter Newton was "intent on developing 'scientific' rules of apocalyptic hermeneutics" in order to make biblical prophecy perspicuous.[27] To this end, one of his basic rules was that interpreters should "chose those interpretations which are most according to the litterall meaning of the scriptures," which for Newton entailed that "but one meaning" be applied "to one place of scripture."[28] In his monograph *William Whiston: Honest Newtonian*, James Force argues that Whiston's lifetime of work in the area of biblical interpretation represents a consistent application of Newton's rules of exegesis.[29] Force's thesis is unassailable, but it must also be emphasized that although Newton undoubtedly has his particularities, the literalism at the centre of the Newtonian "scientific" approach is hardly unique to him. Indeed, the Newtonian emphasis on the "plain sense" is unmistakably Latitudinarian, a fact which comes as no surprise given that like Newton the vast majority of Latitudinarians, including Patrick, Barrow, Tillotson, South, Stillingfleet, and Tenison also studied at Cambridge.[30]

In 1696 Whiston published *A New Theory of the Earth, From its Original, to the Consummation of all Things*. The work proved to be a best seller, and went through six editions from 1696 to 1755.[31] Whiston begins the work by echoing the basic principle of Newtonian exegesis: "The Obvious or Literal Sense of Scripture is the True and Real one, where no evident Reason

---

27. Stephen D. Snobelen, "The Argument over Prophecy: An Eighteenth-Century Debate between William Whiston and Anthony Collins," *Lumen* 15 (1996) 197.

28. For Newton's rules for the interpretation of Scripture see Isaac Newton, "Untitled Treatise on Revelation," Yahuda MS 1.1 f 12r, Jewish National University Library, http://www.newtonproject.sussex.ac.uk/view/texts/normalized/THEM00135.

29. James Force, *William Whiston: Honest Newtonian*, Cambridge, 1985.

30. Margaret Jacob, *The Newtonians and the English Revolution*, Ithaca, NY, 1976, 34. Jacob forges a close relationship between Newtonian science and Latitudinarian political theory in her work. As for Newton, she claims that although Newton was somewhat of a reclusive figure, the churchmen he did associate with were all Latitudinarians.

31. Force, *William Whiston: Honest Newtonian*, 25. Force holds that John Locke was simply giving the opinion of the learned world when he recommended Whiston's *New Theory* as having explained many wonderful and previously inexplicable geological alterations in a letter to Molyneaux.

can be given to the contrary."³² Stephen Snobelen observes that, "This principle would guide Whiston throughout his entire life."³³

Whiston's first published application of the Newtonian hermeneutic to biblical prophecy was *The Accomplishment of Scripture Prophecy; eight Sermons preached at Boyle's Lecture in 1707*, which also proved a bestseller. In his first lecture, Whiston adopts his mentor's approach and outlines ten principles by which he intends to demonstrate the perspicuity of biblical prophecy. The tenth and final principle is as follows:

> I Observe that the Stile and Language of the Prophets, as it is often peculiar and enigmatical, so is it always single and determinate, and not capable of those double Intentions, and typical Interpretations, which most of our large Christian Expositors are so full of upon all Occasions.³⁴

Whiston here intensifies the literalism of the Latitudinarians, dismissing "double Intentions" and "typical Interpretations" on the same basis: the first reason Whiston urges his audience to reject them is that we put "a force upon plain words," acting contrary to our "rational faculties," when we

---

32. William Whiston, *A New Theory of the Earth, From Its Original, to the Consummation of All Things*, London: 1696, 95. Whiston's indication that he is willing to accept the occasional non-literal interpretation echoes statements made by Newton in his rules for interpretation in his untitled treatise on Revelation. Newton acknowledges that the literal sense must be kept "unless it be perhaps by way of conjecture, or where the literal sense is designed to hide the more noble mystical sense as a shell the kernel from being tasted either by unworthy persons, or until such time as God shall think fit". Newton proceeds to suggest that the literal meaning should be upheld "unless where the tenour & circumstances of the place plainly require an Allegory": Newton, "Untitled Treatise on Revelation," Yahuda MS 1.1 f 12v. As for Whiston, his declared openness is seldom, if ever, expressed in his exegesis. Whiston makes it clear in *An Essay towards Restoring the True Text of the Old Testament* that he is willing to go to great lengths to avoid interpreting Scripture non-literally: William Whiston, *An Essay towards Restoring the True Text of the Old Testament, and for Vindicating the Citations of the New Testament*, London, 1722.

33. Snobelen, "The Argument," 198.

34. William Whiston, *The Accomplishment of Scripture Prophecy; Eight Sermons Preached at Boyle's Lecture in 1707*, Cambridge, 1708, 13. Force suggests that the topic for Whiston's Boyle Lectures was likely suggested by Newton himself: Force, *William Whiston: Honest Newtonian*, 194, note 22. O'Higgins argues that it was common at the beginning of the eighteenth century to hold the notion that "Some of the prophecies were regarded as having a double interpretation, one more immediate, the other messianic, which the first typified," James O'Higgins, *Anthony Collins: The Man and his Works*, The Hague, 1970, 159. For a systematic justification of the double sense of biblical prophecy from the period see William Allen, *The works of Mr. William Allen, consisting of thirteen distinct tracts on several subjects*, London, 1707, 645.

attribute more than a single referent to a word.³⁵ Whiston proceeds to apply this principle to the text that would be at the centre of the debate over prophecy, Isaiah 7:

> If we had found, not in a Prophecy, but in the History of the Old-Testament, that in the beginning of the Reign of *Ahaz* King of *Judah a Virgin* did, by the wonderful Power of God, *conceive and bear a Son, and his name was called Emmanuel*; we should have no manner of difficulty, as to the understanding such a passage in that History.³⁶

Whiston has no doubt that history vindicates his belief that Isaiah's prophecy refers univocally to Jesus Christ. Given that there is a one-to-one correspondence between a word and its object, and given that the word "virgin" and the word "Emmanuel" find their objects in the New Testament, there is no reason to fear that historians will discover a second "virgin" or "Emmanuel" alive at the time of King Ahaz.

The second reason prophetic words must be taken to have but one referent is that typology opens the door to "foolish applications of fanciful and enthusiastick Men." Whiston again applies his principle to Isaiah 7:

> If I once was brought to own, that that single beforemention'd Prediction, of the *Conception of a Virgin*, did really foretel such a wonderful event, in the time of King *Ahaz*; and such another event besides in the time of King *Josiah*, it would not be difficult to persuade me, that the same Prophecy was to have many more completions; and that in every Century or two it was again fulfill'd through all future Generations.³⁷

Whiston's third reason follows from the second:

> If we own that we can no otherwise shew their completion, than by applying them secondarily and typically to our Lord, after they had in their first and primary intention been already plainly fulfill'd in the times of the Old-Testament: We lose all the real advantage of these ancient Prophecies, as to the proof of our common Christianity, and besides expose our selves to the insults of *Jews* and *Infidels* in our Discourses with them.³⁸

---

35. Whiston, *Accomplishment*, 14.
36. Ibid.
37. Ibid., 15–16.
38. Ibid., 16.

Whiston believes Christians can be supremely confident that Old Testament prophecies refer singularly to Jesus Christ and he takes this fact to be a deductive proof for the truth of Christianity.

Although Whiston was steadfast in his insistence that typology is to be rejected on the basis of its violation of the principle of singular referentiality and its negation of the apologetic value of messianic prophecies, he was honest enough to consider difficulties inherent in his approach. Sometime between his publication of his Boyle lectures in 1708 and *An Essay towards Restoring the True Text of the Old Testament, and for Vindicating the citations of the New Testament* in 1722 Whiston came to acknowledge that many New Testament texts that claim to be prophetic fulfillments of Old Testament texts could hardly be described as literal fulfillments of them. Whiston, however, refused to adjust either his literalism or his confidence in messianic prophetic fulfillment, and the elaborate theory he developed in his *Essay* allowed him to uphold them both.

The basic contours of Whiston's theory are as follows. Whiston acknowledges that "immense Pains have been taken by the Christian Divines and Expositors, in order to reconcile these Citations with the Texts whence they are cited."[39] Their intricate systems of typological and allegorical fulfillment, however, are entirely unnecessary given that the Hebrew and Greek texts of the Old Testament have been corrupted intentionally by the Jews of the second century in order to obscure the literal correspondence between the Old and New Testaments, and thereby the Christian apologetic. Textual corruption is thus, for Whiston, the mechanism that allows him to uphold the conviction that, "The Texts cited by our Saviour, his Apostles, and the rest of the Writers of the New Testament, out of the Old, were truly cited by them; and in Agreement with the genuine Hebrew and Greek Bibles of that Age."[40]

One intentional textual accretion Whiston claims has been "a very great Disadvantage to the Christian Religion" is the text he had celebrated fourteen years earlier in his Boyle lectures as undoubtedly messianic in orientation: Isaiah 7. Whiston maintains that although St. Matthew and the first Christians quote this passage to prove that the Messiah was to be born of a virgin, the text—as it now stands in all the late Bibles—includes an additional clause "as seems no way applicable to the Messias; and so occasions the *Jews* to triumph, as if the Prediction were meant not of a Virgin, but only of a young Woman, in the Days of *Ahaz*."[41] Whiston argues that

---

39. Whiston, *Essay*, 282.
40. Ibid, 281.
41. Ibid., 229.

while the messianic prediction of a virgin being with child consequently interrupts the flow of the present narrative, it is the "Sum and natural Coherence of several Predictions in the viith, viiith, and the beginning of the ixth Chapters of *Isaiah*." He proceeds to appeal to Tertullian, Justin Martyr and the *Apostolic Constitutions* for a reordering of the text in order to make its messianic orientation credible.[42]

Anthony Collins' forceful critique of Whiston's method has tended to obscure the logic inherent in Whiston's position. Whiston was not engaged in fanciful speculation. He was merely proposing a new application for the well-established tradition of textual criticism that can be traced back to Desiderius Erasmus. Like his Socinian forbearers, Newton himself had undertaken a careful study of extant biblical manuscripts in order to demonstrate that Trinitarian proof texts relied upon textual accretions.[43] And while Whiston lacks the mastery of the textual tradition that the great French textual critic Richard Simon, or perhaps even Newton, demonstrated, his grasp of the tradition is adequate enough to lend credibility to his proposal. He concludes the work by calling upon his fellow textual scholars to undertake a great search for uncorrupt ancient manuscripts, and to employ the extant copies of the Samaritan Pentateuch, the Greek Psalms, the present Hebrew Bible (despite the fact that it has been altered by the Jews), the several Greek editions of the Septuagint, the Syriac Bible, the Chaldean Paraphrases, and Old Testament quotations from Josephus, Philo, New Testament authors and the primitive Fathers, "as we ought faithfully to use all the Helps and Assistances we already have, in order to so truly noble a Design as is this, *of restoring the true Text of the Old Testament, to its original Purity*."[44]

The idea that textual criticism could be employed for the sake of the Christian religion was at the centre of Whiston's proposal, but his opponents seem to have been unable to see textual criticism as anything but an attack on the authority of their Bible and their religion.[45] There can be no doubt as to the association of textual criticism and Socinianism in their minds—an association encouraged by Whiston's own anti-trinitarianism. Furthermore,

---

42. Ibid., 232.

43. Stephen Snobelen, "'To us there is but one God, the Father:' Antitrinitarian Textual Criticism in Seventeenth and Early Eighteenth-Century England," in Hessayon and Keene, eds., *Scripture and Scholarship*, 116–36; Rob Iliffe, "Friendly Criticism: Richard Simon, John Locke, Isaac Newton and the *Johannine Comma*," in Hessayon and Keene, *Scripture and Scholarship*, 137–57.

44. Whiston, *Essay*, 333.

45. David Ruderman claims: "Almost from the moment that Whiston's book appeared, his critics were lining up to challenge his highly controversial conclusions." David B. Ruderman, *Connecting the Covenants: Judaism and the Search for Christian Identity in Eighteenth-Century England*, Philadelphia, 2007, 53.

they were unable to see the need to pursue Whiston's project given the fact that, in the words of James O'Higgins, "Their text was regarded as inviolate."[46] The responses Whiston received therefore tended to reject his proposal as a denial of the canonicity of the Old Testament.[47] Despite this rejection Whiston's *Essay* was to be the catalyst for a series of intense controversies that were to have lasting implications for biblical studies.

ANTHONY COLLINS' REJECTION OF PROPHECY

The controversy surrounding biblical prophecy began in earnest with Collins' response to Whiston's *Essay*, *A Discourse of the Grounds and Reasons of the Christian Religion*. Collins' work sent shockwaves throughout England, and Collins boasts that it provoked no less than thirty-five replies.[48] Of these replies only three—all by Woolston—were in his favor.[49] William Warburton (1698–1779) declared Collins' *Discourse* was one of the most plausible books ever written against Christianity, and in our day it continues to be regarded as Collins' most successful work.[50] For John Drury, the importance of the work resides in the fact that in the early eighteenth century "A thin wall divided the Bible from the acids of criticism. With Anthony Collins that wall was dramatically breached."[51]

Although the strength of Collins position is apparent, it must be added that the force of his argument is sometimes obscured by the fact that he proceeds by quoting his opponents in such a way as to construe their carefully laid-out positions as completely ridiculous. Collins was, nevertheless, a bibliophile of the first order, and his argument is enhanced by the fact that he always manages to find an authoritative commentator to confirm

---

46. O'Higgins, *Anthony Collins*, 155.

47. See William Itchener, *A Defence of the Canon of the Old Testament: or, An Answer to Mr. Whiston's Supplement to His Late Essay*, London, 1723.

48. Anthony Collins, *The Scheme of Literal Prophecy Considered; In a View of the Controversy, occasion'd by a late book, intitled, A discourse of the grounds and . . .*, 2 vols., The Hague, 1726, i, preface.

49. Thomas Woolston, *Moderator; A Supplement to The moderator between an Infidel and an Apostate . . .*, London, 1725; *A Second Supplement to The Moderator between an Infidel and an Apostate . . .*, London, 1725.

50. William Warburton, *The works of the Right Reverent William Warburton, Lord Bishop of Gloucester. In seven volumes*, 7 vols., London, 1788, iii, 500; O'Higgins, *Anthony Collins*, 154.

51. John Drury, "Introductory Essay," in John Drury, ed., *Critics of the Bible, 1724–1873*, Cambridge, 1989, 8–9.

his views.[52] Although Whiston felt Collins had consistently misrepresented him, Collins decisively exposed Whiston's arbitrary application of textual criticism, which "extends to every quotation made from the Old in the New Testament, and gives him liberty and scope to chop and change the whole Old Testament as he pleases"[53] so that "a bible restor'd, according to Mr. W's Theory, will be a mere confounding, and not containing the true text of the Old Testament."[54]

Despite Collins' rhetoric, his *Discourse* has a great deal in common with Whiston's *Essay*. To begin, Collins endorses the application of criticism to the Bible. He also affirms Whiston's theory of language:

> To suppose that an author has but one meaning at a time to a proposition (which is to be found out by a critical examination of his words), and to cite that proposition from him, and argue from it in that one meaning, is to proceed by the common rules of grammar and logick; which, being human rules, are not very difficult to be set forth and explain'd.[55]

Frei takes Collins' reference to the author to be "*an independent factor*," one of two pillars upholding his hermeneutic, and because of this Frei believes that "Collins introduced a new element into the hermeneutical situation of biblical study."[56] For Frei, Collins "assigned the origin of specific meaning to the intention of the individual author" with the result that the words become a clue "to the mind of the author where . . . meaning resides."[57] This fact, coupled with Collins' views regarding "the rules governing the proper use of language," which assumes that the meanings of words derive from their one-to-one correspondence with objects of the external world, leads to a new theory of language signification, which Frei calls "ostensive reference." For Frei, "The upshot of analyzing the ruled use of language is that meaning

---

52. O'Higgins, *Anthony Collins*, 183.

53. Anthony Collins, *A Discourse of the Grounds and Reasons of the Christian Religion*, London: 1725, 222.

54. Collins, *Discourse,* 225. Force interestingly defends Whiston's attempt to "get behind" the Hebrew MSS tradition by appealing to other sources such as the Septuagint and the Samaritan Pentateuch as entirely consistent with the method of contemporary textual critics. If Whiston is to be criticized therefore, it is perhaps on account of the fact that he only applies the rigors of textual criticism selectively to messianic prophecies. He does not, as Collins maintains, "chop and change the whole Old Testament." See Force, *William Whiston: Honest Newtonian*, 81–82.

55. Collins, *Discourse,* 51.

56. Frei, *The Eclipse of Biblical Narrative,* 78.

57. Ibid., 78–79.

becomes identical with ostensive reference. The meaning of a statement is the spatiotemporal occurrence or state of affairs to which it refers."[58]

One of the difficulties of Frei's account is that it fails to demonstrate Collins' reliance upon authorial intent. Frei neglects the fact that the quotation under examination is the only occasion in which Collins mentions the role of the author in the derivation of meaning. Frei also fails to observe that Collins here mentions the author almost in passing: he nowhere pauses to consider the author as "an independent factor." Collins' hermeneutic must not be taken as a move towards the human subject. As he considers the words of biblical authors he shows absolutely no interest in trying to uncover "the mind of the author where . . . meaning resides," to the extent that he comes across as rather dismissive of them. Indeed, whereas appeals to authorial intent are rooted in an acknowledgement of the opacity of language, Collins' account is dominated by confidence in the transparency of language. For Collins, the science of interpretation is entirely public and entirely straightforward. The meanings of texts are—one could almost say mathematically—derived from the common meanings of words and the "rules of grammar and logick."

Frei traces Collins' correspondence theory of language to his mentor, John Locke.[59] This may very well be the case. But it might just as well have been learned from Whiston.[60] As for Whiston, the parallels are striking. Collins and Whiston share, as their foundation, the belief that the meanings of words are "single and determinate," and both reject typology and allegory on this basis.[61] Collins also affirms—with Whiston—that there is a lack of literal correspondence between the Old Testament prophecies and their New Testament fulfillments, and he even admits that this lack of correspondence must be attributed to the corruption of the Old Testament text.[62] These similarities are brought into relief by the fact that Collins diverges from Whiston's path at one crucial point. In a parody of Whiston, Collins states that

> The prophecies cited from the Old Testament by the authors of the New, do so plainly relate, in their obvious and primary

---

58. Ibid., 78.

59. Ibid.

60. Force implies that Collins' theory of referentiality can be attributed to Whiston: Force, *William Whiston: Honest Newtonian*, 79. Whiston and Collins operated in some of the same circles, and Whiston admits that he frequently dined with Collins at Lady Caverly's home before the controversy; Whiston, *Memoirs*, 158.

61. Snobelen, "The Argument," 201.

62. Collins, *Discourse*, 139.

sense, to other matters than those which they are produced to prove; that to pretend they prove, in that sense, what they are produc'd to prove, *is to give up the cause* of Christianity to the *Jews* and other *Enemies* thereof.[63]

At issue between Whiston and Collins is the fact that Whiston takes the referents of Old Testament prophecies to be found in their New Testament fulfillments and Collins confines them to the Old Testament. For Collins, Old Testament prophecies are "literally and obviously applicable" only to their immediate Old Testament contexts."[64]

As for the New Testament, Collins claims it contains merely the *allegorical* fulfillments of Old Testament prophesies. Thus when he turns to the text at the centre of the controversy he observes that, "the *virgin's conception* in *Isaiah*, apply'd by MATTHEW, relates to the virgin MARY in an allegorical sense, *viz.* as a *type*."[65] My contention is that by insisting on the literal correspondence of prophetic texts the defenders of Christianity had made things easy for Collins. Whiston had already done the hard work of demonstrating that many decisive messianic texts of the New Testament did not agree with their supposed antecedents in the Old. All that was left for Collins was to show that Whiston's positive proposal was inadequate: given that they could not possibly hope to restore the text to its Edenic purity, Christians must take the Old Testament text as it now stands and acknowledge the lack of correspondence of prophetic texts. Prophecies can have but one referent, and the lack of correspondence between Old Testament texts and their supposed New Testament fulfillments renders the conclusion that New Testament typology is anachronistic, arbitrary, false—in other words, "allegorical."[66]

In their quest for doctrinal agreement and the comprehension of dissenters, the Latitudinarians had proposed vast simplifications of Christian doctrine. This approach found its zenith in John Locke's *The Reasonableness of Christianity* (1695), in which Locke argued that the one essential truth of Christianity—the one that everyone could agree upon—is that Jesus is the Messiah.[67] In his *Discourse,* Collins takes his friend and mentor's conclusion, and employs it to a radically different end. Collins' argument is as follows: (a) that Jesus is the Messiah can only be proved via the Old

---

63. Collins, *Discourse*, 48. Whiston, *Accomplishment*, 16.

64. Collins, *Discourse*, 124.

65. Ibid., 63.

66. Ibid., 51.

67. John Locke, *The Reasonableness of Christianity with A Discourse of Miracles and part of A Third Letter Concerning Toleration*, I. T. Ramsey, ed., Stanford, 1958, 33.

Testament, through the literal correspondence of Old Testament prophecies with their New Testament fulfillments; (b) no such correspondence exists; (c) therefore Jesus is not the Messiah.[68] With this one simple argument Collins claims to have destroyed, not merely the argument from prophecy, but the very foundation of Christianity.

Most of Collins' opponents denied him his minor rather than his major premise.[69] They assumed that Christianity could only be deductively proved by messianic prophecies and that as defenders of the faith, the mission bequeathed them by the church was to defend the idea of literal prophetic correspondence. Collins' interlocutors—again, with the exception of Woolston—have this in common: they insist that at least some of the messianic prophecies of the Old Testament find their literal fulfillment in the person and work of Jesus Christ.[70]

Respondents to Collins in favor of the literal fulfillment of messianic prophecies in the New Testament can be divided into two camps: those affirming the single sense of prophetic fulfillment, and those affirming the double sense. The most prominent advocates of the single sense of prophetic fulfillment were Whiston, Thomas Bullock (1693/94–1760), Samuel Chandler (1693–1766), Thomas Jeffery (1698–1729), and Arthur Ashley

---

68. O'Higgins admits that Collins is somewhat of an enigma, for although he seems to be intent on destroying Christianity in many of his writings, he took himself to be a good Anglican. He likely understood himself as purifying Anglicanism by removing all doctrinal particulars in order to make Anglicanism consistent with "moral religion": O'Higgins, *Anthony Collins*, 171–74.

69. Those who did deny the major premise tended only to quarrel with the notion that the argument from prophecy was the *only* proof of Jesus' messiahship, reminding Collins that they also had recourse to His miracles: Samuel Chandler, *A Vindication of the Christian Religion*, London: 1725; Samuel Clarke, *A Discourse concerning the Connexion of the Prophecies in the Old Testament, and the Application of them to Christ*, London, 1725. Two of Collins' more obscure opponents, John Green and Theophilus Lobb, in opposition to this general tendency, made the defense of miracles central to their defense of Christianity. Their approach anticipates the fact that the argument concerning the nature of the miracles of Jesus was to take center stage following the publication of Woolston's six vitriolic *Discourses on the Miracles of Our Saviour*, London, 1727–29; John Green, *Letters to the Author of the "Grounds and Reasons of the Christian Religion,"* London, 1726; Theophilus Lobb, *A Brief Defence of the Christian Religion*, London, 1726. See also O'Higgins, *Anthony Collins*, 176–77; Trapnell, *Thomas Woolston*, 57–67.

70. Collins' *Discourse* gave Woolston the opportunity he had been waiting for—he seems to have mistaken Collins as a prominent ally in his quest for the re-establishment of patristic allegorical exegesis: Force, *William Whiston: Honest Newtonian*, 68. The Anglican establishment seems to have embraced Collins' pejorative definition of allegory and therefore rejected Woolston's *Moderator*. Woolston's foray into the debate merely entrenched the conviction that allegory was to be avoided at all cost.

Sykes.[71] Sykes offers a helpful summary, both of his position and the larger controversy:

> In the Prosecution of my Argument, I think, I have made it evident upon what Foundation in the Old Testament Christianity stands: And if *Prophesy*, clearly such, and exact corresponding *Event*, be *Proof*, as 'tis without dispute, then is Christianity true. But because much Dispute has been about the meaning of some Passages of the Old Testament, cited by the Authors of the New; and Learned Men have been perplexed about those Citations; Some pleading a *Corruption* of the Books of the Old Testament, Others insisting upon *double Completions*, and Others still pretending a strange *allegorical*, absurd, way of Reasoning in the Apostles: I am not willing to leave this point unconsidered ; and therefore submit the following Reflexions to every candid Reader who feels the Difficulty. But before I proceed I must observe, That such a *wilful Corruption* as Mr. *Whiston* has contended for in order to get rid of the Difficulty, and That to be made at the time when 'tis said by Mr. *Whiston* to be made, is as great a Difficulty as that which he endeavours to account for. A *Double Sense* of Prophecies, where the Prophet has not declared such a *double* Sense, is making Prophecy useless; because when Prophecies have no *One* determinate Sense, they will be equally capable of as many Accomplishments as every *Enthusiast* pleases. And the *Allegorical* way of interpreting Prophecies and arguing from them, is, generally speaking, so wild and extravagant, that those who judge of things from the actual Agreement or Disagreement of Ideas, can never be made Converts by such a method of Reasoning.[72]

Three observations are in order. The first is that Sykes articulates his position not merely in opposition to Whiston and Collins, but quite consciously in opposition to proponents of the "*Double sense* of Prophecies" and the "*Allegorical* way of interpreting Prophecies."[73] The second is that this opposition is motivated by apologetic concerns: like Whiston, Sykes rejects typology and allegory as apologetically useless. The third is that while Sykes

---

71. Thomas Bullock, *The Reasoning of Christ and His Apostles in Their Defence of Christianity Considered* . . ., London, 1725; Chandler, *A Vindication;* Thomas Jeffery, *The True Grounds and Reasons of the Christian Religion*, London, 1725; Thomas Jeffery, *A Review of the Controversy between the Author of a Discourse of the Grounds and Reasons of the Christian Religion, and His Adversaries*, London, 1726; Arthur Ashley Sykes, *An Essay upon the Truth of the Christian Religion*, London, 1725.

72. Sykes, *An Essay*, 177–78.

73. Ibid., 178, 204, 205.

follows Whiston in holding that prophetic signification is not enclosed within Old Testament texts he acknowledges that the texts must have meant something to the Jews who wrote them. Sykes thus dedicates the first two chapters of his tome to the consideration of the nature of Jewish messianic expectation and strongly endorses the study of rabbinic literature in order to appreciate the quotation techniques of New Testament authors.[74] While Sykes continues to hold Whiston and Collins' views concerning singular referentiality he is also opening up to the idea that messianic prophecies must be placed within a larger messianic framework.

The most prominent opponents of Collins who affirmed the double sense of prophetic signification were Edward Chandler, Samuel Clarke (1675–1729), and Thomas Sherlock (1678–1761).[75] The final section of this essay will treat Chandler's reply in detail. But before proceeding it is worthwhile to consider the work of one of Collins' more obscure opponents, Herbert Crofts. Crofts' reply to Collins, *The Christian Religion Not founded on Allegory* (1724), stands out for two reasons. The first is its scornful vituperation. The second is Croft's attempt to reconcile singular referentiality and typology in his demonstration that "*Jesus* in the New Testament did demonstrate himself to be the *Messiah* of the *Jews*, and the Saviour of the *Gentiles* promis'd in the Old Testament."[76]

The task Crofts establishes for himself in his discussion of Isaiah 7, not surprisingly, is to justify Matthew's interpretation of it.[77] Crofts rejects what he calls the Jewish interpretation of the passage, which he believes assigns the word "emmanuel" to Hezekiah the Son of Ahaz, on account of the fact that Hezekiah "must have been born several Years before the time of this Prophecy."[78] After summarily dismissing the allegorical solution, and Whiston's text critical one, Crofts offers his own theory: "The words, as they stand, may be fairly reconcil'd to St. *Matthew*'s Citation; if the 14th Verse only be apply'd to the Birth of the *Messias*, and the 15th and 16th Verses be understood of *Shear-jashuh* the Prophets Son."[79] Crofts admits that, "The transition from *Emmanuel* to *Shear-jashuh* may be thought too nice and

---

74. See n. 91 below.

75. Edward Chandler, *A Defence of Christianity from the Prophecies of the Old Testament*, London: 1725; Samuel Clarke, *The Connexion*; Thomas Sherlock, *The Use and Intent of Prophecy, in the Several Ages of the World . . .*, London, 1732.

76. Herbert Crofts, *The Christian Religion not Founded on Allegory*, London, 1724, 131.

77. Ibid., 100.

78. Ibid., 101.

79. Ibid., 103–4.

imperceptible ... but if it be granted, all other difficulties vanish."[80] Unable to deny the fact that many referents in the passage point unmistakably to Isaiah's own context, Crofts excises verse fourteen from Isaiah's context, places it in Matthew's, and is therefore able to uphold Matthew's application of the text and his theory of singular referentiality.

Crofts wonders whether he will be "happy enough to have any Commentators agree in this Opinion" but the implausibility of his scheme speaks for itself.[81] Like Whiston, Crofts must inevitably hold that the quotation of an Old Testament word in the New Testament requires that it be assigned no Old Testament referent. But whereas Whiston holds that Old Testament narratives must be consistent in their referentiality, and that New Testament authors must have rightly discerned this referentiality, Crofts is happy to sever referentiality from narrative context. Crofts' peculiar exegesis clearly demonstrates the difficulty Christian interpreters faced as they struggled to reconcile literal interpretation and messianic fulfillment, and the inadequacy of Crofts solution may be attributed to the fact that Crofts attacks what he considers to be Whiston and Collins' destructive applications of singular referentiality rather than the theory itself. Indeed, the success of Chandler's account may be attributed to the fact that he offers an alternative account of language signification.

EDWARD CHANDLER'S APPEAL TO AUTHORIAL INTENT

Collins' opponents certainly took Chandler to be their primary spokesman, and some made use of Chandler's work, *A defence of Christianity from the prophecies of the Old Testament* (1725), in their own.[82] Collins took Chandler to be his principle opponent, and his supplement to his *Discourse*, entitled *The Scheme of Literal Prophecy Considered* (1726), focuses almost entirely on Chandler's work. It is clear that by this point the controversy was taken by most to be a dispute between Collins and Chandler, despite the fact that Whiston wrote no less than three replies to Collins.[83]

80. Ibid., 104–5.
81. Ibid., 105.
82. See, for example, Jeffery, *A Review*, 51, 59, 71, 140, 142, 147, 160, 196, 206; William Lowth, *A Commentary upon the Prophecy of Daniel*, 2 vols., London, 1726, i, 8; Nathaniel Lardner, *The Credibility of the Gospel History*, London, 1727, 282.
83. O'Higgins, *Anthony Collins*, 179. Whiston's three responses were *A List of Suppositions Or Assertions in the Late Discourse of the Grounds and Reasons of the Christian Religion which are Not Therein Supported by Any Real or Authentick Evidence*, London, 1724; *Literal Accomplishment of the Scripture Prophecies, being a Full Answer to a Late*

Although there can be no doubt as to the force of Collins' argument—which he strengthened in his *Scheme* by admitting that arguments from prophecy were not the only arguments that could demonstrate the truth of Christianity—Chandler's erudition was considered by the controversialists to have won the day. He had a vast knowledge of the targums and later Jewish writers, including Maimonides, and was able to demonstrate that they interpreted the Old Testament prophetic texts literally and typologically rather than allegorically. Collins, of course, dismissed them all as allegorizers, but few of his contemporaries were convinced.[84]

Chandler's articulation of the Jewish anticipation of the Messiah was central to his argument and occupies the first half of the book (Chapters 1–3). He begins by arguing that there was a general messianic expectation at the time of Jesus Christ that can be traced back to their return from Babylon (1–57). He then proceeds to demonstrate that this general expectation was grounded in the prophecies of the Old Testament (58–74), which can be understood as having either literal (75–194) or typological (194–265) signification. It is only once he establishes the foundation of Jewish messianic expectation in the concrete words of the Old Testament that Chandler turns to justify New Testament applications of Old Testament texts as consistent with Jewish tradition (Chapters 4–6).

Important in Chandler's scheme is the new role he assigns to the fulfillment of literal prophecies. They continue to occupy an important place in his argument and, indeed, he spends one hundred and twenty pages treating twelve Old Testament prophecies, which he claims, "refer literally and singly" to the coming of the Messiah.[85] Nevertheless, they do not stand on their own as indisputable proofs as they do for Whiston and many of Collins' other opponents. For Chandler, the literal prophecies of the Old Testament only find their meaning within the larger framework of Jewish messianic expectation. This expanded framework gives rise to a new concern: the concern to unearth and understand what the Jewish people felt, saw, anticipated, hoped, and prayed. Chandler gives particular attention to Jewish prayers, first, because they are able to teach us about their "ancient faith" and second, because they demonstrate not only the messianic nature of the Jewish religion, but the messianic nature of the prophetic texts they quote.[86]

Discourse, of the Grounds and Reasons of the Christian Religion London, 1724; *Supplement to the Literal Accomplishments of Scripture Prophecies*, London, 1725.

84. Ibid., 183.
85. Chandler, *Defence*, Contents.
86. Ibid., 60–61.

Change and Transformation

What emerges in Chandler's discussion of Jewish messianic expectation is a different answer to the question, "on what basis is an Old Testament text established to be prophetic?" For Chandler, a text is prophetic if the Jews believed it to be prophetic. Thus, the fact that the Jews prayed a text prophetically confirms its original authorial messianic orientation and justifies its messianic application in the New Testament. Accompanying this redirection is a redefinition of the literal sense.[87] In a word, what emerges is a new and decisive role for what has come to be known as hermeneutics. For Chandler, language is not transparent, as it is for Whiston and Collins.[88] Language is polyvalent—the quest for its literal sense far from straightforward. For Chandler we must uncover the authorial intent imbedded within a text to find its literal sense. Until this point in the dispute over prophecy, authorial intent was taken for granted as synonymous with the "plain sense" of the words themselves. Now, a fissure between them emerges that enables interpretations that violate the "plain sense" to nevertheless be authorized as authorial.[89]

87. It would be anachronistic to identify Chandler as an early proponent of reader response theories of textual meaning despite Chandler's nod in that direction of communal meaning. That the Jewish community identified a text as messianic is a preliminary argument used by Chandler to demonstrate that the messianic applications of Old Testament prophetic texts by New Testament authors are traditional. It serves to buttress his primary argument that their original Jewish authors intended the prophetic texts used by New Testament authors to be understood as messianic.

88. Collins continued to affirm the transparency of language in his response to Chandler, insisting that the meaning of words "is most commonly plain, or may be made so by the rules of common sense, viz. of grammar and criticism": Collins, *Scheme*, 270. My contention is not that Chandler is the first biblical interpreter to engage in hermeneutical enquiry, but rather that his engagement must be recognized as an important development within his context given the prevailing confidence in the transparency of language. St. Augustine's *De Doctrina Christiana* is the classic Christian text on the distinction between basic literacy and the interpretive act. See R. A. Markus, *Signs and Meanings: World and Text in Ancient Christianity*, Liverpool, 1996; Brenda Deen Schidgen, "Augustine's Answer to Jacques Derrida in the *De Doctrina Christiana*," *New Literary History* 25 (1994) 383–97; Kathy Eden, "The Rhetorical Tradition and Augustinian Hermeneutics in *De doctrina Christiana*," *Rhetorica: A Journal of the History of Rhetoric* 8:1 (1990) 45–63.

89. A possible source of Chandler's understanding of authorial intent as being in distinction from the "plain sense" is the debate surrounding the question of Arian subscription to the 39 Articles. Daniel Waterland insisted on a rigorous Trinitarian interpretation of the articles on the basis of the Trinitarian design of the original authors, whereas Arthur Ashley Sykes argued that this insistence is arbitrary given the fact that authorial intent is obscure. See Daniel Waterland, *The Case of Arian-Subscription Considered: And the Several Pleas and Excuses for It Particularly Examined and Confuted*, Cambridge, 1721, 10–11; Arthur Ashley Sykes, *The Case of Subscription to the XXXIX Articles Considered. Occasioned by Dr. Waterland's Case of Arian Subscription*, London, 1721, 18–19, 34. Despite this initial rejection of the quest for authorial intent Sykes

The newfound importance of authorial intent is most clearly seen in Chandler's most creative contribution: his reconfiguration of the distinction between typology and allegory. Chandler begins his third chapter as follows:

> We are now come, to enquire into another way of prophesying, used very early among the Jews, which we call Typical. And this I distinguish from the strictly Allegorical method, that prevailed in and before our Savior's days; the sense whereof oft-times was not so much the mind of the prophet, as of him that formed the [מדרש] *Midras* from thence; of him that applied, or those that formerly so understood, the word of the Prophet.[90]

Chandler's approach is consistent with his earlier discussion of literal prophecies, as he here continues to display keen interest in Jewish intentionality: whereas typological predictions were intentionally construed as such by their Jewish authors, allegorical predictions were predictive only in lieu of later figurative applications.[91] Chandler continues:

---

is much more open to it in his response to Collins. Like Chandler, Sykes' developing interest in authorial intent can be attributed by his desire to uncover the nature of Jewish messianic expectation; Sykes, *An Essay*, 213. See also Ruderman, *Connecting the Covenants*, 70.

90. Chandler, *Defence*, 195.

91. Stephen Leslie claims that Chandler approved of allegory: Stephen Leslie, *History of English Thought in the Eighteenth Century*, New York, 1962, 187. Trapnell and Ruderman echo this opinion: Trapnell, *Thomas Woolston*, 93. Ruderman rightly observes that Chandler seems quite comfortable with the tradition of Jewish allegorization: Ruderman, *Connecting the Covenants*, 68–96. What Ruderman fails to note is that while Chandler approves of the fact that both the rabbis and New Testament authors used allegory, his is a qualified acceptance. In Chandler's discussion of Pauline allegory he says: "He had the same right to argue with the *Jews*, from their midrashes, however, they were grounded: He had as good authority to raise a Christian doctrine, from the history of the Old Testament, as any *Jewish* doctor before him, to build thereupon, a purely *Jewish* doctrine. It is, however, to be remembered, that these proofs were used only with the *Jews*, and not with them, before they were Christians. When their conversion was labored, other arguments were offered from miracles, the gifts of the Spirit, Christian predictions, and literal prophecies of the Old Testament; and upon these arguments alone, the Christianity of the *Jews*, was truly grounded. All besides, were *ex abundanti & ad hominem*, more than was needful, and for their sakes alone, that relished such reasonings. But how then will *Christianity* be made out, to be *an allegory*? Let him look to it, who hath asserted it, with much assurance. The author of *Grounds and Reasons* is fond of the notion: And rather than part from it, he hath spent one whole chapter, and part of another to maintain, that Christianity is nothing else than mystical *judaism*, and that the *allegorical reasonings* of the apostles were designed as *absolute proofs* of Christianity, and not *ad hominem* to the *Jews*." Chandler, *Defence*, 364–65. Woolston was quick to detect Chandler's ambivalence towards allegory and thus complains that what brings him offence is Chandler's claim that Paul "suffer'd in the Esteem of the Jewish Christians for a Neglect of Allegories, and seems to be brought

Change and Transformation

> Typical prophecies, I take to be those, which are interpreted, of the Messias for instance, according to the primitive, and direct intention of the writer, or the spirit of God in him, though they be spoken in the Prophet's name or in the Name of some other man, who is made to personate the Messias; and the prediction be intermingled with matters that also concern other Persons. These, where they regard the Messias at all, belong to him directly and principally, and to others indirectly, and secondarily; and where they pass, from the Messias to the person representing, they concern him properly, and the Messias improperly. On the contrary, Allegorick predictions, throughout regard other things, in their obvious and literal sense, and the Messias only, by accomodation and allusion.[92]

A threefold typology of authorial intent might therefore be conceived as follows: literal prophecies are intended by their authors to refer solely to the Messiah. Typological prophecies are intended by their authors to refer primarily to the Messiah, and secondarily to other matters. Allegorical prophecies, on the other hand, were originally intended to refer to matters other than those to which they were later applied.

Chandler is consistent in the application of these definitions. Thus, when he comes to justify St. Matthew's exegesis of Isaiah 7, he justifies it as typological, which is to say, on the basis of Isaiah's intentionality. Chandler couches his exegesis in a colloquial paraphrase of Isaiah's oracle:

> I give you a sign, in my son, which shall be born of my wife, and be called *Immanuel* a sign that none of these evils shall happen.

---

into the Use of them against his own good liking": Woolston, *Moderator*, 127–28. Ultimately it seems that as a scholar of Judaism Chandler is more than happy to celebrate the beauty of allegory, but his apologetic stance forces him to draw the line between Jews and Christians. This distinction is inherent in his strategy to salvage the apologetic force of messianic typology. Because Chandler justifies both typical and literal prophecies on the basis of authorial intent, he draws them together, and, in the process, entrenches the divide between typology and allegory, with the result that allegory is seen as merely a literary device.

92. Chandler, *Defence*, 195–96. Chandler's passing reference to the "spirit of God" makes it clear that he does not interpret human intentionality and divine intentionality as necessarily in conflict. Furthermore, the contemporary prominence of the Newtonian design argument suggests that many in Chandler's day many took the identification of secondary causes as giving even greater prominence to God's role as first cause. Despite this fact it is clear that for Chandler, human intention carries the weight, as the way to uncover divine intention is to uncover human intention, rather than vice versa. The Romantic emphasis on the Spirit of the prophet, so evident in Robert Lowth's work, can potentially be seen as a reaction against an overemphasis on human intention: Robert Lowth, *Lectures on the Sacred Poetry of the Hebrews*, London, 1787.

> The imposition of so auspicious, so august a name, shews that this son, is not your expected Saviour, but a type of him, who shall be born of a pure virgin, and fully answer, the import of the name *Immanuel*. Herein only, is my child an *Immanuel*; as portending deliverance from your present dangers.[93]

Because words, for Whiston and Crofts, can have but one referent, they assign the referents of some words to the Old Testament, and others to the New. Chandler, on the other hand, is happy to assign more than one referent to a single word. For Chandler, the word "Immanuel" carries a double sense: Isaiah calls his son "Immanuel" first, in reference to the coming Messiah, and second, in reference to the present deliverance of Israel. In his own person Isaiah's son is only "Immanuel" in a secondary, typical sense. While this approach seems to give priority to the New Testament appropriation of the text, it must be noted that there is, in actual fact, nothing "new" about this appropriation. Matthew can only offer a messianic interpretation of the text because such an interpretation is already present in the mind of Isaiah.

There is a sense in which Chandler's answer to Whiston's problematic is a *formalist* resolution to the problem. Chandler is able, by his reclassification of interpretive strategies, to salvage the messianic import of Old Testament texts without having to alter them. With Whiston, Chandler can comfortably affirm the messianic import of Old Testament texts that were quoted verbatim by New Testament authors as "literal." As for the texts with significant verbal agreement, they are not to be considered corrupted texts (Whiston) or allegorical fancies (Collins), but are merely "typical" prophecies. And as for those problematic texts with a complete lack of verbal agreement, Chandler simply removes them from the forum of controversy by classing them as "allegorical" musings rather than messianic proofs.

Classification is not, however, the only, or even the primary element of Chandler's solution. At the heart of his approach is the anti-formalist rejection of Collins' flat use of language. New Testament appropriations of Old Testament texts need not agree with the ruled use of language given that authors often intend that the words they use should refer to more than one thing. Chandler's appeal to authorial intent thus threatens to re-engage the figurative use of language. While with Chandler it is not possible, with Aquinas, to say that words refer to things and that these things refer to other things, it is at least possible to say that words refer to things and other things.

---

93. Chandler, *Defence*, 321–22.

Change and Transformation

CONCLUSION

Chandler's legacy was such that he was considered to be the great defender of biblical prophecy throughout the eighteenth century. In 1750 Benjamin Andrewes Atkinson (1680–1765) vividly recalled the controversy between Collins and Chandler, summarizing it as follows:

> A little smattering in *Latin* and *Greek*, with a ready Pen and a voluble Tongue, made the Gentleman so vain, that he imagined with one Puff of his Breath he could blow away All the Old Testament Prophecies concerning our Blessed Lord and Saviour Jesus Christ; or with one Dash of his terrible Pen, he could cancel them, and write, NON PROBATUM EST. But the Learned and Pious Dr. *Chandler*, now Bishop of *Durham*, with great Learning confuted this mighty Boaster.[94]

Atkinson's comment serves as an appropriate *entrée* to the second half of the eighteenth century, which was to be the high water mark of the argument from prophecy. The great apologetic work in defense of prophecy written at the beginning of the period—Thomas Newton's (1704–82) *Dissertations on the prophecies* (1754) quotes Chandler extensively.[95] The premier apologist of the late eighteenth century, William Paley (1743–1805), held him in similar regard, and he begins *A View of the Evidences of Christianity* (1794) by declaring that the reader that is interested in the fulfillment of Old Testament prophecies in gospel history "will find them disposed in order, and distinctly explained in Bishop Chandler's treatise upon the subject."[96] In the intervening years scholars and divines treating the subject of biblical prophecy understood that they had to deal with Chandler's account, and a surprisingly large number quote his work.

In the tradition of the Latitudinarians Newton appealed to the "plain sense" of the words themselves, arguing, for example, that Jesus must be taken to be the sole fulfillment of a prophecy on the basis of the fact that the prophet God promises to raise up is described in the singular rather than plural sense.[97] Newton, like Chandler, however, was also deeply interested in Jewish religion, and like Chandler, he felt compelled to defend the messianic

---

94. Benjamin Andrewes Atkinson, *A Defence of the Bishop of London's Connection of the Old Testament Prophecies concerning Christ . . .*, London, 1750, 21.

95. Thomas Newton, *Dissertations on the prophecies, which have remarkably been fulfilled, and at this time are fulfilling in the world*, 3 vols. London, 1754. Newton's work went through ten editions by the end of the eighteenth century.

96. William Paley, *A View of the Evidences of Christianity*, 2 vols., London, 1794, ii, 12.

97. Thomas Newton, *Dissertations*, i, 161.

orientation of prophecy on the basis of the fact that the Jews "understood and applied this prophecy to the Messiah, the only prophet whom they will ever allow to be as great or greater than Moses."[98]

Newton's work testifies to the fact that although the celebration of the literal fulfillment of messianic prophecies continued in the years following the dispute between Collins and Chandler, the dispute also gave rise to a growing interest in the study of the Old Testament as a monument of the Jewish religion.[99] Chandler's work signaled the rise of Jewish studies in England, and the eighteenth century witnessed the publication of great tomes on Jewish religious observance and ritual signification.[100] Scholars of Judaism saw their work excavating the monuments of Jewish religion as building upon Chandler's insight that the study of Jewish culture required an appreciation of the figurative aspect of action and sensible sign.[101] Detailed scholarship on Jewish understandings of the Jewish scriptures, however, inevitably led to the conclusion that they had one meaning for the Jews, and another for Christians, a development that Henry Owen (1716–95) deemed most unfortunate:

> It has been asserted by various authors, to whom I can by no means assent, that several of the quotations made by the Evangelists are to be considered as mere *allusions*, delivered at first on *particular* occasions, but equally *accommodated*, and consequently *applied* to *other* transactions of a *similar* kind. Thus they say, that our Saviour applied to the Jews of *his* own time . . . what the Prophet Isaiah had, above seven hundred years before, alleged against *those* of *his* time.[102]

98. Ibid., 163.

99. Peter Harrison helpfully traces the development of the concept of "religion" that was to prove so important in the eighteenth century. Peter Harrison *'Religion' and the Religions in the English Enlightenment*, Cambridge, 1990.

100. William Lowth, *A Commentary*; William Warburton, *The Divine Legation of Moses Demonstrated . . .*, London: 1738; John Gill, *An Exposition of the Old Testament, in which are Recorded The Original of Mankind . . .*, London, 1764–65; Duncan Shaw, *The History and Philosophy of Judaism . . .*, Edinburgh, 1787; John Collier, *Historical and Familiar Essays, on the Scriptures of the Old Testament*, High-Wycombe, 1791; Robert Lowth, *Lectures*; Robert Gray, *A Key to the Old Testament and Apocrypha: In which Is Given an Account of Their Several Books, Their Contents, and Authors, and of the Times . . .*, Dublin, 1792; Thomas Wintle, *Daniel, an Improved Version Attempted; with a Preliminary Dissertation, and Notes Critical, Historical and Explanatory*, Oxford,1792; John Hey, *Lectures in Divinity, Delivered in the University of Cambridge . . .* 4 vols., Cambridge, 1796–98.

101. See Richard Hurd, *Sermons Preached at Lincoln's-Inn, between the Years 1765 and 1776 . . .*, London, 1776, 80, 270.

102. Henry Owen, *The Modes of Quotation Used by the Evangelical Writers Explained*

Change and Transformation

It seems thus, that while the appeal to authorial intent was initially able to bind the Old and New Testaments together after the appeal to the "plain sense" had faltered in this regard, the victory was far from decisive.

Chandler, of course, had bound the testaments together by assigning a messianic meaning both to Old Testament prophetic texts and their New Testament appropriations. In opposition to Frei's analysis, Chandler's appeal to "authorial intention" constituted a movement away from Whiston and Collins' definition of the literal sense as one-to-one "correspondence with external reality," and was thus able, in refutation of them both, to demonstrate that lack of exact verbal correspondence between Old and New Testament texts does not warrant the rejection of typological interpretation. Despite this reaffirmation of typology there is reason to believe that Chandler's solution does not signal a return to the multivalent relationship between words and things, but rather, a further movement away from it. In Whiston and Collins' literal frame the meanings of words continue to be derived from their correspondence with the external world. In Chandler's frame correspondence with the world becomes secondary, and the path towards the view that meaning is entirely subject to human intention is forged.

In such a configuration it is evident that when Matthew uses the term "virgin" he intends to refer to Mary the mother of Jesus, a woman that, for Isaiah, had yet to be born. It also becomes apparent that even when canonical authors use terms similarly, the way they employ them is uniquely theirs. Authorial intent can only bind canonical books, and the testaments, together with great difficulty. And it can only do this, evidently, through a process of abstraction in which, for example, Matthew's employment of the term and Isaiah's employment of the term "virgin" are harmonized as generically "messianic" through the removal of historical particularity. In such a deployment prophetic texts in the Old Testament can only be monuments to the "messianic" element of Judaism, and New Testament appropriations of them become Christian impositions upon Jewish messianism. Reading through the lens of human intentionality is unable to locate Christ in the Old Testament and Israel in the New. It fails, in other words, to accommodate the movement from the literal to the spiritual reading of Scripture, which as Aquinas reminds us, is rooted in the acknowledgement that the author of Scripture is God

---

and Vindicated, London, 1789, 103–4.

5

Spiritual Transformation in Sarah Trimmer's *Essay on Christian Education*

HEATHER E. WEIR

SARAH TRIMMER (1741–1810) WROTE *An Essay on Christian Education* late in her life and writing career.[1] The essay was first published in serial form in her journal, *The Guardian of Education* (1802–5), and Trimmer was revising it for publication in a single volume at the time of her death. The *Essay* contains the clearest outline of her plan for the education of Christian men and women of the middling ranks of English society. Trimmer based her educational plan on the Christian religion, as revealed in the Bible and as practiced in the Church of England. Parents, aided by the Holy Spirit, were the primary agents of this education. The spiritual transformation of a person was to take place gradually from birth to adulthood. The result of a Christian education would be adults ready to take their place in Christian society who were able to guide their own children in this spiritual transformation.

---

1. Sarah Trimmer, *An Essay on Christian Education*, London, 1812.

Change and Transformation

Trimmer was an ardent educator. Born Sarah Kirby, on January 6, 1741, in Ipswich, England, her father, Joshua Kirby (1716–74), was an artist, architect, and published author.[2] Kirby directed his daughter's education after the family moved to London in 1755. Kirby was appointed clerk of the works at Kew and Richmond by George III in 1761,[3] and the Kirby family's subsequent residence at Kew resulted in the marriage of Sarah to James Trimmer of Brentford. James Trimmer (1739–92) worked with his father managing their brickworks in Brentford. The Trimmers had twelve children, eleven of whom lived past infancy.[4] Trimmer's interest in education was prompted by her growing family, whose education was her primary concern: "She would say, that as soon as she became a mother, her thoughts were turned so entirely to the subject of education, that she scarcely read a book upon any other topic, and believed she almost wearied her friends by making it so frequently the subject of conversation."[5]

Trimmer first taught her own children. Then, urged on by friends who saw potential in the work she had done with the younger Trimmers, she wrote to assist other mothers in educating their children. She became interested in Sunday schools, and her educational interests moved outside of the homes of the middle ranks of English society. Based on her experiences in a local Sunday school she wrote to advise others how best to found and run similar schools.[6] She then wrote curriculum and advice for teachers

---

2. The basic outline of Trimmer's life follows the unsigned memoir that introduces her published journals and letters. Most biographical sketches of Trimmer follow this memoir: [Sarah Trimmer] *Some Account of the Life and Writings of Mrs. Trimmer, with Original Letters, and Meditations and Prayers, Selected from Her Journal*, 2 vols., London, 1814, i, 1–64. See also D. M. Yarde, *The Life and Works of Sarah Trimmer A Lady of Brentford*, Hounslow, 1972.

3. See Felicity Owen, "Kirby, Joshua (1716–74)," in *Oxford Dictionary of National Biography*, ed. H. C. G. Matthew and Brian Harrison, Oxford, 2004, 31: 765. Note that many of Trimmer's biographies follow the introduction to *Some Account*, and give the date of the move to Kew as 1759, however this date is probably in error. Kirby's appointment followed the ascension of George III to the throne in 1760. Owen cites court documents giving 1761 as the correct date, and I have followed her here.

4. The Trimmer children were Charlotte (1763–1836), Sarah (called Selina) (1764–1829), Juliana Lydia (1766–1844), Joshua Kirby (1767–1829), Elizabeth (1769–1816), William Kirby (1770–1811), Lucy (1772–1813), James Rustal (1773–1843), John (1775–91), Edward Decimus (b. & d. 1777), Henry Scott (1778–1859), and Annabella (1780–86). See Yarde, *Life and Works*, 20, 29.

5. [Trimmer], *Some Account*, i, 14.

6. Sarah Trimmer, *The Œconomy of Charity, or, an Address to Ladies Concerning Sunday-Schools; the Establishment of Schools of Industry under Female Inspection; and the Distribution of Voluntary Benefactions. To Which Is Added an Appendix, Containing an Account of the Sunday-Schools in Old Brentford*, London, 1787.

of Sunday schools.[7] Trimmer was driven by her sense of vocation and her ambition for God. Her strong sense of calling compelled her to campaign to have her works accepted for publication by the Society for Promoting Christian Knowledge (SPCK).[8] Publication by this society would ensure the wide circulation and use of her books. She not only wrote books for use by parents and teachers, she also wrote books about how to use her works. She had a clear educational vision which she shared in her works, so that others could follow her plan.

Trimmer's *Essay* is divided into two parts. She based the first part on the baptismal service of the Church of England, and the second part on its catechism.[9] She often referred to the wording of the baptismal service and the catechism as printed in the *Book of Common Prayer*.[10] Each part of the *Essay* is further divided based on the age of the children under consideration. The first part of the *Essay*, based on the child's baptism, is concerned with children aged 0–3 years, then 4–7 years. The second part, based on the catechism, is concerned with children aged 7–12 years, then 12–16 or 17 years when the young person would be confirmed. Christian education, according to Trimmer, began with baptism and culminated in confirmation. The spiritual transformation that took place between these two events meant that the young person could take responsibility for their baptismal vows. At that time they also took responsibility for their continued learning and growth in the Christian faith. This discussion of Trimmer's *Essay* will follow her organization of the material in parts and by ages.

---

7. See, for example, Sarah Trimmer, *The Charity School Spelling Book*, London, 1792, and *The Teacher's Assistant; Consisting of Lectures in the Catechetical Form: Being Part of a Plan of Appropriate Instruction for the Children of the Poor*, 2 vols., London, 1820.

8. [Trimmer], *Some Account*, ii, 15–16.

9. "In the first part of this Essay the Office of the Administration for the Sacrament of Baptism was our Text Book, for that which follows the Church Catechism, which contains within a very small compass, a complete compendium of Christian Faith and Practice, built upon the foundation of Scripture, will serve the purpose." Trimmer, *Essay*, 209.

10. Trimmer would have used the *Book of Common Prayer* as printed in her lifetime, which would have been reasonably close to the 1662 version. References in this paper are to the Everyman edition of *The Book of Common Prayer*, London, 1999. For a history of the revisions of the *BCP* to the beginning of the twentieth century, see F. E. Brightman, *The English Rite: Being a Synopsis of the Sources and Revisions of the Book of Common Prayer*, London, 1915.

EDUCATION BASED ON BAPTISM

In her introduction, Trimmer pointed out how her work differed from other books on religious instruction she had read: "I do not recollect any System that carries this instruction back to the early season at which I conceive a Christian Education should begin, or that has for its foundation the Holy Sacrament, by which infants are received into the Christian church, and to which, surely, constant regard should be had through the whole course of a child's education."[11] Trimmer argued that baptism must be foundational for Christian education as it is the only way a person can become a member of the Christian church.

The first chapter of the *Essay* walks the reader through the process of baptism, and includes a detailed commentary on all aspects of the service as it is found in the *Book of Common Prayer*. Readers are to imagine the child with his or her parents and godparents before the minister. Trimmer clearly expected her readers to have the prayer book open to the service. In her comment on the exhortation on the gospel reading, Trimmer called her readers to pray with the imagined godparents and congregation:

> Since Baptism is the only means by which Infants can now be brought to *Christ*, the godfathers and godmothers may rest assured that *God* is well pleased with their charity, in bringing so fit an object of his mercy; they may therefore proceed in the good work they have undertaken without the least doubt of its efficacy; but before they answer for the Infant it is very proper that they should acknowledge the goodness of *God* to *themselves*, and pray for an increase in divine knowledge, and a confirmation of their Faith, and offer up at the same time their supplication in behalf of the Infant; for this purpose the following Thanksgiving and Prayer is added, in which everyone present should devoutly join. Let us therefore do so, calling to mind at the same time our own baptismal vow.[12]

This first chapter reminds parents and godparents of the basic theology of baptism. Trimmer commented on every aspect of the service, drawing out lessons and obligations for parents and godparents. The vows undertaken on behalf of the child are the basis for the child's Christian education. Godparents are charged in the service to ensure that the child learns the Creed, the Lord's Prayer, and the Ten Commandments as well as the church catechism.[13]

---

11. Trimmer, *Essay*, 1.
12. Ibid., 13.
13. "Forasmuch as this Child hath promised by you *his* sureties to renounce the

Trimmer recognized that godparents often lived at some distance from the child, so that parents were "under a double obligation to bring their children up in *true faith*; that is, according to their *baptismal vows*."[14] Trimmer wrote this extended and careful exposition of the baptismal service "with the hope of leading parents and others, who are engaged in the education of children, into a serious consideration, not only of the importance of this *Holy Sacrament as a means of grace*, but of its use and advantages as the *foundation of a Christian Education*."[15]

Before giving explicit instruction on the education of infants and children, Trimmer first ensured that parents, particularly mothers, understood the "proper idea of the spiritual condition of infants after they have been baptized."[16] The second chapter of the *Essay* is devoted to this task. It contains an extended argument for the innocence of a child after baptism, followed by instructions for regulating an infant's first year as a foundation for religious instruction.

Trimmer acknowledged that while there was controversy regarding the spiritual condition of children after they had been baptized, she attempted to present what was taught by the Church of England about the efficacy of baptism, and then draw conclusions from that teaching:

> The baptised infant, through the efficacy of the spiritual grace bestowed in that Holy Sacrament, is cleansed from the defilement of *original sin*, freed from the penalty of everlasting death, adopted as the child of *God*, and made an inheritor of the Kingdom of Heaven. If such be the condition of the baptized infant I conceive that instead of regarding him as a *corrupt creature*, disposed to evil and averse to all goodness, we are to consider him as a *new-born creature*, in whom a new principle, *the seed of Divine Grace*, is implanted, to eradicate the evil principle derived

---

devil and all his works, to believe in God, and to serve him: Ye must remember, that it is your parts and duties to see that *this Infant* be taught, so soon as *he* shall be able to learn, what a solemn vow, promise and profession *he* hath made by you. And that *he* may know these things the better, ye shall call upon *him* to hear sermons; and chiefly ye shall provide that *he* may learn the Creed, the Lord's Prayer and the Ten Commandments in the vulgar tongue, and all other things which a Christian ought to know and believe to his soul's health; and that *this Child* may be virtuously brought up to lead a godly and a Christian life . . . Ye are to take care that *this Child* be brought to the Bishop to be confirmed by him, so soon as *he* can say the Creed, the Lord's Prayer and the Ten Commandments in the vulgar tongue, and be further instructed in the Church Catechism set forth for that purpose." BCP, 273–74.

14. Trimmer, *Essay*, 25.
15. Ibid., 27.
16. Ibid., 28.

> from Adam, and to dispose him to goodness, and virtue. To think of a baptized infant in any other light, is in fact to deny the sanctifying and vivifying efficacy of that Holy Sacrament which was ordained by *Christ* himself as a means of purification and regeneration.[17]

Children are thus free from sin until they reach an age where they can understand and willingly chose to disobey God's laws. Only then could such actions be considered sin.[18] The baptized child is not only free from original sin after baptism, he or she is also given the gift of the Holy Spirit:

> And the gift of the *Holy Ghost* is evidently necessary for securing to Infants the blessings of the Christian Covenant; for they stand in need, even in their earliest years, of the help and influence of the *Holy Spirit* that they may grow up with good dispositions, and in virtuous habits, and be gradually prepared to live a Christian life, when they shall be capable of performing the conditions of the Christian covenant.[19]

The Holy Spirit is an essential partner in the Christian education of all children, both influencing the children and aiding the parents.[20] Once the parents understand that their child is innocent and has the help of the Holy Spirit, they are ready to begin the task of educating the child entrusted by God to them.[21]

THE EARLIEST CHRISTIAN EDUCATION: AGES 0-3

In the earliest years, Trimmer argued, parents represent God to the child. Thus, the required attitudes of humanity toward God, love, honor, obedience, but not worship, should be required of children to parents:

---

17. Trimmer, *Essay*, 28-29. Spelling in Trimmer's work has not been regularized and I have rendered her words from the original. Though inclusive pronouns and language for human beings are employed in this essay, Trimmer did not do so. I have not flagged Trimmer's use of the masculine pronoun as inclusive after this quotation. This has been done so that Trimmer's voice may be heard more clearly.

18. Ibid., 31.

19. Ibid., 35.

20. Ibid., 36-37, 45.

21. "Let not Parents however suppose that their Infants are absolutely given up to their will, they are only consigned to them by their Heavenly Father, as a sacred deposit to be accounted for to him, and severe will be the punishment of those who abuse or neglect this important trust." Trimmer, *Essay*, 37.

> Parents will surely endeavor to gain the love of their children, and to make them dutiful and obedient to *themselves* in their early years; not merely for the *personal comfort* they may reasonably hope to enjoy in return; but especially, that, by the habitual exercise of *filial affection* and *obedience* towards their *visible* benefactors, their *earthly Parents*, they may be prepared to *love, honour,* and *obey* their *heavenly Father*, when their intellectual faculties shall be sufficiently strong to receive the idea of an *invisible Creator*, the author, preserver, and protector of all things.[22]

As God's representatives, parents must act toward their children as God acts toward humanity. They must supply children with "the necessities of life," as God supplies humans with the good things needed for human life. As God guides humanity, providing humans with divine revelation, so parents must assist children in judgment, and teach children what God has revealed to humans.[23]

Trimmer connected nursing a baby with the providence of God in providing food for Adam and Eve in the Garden of Eden, then for Noah and his family after the flood. She then argued that the Christian mother will gladly nurse her baby herself:

> Is there no food that is good for Man in his tender years? Thanks to Divine Providence there is an abundant supply! And can the mother, to whom this supply is intrusted, withhold from her infant what his heavenly Father has bestowed expressly for his nourishment? Surely no. Whatever the giddy votaries of fashion and dissipation may do, the Christian mother (unless prevented by those insuperable obstacles which sometimes unfortunately occur) will, on the contrary, obey with delight the impulse of natural affection, and the demands of duty, and while she dispenses to her child the food which his heavenly Father has provided for him, she will rejoice in the thought, that no *child of poverty* is deprived of his allotted portion through her fault.[24]

Nursing her own child is the beginning of a Christian mother giving her child a Christian education. The child is fed by his or her parent, just as humanity is fed by God. Furthermore, another baby is not deprived of food because of the need to employ a wet nurse.

---

22. Ibid., 39–40.
23. Ibid., 40–41.
24. Ibid., 43.

Change and Transformation

Trimmer gave mothers extended advice on regulating the nursing child's appetite so that the child would learn the Christian virtue of temperance early. As the child grows, the mother should continue forming regular habits to assist him or her in learning to love God and neighbor.[25] As the child learns to walk and to talk, he or she should be encouraged to amuse themselves with appropriate toys; the child should have his or her needs met, but not every wish indulged. The more time a Christian mother actually spends with her children the more she can ensure that these instructions are followed to best effect.[26] Trimmer's own experience led her to encourage mothers to engage in the task of parenting because "having once experienced the delight and comfort of educating her own children, she will not easily be induced to forgo the employment; for as her family multiplies around her, it will grow more and more interesting."[27]

As the child learns to walk, talk, and interact with those around him or her, the child should be guarded from temptation from the devil, the world, and the flesh.[28] Following James 4:7, the *Essay* advises parents to resist the devil by use of "the *means of grace*, which, in respect to Infants, are, after *baptism*, the prayers of the Parents, and the authority given to them to control the appetites and desires of their children within the bounds prescribed by the laws of God. The first should be daily offered up, and the latter constantly exerted."[29] Vanity and pride are the primary temptations of the world for the young. The *Essay* advises mothers to cultivate humility and modesty in their children, especially daughters.[30] Greed, particularly greed related to food, is the key temptation of the flesh to be guarded against in the young. Children should eat with the family, and parents should regulate what they eat. They should be given good, nourishing food, enough for their physical growth, but they should not over-indulge their appetites.[31] By appropriately attending to the needs of their children from infancy, parents cultivate habits that are a vital part of a child's religious education.

Not only should vice be guarded against in small children, but virtue, especially love, should be cultivated in them. A child learns to love others first at home in loving parents, siblings, and other relatives. The *Essay* then

25. Ibid., 47.
26. Ibid., 43–72.
27. Ibid., 70–71.
28. Trimmer, *Essay*, 75. The baptismal vows taken for the child include the promise to "renounce the devil and all his works, the vain pomp and glory of the world, with all covetous desires of the same, and the carnal desires of the flesh." *BCP*, 270–271.
29. Trimmer, *Essay*, 77.
30. Ibid., 79.
31. Ibid., 85–87.

calls on parents to teach the child benevolence to those outside the family, as well as care for animals.[32] Once love and benevolence are taught, the child can move on to learn piety and devotion along with other aspects of Christianity.

The first five chapters, or a little over a third of the *Essay*, deal primarily with issues of parenting young children. Trimmer called Christian parents to think of their work in raising their children as an essential part of Christian education. Trimmer pointed out that everything that happens in a Christian home is part of training in the faith. She based her parenting advice not only on her extensive experience, but also on her understanding of, and reflection on, the baptismal service found in the *Book of Common Prayer*. She argued that Christian parents should see their children as fellow Christians in whom virtue should be cultivated and vice regulated. The Holy Spirit would help both the parents and children in this process.

BEGINNING RELIGIOUS INSTRUCTION: AGES 4-7

Trimmer urged parents not to neglect specifically religious conversation as part of parenting young children, even before the age of four. Often children will themselves ask questions which provide opportunities for instruction. She gives the example of a young boy, about four years old, who stopped in the middle of his repetition of the Lord's Prayer and would not continue until the word temptation had been explained to him.[33] Later that night, "he was supposed to be asleep, he raised his head from the pillow, and said to his attendant, 'Nurse! I know what *temptation* means, and I will tell you what *my* temptation is—*When I am in a Toy-shop!*' Will it be carrying our ideas too far to say, that we may in this instance perceive, that children, of four years old, are capable of *religious meditation*?"[34] This kind of conversation with young children should be a natural part of the Christian home. Trimmer cited Deuteronomy 6:4–7 often to remind Christian parents of the need for conversations about faith with children.[35]

---

32. Ibid., 107–9.
33. Ibid., 135.
34. Ibid., 135.
35. In the Authorized Version, these verses read as follows. "Hear, O Israel: The *Lord* our God is one *Lord*: And thou shalt love the *Lord* thy God with all thine heart, and with all thy soul, and with all thy might. And these words, which I command thee this day, shall be in thine heart: And thou shalt teach them diligently unto thy children, and shalt talk of them when thou sittest in thine house, and when thou walkest by the way, and when thou liest down, and when thou risest up."

Change and Transformation

While faithful conversation could happen in any situation during the day, Trimmer suggested two particular objects of discussion, the natural world and the Bible:

> But though I would strongly recommend to the Christian Mother frequently to examine with her children the *great book of Nature,* in order to shew them, that "*On every leaf Creator God is writ,*" and to confirm what she tells them of His power, wisdom, goodness, and providence; I would by no means advise a reliance upon this measure alone; Children should frequently hear their Parents talk of the *Bible,* as the book in which a knowledge of God and heavenly things are revealed: they should also be led to understand, that their Parents make the *Bible* their own study, for the purpose of acquiring that knowledge which alone can make mankind happy here and hereafter.[36]

The natural world should be brought to a child's attention "by pointing out to him, *even as she walks by the way,* the most obvious proofs of the being and attributes of the Deity, as displayed in the works of the creation, and in his gracious dispensations of the common blessings of life."[37] The Bible can be taught using catechisms as well as "*Scripture Histories, with prints,* adapted to the capacities of children."[38] Trimmer advised parents to use the published materials available to them to help them teach their children: "Nothing is wanting to enable mothers to teach their children to read, to give them general ideas of the works of nature, and to lead their minds to God, but patient perseverance in the use of the means provided to their hands."[39]

Trimmer frequently mentioned works by other authors in her *Essay,* for example, quoting at length from Charles Rollin (1661–1741), a French Roman Catholic writer; commending the works of Isaac Watts (1674–1748), a dissenting minister; and mentioning works by Hannah More (1745–1833), Trimmer's friend and correspondent. Trimmer did not name her own educational works, though these seem to be assumed as a background for parts of the *Essay.* Trimmer provided details in the *Essay* about teaching children to pray and learn the Lord's Prayer by heart,[40] but she did not provide details for lessons involving nature, or the use of scripture history prints and

---

36. Trimmer, *Essay,* 138.

37. Trimmer, *Essay,* 165. Notice that Trimmer referenced Deut 6:7 in the italicized phrase, "*as she walks by the way.*"

38. Trimmer, *Essay,* 182–83.

39. Ibid., 183.

40. Ibid., 141–42.

lessons. Those details are in her other works, *An Easy Introduction to the Knowledge of Nature and the Reading of the Holy Scriptures* and scripture prints and lessons from both the Old and New Testaments.[41]

An Easy Introduction to the Knowledge of Nature and the Reading of the Holy Scriptures (1780) contains lessons taught by a mother to her young daughter and son, Charlotte and Henry.[42] The knowledge of nature is introduced in the first two-thirds of the book. Both Charlotte and Henry learn about nature while walking in the gardens and fields around their home with their mother. The final third of the book is comprised of the introduction to reading scripture. Mother teaches only Charlotte the lessons on scripture, as Henry is too young to be able to read the Bible. This clearly follows the plan Trimmer lays out in her *Essay*. Any actual reading of selections from the Bible comes after children learn about God through creation and after they hear Bible stories from the "Universal History" Prints and lessons series.

Readers easily identify the Mother character in *An Easy Introduction* with Trimmer herself. The memoir of Trimmer's life, written by one or more of Trimmer's own children, noted that Mother's voice in *An Easy Introduction* was very like Trimmer's: "In composing it [*An Easy Introduction*] Mrs. Trimmer seemed to fancy herself conversing with her own children in her accustomed manner. It appeared to her only like putting down on paper some of the instructions she was in the daily habit of giving."[43]

What did Trimmer, as Mother, teach to her readers? Together Charlotte and Henry learned about plants, animals, and insects on walks around their house. With the aid of a globe on rainy afternoons they also learned some geography, physics, astronomy, and cosmology. Mother began with things in her children's immediate experience and then added to their knowledge by discussing objects and events the children had not yet seen or experienced. She directed the children's observations, and by her example taught them to learn from everything around them. For example, when resting under an oak tree, she asked Charlotte to pull up a small sapling next to the

---

41. For a more detailed discussion of these works see Heather E. Weir, "Teaching the Bible with Sarah Trimmer," Th.D. diss., University of Toronto, 2008, chapters 2 and 4.

42. Sarah Trimmer, *An Easy Introduction to the Knowledge of Nature and the Reading of the Holy Scriptures*, London, 1780. Bill Marsden suggests that the teacher in this work is "at least a mother-figure." Bill Marsden, "Book of Nature and the Stuff of Epitaphs: Religion, Romanticism and Some Historical Connections in Environmental Education," *Paradigm* 1/24 (1997), http://faculty.ed.uiuc.edu/westbury/Paradigm/Marsden.html. The teacher's relationship to the children's father indicates that she is indeed their mother, and I refer to her as Mother in this essay. See Trimmer, *Easy Introduction*, 103, 241.

43. [Trimmer], *Some Account*, i, 43.

tree so that the children can see that the acorn from which it grew was still on the root of the young tree.[44] Later, after directing the children to look closely at birds' feathers, Mother told them that "I would have you accustom yourselves to look at every thing, that is the way to gain Knowledge."[45] When teaching Charlotte and Henry about animals, Mother began with farm animals and pets, including Charlotte's cat,[46] then moved on to unseen animals, including, "Lions, Tygers, Leopards, Panthers, Wolves, and others."[47] While Mother had seen some of those beasts at the Tower of London, the children had no experience of them.[48]

The kinds of lessons described in *An Easy Introduction* match the briefer outline of children's studies of the natural world in the *Essay*. Trimmer did not repeat what she had written elsewhere, but allowed her well-known and well-received previous work to instruct parents in using conversations on nature to further a child's Christian education. Though *An Easy Introduction* was primarily intended to be read to or by children, it also provided parents with a guide to possible activities they could undertake with their children.

Trimmer also published a universal history series in pairs of volumes, with the prints depicting the events bound in a separate volume from the descriptions, or lessons, associated with them. The series included prints and lessons on ancient history, Roman history, and English history, as well as the scripture history prints and lessons,[49] and the New Testament.[50] The titles of the universal history volumes indicate that the prints were the focus of the series. The lessons accompanied the prints, rather than the prints illustrating the lessons. The written lessons were titled using the formula "A

44. Trimmer, *Easy Introduction*, 13–14.
45. Ibid., 71.
46. Ibid., 58.
47. Ibid., 60.

48. See *Easy Introduction*, 62. The Tower of London housed the Royal menagerie until the 1830s when the animals were given to the London Zoological Society. For an entertaining history of the Tower menagerie, see Daniel Hahn, *The Tower Menagerie*, London, 2003.

49. Sarah Trimmer, *A Series of Prints of Scripture History, Designed as Ornaments for Those Apartments in Which Children Receive the First Rudiments of Their Education*, London, [1786]; Sarah Trimmer, *A Description of a Set of Prints of Scripture History: Contained in a Set of Easy Lessons*, London, [1786].

50. The date is taken from the dated prints. Sarah Trimmer, *A Series of Prints Taken from the New Testament, Designed as Ornament for Those Apartments in Which Children Receive the First Rudiments of Their Education*, London, [1790]. Sarah Trimmer, *A Description of a Set of Prints Taken from the New Testamenc [Sic]. Contained in a Set of Easy Lessons*, London, [1790].

Heather E. Weir Spiritual Transformation in Essay on Christian Education

Description of a Set of Prints of . . . Contained in a Set of Easy Lessons" where the subject matter (Scripture history, Roman history, etc.) was inserted at the ellipsis. The prints were presented as the text that pre-literate children could "read." The written material supported the prints and assisted parents and teachers in helping children to read the prints. This understanding of the series means that the implied readers of the written lessons were adults, who read the lessons aloud to children who could not yet read, or were in the early stages of learning to read. Both adults and children had access to the prints, which were separate from the written text. Children more advanced in learning to read might be able to read parts or all of the lessons for themselves.

The prints were intended as decorations for the walls of nurseries or schoolrooms as indicated in their titles. Both the prints and descriptions are contained in small books: each volume is approximately 9 cm wide by 11 cm tall. Mary Jackson describes the books as pleasing to handle:

> It is not possible to realize the appeal of these squat little volumes, nearly four inches square, unless one has the fortune to examine them for oneself. The print is large and spaced for easy readability; the prints are clear, plentiful, well executed—most are pleasing if not imaginative. The books were enormously and enduringly popular and went through numerous reprintings and new editions with their original publishers and others.[51]

The prints (approximately 7.5 cm square) are numbered, but without captions; all the information about the subject of each print comes from the descriptions printed in the companion volume. The descriptions are printed in a large font, as noted by Jackson, and as promised in the introduction to the first book of prints.[52] The descriptions, or lessons, are numbered and the corresponding print number is noted and some library copies have titles handwritten above the prints that correspond to the titles given in the lesson. The prints depict a particular moment in a Bible story while the lessons include more information about the whole story, and, at times, a moral to be learned from the episode.

---

51. Mary V. Jackson, *Engines of Instruction, Mischief, and Magic: Children's Literature in England from Its Beginnings to 1839*, Lincoln, NE, 1989, 135.

52. "Each Set of Prints will be accompanied by a small Volume, printed in a large clear Type, containing an explanation of the Plates in easy Language adapted to the Capacities of those for whose Amusement the Prints are designed." Trimmer, *Scripture History Prints*, 4.

Change and Transformation

Trimmer extensively revised the Old Testament material found in the *Scripture History* volume in 1797.[53] The lessons in this revised edition followed the text of the Old Testament more closely than the *Scripture History Lessons*. The revised version of the prints and lessons also gave parents and children a more comprehensive introduction to the Old Testament than was previously available since the number of lessons and prints available to them increased. The Old Testament episodes depicted in *Old Testament Prints* supplemented those in *Scripture History Prints* and there was little duplication of the earlier prints in the second set. Trimmer's references to *Scripture History Prints* in *Old Testament Lessons* show that this was intentionally done so that families who had invested in *Scripture History Prints* could supplement their collection with *Old Testament Prints*, or use the new *Old Testament Lessons* with the earlier prints. The two sets of prints provided families or schools with ninety-six pictures that portrayed biblical scenes appropriate for children.

Trimmer's *Easy Introduction* along with her *Old Testament Lessons, Old Testament Prints, New Testament Lessons,* and *New Testament Prints* provided parents with ample material for a child's Christian education until he or she reached about 7 years old. Trimmer summarized this early education in the faith in this way:

> Whilst the child is thus learning from time to time, in familiar conversation, the fundamental doctrines of Christianity [in conversations like those in *Easy Introduction*], it will be proper to let him read some easy *Scripture Lessons*, in which he should be instructed to observe, as they occur, the confirmation of things he has before been told; and he should be made to understand that these Lessons are taken from the *Bible*, and only shortened to make them easier for children; but that when he is older, and has more understanding, he shall read these and many other things in the *Bible* itself. I refer the reader to what is quoted in the last Chapter, respecting the use of *Scripture Prints* in the early religious education of children. I also recommend, that the words of the *Church Catechism* be taught at this stage of a child's education; also a Morning and Evening Prayer (to be said before the *Lord's Prayer*), containing a petition for the help of the Holy Spirit , and ending with asking *in the name of Christ*; that he also learn by heart some of Dr. Watt's Divine Songs for Children, and of Mrs. Barbauld's Hymns in Prose; and

---

53. Sarah Trimmer, *A Series of Prints from the Old Testament Designed to Accompany a Book Intitled Scripture Lessons*, London, [1797]; Sarah Trimmer, *Scripture Lessons Designed to Accompany a Series of Prints from the Old Testament*, London, [1797].

if his parents take him to church, he should likewise be taught to repeat by heart , so as to join with the congregation, the *General Confession*, the *Te Deum*, and other parts of the Church Service; which will make church pleasant to him, till he is able to read fluently in his Prayer Book.[54]

Trimmer advised parents to use Charles Rollin's *Belle Lettres* as the foundation for the other lessons a child should be taught.[55] She thought that the course of Christian education she described would "leave time for every necessary acquirement, according to M. Rollin's plan."[56] Trimmer urged that a child's religious education be appropriate to his or her age and should be a pleasurable subject. She advised, "that in teaching Religion to children, the parent must be very careful not to make it an irksome task; she should teach but a little at a time, and in a lively cheerful way, so as to shew that she herself takes pleasure in the subject."[57] Trimmer admonished the Christian mother to "proceed with humble confidence in the delightful task of teaching her child what she herself has learnt from her *Bible*."[58] Because the "various intellectual faculties unfold themselves"[59] at this age, teaching should become appropriately more complex as the child became able to reason better.

CHRISTIAN EDUCATION BASED ON THE CATECHISM

While the first part of Trimmer's *Essay* followed the baptismal service in the *Book of Common Prayer*, the second part was based on the church catechism. Trimmer described the Catechism as containing "within a very small compass, a complete compendium of Christian Faith and Practice, built upon the foundation of Scripture."[60]

Trimmer introduced this section with some instructions on beginning to teach the Catechism to children aged 4–7 years. Children should memorize the catechism at this age, and have it explained to them up to the section

---

54. Trimmer, *Essay*, 202–3. See Isaac Watts, *Divine Songs for Children*, London, 1715, and Anna Barbauld, *Hymns in Prose for Children*, London, 1781.

55. There are many English editions of Rollin's *Belles Lettres* translated from the French, and it isn't clear which edition Trimmer owned. Charles Rollin, *The Method of Teaching and Studying the Belles Lettres*, 4th ed., London, 1749.

56. Trimmer, *Essay*, 203.

57. Ibid., 203.

58. Ibid., 206.

59. Ibid., 205.

60. Ibid., 209.

on the Lord's Prayer.[61] The explanation of the sacraments could come at a later stage of the child's education. Trimmer admonished mothers to keep the child studying the catechism as a reminder "that he has been made *a member of Christ, the Child of God, and inheritor of the kingdom of heaven.*"[62] The detailed instructions on explaining the first part of the catechism to children between four and seven matches the imagined participation of readers in a baptism service in part one. Trimmer reminded her readers what the catechism said by providing a detailed review of it. She established the framework for the second part of the *Essay*.

Following the detailed review of the first part of the catechism, Trimmer advised the Christian mother to help her child understand when he or she had acted against his or her Christian duty in order to awaken the child's conscience. Children should attend church on Sundays, though "a few instructions may be necessary to make him comprehend the nature of public worship."[63] Trimmer detailed the kinds of instructions that might help a child better appreciate the service, expanding her previous advice to have the child memorize parts of the service.[64] Trimmer then reiterated her earlier advice to teach children of this age "the principal events of the Old *and* New Testament."[65] She added weight to her argument for teaching children the Bible by relating several anecdotes about different children's reflections on the Bible. One boy thought that when he went away to school some other boys might want him to worship idols:

> "One will say, *Tom*, worship *my* idol; and another will say, *Tom*, bow down to *mine*. But I shall say, I will not bow down and worship any idols; I will worship the *Lord God*, for there is no *true God* but he." May we not regard this as a proof of *pious resolution* in the mind of an infant.[66]

Trimmer took care to caution parents not to pour the instructions she suggested too quickly, or without thought, into a child's mind during this second stage of Christian education: "The mother will of course enlarge upon the different parts of them [the provided lessons] as her child's enquiries, or her own judgment, may direct her."[67]

61. See *BCP*, 289–93.
62. Trimmer, *Essay*, 219.
63. Ibid., 220.
64. Ibid., 202–3, 220–21.
65. Ibid., 221.
66. Ibid., 223.
67. Ibid., 225.

Heather E. Weir *Spiritual Transformation in* Essay on Christian Education

Trimmer thought that before introducing a child of seven to reading the Bible the child should first be exposed to theological reflection. Nature may be a helpful handmaid to an introduction to theology as learning about the natural world may lead "the mind to the contemplation of the Great Creator."[68] Trimmer provided a detailed account of how to use the study of the natural world as an introduction to theological reflection in *An Easy Introduction*. The final third of the book contains lessons on theology and reading the Bible taught only to Charlotte, who is about seven years old.

Before Charlotte can begin to read the Bible, Mother first makes a sophisticated argument for the existence of God based on Charlotte's knowledge of the natural world. Mother first works to convince Charlotte that humans are superior to animals. She then uses a version of the design argument.[69] The design argument begins with the argument that aspects of the natural world appear to have a purpose, and by analogy with objects with a purpose made by humans, these natural objects must have a designer.[70] This designer is God. In Mother's version of this argument, she first rhetorically asks if a watch or house could make itself, or grow spontaneously from the ground.[71] Since these carefully designed items are not spontaneously formed, but built by humans, Mother then argues that other natural objects, which humans cannot make, require a designer superior to humans:

> It is not in the power of the wisest man in the World, to make even a blade of grass, and less must be expected from the Animals, which I have shown are inferior to us. It is evident, from the construction of every part of Nature, from the noblest to the most insignificant, that they are admirably formed; they must therefore have been the Work of some wise powerful Being, infinitely our superior. We can no otherwise account for our Existence, than by supposing that we are likewise the Work of

---

68. Ibid., 255.

69. For a more detailed discussion of the design argument, see Stephen T. Davis, *God, Reason and Theistic Proofs*, Grand Rapids, 1997, 97–120.

70. This analogical aspect of the design argument is often glossed over in discussions of the topic. See Frederick Ferré, "Design Argument," in *Dictionary of the History of Ideas: Studies of Selected Pivotal Ideas*, Philip P. Wiener, ed., 5 vols., New York: Scribner, 1973–74, 670.

71. Trimmer, *An Easy Introduction*, 208–9. The house and watch examples were regularly used in design arguments of the eighteenth century. The watch analogy is commonly associated with William Paley's *Natural Theology* (1802), but both Trimmer and Paley were drawing on a tradition of comparing the world to machines. See Neal C. Gillespie, "Divine Design and the Industrial Revolution: William Paley's Abortive Reform of Natural Theology," *Isis* 81/2 (1990) 215. Also see Gerald Bray, *Biblical Interpretation Past & Present*, Downer's Grove, 1996, 252.

his Hand, for we know that we did not create ourselves, nor have we yet met with any Creature that could form us.[72]

Nature gives us some knowledge of God, Mother tells Charlotte, but the Bible is needed to give us the detailed information we need about the proper worship of God, our Maker. With a clear reason for the Bible in place, Charlotte and Mother begin to look at this important book. While they will begin reading together in Genesis, before that can happen, Mother argues that the Bible really is the inspired word of God by looking at the story of Moses, the presumed author of Genesis. Once Mother has carefully established that there is a God, and that the Bible is God's revelation to humans, then Charlotte and Mother begin to read selections from scripture together. As will be seen below, Trimmer instructed parents to follow this example, though she did not directly cite *An Easy Introduction*.

BEGINNING TO READ THE BIBLE: AGES 7–12

Trimmer firmly stated that "no *human compositions*, ought to be used as *substitutes* for the *Bible* itself."[73] With this in mind, as soon as a child "can read fluently, and is capable of having any part of the Scriptures explained to him, in a *practical way, that part* should be put into his hands, and *other parts in succession*, till he has obtained such a general knowledge of the contents of the Bible, as may enable him to read any portion of Scripture with pleasure and edification."[74] With this end in mind, Trimmer suggested that selections from the Bible be given to children in the following order:

> 1st. *From the Historical Books of the Old Testament.*
> 2d. *From the Historical Books of the New Testament.*
> 3d. *From the Proverbs, Psalms,* &c.
> 4th. *From the Prophetic Books* and *the Epistles.*[75]

Notice that Trimmer does not think the child should be given the Bible to read indiscriminately, but only selections that he or she can easily understand. Before beginning to read these selections, the child should be taught some basic facts about the way the Bibles that we have are organized, and given a brief theology of revelation:

---

72. Trimmer, *An Easy Introduction*, 209–10.
73. Trimmer, *Essay*, 257.
74. Ibid., 257–58.
75. Ibid., 258.

Heather E. Weir *Spiritual Transformation in* Essay on Christian Education

> Previously to putting the Selection into the child's hands, it will be advisable for his mother to turn over the *Bible* with him, to shew him how it is divided, first, into two principal parts, the *Old* and *New Testament*; and, these parts into books, chapters, and verses; and to tell him that the first part gives the history of God's goodness to mankind before the coming of our Saviour; and the latter, the history of our Saviour's life and death, his doctrines and resurrection, and the preaching of his apostles. It will also be proper to give him some short account of the sacred writers; and to tell him, that though these good men, from living at different periods of time, or in distant places, had no opportunity of consulting one another, their writings agree together so as to form one complete book, such as no man, or set of men, could have written, but by the immediate inspiration of the *Holy Spirit*. That he is therefore to regard *the Bible* as the *Word of God*, as much as if he had heard the Almighty speak what is written in it.[76]

This brief introduction to the Bible and the idea of revelation summarizes the main ideas Mother taught Charlotte in the final section of *An Easy Introduction*, though the order of the lessons found there (as described above) is reversed. In the *Essay*, Trimmer presented an argument first from the Bible, and then from Nature.[77]

Trimmer told parents to use "selections" from the Bible for children. She provided a set of scripture selections for parents to use in her six-volume work, *Sacred History selected from the Scriptures: with annotations and reflections, particularly calculated to facilitate the study of the Holy Scriptures in schools and families* (published between 1782 and 1785).[78] Trimmer had introduced her readers to the Bible and the opening chapters of Genesis in *An Easy Introduction*, and she wanted them to continue to read scripture. Thus, *Sacred History* was written so that children could continue to read the Bible with a qualified guide. The first four volumes of *Sacred History* follow the narrative thread of the Old Testament from the creation story to the intertestamental period.[79] The final two volumes cover the narrative thread

---

76. Ibid., 259–60.

77. Ibid., 265.

78. For a more detailed discussion of *Sacred History*, see Weir, "Teaching the Bible with Sarah Trimmer," chapter 3.

79. The inter-testamental period is covered in a section titled "A Supplement to the Bible History of the Jewish Nation": Sarah Trimmer, *Sacred History Selected from the Scriptures, with Annotations and Reflections, Suited to the Comprehension of Young Minds*, 6 vols., London, 1782–85, iv, 397–504. Trimmer based this section of *Sacred History* on the work of Humphrey Prideaux (1648–1724), the prophecies of Daniel and

of the New Testament, ending with a discussion of the book of Revelation and the future "consummation of all things."[80]

Each of the six volumes of *Sacred History* is divided into a number of sections with two parts: first, a selection from the Authorized Version of the Bible, and second, an explanation of the passage entitled "Annotations and Reflections."[81] The excerpts from the Bible vary in length, and usually contain one or two chapters from the Authorized Version. Trimmer attempted to keep one complete story together, thus excerpts do not necessarily follow chapter divisions. Trimmer arranged the Bible selections chronologically and included only "those parts which appear to me proper to be read by young persons."[82] Trimmer's notes and reflections consist of a theological explanation of the passage that led to applications to readers' lives. Applications might come from a new understanding of God, or from examples or warnings in the behavior of characters in the biblical narrative. The annotations and reflections reflect Trimmer's opinion that though a child can read the historical narrative and understand the facts, "the child will not perceive, at this early age [6 or 7], unless they are pointed out to him, those divine truths and instructions."[83] Parents should explain lessons to children, just as Trimmer explained the selections in *Sacred History*.

In *Sacred History*, Trimmer dropped the fictional characters used in *An Easy Introduction*, and spoke to her readers, as a mother would her children.[84] Thus, in the annotations, Trimmer called readers "my dear."[85] While Trimmer included herself in the applications of the biblical text, using the first person plural "us" and "we" in many cases[86] if an application was di-

---

Ezekiel, and the Apocrypha. See Humphrey Prideaux, *The Old and New Testament Connected in the History of the Jews and Neighbouring Nations from the Declension of the Kingdoms of Israel and Judah to the Time of Christ*, London, 1718.

80. Trimmer, *Sacred History*, vi, 477.

81. Trimmer described the work as consisting "of extracts from the holy Scriptures, divided into distinct sections, with explanatory notes and practical reflections." Trimmer, *Sacred History*, i, preface unnumbered.

82. Ibid.

83. Trimmer, *Essay*, 261.

84. "In a former work [*An Easy Introduction*], I introduced myself to the world as a mother instructing her own children; and having had the satisfaction to hear that it was agreeable to my young readers have endeavoured to keep up the same idea in my present performance; in hopes, that those to whom these lessons are adapted will appropriate them, and fancy that they are the parties concerned." Trimmer, *Sacred History*, i, preface unnumbered.

85. Trimmer, *Sacred History*, i, 103.

86. For example, in discussing Elijah's ascension to heaven in a chariot of fire (2 Kgs 2:1–18), she wrote: "How his body was changed, and rendered fit for a celestial

rected toward a younger audience, Trimmer changed to the second person "you."[87]

Trimmer intended parents to repeat the selections more than once: "The *historical Selections* should not be laid aside after the first reading, they should be read again and again.—There will be no danger of the young reader's growing tired of them."[88] Furthermore, given the order in which Trimmer suggested reading the Bible in the *Essay*, parents would probably not use all the selections the first time a child went through the volumes. In *Sacred History*, Trimmer placed passages from the Prophets next to the fulfillment of the prophecy, particularly in the gospel accounts. For example, the section on the crucifixion is preceded by a section on Isaiah 50 and followed by a section on Psalm 22. Other Psalms were placed throughout the life of David. On a first reading of *Sacred History*, parents could omit the selections from the Psalms and Prophets and then add these sections at a later reading.

Based on the arrangement of the first edition of *Sacred History*,[89] if a child read and discussed only one scripture selection per week with his or her parent, it would take almost eight years to go through the entire work—that means if a child started at age 7 he or she would finish by the age of fifteen. If the lessons occurred once a day for six days of the week, it would take a little over seventeen months to work through all six volumes. These more frequent lessons would allow a student to read the set at least three times in four years.

Trimmer's motherly tone cannot disguise that parts of *Sacred History* contain reflections of some theological depth that would be difficult for younger children to understand. Because the book was designed to be read by children several times, and given the depth of the lessons, Trimmer may

---

existence, is a vain enquiry, for it is impossible for us to know." Trimmer, *Sacred History*, iv, 30. Also see Trimmer's discussion of the crossing of the Red Sea for examples of her use of 'we' in applications and lessons to be learned: Trimmer, *Sacred History*, i, 322–23.

87. For example, in Trimmer's notes on the Flood, she encouraged her younger, less experienced reader not to doubt God: ". . .and if, in your future life, my dear child, you should find yourself in any circumstances of distress, think of their miraculous preservation, and never despair so long as you have an Almighty protector to flee to, who will either relieve you, or strengthen you to bear whatever befalls you in this world." Trimmer, *Sacred History*, i, 53.

88. Trimmer, *Essay*, 265.

89. In the first edition, volume 1 has 49 sections and 453 pages; volume 2 has 68 sections and 482 pages; volume 3 has 62 sections and 487 pages; volume 4 has 57 sections and two supplements for a total of 512 pages; volume 5 has 102 sections and 430 pages, and volume 6 has 71 sections and 480 pages. The first edition contains a total of 409 sections and 2,844 pages. Note that the average length of a section drops from about 9 pages in the first volume to just under 7 pages in the final volume.

have aimed her reflections at the teens comprising the older spectrum of readers. It is possible that by the time a young person was thirteen or fourteen they would be expected to read *Sacred History* without input from a parent, but younger children would require guidance when using the book.[90]

Trimmer advised parents that indiscriminate reading of the "*Poetical Books of Scripture*" might not be edifying for children "because they abound with *figurative expressions*" which may be difficult to explain.[91] Trimmer did not think that all figurative language should be excluded from Bible reading otherwise, as she pointed out, many narrative passages would also have to be excluded. Figurative language should be explained to children when it is encountered, however it appeared clear to Trimmer that "some parts of the *Poetical Books* of the Bible are unquestionably beyond the capacity of children," thus, she advised parents to make selections from Proverbs and Psalms for their children to read.[92] As the "young *Christian Scholar*" reads the selections from biblical poetry, he or she should memorize passages of the Bible, both poetry and historical narrative.[93]

After working through selections from the poetry of scripture the young Christian could move on to selections from the prophets and the epistles. Trimmer argued that though these parts of the Bible are difficult to understand, they are necessary for a complete Christian education. The epistles, in particular, contain "much of the *practical part* of Christianity."[94] Trimmer thought that "a well-educated child may fairly go through this course of instruction before he is twelve years old; and that, without preventing his pursuing any other branches of education compatible with the acquisition of Christian Knowledge."[95] Thus, in Trimmer's scheme, by the time a child reaches twelve, he or she will have read through the historical narratives of the Old and New Testaments more than once, will have read and memorized a selection of Psalms and Proverbs, and will have been introduced to reading the prophets and the epistles. The lessons to be learned from reading the Bible would continue the child's instruction in virtue and vice begun in infancy. It also would provide the child with a broader understanding of the faith he or she was initiated into at baptism.

---

90. One other educational writer produced a preliminary work for use by younger children prior to using Trimmer: A. C., *The Footstep to Mrs. Trimmer's Sacred History*, London, 1795.

91. Trimmer, *Essay*, 267.

92. Ibid., 268.

93. Ibid., 270.

94. Ibid., 274.

95. Ibid.

Heather E. Weir *Spiritual Transformation in* Essay on Christian Education

Trimmer thought that Sundays should have a different kind of Christian education than regular weekdays:

> I would advise that on Sundays the Selections be laid aside, and the Bible produced, in which the child should be required to find the Lessons for the day before he goes to church, and to read them to himself after the minister when he is there; he should also be required to look for the texts of the sermons he hears on that day, and in the hours of instruction, he may be examined concerning them; also concerning the Collects, Epistle, and Gospel, and Psalms for the day.[96]

Trimmer provided a detailed sample set of explanations and questions on the readings and collect for the first Sunday in Advent as found in the *Book of Common Prayer*.[97] Trimmer claimed: "Children in general will take great pleasure in these examinations, if those who instruct them are careful not to put questions to them which are too difficult for them to answer; they should be led on gently by occasional explanations, when they are not able to understand the meaning of the texts without assistance."[98] The kind of detailed questions Trimmer provided, covering 14 printed pages, may "appear so minute and copious, as to require more time than can be spared for *religious instruction*, let the importance of this instruction be remembered; and let it also be considered that the course here recommended is designed for children from eight to twelve years of age, and that a whole family or class may be instructed at the same time."[99]

Trimmer wrote a book that families could use as another resource for Sunday instruction in 1791.[100] In this earlier work, Trimmer provided detailed notes on all aspects of the services as printed in the *Book of Common Prayer*. Her commentary on the baptism service and on the catechism is similar to that found in the *Essay*. Trimmer intended the *Companion* to be used to instruct young people in the liturgy of the Church of England.[101] This volume can be seen as supporting material to the lessons around Sunday services detailed by Trimmer in the *Essay*.

---

96. Ibid., 277.
97. Ibid., 277–291.
98. Ibid., 291.
99. Ibid., 292.
100. Sarah Trimmer, *A Companion to the Book of Common Prayer of the Church of England: Containing a Comment on the Services for Sundays; including the Collects, Epistles and Gospels*, London, 1791.
101. Trimmer outlined her vision for the work in the dedication to the Princess Royal: Trimmer, *Companion*, iii.

Change and Transformation

Many boys from the kind of family Trimmer addressed in the *Essay* were sent away to school around age eight. Up to this point in the *Essay*, Trimmer made no distinction in the education of a male or female child since "in respect to what particularly belongs to Christian Education, the same method will in general equally apply to both sexes."[102] Trimmer encouraged parents to continue the Christian education of sons sent to boarding school during the holiday months. Trimmer wrote with those whose education took place entirely at home, whether male or female, in mind. She conceded that school-aged daughters often learned "ornamental accomplishments," and addressed those particularly in discussing the integration of religious instruction with a general liberal education.[103] Trimmer acknowledged music, dancing, and drawing as ornamental accomplishments. Music, Trimmer thought, was especially appropriate as part of religious instruction as singing to praise God is an important part of worship. Trimmer urged moderation in the practice of all accomplishments so as not to "excite vanity"[104] in the young women engaged in them. She also acknowledged that any of these accomplishments could be used to honor or dishonor God; children should be taught to honor God in all that they do. For further assistance, Trimmer recommended Hannah More's *Strictures on Female Education* as useful to parents in a daughter's education.[105]

Trimmer discussed the matter of dress as a branch of fashionable education at length. She thought attention must be paid to dress because "girls, at a time when their attention should be directed to mental improvement, are allowed, nay encouraged, to exercise their taste for variety of dress and personal ornament to the exclusion of every serious thought."[106] Trimmer noted that the Bible has a lot to say about dress, citing 1 Timothy 2:9–10, Psalm 95:13–14, and Proverbs 31:21–22. Trimmer argued that all of these texts show that women should choose "apparel as shall convey to the eyes of the beholder an image of a virtuous and delicate mind, in which *vanity* is totally subdued, and no desire of general admiration prevails; but in which a regard to the practice of Christian virtues is strikingly predominant."[107] In

---

102. Trimmer, *Essay*, 297. With this statement, Trimmer clarified that she saw the male singular pronoun she used of "the child" as inclusive of both genders.

103. Trimmer, *Essay*, 297. Part II, Chapter V of the *Essay* is entitled "On the Practicability of making the various Branches of a liberal Education subservient to the great End of Religious Instruction; and on the Care which is requisite in the Choice of Books for Children." Trimmer, *Essay*, 295–312.

104. Trimmer, *Essay*, 301.

105. Ibid., 301, note.

106. Ibid., 301.

107. Ibid., 303.

the matter of dress, Trimmer reduced the "*Science of Dress*"[108] to two rules: first, the material for clothes must be within the budget of the purchaser, and should be sturdy enough to last until another purchase can be made; second, the style of clothes made from the material should be "suitable to the *rank, age,* and *condition* of the person for whom it is designed, in respect to her own character, the credit of her sex, and the honour of Religion."[109]

Trimmer wrote extensively on the choice of books for children's reading. She wrote regular reviews of children's books in the *Guardian of Education*, the periodical in which the *Essay* was first published in serial form.[110] In the *Essay*, she firmly stated that children should consider it a duty to consult their parents regarding which books to read, since books could be made "an engine of mischief."[111] Despite this danger, Trimmer still considered reading to be a vital part of a child's education: "Between the ages of *eight* and *twelve years* children of both sexes may lay in a considerable stock of literary knowledge, if their school exercises are so managed as to prevent the encroachment of ornamental accomplishments at the hours which should be devoted to better purposes."[112]

Between the ages of 7 and 12, Trimmer added reading selections from the Bible to the discussions of theology, virtue, and vice which arise during daily life. In addition to reading the Bible, children began to learn in more detail what lies behind the catechism of the Church of England. Further, parents assisted their children in understanding the liturgy and sermons by regularly discussing the Scripture lessons and prayers with them. As children grew in their ability to think, they began to read parts of the Bible that were more difficult to understand. All aspects of a child's education were integrated with religious instruction, so that a child learned to apply biblical lessons to all areas of their lives.

---

108. Ibid., 304.

109. Ibid., 305.

110. Trimmer's reviews have been the subject of much discussion among scholars specializing in children's literature. The *Guardian of Education* has been indexed to provide access to the reviews. See, Andrea Immel, *Revolutionary Reviewing: Sarah Trimmer's Guardian of Education and the Cultural Politics of Juvenile Literature. An Index to The Guardian*, Los Angeles, 1990. The *Guardian* has also been republished with notes, see M.O. Grenby, *The Guardian of Education: A Periodical Work (1802–1806) by Sarah Trimmer. A new edition with an introduction and notes*, Bristol, 2002.

111. Trimmer, *Essay*, 310.

112. Ibid., 307–8.

PREPARATION FOR CONFIRMATION: FROM AGE 12

After the age of 12, a child's study of the church catechism should be extended to include the sacraments. Trimmer delayed the introduction of the last part of the Catechism on baptism and the Lord's Supper until the child "learned the first elements of Christianity."[113] Trimmer provided parents with a detailed commentary on the second part of the catechism,[114] and recommended parents make use of the many other books published on the catechism by "many learned and pious authors."[115] In addition to parental instruction on the sacraments from the sacraments, following Trimmer's model, the student should continue his Bible studies, and read daily books in dialogue form that explain "the Catechism, Confirmation, the Sacrament, and the Liturgy."[116] Trimmer admonished parents to frequently take communion themselves, and to encourage their children to be confirmed and receive the sacrament of the Lord's Supper.[117]

The young Christian's education did not end once he or she had been confirmed and taken communion. Following this entry into adult participation in the church, "it will be highly proper that he should study the *Articles of Religion* in the Common Prayer Book, with the help of some good author for the illustration of them. The Liturgy should also be studied and the Scriptures read with a good commentary upon them."[118]

SUMMARY AND CONCLUSION

Sarah Trimmer proposed a system of Christian education based upon the sacrament of baptism and an understanding that a baptized child was a Christian, indwelt by the Holy Spirit. Parents were the primary agents of their children's Christian education. By raising a child to prefer virtue to

---

113. Ibid., 320.

114. Ibid., 322–334.

115. Ibid., 321. Trimmer does not specifically recommend any of this multitude of works.

116. Ibid., 334.

117. Ibid., 335–37.

118. Trimmer, *Essay*, 337. Note that Trimmer wrote a commentary on Scripture to assist those reading the Bible: Sarah Trimmer, *A Help to the Unlearned in the Study of the Holy Scriptures: Being an Attempt to Explain the Bible in a Familiar Way*, London, 1805. For a discussion of Trimmer's commentary see Weir, "Teaching the Bible with Sarah Trimmer"; and Weir, "Helping the Unlearned: Sarah Trimmer's Commentary on the Bible," in Christiana de Groot and Marion Ann Taylor, eds., *Recovering Nineteenth-Century Women Interpreters of the Bible*, Atlanta, 2007, 19–30.

vice, to learn and understand the principles of the Christian faith, building on this knowledge as the child grew in ability to understand, parents could ensure that by age twelve a child may have made "considerable progress in Christian knowledge and practice."[119] Trimmer did not call this progress a spiritual transformation; rather, she saw the transformation as a rational one. As a child's power of reason grew, his or her Christian belief and practice would become stronger. For Trimmer, the child's key spiritual transformation took place at their baptism when the child received the Holy Spirit:

> I am fully persuaded, that by the gift of the Holy Ghost bestowed upon them in Baptism, they are *disposed to goodness*; but the animal nature in children, as I have before observed, gains strength whilst their reason is weak and imperfect, and if left to themselves, passion and appetite will certainly increase. If this happen it is from the neglect of the parent, not from any evil propensity inherent in the soul. However, that the *Enemy will sow Tares* while those who watch over them to cultivate the *good seed* sleep, and that it will spring up, more or less, I cannot deny; and I am also sensible, that no human creature can do any good thing without the special grace of God; this, therefore, children should be instructed to seek for as soon as they are capable of being taught.[120]

Trimmer saw no need for a child, or indeed any person baptized as an infant, to undergo a radical conversion as preached by the Methodists. Rather, Trimmer saw spiritual transformation as initiated at baptism, then inculcated carefully by parents as children grew. Spiritual growth, for Trimmer, was thus strongly connected to mental maturation. As a child's powers of cognition developed, the child could and would grow as a Christian, if provided with the right instruction, and protected from the vices of the world around them.

---

119. Trimmer, *Essay*, 313. Note that Trimmer used a phrase from Isa 28:10 and 13 "precept upon precept and line upon line" to support her suggestion that children should be taught the faith little by little. Unfortunately the King James Version translates the phrases poorly, and the phrase does not have a positive sense in the larger context of the passage. Trimmer's commentary, *A Help to the Unlearned*, shows that she understood the negative intent of the passage; it is not clear why she still chose to use this phrase repeatedly as her text for educating children gradually as their abilities grew.

120. Trimmer, *Essay*, 319.

6

"Of No Small Importance"
Curricular Change in the School Of Divinity, Trinity College Dublin, 1790–1850

THOMAS P. POWER

> "There are studies connected with its [i.e. Protestant faith] elucidation and defence which are of no small importance; and its enlightened character demands, on the part of those who are about to become its advocates and preachers, a close and diligent attention to everything that may be calculated to advance its interests, or to do justice to its claims."
>
> "Trinity College" *The National Magazine* 2/4 (1831) 467

SOME CENTRAL QUESTIONS SUGGEST themselves in regard to theological education: what is the relationship between theological education and a professional degree? Should bishops have any influence in determining the curriculum? What place should divinity studies have within a university context? Is there a discernible coalescence in quality between the caliber of the faculty, the demands of the curriculum, and the ability of the students? Is competence tested? A case study of the reforms implemented in Trinity College Dublin in the 1830s illustrates how such questions can be answered in the context of curricular change.

INTRODUCTION: 'A MATTER OF ACADEMIC ARRANGEMENT'

At the outset of the nineteenth century the University of Dublin, like Oxford and Cambridge, had no further professional education available beyond the BA degree for those wishing to enter the ministry of the Church of Ireland. From its foundation in 1592, Trinity College (the only constituent college of the University of Dublin) held the teaching of divinity as central to its educational purpose, something that aligned with the strong Anglican character of the institution.[1] A focus on Greek and Latin along with an emphasis on the study of the Bible in its original languages was complemented by study of the history and doctrines of the church.[2] In 1637 provision was made for a lecturership in Hebrew and in 1761 it was made a professorship.[3] Though there was, early, a professor of "theological controversies," and later a "public professor of divinity," little is known of the content of their courses.[4] However, early professors of divinity likely engaged in biblical exposition, preaching, and replying to the doctrinal issues of the day.[5]

---

*I would like to thank Alan Hayes and Susan Parkes for comments on an earlier draft of this paper. I alone am responsible for any errors of fact or interpretation that remain.

1. For general surveys, see R. B. McDowell and D. A. Webb, *Trinity College Dublin, 1592-1952: An Academic History*, Cambridge, 1982; J. V. Luce, "The Church of Ireland and Trinity College Dublin, 1592-1992," *Search* 15/1 (1993) 9-17; John R. Bartlett, "From Divinity to Theology in Four Centuries," in C. H. Holland, ed., *Trinity College Dublin and the Idea of a University*, Dublin, 1991, 224-37; John Crawford, *The Church of Ireland in Victorian Dublin*, Dublin, 2005, 91-93, 96; for an earlier period, see T. C. Barnard and W. G. Neely, ed., *The Clergy of the Church of Ireland, 1000-2000*, Dublin, 2006, 85-91. See also, F. W. B. Bullock, *A History of Training for the Ministry of the Church of England in England and Wales from 598 to 1799*, St. Leonard-on-Sea, 1969, 125-26; F. W. B. Bullock, *A History of Training for the Ministry of the Church of England in England and Wales from 1800 to 1874*, St. Leonard-on-Sea, 1955, 149-51; Joseph Liechty, "Irish Evangelicalism, Trinity College Dublin, and the Mission of the Church of Ireland at the End of the Eighteenth Century," PhD diss., St. Patrick's College, Maynooth, 1987, does not treat of divinity education.

2. Bartlett, "From Divinity to Theology in Four Centuries," 224.

3. The chair was established through an endowment from the Board of Erasmus Smith, which made the appointment to the position from a recommendation from the Board of Trinity College; *DUM* 30 (1847) 611.

4. J. T. O'Brien, *An Introductory Lecture Delivered in the Divinity School in Trinity College Dublin*, Dublin, 1838, 58-59.

5. J. E. L. Oulton, "The Study of Divinity in Trinity College, Dublin, since the

Change and Transformation

In 1607 the scholarly James Ussher was the professor of divinity, in 1674 the position was endowed, and in 1761 it became a regius professorship.[6] In 1718 the archbishop of Dublin, William King, endowed a lecturership in divinity.[7] Yet, despite the existence of the regius professor and Archbishop King lecturer, there was not until the early nineteenth century a school of divinity as such at Trinity.

How then did the transition occur from an undergraduate program where the emphasis was on the classical languages, mathematics, and a liberal education (that together constituted preparation for the ministry), to one dedicated to divinity studies? Three phases can be discerned: a preparatory phase between 1790 and 1833; the reforms of 1833; and finally the phase of implementation after 1833.

'LAUDABLE STEADINESS' 1790-1814

The stirrings of change in divinity studies became apparent from the 1780s onward in response to external circumstances, and as a result of initiatives by the Irish bishops. Change occurred because the prospects for ministerial openings were not auspicious, and the quality of the Trinity degree as preparation for ministry was questioned.

Difficult Prospects

The broader context in the eighteenth century was that the number of vacancies arising annually in the Established Church in Ireland was insufficient to provide openings for ordinands.[8] The situation became acute in the 1780s. Situating the problem in the context of overall numbers, the archdeacon of Cork, John Forsayeth, cited evidence that Trinity's then current undergraduate enrollment stood at 560, that the average annual intake over a ten-year period was 144, and that the annual average of arts graduates in the same period was seventy-eight.[9] Of the latter, the majority (two-thirds

---

Foundation," *Hermathena* 58 (1941) 11.

6. DUC report (1852–53), 15.

7. O'Brien, *Introductory Lecture*, 61–62. No new lecturership materialized at the time, it became an annual office, and often the lecturership and the professorship were held jointly until a 1761 statute made them distinct.

8. T. C. Barnard, *A New Anatomy of Ireland: The Irish Protestants, 1649–1770*, New Haven, 2003, 82.

9. [J. Forsayeth], *Thoughts on the Present State of the College of Dublin Addressed to the Gentlemen of the University*, Dublin, 1782, 21–22. The work is sometimes attributed

or fifty-two) were intent on holy orders. But by Forsayeth's calculation, one third of them would be un-provided for in the church.[10]

To compound the problem there was the practice of foreign-educated clergy intruding themselves on the Irish scene. In the early eighteenth century up to 90 percent of the beneficed clergy officiating in Ireland had been educated there.[11] However, by the 1780s of the thirty-six annual vacancies in the Church of Ireland, many were filled by non-Trinity graduates who came primarily from Scotland and who were ordained by the Irish bishops, thus creating a more difficult situation for Trinity's graduates.

The problem of ecclesiastical preferment was exacerbated by the prevailing practice of appointing English clergy to some of the more lucrative positions in the Irish church (in which stipends were typically more generous), to the extent that it was calculated that they enjoyed one quarter of the entire revenues of the clergy in Ireland.[12] They in turn used their influence to gain curacies or small livings for their friends, thus compounding an already difficult and competitive situation for Irish candidates. Others had found their way into the church without qualification of any kind whether from Dublin, Scotland or England.[13] For these reasons, then, there was an oversupply of ordinands in the Irish church in relation to the number of vacancies, a situation worsened by a pattern of preferment of clergy from England (who took a quarter of church revenues) and the intrusion of aspirants with Scots degrees.

Educational Inadequacy

On paper, at least, the academic requirements were rigorous. Competence in the Bible was required as part of the entrance requirements. Between

---

to Arthur Browne.

10. Ibid., 22. He calculated that of the not more than 1,200 clergy then officiating in the country, only 36 would die each year, thus leaving about one-third of the 52 ordinands un-provided for annually: Ibid., 22–23. The number of 1,200 clergy was not an increase on what prevailed in the early eighteenth century: Barnard, *New Anatomy*, 82. Forsayeth's calculation of annual mortality was based on an urban context, for he conceded that in rural areas (where most clergy lived) the average death rate would be less given that in such areas clergy lived "more temperate lives." [Forsayeth], *Thoughts*, 23n. Rural unrest in the 1780s likely contributed to the surfeit of openings: Thomas P. Power, *Land, Politics, and Society in Eighteenth-century Tipperary*, Oxford, 1993, 188–90, 204–9.

11. Bernard, *New Anatomy*, 88, 99. Also an education for the church was becoming more expensive: Ibid. 82, 87.

12. [Forsayeth], *Thoughts*, 25–26.

13. Ibid., 41–43.

Change and Transformation

1769 and 1825, among the works examined for entrance were the Greek testament, the four gospels and Acts, a practice that largely subsisted until 1849.[14] Trinity placed an important emphasis on the formation gained through study of mathematics, moral and natural philosophy, and the ancient languages, as foundational to divinity studies. In 1815, Richard Graves, who combined the regius professorship and the King lecturership, told the divinity students: "You come to this study with advantages which render you fully adequate to such labour and such extended enquiries."[15] As expressed by Joseph Singer, a later regius professor, such studies

> connect the education in Arts with that in Theology, and render the one an introduction to the other; and assuredly neither the interests of religion or sound learning will be consulted, nor the pious intentions of our great founder fulfilled . . . , if any separation should take place between Theological Education and well-arranged and ascertained Education in Arts.[16]

What Graves and Singer highlighted was that undergraduates were exposed to the New Testament in the original Greek language, Latin and Hebrew, all of which was an excellent preparation for the study of Scripture. Of the value of the fields of mathematics, moral and natural philosophy, Graves commented that the student

> brings with him a mind rendered acute and discriminating by logical disquisition, patient, attentive and vigorous by mathematical research, expanded and elevated by tracing the laws by which the Creator regulates the system of nature, and by contemplating the grandeur and extent of that system itself, and above all, he has been instructed in the principles of moral truth, and acquainted with the history of human nature, prepared by the former to admire the pre-eminent excellence of Scripture morality, and by the latter to feel the necessity of a divine interposition to sustain the interests of virtue.[17]

---

14. DUC report (R), 1852–53, 64.

15. *The First Praelection Delivered as Professor of Divinity by the Very Rev. Richard Graves*, Dublin, 1815, 10.

16. DUC report (E), 1852–53, 20. Singer was associated with the founding of the Hibernian Bible Society, in 1828 was involved with the founding of the Established Church Home Mission for the evangelization of Roman Catholics, and with J. T. O'Brien was known for his "Calvinist" views: Timothy C. F. Stunt, *From Awakening to Secession: Radical Evangelicals in Switzerland and Britain, 1815–35*, Edinburgh, 2000, 158.

17. *The First Praelection*, 12–13.

Students exposed to logic, mathematics and physics acquired inductive habits, classes in moral and metaphysics allowed them to make connections to important issues in theology, and an acquaintance with ancient languages and classics was clearly advantageous for biblical studies.[18] Even the final year course of study in science was considered light enough and "so much akin to theology" that it was deemed appropriate to begin study of divinity in that year.[19] Examinations for the degree of BA required that students be able to translate into Latin the entire Greek New Testament, have knowledge of Hebrew grammar, and be capable of translating the first two Psalms from Hebrew into Latin.[20] There were clear advantages in having formative undergraduate studies that laid a broad foundation, not only in terms of content but also with reference to reasoning skills and mental discipline that complemented studies in divinity. Indicative of the rigor of the Trinity course of studies are the statements of clerical commentators who claimed that the divinity degree obtained in the Scottish universities was inferior to that given at Dublin since students in the former were not required to pass an examination but merely to attend lectures, and that those Irish who could not succeed at Dublin had recourse to the Scottish schools where they could attain their degrees more easily.[21]

Despite such assertions of Trinity's academic rigor some graduates left the college not feeling well prepared for ministry. Of his first appointment to Castlecomer, Co. Kilkenny, in the 1790s, Rev. Henry Irwin later commented that "on entering upon the duties of our office, we soon were made deeply sensible of our manifold and great deficiencies. We had not enjoyed the advantages which divinity students now [i.e. 1858] possess in Trinity College."[22] As late as 1823 the new bishop of Limerick, John Jebb, in his first diocesan charge, declared his conviction that the education in divinity received at Trinity was inadequate given that the large numbers in class made direct instruction a challenge, aggravated by long intervals and spasmodic attendance by students. The result was that some who graduated even with first class honors had within a year "retrograded rather than advanced, and

---

18. DUC report (E), 1852–53, 20.
19. O'Brien, *Introductory Lecture*, 56.
20. Oulton, "The Study of Divinity in Trinity College, Dublin," 4.
21. [Forsayeth], *Thoughts*, 33–34.
22. *Remains of the Venerable Henry Irwin, Archdeacon of Emly and Chaplain of Sandford, Dublin*, Dublin, 1858, 244. Irwin found support and encouragement in his ministry in the newly formed Ossory Clerical Association which met monthly for prayer and fellowship; ibid., 244–46.

betrayed a degree of ignorance, which it is painful to think upon."[23] How was such a serious deficiency to be accounted for?

Teaching Staff

In part, the divergence between reputation and graduate preparedness can be ascribed to the situation of the teaching staff. On the one hand, they benefited from the system. In terms of academic reputation and ability, the fellows of Trinity had a distinguished lineage, going back to Ussher, but by the 1780s in the opinion of one observer, "inactivity and seeming despondency" prevailed.[24] Fundamentally the teaching staff were pluralists who held multiple offices (including in the church, which necessarily implied absence from college), were under no compulsion to teach, and did not hold academic research and publication in high regard.

On the other hand, they were victims of the system. After a grueling process of study and examination, an aspiring teacher might become a tutor, a time-consuming position that did not allow for serious academic writing and one in which he might continue for up to twenty years when fellowship might be achieved through examination, after which one waited for a vacancy.[25] Upon attaining fellowship status a comfortable income ensued but it involved a statutory commitment to celibacy as well as additional, unenviable tasks in the administration of the college that precluded academic research and writing.[26]

In part these circumstances were a reflection of differing status and rewards. The junior fellows received meager recompense, which did not conduce to commitment, though they and the senior fellows were able to supplement their emoluments through the fees paid by students for tuition. A major inequity existed between the junior and senior fellows, with the former having to devote their entire time to tuition; only when elected to the board did they have the time to devote to scholarship. There was recognition of the need to increase the number of fellows of both categories, and have a more equitable proportion of income between the two.[27] Some

23. *A Charge Delivered to the Clergy of the Diocese of Limerick at the Primary Visitation in the Cathedral Church of Saint Mary on Thursday, the 19th of June, 1823* printed in John Jebb, *Practical Theology Comprising Discourses on the Liturgy and Principles of the United Church of England and Ireland* [etc], 2 vols., London, 1830, i, 362.

24. [Forsayeth], *Thoughts*, 6. A contemporary ascribed this lethargy squarely to neglect by the government despite Trinity's continued expressions of loyalty; ibid., 7,11.

25. Ibid., 14–16.

26. Ibid., 16–20.

27. This was an issue only addressed by Provost Lloyd in 1833: TCD Ms 2770/47.

professors, including the incumbents of the regius professorship in divinity and some senior fellows, had a more permanent status, but the junior fellows were a more shifting entity. Additionally, the assumption of office was always subject to the vagaries, personalities, and staff preferences prevailing at a particular time. In 1790, for instance, the vacant King's lecturership was initially declined by all the senior fellows and was only filled when an additional £200 was added to its emoluments.[28]

Thus a situation in the 1780s of difficult career prospects for ordinands was paralleled by inadequacies in the teaching staff who were both beneficiaries and victims of the system of which they were part.

Episcopal Initiatives

In the 1790s the initiative in confronting these issues was taken by the bishops who may have been responding to criticisms from such sources as the archdeacon of Cork.[29] In 1790 half of the complement of Irish bishops (eleven out of a total of twenty-two) resolved that for the future they would not ordain any person who was not a graduate in arts and who was not able to produce a certificate of one year's attendance at the lectures of the regius professor and the King lecturer, a resolution, the "pious intentions" of which, the board of Trinity (comprising the provost and senior fellows) was willing to accede to.[30] In that spirit in 1794 the board stipulated that in order to obtain credit students in divinity had to attend two-thirds of all lectures in a particular term.[31] These developments were of great significance, for the bishops committed themselves to requiring evidence of a year's attendance at divinity lectures as a prior condition of ordaining candidates. Also, while there was no direct control of the course of studies in divinity

---

In the short term, an increase in enrollments in the 1790s brought some relief as it necessitated the appointment of additional fellows; TCD Board minutes, 1784–1810 (MUN V/5/5/226).

28. TCD Board minutes, 1784–1810 (MUN V/5/5/87v, 88r–88v, 89r–p.160). In April 1790 Dr. Drought was elected to the King's lecturership having resigned his fellowship. In 1800 Drought had to be deputized for because of illness caused by "weakness of sight," TCD Board minutes, 1784–1810 (MUN V/5/5/345). In 1812 there was a proposal that Drought be encouraged to resign which happened in 1814 when Richard Graves was elected lecturer, Board Minutes, 1810–1830 (MUN V/5/6/55–56, 116–117).

29. [Forsayeth], *Thoughts*, 48–49.

30. TCD Board minutes, 1784–1810 (MUN V/5/5/89r–p.160); DUC report, 1852–53, 25; J. W. Stubbs, *The History of the University of Dublin from Its Foundation to the End of the Eighteenth Century*, Dublin, 1889, 259–60; Oulton, "The Study of Divinity in Trinity College, Dublin," 15; O'Brien, *Introductory Lecture*, 63–64.

31. TCD Board minutes, 1784–1810 (MUN V/5/5/248).

by the bishops, significantly the initiative shows that their views were taken account of by the board.

Furthermore, the bishops also submitted to the board in May 1790 a recommended list of texts for study, which they would examine candidates on in future for the orders of deacon and priest.[32] The list included, for deacons, works by Grotius and Thomas Secker, commentaries on the Old Testament by Simon Patrick and William Lowth and Robert Gray, commentaries on the New Testament by Thomas Percy and Daniel Whitby, Moses Lowman on Revelation, Locke and Taylor on Romans, and Bishop Burnet on the Thirty-Nine Articles; and for priests, in addition, Samuel Clarke on Christian revelation, Hugh Hamilton on the existence of God, Thomas Newton, *Dissertations on the prophecies*, and Charles Wheatly on the Book of Common Prayer.[33] Of these texts, that of Bishop Burnet on the Thirty-Nine Articles, was particularly highly regarded in Dublin not merely for the quality of its information and treatment but for the potential it allowed lecturers for elaboration, something they along with students took advantage of.[34] The board was cooperative in this episcopal initiative recommending that the teachers in divinity be provided with the list of texts in order to prepare the students for the episcopal examinations.[35] Further, board acceptance of episcopal recommendations of texts was a practice that continued thereafter.[36]

In respect of graduates seeking to enter the church, if college examinations were generally absent and lecture attendance variable, then at least the bishops in their capacity as examiners of candidates prior to ordination were able potentially to gauge competence. While bishops came and went, and while commitments by one occupant of a see might not be binding on a successor, nevertheless the bishops' initiative of 1790 was something that their successors generally subscribed to.[37] Thus, evaluating the episcopal

32. TCD Board minutes, 1784–1810 (MUN V/5/5/165–6). Each candidate would be required to write in Latin on some "sacred subject" as well as being examined in the Greek New Testament.

33. TCD Board minutes, 1784–1810 (MUN V/5/5/165–6); RCB Ms 103 Copy by A. Erck of "A Compendium of Locke on Human Understanding . . ." with an appendix containing details of subjects including for priests and deacons orders, 1791. However, in the view of one student the attempt to get through all thirty-nine articles from November to July was abortive: *The Christian Examiner and Church of Ireland Magazine* 2 (1833), 175.

34. O'Brien, *Introductory Lecture*, 71.

35. TCD Board minutes, 1784–1810 (MUN V/5/5/165–6).

36. TCD Board minutes, 1784–1810 (MUN V/5/5/165–6); also found in DUC report (E), 1852–53, 16; O'Brien, *Introductory Lecture*, 69–70.

37. O'Brien, *Introductory Lecture*, 64.

initiative of the 1790s from the vantage point of the 1830s, James T. O'Brien, the then Archbishop King lecturer and a future bishop, considered that it was "acted upon generally with very laudable steadiness, and with the happiest effects."[38] The effect of these developments in the 1790s was that candidates for ordination henceforth had to demonstrate competence through presentation of certificates of attendance at lectures by the divinity faculty, familiarity with a list of prescribed books, and an ability to write in Latin and read New Testament Greek.[39] These developments were well in advance of the situation in England where even as late as the 1840s there was no unanimity among the bishops as to the texts on which they would examine ordinands.[40] The Irish bishops, therefore, in 1790 made an important decision, for in addition to their existing insistence that they would only ordain those who were graduates, was now the requirement of proof of attendance, though this as we shall see was dependent on college enforcement.

Board Initiatives

While episcopal initiative was to the fore, the board itself was also active. Already in 1781 it had resolved for the future to insert in student graduation certificates (testimoniums) a statement as to attendance at lectures in divinity, "whenever that fact shall warrant such insertion."[41] Given such latitude the resolution was in effect more of a recommendation than a requirement and the bishops at the time are likely not to have required it. However, board cooperation with episcopal initiative was enhanced by the fact that in the 1790s the college was the beneficiary of significant bequests, a number of which benefited the broad divinity curriculum. In 1794, for instance, it received a legacy of £1243 to be designated for the encouragement of "religion, learning, and good manners," the annual interest from which was to support six sermons to be delivered in the college chapel by the senior fellows, with four out of the six to be published.[42]

The 1790s also saw enhancements to the study of divinity through external bequests and board initiatives. In 1796 a bequest of £1,000 from William

---

38. Ibid.

39. TCD Board minutes, 1784–1810 (MUN V/5/5/381).

40. David A. Dowland, *Nineteenth-Century Anglican Theological Training: The Redbrick Challenge*, Oxford, 1997, 187.

41. Quoted in O'Brien, *Introductory Lecture*, 63.

42. TCD Board minutes, 1784–1810 (MUN V/5/5/249–250). The first series of sermons to be given was on the topic: "Proof of Christianity derived from the miracles recorded in the New Testament." (TCD Board minutes, 1784–1810 (MUN V/5/5/250).

Downes, bishop of Waterford and Lismore, established the Downes prizes in recognition of excellence in written composition, oratory, and reading the liturgy with the goal of encouraging the skills of reading and speaking.[43] For the determination of prizes, so far as oratory is concerned, qualified students (that is those who had attended at least four terms in divinity and oratory) were to appear before the board and the professor and lecturers in divinity and deliver a discourse not exceeding fifteen minutes duration on a "moral or controversial" topic to be determined by the lecturer in divinity.[44] Prizes were also offered under the Downes bequest for proficiency in the reading of the liturgy.[45] In subsequent years the Downes prize acted as a strong motivator for some students to display their ability. Between 1797 and 1834, for instance, almost two-hundred prizes were awarded for written composition, extempore speaking, and reading the liturgy.[46] Some of the award recipients in time proceeded to be either important figures in the Irish church, like John Jebb (1797) who became bishop of Limerick, Ardfert, and Aghadoe, and John Russell (1815) who became archdeacon of Clogher; authors, such as Benjamin W. Matthias (1797) (*Doctrines of the Reformation* and *History of the Council of Trent*), and William Cooke Taylor (*History of*

---

43. TCD Board minutes, 1784–1810 (MUN V/5/5/292); W.B.S. Taylor, *History of the University of Dublin*, London, 1845, 106-7. For the print version of the first oral composition to receive the prize, see "A Divinity Treatise" in John Jebb, *Practical Theology*, ii, 213–24.

44. TCD Board minutes, 1784–1810 (MUN V/5/5/303). In 1803, for instance, candidates were expected to discourse on the following: "That the Chr[istian] religion proposes the most exalted scheme of benevolence supported and enforced by the strongest motives: and that whilst the cultivation of virtuous private friendship and the laws of our country are recommended by the example of our blessed Lord and his apostle to the practice of Christians, the omission of a spiritual precept that should in particular enjoin them is so far from being an objection to the system of gospel morality, that on the contrary it renders it preferable to every system of morals or institution of religion that ever appeared in the world." TCD Board minutes, 1784–1810 (MUN V/5/5/410). Later topics included the consequences for the gentile world of the conversion of the Jews, and the anointing of the sick by the apostles as not being an obligatory rite. TCD Board minutes, 1810–1830 (MUN V/5/6/37, 154).

45. TCD Board minutes, 1784–1810 (MUN V/5/5/304).

46. *The Dublin University Calendar MDCCCXXXV*, Dublin, 1835, 34–38. This does not include the years, 1798–1810 inclusive, 1816, 1822, and 1829 for which no awards are recorded. The figure includes those who may have received prizes for more than one category, or awards to the same individual given in different categories in different years. See also, *Discipline of Dublin University Being a Concise Account of All the Duties of Students in Trinity College from Entrance to the Time of Being Candidate for the Degree of A.M.*, Dublin, 1823, 23–4; TCD Ms 2770/5.

the Mohamedanism); fellows, such as Daniel Mooney; or controversialists, like Mortimer and Samuel O'Sullivan.[47]

A further initiative came in 1794 when the board considered various ways in which to support the study of Hebrew, which resulted in a stipulation that premiums offered for proficiency in the language be spent on books in Hebrew or divinity and that distinguished student attendance at classes in Hebrew be recognized by the insertion of a clause to that effect in their testimonium.[48] In 1800 additional encouragement to the study of Hebrew came with an endowment by the archbishop of Armagh, William Newcome, of £100 in annual prizes, a practice continued by his successors.[49] In the years after 1800, the Hebrew prize established itself as a prestigious award, some of its recipients proceeded to fellowship, a few to professorships (e.g. Charles W. Wall, professor of Hebrew), some as authors of works in the language (e.g. George Downes, *A Hebrew Grammar in the English Language* (London, 1823), and others to positions in the church (e.g. Samuel R. Kyle, archdeacon of Cork).[50] Nevertheless, as with Greek, while Hebrew had received worthy promotion, it remained outside direct association with the teaching of divinity.[51]

Other developments advantageous to the study of divinity took place as the result of board initiative. In this decade it agreed to sponsor in part the publication of the sermons of James Ussher, to donate twenty copies of Robert Gray, *Key to the Old Testament* to the college library if the college printers consented to publish it, and subsequently it sanctioned the publication of the New Testament and a new edition of the authorized version of the Bible, among other initiatives.[52] By royal patent in 1811, the college was

---

47. *Dublin University Calendar,* 1835, 34–36 passim; for the O'Sullivans: Desmond Bowen, *The Protestant Crusade in Ireland, 1800–1870,* Dublin, 1978, 117–22.

48. TCD Board minutes, 1784–1810 (MUN V/5/5/250–251).

49. DUC report (R), 152–3, 47. The Board gave additional encouragement through prizes and an entrance sizarship: TCD MUN V/5/8/35. These Primate prizes, as they became known, continued to be awarded, e.g. *DUM* 3 (1834), 341; *Dublin University Calendar,* 1835,, 39; TCD Ms 2770/14.

50. *Dublin University Calendar,* 1835, 40–47. This lists the recipients for 1800–1834 (except for 1809–1811).

51. On the foregoing see DUC report (R), 152–53, 46–47. The board, recognizing that an inordinate amount of time was given over to teaching Hebrew grammar (an area in which many acquired competence in school before entrance) in preparation for the prize examination, in 1830 rectified the anomaly by extending eligibility to bachelors, increasing the number of opportunities to take the exam, and by including chapters in Genesis: *Dublin University Calendar,* 1835, 38–39, 76.

52. TCD Board minutes, 1784–1810 (MUN V/5/5/164, 173), 1830–1840 (MUN V/5/7/3–4). In 1831 the board approved the use of the college printing house for the printing of the New Testament by the Hibernian Bible Society, in a small size edition,

Change and Transformation

given the privilege (shared with the king's printer) of printing bibles and testaments, a right that was to extend to forty years.[53] A further act of 1818 exempted from tax the paper used in the printing of bibles at the university press.[54] In these various ways the bishops' initiative led to some advances in the divinity course, followed by new inducements for student attainment in Hebrew, and by board advances in publishing, printing, and library resources in divinity-related areas.

Assessment

The bishops in 1790 deferred to the college as to the content of the divinity course and what the attendance requirements should be. Yet the intention was that award of the certificate (testimonium) should reflect attendance at the divinity lectures. What attendance constituted was made clear by a regulation of 1801, which stipulated that success at an examination and the award of a testimonium were made conditional on attendance at the lectures of the professor and the lecturer during four complete terms (attendance being interpreted as not less than three-quarters of the total number of lectures).[55] Though this attendance rule continued in force into the late 1830s, in practice attendance at the divinity lectures was not enforced and typically the certificate was given to all who attended the four academic terms with an assistant lecturer.[56] By such means the education and examination of candidates for the ministry resided firmly in the hands of the college, though the bishops reserved the right to examine candidates themselves prior to ordination. This established what was to become long-term practice, for the bishops retained the right of ordination, while the university prescribed the academic program that the candidate had to pass.[57]

All this is to indicate that in the 1790s there were some significant changes. While these were not perfect, with one commentator judging that the course of study was limited only "by the exertions both of students and

---

in several parts; and in the same year it sanctioned the publishing of an edition of the Wyclif bible and ordered that a manuscript copy in the college library be utilized for that enterprise (MUN v/5/7/16–17, 20).

53. *Dublin Penny Journal*, 4 no.171 (Oct. 10, 1835), 116.
54. Ibid.
55. TCD Board minutes, 1784–1810 (MUN V/5/5/381).
56. O'Brien, *Introductory Lecture*, 67–68.
57. McDowell and Webb, *Trinity College Dublin*, 138.

lecturers," nevertheless they were deemed "highly efficient" and of benefit to the church.[58]

"STRENGTH AND EFFICIENCY": BEGINNINGS OF REFORM, 1814–1832

The number of incumbents in the country grew from 1200 in the mid-1780s to 1625 in 1830.[59] This growth was paralleled by the rise in student numbers in the college as a whole, and in divinity in particular. It was estimated that the number of students on the books increased four-fold from about five-hundred in 1805 to two-thousand in 1835.[60] Already in 1816, an enrollment of eighty-eight students in divinity necessitated the appointment of additional staff to be assistants.[61]

Within this context of growth of overall numbers, what distinguishes the two decades before 1833 was the reforms introduced by the regius professor in attendance and examinations; the more intentional catechetical program for junior undergraduates; new rules to do with celibacy; and more stringent requirements of competence by a select number of influential bishops.

Regius Professorship

Prior to his election as professor of divinity, Richard Graves had in 1813 advanced proposals to reform theological education in the college, and these eventually emanated in new statutory regulations published and implemented in 1814.[62] The reforms centered on three areas: appointment to the regius professorship, student attendance, and examinations.

Appointment

The statute widened eligibility for appointment from its previous limitation to senior fellows to include any fellow who possessed a doctorate in divinity;

---

58. O'Brien, *Introductory Lecture*, 3–4.
59. [J. Forsayeth], *Thoughts*, 22–23; Barnard, *New Anatomy*, 361, n.6.
60. *Dublin Penny Journal* 4/171 (Oct. 10, 1835) 115.
61. TCD Board minutes, 1810–1830 (MUN V/5/6/192). The board decided that for the future the number of assistants in divinity should be based on student enrollment, although the ratio remained unspecified.
62. TCD Board minutes, 1810–1830 (MUN V/5/6/103, 110, 116).

the salary of the professorship was increased, additional duties were prescribed, and provision was made for the appointment of a deputy should circumstances require it.[63] The only qualification was that he be either a senior or junior fellow, possessed of a DD, and be considered a "discreet and learned man."[64] The statute of 1814 also stipulated that the position was for life, resignation being only required if the incumbent was appointed to a bishopric.[65] The regulations of 1814 required the incumbent to deliver four public lectures annually that explained Scripture and expounded controversies.[66]

Attendance and Examinations

While attendance at the lectures of the regius professor was always voluntary, attendance at those given by Richard Graves (1814–29) and his successor, Charles R. Elrington (1829–50), was considerable.[67] This was despite the fact that many students were happy to take the minimal number of divinity lectures in order to graduate and prior to 1833 these did not include those offered by the regius professor.[68] They were regarded as supplementary and hence not necessary.

Graves' suggestion as incorporated into the 1814 statute made provision for special annual voluntary examinations for students in divinity.[69]

63. DUC report (R), 1852–53, 18; DUC report (E) 1852–53, 15–17; O'Brien, *Introductory Lecture*, 60n. Ironically there was no attempt at this stage to extend eligibility to ex-fellows (which was to be a recommendation of the royal commission of 1853), that is those who had resigned their fellowship for the purpose of taking up a church living and thereby gain practical experience of ministry: DUC report (R), 1852–53, 18.

64. DUC report (E), 1852–53, 15.

65. DUC report (E), 1852–53, 15. Provision was also made for the appointment of a deputy in the event of illness or absence, and if either extended to more than one year, then £400 from the salary of the regius professor was to be allocated to the deputy: Ibid.,16. The statutes of 1761 and 1814 empowered the board to discipline the incumbent in cases where neglect was apparent, and if he was called twice to appear before a disciplinary hearing, upon conviction he was to be removed: DUC report (E), 1852–53, 17.

66. TCD Board minutes, 1810–1830 (MUN V/5/6/150).

67. In 1829 Rev. C. R. Elrington succeeded Richard Graves as King's lecturer of divinity. He had deputized for Graves since August 1827 due to the latter's health problems: TCD Board minutes, 1810–1830 (MUN V/5/6/405, 426).

68. O'Brien, *Introductory Lecture*, 61.

69. DUC report (E), 1852–53, 17. All candidate bachelors and those of higher degree could attend lectures as divinity students. Names had to be on the college books and students had to have completed the junior divinity year. The statutes required that auditors must be BAs and masters of first and second year. As divinity students they

These were to be held over two days in November for four hours each day with tests on the Old Testament, New Testament, church history, and the creeds, articles and liturgy of the Church of England. In time, recommended texts for student preparation for these special exams were advertised.[70] None of the lectures or exam papers were required to be published; however, questions asked at the professor's exam were usually printed for circulation and were published in the university calendar (from 1834).[71]

Under the new rules no student could take the divinity exams who was not already of BA standing and had attended two terms of divinity lectures; those intending to take the exams were required to submit their names in advance to the professor of divinity; and credit had to be obtained for passing the divinity exam before one could be considered for the Downes prize.[72] The board allocated funds to reward proficiency.[73]

However, despite these strictures and the incentives from the board, it was found that since attendance was voluntary and given the regimen of the exams, the number of those presenting themselves was never extensive. Nevertheless, those few who did prepare were deemed to be of benefit to the church.[74] From 1814 onwards two premiums were awarded annually and the recipients included a number who proceeded to be the authors of works in theology or classics.[75] Particularly, proficiency was to be recorded

---

paid nothing, but to keep their names on the college books they continued to pay ordinary college fees of £7.10s half yearly for pensioners, which may be regarded as paid for attendance on divinity lectures as this required longer residence in college than would be necessary simply for taking the BA. This fee, the payment of which was dependent on whether the student was in attendance regularly, was paid half yearly. Attendance was voluntary except for scholars who had graduated with BA who could attend the classes either of the regius professor, the Archbishop King's lecturer, or their assistants: DUC report (E), 1852–53, 17, 19.

70. *Dublin University Calendar*, 1835, 30–31. In an accompanying note so far as the study of commentaries in this list was concerned, the regius professor, C. R. Elrington, in the early 1830s made it clear that he did "not so much require a knowledge of the opinions of any particular commentator, as a general acquaintance with the Bible itself." Ibid. 30; see also TCD Ms 2770/18.

71. DUC report (E), 1852–53, 17. Though the lectures given by the incumbent were public, those of his assistants and the exams were private except the voluntary exam for the professor's premium which was public.

72. TCD Board minutes, 1810–1830 (MUN V/5/6/131–2). In the first of implementation of the new regulation, thirty students indicated their intention to take the exam: Ibid., 138, 144; see also: *First praelection*, 31–32.

73. *First Praelection*, 7–8, 31–32. For the list of prescribed texts; ibid., 33–35.

74. O'Brien, *Introductory Lecture*, 61.

75. *Dublin University Calendar*, 1835, 31–32. This lists the 41 recipients between 1814 and 1833 inclusive. Thomas Keightley (1815) was the author of works in classics, George Jones (1818) was the author of *A Comprehensive Hebrew Grammar*, Dublin,

on the student's testimonium, which he then could present to the bishop for examination and ordination, something Graves hoped would be taken notice of by the bishops.[76]

Catechetical

An additional strength to the undergraduate program as preparatory for the study of divinity was catechetical instruction. The statutes of the college required that one of the senior fellows act as catechist.[77] His duties included weekly instruction and examination of all students in the catechism, lectures on specifically difficult passages of the same, and covering the entire in the course of the year. This system was observed until 1807 when the board created the position of catechetical lecturer the holders of which were responsible for instruction (normally on Saturday mornings during term in the chapel) in the Bible, holding examinations (including questions from Archbishop Secker lectures on the catechism), and granting prizes for effective answering at exam time.

From 1815 the practice prevailed of having the two junior classes catechetically instructed in scriptural knowledge and history, as well as key doctrines of the Christian faith.[78] The lectures were intended for students living within a defined radius of the college (those living at a distance simply attended the examinations); though senior students neglectful of their own course of studies could attend the catechetical lectures in lieu. For the catechetical term exams junior freshmen were tested on the gospel of Luke, the Acts of the Apostles, and Archbishop Secker's lectures on the creed; and senior freshmen were examined on Genesis and Exodus, other historical books of the Old Testament, and Isaiah.

Celibacy

The college statutes required that the fellows be celibate, the consequence of marriage being that they would be deprived of the privileges of office. Their original intent was as an incentive to academic endeavor towards fellowship. As expressed by the duke of Cumberland, chancellor of the university,

---

1826, and John Russell became archdeacon of Clogher; ibid. See also *Discipline of Dublin University*, 24.

76. *First Praelection*, 8.

77. For what follows see DUC report (R), 1852–53, 70; *Discipline of Dublin University*, 9–10, 13–17.

78. *First Praelection*, 13.

in 1836, the purpose of the celibacy rule was "to hold out to young men an inducement to study and to obtain intellectual eminence to qualify for their fellowships, and that marriage was one of the most likely means of inducing fellows to vacate."[79] It was maintained, however, that the statutes did not specifically seek to enforce celibacy, rather only if it could be legally proven that any of the fellows married, would the rule be used to deprive them of the rights of fellowship.[80] Yet in the 175 years of the statute's operation (1637–1812), only two instances of such were on record.[81] Over the years those who contravened the statute by marrying received a royal dispensation that allowed them to continue in office.[82] In effect this made the requirement obsolete, and it was incongruous because the provost and senior fellows were exempt from the statute.

By 1811, sixteen of the twenty-three fellows were married, so in that year the provost, Rev. George Hall, introduced a new statute enforcing a more strict compliance with the celibacy requirement.[83] This elicited a protest from fifteen of the fellows who argued that they had been "consumed" preparing for the achievement of fellowship but would never have done so had they known that upon marrying they would be disqualified from holding the fellowship.[84] The result of such protests was the development of a more streamlined system of dispensation whereby, for the future, fellows marrying were, in three months, to notify the provost of the fact and be able to continue to hold their fellowships for a period of a year from the date of their marriages.[85] Failure to give such notice would result in a voidance of fellowship and its vacancy thereby entitling others to apply. During that one-year period the fellow would be entitled to avail of his choice of any vacant church living in the college's gift.[86] Despite the system of dispensation, the requirement was antiquated and difficult to justify, it represented an open evasion of one of the statutes of the college, it proved highly unpopular

---

79. Cumberland to Primate, 31 Mar. 1836 (TCD Ms 2770/148).

80. *DUM* 15 (1840), 355.

81. Ibid.

82. TCD Board minutes, 1784–1810 (MUN V/5/5/229, 258–9).

83. McDowell and Webb, *Trinity College Dublin*, 107; TCD Board minutes, 1810–1830 (MUN V/5/6/17, 18, 26–27).

84. TCD Board minutes, 1810–1830 (MUN V/5/6/44).

85. TCD Board minutes, 1810–1830 (MUN V/5/6/27–33, 39, 43–46); MUN D 1687.

86. TCD MUN D 1688; *DUM* 15 (1840), 355. In a separate development, provosts were to be permitted to marry, and senior fellows were freed from the constraints of the statute: Ibid.

among those who had or hoped to attain fellowship, and the fellows continued to request a repeal of the statute.[87]

On the other hand, there were those that recognized the practical benefits of the statute, in particular, the fact that it allowed for rotation among the fellows and the inducement for the fellow of accepting a college living was that it held out the prospect of marriage.[88] However, there were fears that, should the statute be repealed, the livings in the gift of the college would not be so adequately filled as before. This was because if marriage was allowed with fellowship, few fellows would take up a college living, leaving the college with no choice but to dispose of the livings to students who were not fellows.[89] In the absence of such a prospect, there was no inducement for a fellow to leave the college and accept a living.[90] As we shall see, the issue of celibacy was not to be finally resolved until its abolition in 1840.

Bishops

The initiative of the 1790s by a group of bishops was continued by some, yet on the whole the role of the bishops in the examination of candidates for ordination could have been more rigorous. In 1833 it was stated bluntly: "The system of examination usually pursued, previous to ordination, has (I fear in many instances deservedly) fallen into general disrepute."[91] As an example of this in 1831 the bishops of Elphin and Raphoe ordained "several persons" who were not in possession of certificates.[92] Yet there were those bishops who were conscientious. Thus John Jebb, bishop of Limerick (1823–33), in his first charge to clergy in the diocese delivered in June, 1823, identified the study of divinity as consisting of the critical and the practical, the former comprising the content of theology, the latter pertaining to the spiritual and devotional application of the same, the one being necessary to the other.[93] While he conceded that such a division might seem obvious, he

---

87. TCD MUN V/98/7.

88. Charles W. Wall to Primate, 27 Jan. 1832 (TCD Ms 2770/49).

89. John [bishop of], Cloyne, Cloyne to the Primate, 26 Nov. 1831 (TCD Ms2770/45).

90. Charles W. Wall to Primate, 27 Jan. 1832 (TCD Ms 2770/49).

91. *Christian Examiner and Church of Ireland Magazine* 2 (1833) 177.

92. C. R. Elrington, Trinity College to Primate, 26 Nov. [1831] (RCB Ms 853).

93. *A Charge Delivered to the Clergy of the Diocese of Limerick* . . . printed in John Jebb, *Practical Theology*, i, 359–60.

was keen to point out that all too often clergy assumed that their theological education ceased with their academic study at university.[94]

In pursuance of improving levels of competence among clergy, Jebb raised the standard of examination for ordinands in his diocese, having previously been examining chaplain to the archbishop of Cashel, Charles Brodrick, and having contacts among bishops in England who were advocates of reform in theological education.[95] The examination conducted by Bishop Jebb was spread over three days (six hours duration per day) and it required candidates, among other things, to read aloud a portion of the liturgy, to translate a passage from the Greek testament, and to submit reading notes from texts they had read, all of which had the goal of inculcating a more vital professionalism.[96] Upon his appointment to the see of Dublin in 1831, Richard Whately made the ordination examinations for his diocese more demanding.[97] These initiatives among the bishops presaged reform in the school of divinity itself.

Efforts and developments in the two decades prior to 1833 represented an advance, but they were limited in their impact. Thus the system of voluntary November exams introduced by Graves was supplementary to the main course and hence only appealed to the more capable students; the celibacy requirement remained a restrictive barrier; catechetical arrangements were confined to the first two undergraduate years; and episcopal articulation of needs and expectations was confined to a select group of committed bishops. It was recognized that while the changes were beneficial and worked well, there was a need to extend the period of study, enlarge the course of study, and alter the way in which the divinity program operated.[98]

A GREAT CHANGE: 1833

The reforms of 1833 can be considered from external and internal perspectives. Externally, the wider historical context c.1830 was not auspicious for the established church in Ireland. Indeed all the indicators were that the Whig administration was intent on dismantling the privileged position of the Church of Ireland. Admittedly since 1800 a series of reforms addressed some of the more serious abuses (non-residence, pluralism, political interference), the number of churches increased by about one third, the rise of an

94. Ibid., i.362.
95. Bullock, *History of Training from 1800 to 1874*, 149.
96. Ibid., 150.
97. Ibid.
98. O'Brien, *Introductory Lecture*, 5.

evangelical strain animated its ranks, and financial reform (e.g. state initiative in regularizing the inequities of the tithe system) was apparent.[99] Yet despite these reforms the church was still in a precarious position. Specifically, increased political mobilization by Irish Catholics resulted in significant political concessions, notably the relief act of 1829 popularly known as Catholic emancipation, which allowed Catholics to enter parliament, belong to any corporation, and hold higher military and civil offices. This was a major dent in Anglican dominance of the political system. The assault continued with an attack on the legal privilege of the Church of Ireland. The Church Temporalities Act (1833) reduced the number of archbishoprics from four to two, the number of bishops by ten, and appointed ecclesiastical commissioners with powers to divide livings, suspend appointments, and allocate revenues. Further, in Oxford in July 1833 John Keble delivered his famous assize sermon on "National Apostasy," an event seen in retrospect as inaugurating the Oxford Movement. No doubt there were fears that the latter would impact the Church of Ireland. All this was not auspicious for the Anglican ecclesiastical polity in Ireland. To exacerbate the situation, in 1831 the introduction by the Whig government of a national system of non-denominational education was seen as an attack on an area that hitherto many Anglicans regarded as their prerogative. Further, as the 1830s progressed pervasive agrarian violence was to coalesce around the unresolved issue of tithe. All this demonstrated how vulnerable the church was in the face of a resurgent Catholicism (in which a Maynooth-educated clergy figured prominently), and how susceptible it had become to government intervention in the cause of reform. It seemed opportune to respond by strengthening the church from within. One expression of this was improving the quality and training of its clergy in order to defend the position of the Established Church.

The reforms also had their own rationale from an internal administrative perspective. In 1833 the provost, Rev Bartholomew Lloyd and Rev Charles R. Elrington undertook a major reform. Lloyd had become interested in the general academic reform of the college following his appointment to the chair of mathematics in 1813, and the opportunity to implement reformist ideas came with his assumption of the provostship in 1831.[100] So far as Elrington is concerned, he had had a distinguished academic career at the college, being elected to fellowship (1810), a position he resigned upon election to the regius professorship in divinity in 1829, which he held for

---

99. For a detailed analysis of these reforms see D. H. Akenson, *The Church of Ireland: Ecclesiastical Reform and Revolution, 1800-1885*, New Haven, 1971, 71-142.

100. *DUM* 11 (1838), 112-14.

over twenty years. While many, including Lloyd, recognized the merits of the course of study in divinity as it existed, and in particular the efforts of "the active and able" professor of divinity, there was a desire to improve it without extending the period of study unduly.[101]

Already in 1831 Lloyd delegated Elrington to devise a plan to extend the time of attendance and to lengthen the duration of the course, in order that apologetics and biblical criticism were accommodated.[102] As part of his remit, Elrington consulted with the primate, Archbishop John George Beresford, who was also vice-chancellor of the university. Already in 1827 at their annual visitation of the college, the archbishops of Armagh and of Dublin, while they expressed approval of the system of examinations in divinity, suggested that an addition to the number of divinity lecturers might be "expedient."[103] Primate Beresford, in particular, was interested in reform and some of the ideas later implemented by Provost Lloyd—for instance, beginning the course in the final undergraduate year and extending it for a further year—coincided (if not originated) with those of the primate.[104]

The primate's specific recommendation was that a two-year course of study in divinity should begin in the senior sophister (final) year of the bachelor's degree, a year during which students did very little, a fact recognized by the board.[105] To Elrington's mind this proposal would greatly inconvenience students on the basis that since the vast majority of them in the Dublin area took their degree before they reached twenty-two years of age they would have to wait an extra year before ordination (the canonical age being twenty-three), added to which was the extra expense of attending the divinity lectures.[106] The main issue in the estimation of the board was the assistants to the professor of divinity who were too engaged with other duties to be sufficiently supportive of the regius professor.[107]

Complementary to these considerations, Lloyd proposed a revision of the existing statutes that were restrictive or cumbersome. These included reducing the number of terms in the academic year from four to three; lessening the number of daily chapel services; allowing tutors to have the

---

101. Provost and senior fellows to Primate, 5 July 1831 (TCD Ms 2770/22); for a brief survey of the reforms: McDowell and Webb, *Trinity College Dublin*,161–4.

102. C. R. Elrington, Trinity College to Primate, 26 Nov. [1831] (RCB Ms 853).

103. TCD Board minutes, 1810–1830 (MUN V/5/6/443, 448).

104. Edward Stopford to Primate, 18 Aug. 1831 (TCD Ms 2770/32); C.R. Elrington to same, 23 Dec. 1831 (TCD Ms 2770/46).

105. Provost and senior fellows to Primate, 5 July 1831 (TCD Ms 2770/22); C. R. Elrington to same, 23 Dec. 1831 (TCD Ms 2770/46).

106. C. R. Elrington to Primate, 23 Dec. 1831 (TCD Ms 2770/46).

107. Ibid.

assistance of non-fellows; and choosing the best qualified junior fellows to assist in fellowship exams instead of the current practice based on seniority.[108] A preliminary draft of the changes circulated among the senior and junior fellows only elicited one dissenting voice.[109] With these restrictions dispensed with, the way was open for Lloyd to advance specific proposals for the instruction in and management of divinity studies.

Reform Elements

At the board meeting of March 30, 1833, five key proposals were presented and approved. First, from November 20 onward the position of Archbishop King's lecturer was to be filled from the ranks of the junior fellows. Second, upon assuming the King's lecturership the junior fellow was to cease being a tutor or hold any other office except that of preacher, who was to remain in it until he was elected a senior fellow. No longer was it to be an annual office rotating among the senior fellows at a small salary. Third, the salary of the King's lecturership was raised to £700 annually. Fourth, to obtain a divinity testimonium students were required to attend divinity lectures for two years instead of one: the first year with the King's lecturer, the second under the regius professor of divinity. Finally, more rigorous rules of attendance were to apply to those entering their studies in future.[110] In sum, the period of study of divinity was extended, the course of study itself was expanded, and the means whereby it was conducted was changed. In effect the changes inaugurated a formal school of divinity within the university. The most significant change was in the status and duties of the King's lecturer.

108. Lloyd to Primate, [] July, 1831, 28 Jan. 1832 (TCD Ms 2770/28, 50). Lloyd was confident that consultation with the board was unnecessary where a request for a new statute was concerned on the basis that it could be obtained from the crown based on the recommendation of the visitors.

109. Lloyd to Primate, n.d. [post April, 1832] (TCD Ms 2770/64); the primate opposed revision of the statutes: Primate to Provost, 16 July 1831 (TCD Ms 2770/27). O'Brien, *Introductory Lecture*, 66 (quotation). It is apparent that Lloyd's revision of the statutes was conducted without prior consultation with the board (TCD Ms 2770/54, 58, 60, 61). See also TCD Ms 2770/63, and 2770/156 for staff support of the reforms.

110. TCD Board minutes, 1830–1840 (MUN V/5/7/56, 66). These proposals passed with only two dissenting voices, those of Drs. Phipps and Prior, who argued that the plan would discourage succession among the junior fellows (already a slow process), and it wrested entitlement to the office of Archbishop King's lecturer from the senior fellows and bestowed it on the junior fellows: Ibid., 57.

King Lecturer

The position of Archbishop King's lecturer was enhanced and given a new status of permanence. Until 1833 the lecturership remained a virtual sinecure granted on an annual basis to one of the senior fellows in order to enhance his income and combine it with other college offices. The defect of this arrangement was that there was a lack of continuity in teaching and no incumbent could seriously get to know his subject in depth. Henceforward, the salary was raised to £700 (to compensate for the loss of fees from tutoring) putting the King lecturer on a par with the professors of moral and natural philosophy. Qualifications were not to be based on seniority or examination, but on the choice of candidate by the board.[111] It was the opinion of a later occupant of the position, Rev Thomas McNeece, that the board would always elect a junior fellow to the position "if they can find one willing and competent" but if not they were likely to select from among the ex-fellows.[112] This was a provision designed to exclude the senior fellows from holding the position. Central to the new arrangements was the desire to unencumber the lecturer from the responsibility for tutoring in order to free up his time to devote to lectures and exams.[113] Associated with this was an increase in the number of assistants from one in 1783, to two in 1795, to six, and to eight by mid-century.[114]

Under the new arrangement the position of lecturer was offered to James T. O'Brien, someone Lloyd favored because he had "excited the greatest interest among the divinity students by his preaching and lectures," and touted his "intellectual powers and profound research."[115] However, in 1836 in a reversal of policy O'Brien had his request approved that he be allowed to resign his fellowship and be appointed to a college living while still retaining his lecturership.[116] In addition, upon reaching the status of senior fellow

---

111. DUC report (R), 1852–53, 19; *DUM* 7 (1836), 346.

112. DUC report (E), 1852–53, 24. One contributor to the *Dublin University Magazine* in 1834 advocated that the professorships be taken out of the hands of the fellows (who, he maintained, had many other duties to fulfill) and be opened to graduates who would sit an examination to qualify for consideration: *DUM* 3 (Jan., 1834), 90.

113. Provost to Primate, 21 Feb 1833 (TCD Ms 2770/94).

114. DUC report (R) 1852–53, 19. The eight assistants were junior fellows, in orders, and chosen on seniority.

115. Provost to Primate, 21 Feb 1833 (TCD Ms 2770/94). The students knew about O'Brien's gifts as he substituted for Elrington who was on leave of absence: Ibid.; *DUM* 3 (Jan., 1834), 91.

116. TCD Board minutes, 1830–1840 (MUN V/5/7/121–2); DUC report (R), 1852–53, 19. Prior to its acceptance by O'Brien, the living had been offered to each of the senior fellows who had refused it (TCD Board minutes, 1830–1840 (MUN

Change and Transformation

he was to resign the lecturership and have the choice of a different living.[117] In 1841 O'Brien accepted the deanery of Cork and resigned his living, but with the permission of the board he was allowed to retain the lecturership in divinity.[118] Within four months, however, O'Brien was elevated from the deanery to the see of Ossory, and with resignation being mandatory upon election as bishop, a vacancy in the lecturership was created that was filled by Thomas McNeece.[119] The practice of combining an academic position with church livings was continued (and tolerated by the board) into the 1880s, largely to the detriment of the parishes concerned.[120] Thus, although later enforcement wavered, in the short term in 1833, with an enhanced salary and freedom from other duties, this reform brought stability and continuity to the King's lecturer position, and in turn created the expectation that the occupant would devote energy to the subject.[121]

Attendance

Expectations around attendance were raised. From 1833 students had to spend two years or six terms in divinity studies: the first year with the King's lecturer and the second with the regius professor, as well as the lectures of their assistants.[122] To obtain a certificate of attendance, a student had to be of senior sophister or higher standing, and have his name on the college books. Once he completed his first or junior year, the student then proceeded to attend the lectures of the regius professor.[123]

V/5/7/122). The report of the royal commission into the affairs of the college in 1853 recommended that this innovation of 1836 be repealed and a return made to the situation of 1833: Ibid. In 1840 O'Brien was permitted to use a deputy to deliver his lectures for the Michaelmas Term: TCD MUN V/5/8/19.

117. TCD Board minutes, 1830–1840 (MUN V/5/7/121). Although it was a majority decision, there were three dissenting senior fellows, one of whom, Robert Phipps, recognized the impossibility of the incumbent devoting himself to full-time teaching, while at the same time dividing his time with his parish responsibilities, such that he had to become the absentee to one and appoint a deputy (TCD Board minutes, 1830–1840 (MUN V/5/7/121).

118. TCD MUN V/5/8/67–69, 79.

119. TCD MUN V/5/8/72, 82–3, 84.

120. McDowell and Webb, *Trinity College Dublin*, 162.

121. DUC report (E), 1852–53, 23. The salary was a fixed amount of £700, the bulk of which derived from college funds rather than the Archbishop King endowment.

122. *DUM* 2 (July 1833) 114–15.

123. DUC report (E), 1852–53, 28.

On the issue of student attendance in general, it must be remembered that degrees in arts at Trinity could be achieved merely by passing the required examinations without residence in Dublin or attendance at lectures. However, those studying divinity were obliged to reside, but were not required to attend the courses.[124] Prior to 1833 it was possible to get the testimonium by one year's attendance at lectures of the assistants in one's final undergraduate year.[125] Attendance at divinity lectures continued to be voluntary, except in the case of scholars who were BA graduates.

Now with the revised expectations of 1833, to attain the divinity testimonium, a student had to attend six terms, three in each year of two. In the junior year, each student had to attend at least three-quarters of the lectures of the professor and his assistants each term. For senior year students, six weeks per term was the minimum attendance required. Students could not attend senior year divinity lectures, unless they had first completed their bachelor degree and their junior year.[126] Students could attend the lectures given by the professors of Hebrew, Moral Philosophy, Biblical Greek or Ecclesiastical History (who were not required to participate in the exams of the divinity school) on a voluntary basis.[127] In 1849 students in divinity were allowed to substitute attendance at divinity classes for classical lectures and exams in the senior sophister year.[128]

Arts Requirement

A related requirement was that the testimonium only be awarded to those who had completed the arts course prior to entering the senior divinity year. The strength of the course of study at Trinity was that after 1833 the study of divinity began in the final undergraduate year making it a requirement that no certificate (testimonium) in divinity would be granted except to those who had graduated as bachelors in arts. To attain this the students in divinity had either to attend catechetical classes or pass catechetical exams

---

124. DUC report (R) 1852–53, 68.

125. TCD Board minutes, 1830–1840 (MUN V/5/7/57, 66). In addition, students who had attended two terms of divinity lectures might qualify for the Downes' divinity premiums: DUC report (E), 1852–53, 17.

126. TCD MUN V/5/8/197, 251. The only advantage of regular attendance, apart from attainment of the divinity testimonium, was that scholars and students holding exhibition scholarships would keep their emoluments since they were conditional on attending two courses of lectures, one of which could be divinity: DUC report (E), 1852–53, 17.

127. DUC report (E), 1852–53, 18.

128. TCD MUN V/5/9/79.

in their freshman (or junior undergraduate) years, while in their senior (sophister) year they had to attend classes and pass exams (or pass exams only) in moral philosophy and the evidences of Christianity.[129]

The requirement of an arts degree continued the strong link that already existed between arts and theology. In recognizing the valuable connection between an education in the humanities as preparatory for one in theological education, Thomas McNeece, Archbishop King's lecturer said:

> "It would be a serious mistake to look upon the professional education of divinity students as the only education which it is important for them to receive: on the contrary, I am convinced that if the principle of severing the theological education of our clergy from education in arts were acted on, the result would be most detrimental to the cause of religion and learning."[130]

While it was conceded that ideally the undergraduate course should have been completed before theological studies began, it was recognized that the additional two years would place heavy demands in terms of time and expense on divinity students.[131] Against this had to be weighed the fact that some like James T. O'Brien regarded this arrangement as temporary as it gave the average student more than enough to do and thus had the potential to reduce the number of candidates needed for ministry in the church.[132] Nevertheless, from 1833 the board permitted senior sophisters as well as BAs to attend divinity lectures of the junior year, thereby allowing the junior divinity year to start in the senior undergraduate year.[133]

Content

A new clarity around the content of the courses taught by the respective professors of divinity was achieved as a result of the reforms of 1833.

---

129. DUC report (R) 1852–53, 20; *Dublin University Calendar*, 1835, 74–75.

130. DUC report (E), 1852–53, 28.

131. O'Brien, *Introductory ecture*, 55–56.

132. Ibid., 56. See RCB Ms 769 for his lecture notes on Ecclesiastes. O'Brien was the author of *An attempt to explain and establish the doctrine of justification by faith only in ten sermons upon the nature and the effects of faith preached in the chapel of Trinity College Dublin*, London and Dublin, 1833. See RCB Ms 783. For a review of the work, see *The Christian Examiner and Church of Ireland Magazine* 3: 31 (1834), 289–302.

133. DUC report (E), 1852–53, 28.

Archbishop King's Lecturer

For the junior or first divinity year the King's lecturer lectured for the first two terms on the evidences of natural and revealed religion including prophecy and in the last term on the Socinian (or Trinitarian) controversy. He or his assistants covered the evidences for Christianity (with Paley, *Evidences of Christianity*, as a text), the gospel of Luke in Greek, successively Acts of the Apostles, Galatians, and Philippians (the first of which was a set text while the other two could change), and John Pearson, *An exposition of the Creed*.[134] At the end of Trinity Term a final examination of the entire class was conducted based on prescribed texts and topics. He also conducted a special, voluntary examination for junior divinity students for the Archbishop King divinity prizes, established for the purpose by board in 1836.[135]

Regius Professor

By statute, the regius professor was required to deliver about thirty-six lectures annually.[136] In the first term he covered biblical criticism and interpretation; in the second, the liturgy and the articles of the church; and in the third, controversies with the Roman Catholic Church. Little of the content changed as a result of the reforms of 1833. Thus in their second year students were instructed on criticism and interpretation of the Bible, the Thirty-Nine Articles and the liturgy, and controversies with Catholics. The second or senior year students studied the epistle to the Hebrews in Greek; church history (covering the first three centuries and the sixteenth with Mosheim, *Institutes of ecclesiastical history* as a text); liturgy and church polity (Wheatly, *Book of Common Prayer*, and Potter, *Church Government* as texts); and Roman Catholic controversies (with Leslie, *Case stated between the Church of England and the Church of Rome*, and Leslie, *The true notion of*

---

134. *Dublin University Calendar*, 1835, 24; O'Brien, *Introductory Lecture*, 28, 33, 34, 36–38, 39, 40–41, 79; DUC report (E), 1852–53, 27.

135. O'Brien, *Introductory Lecture*, 80. He also administered other prizes including the prestigious Downes prize. There were two annual prizes (value £20) for the junior divinity class. He often gave extra prizes of £3 or £4. Dr. Downes' premiums were open to students in the junior divinity class. There were two premiums for written composition (value £33), two for extempore preaching (value £20), and two for reading the liturgy (value £12). There were other smaller prizes granted by the board, which also put prizes (£15) at the disposal of the professor of Biblical Greek. There were no medals, exhibitions or scholarships awarded in the junior year: DUC report (E) 1852–53, 28–9. By the mid-nineteenth century there were fifteen annual prizes valued at £165 awarded to students for proficiency: DUC report (R), 1852–53, 74.

136. DUC report (E), 1852–53, 18.

the Catholic Church).[137] Joseph Singer, regius professor from 1850, admitted that these topics were too extensive and important to be covered satisfactorily in lectures, so he strove to give students "a general view of their extent and nature" which he supplemented with directed readings to "guard their minds against the errors that are prevalent."[138] This instruction was supplemented by that offered by assistants which consisted of church history (with Mosheim as a text), the epistle to the Hebrews (in Greek) in the first term, and Burnet, on the Thirty-Nine Articles in the second and third.[139]

While the classes of the regius professor and Archbishop King's lecturer were professorial, those of the assistants were catechetical. Thus, the entire class attended the King's lecturer, but were dispersed in smaller groups among the different assistants; and similarly with the regius professor in their second year. They explained and examined prescribed parts of texts previously prepared by the students.[140] Dublin, as well as the English universities, placed an emphasis on the catechetical method which was more constraining, in contrast to the continental and Scottish model which was professorial and gave more freedom. Though the catechetical approach continued even after the reforms of 1833, particularly when conducted with the examinations, there were some, like James T. O'Brien, who maintained that a combination of the catechetical and professorial approaches would be advantageous.[141] In his view, this combination was to some degree achieved, for the lectures of the regius professor and the King's lecturer were in effect professorial, while those of their assistants were catechetical. This combination of academic and catechetical, professorial and tutorial instruction, benefited students and distinguished the Trinity approach, made it highly regarded, and in the opinion of one bishop, "one without which few of our students could obtain other than a very superficial knowledge of theology."[142]

---

137. O'Brien, *Introductory Lecture*, 77–78.

138. DUC report (E), 1852–53, 18. Singer eschewed topics that were divisive in the contemporary church, though he felt free to offer his own opinion: Ibid. In 1848 the number of lectures given weekly was reduced to two in Trinity Term to allow students adequate time for preparation: TCD MUN V/5/9/62.

139. *Dublin University Calendar*, 24; O'Brien, *Introductory Lecture*, 71–72.

140. DUC report (E), 1852–53, 18, 27; report (R), 73. When the divinity course was extended to two years, provision was made for the appointment of assistants to the regius professor, which had not pertained previously. The number of assistants, who had to be junior fellows and in orders, grew to seven who were appointed annually (normally based on seniority) by the provost and senior fellows and renewable depending on satisfactory performance. The board not the regius professor was responsible for their oversight: DUC report (E), 1852–53, 16.

141. O'Brien, *Introductory Lecture*, 73.

142. DUC report (R), 152–3, 73–74; DUC report (E), 1852–53, 18.

Many of the texts used in Dublin (which were approved by the board which also controlled the lectures and examinations) were similar to those studied at Oxford with the works of Paley, Pearson as well as the four gospels and Acts (in Greek), the Articles, Old Testament, being in common, a program that has been judged as an example of "best practice."[143] Even with the reforms of 1833, the entrance examination at Trinity required study of the four gospels and the Acts of the Apostles in Greek.[144] The texts recommended by Elrington, the regius professor (1829–50), for students wishing to study for the prizes, contained three works (Joseph Butler, *Analogy of Religion*, William Paley, *Horæ Paulinæ, or the truth of the scripture history of St. Paul evinced*, and Hooker, *Ecclesiastical Polity*, book V) which continued to be required until the mid-twentieth century.[145]

Attendance/Examinations

The 1833 reforms viewed attendance at lectures and passing examinations as at the core of assessing competence. Students were required to attend at least three quarters of the classes of the professor and lectures of the assistants each term.[146] Previously there had been no incentive on the part of ordinands to engage in serious study because of the absence of formal examination.[147] Now a general examination was required at the end of each year which all divinity students had to pass, that in the final year be-

143. Trevor Park, "Theological Education and ministerial training for the ordained ministry of the Church of England, 1800–1850," Ph.D. thesis, Open University (1999), 2 vols., i, 69. In 1837 Edward Pearson, *Remarks on the controversy subsisting or supposed to subsist, between the Arminian and Calvinistic ministers of the Church of England*, London, 1802 was substituted for Paley, on the recommendation of O'Brien, King's lecturer: Board Minutes, 1830–1840 (MUN V/5/7/136).

144. DUC (1835) 11.

145. Oulton, "The study of Divinity in Trinity College, Dublin," 17; Taylor, *History*, 179, 180. Butler survived at Trinity but at Oxford it was removed because of Newman's acknowledgement of how formative it had been in the evolution of his thinking.

146. DUC report (E), 1852–53, 17–18. The text of the testimonium stated: "Testamur A.B. per biennium sedulo interfuisse praelectionibus, atque examinationibus, in Sacra Theologia requisitis. E. Coll.SS.Trin. juxta Dublin. [Signed] Professor Reg. in Sac. Theol. [and] Praelector in Sac. Theol." O'Brien, *Introductory Lecture*, 78.

147. Attendance at the divinity lectures were voluntary, except in the case of scholars who had graduated with a BA. Students may attend at their own choice. The only advantage in attendance, besides the divinity testimonium, was that scholars and students holding exhibitions preserved their emoluments which were conditional on attendance at two courses of lectures, one of which could be in divinity. No fees were charged for attendance at the regius professor's lectures or exams, and there were no fees for the granting of the divinity testimonium: DUC report (E), 1852–53, 21.

ing especially important for upon it award of the divinity testimonium was dependent.

The first day of each term students in their junior or senior year were tested on a prescribed text of the Greek New Testament (e.g. Paul's epistles to Timothy and Titus), which had to be taken again at the end of the term in cases of non-attendance or defective answering. In addition, on two days (with mandatory attendance at one) each term students had to write an essay on subjects or texts of Scripture. In the second and third terms on the first day of term the test was again on prescribed parts of the Greek testament (e.g. Ephesians and Colossians), the choice being changed occasionally.[148] The year-end final test was based on the letter to the Hebrews (in Greek); Old Testament history; the Book of Common Prayer; church government; the Thirty-Nine Articles; Catholic controversies; and a subject for English composition.[149] By 1837, the junior year-end examination was comprised of three areas: firstly, the four gospels and the epistle to the Romans all in Greek; secondly, the evidences for Christianity based on three texts: Thomas Chalmers, *On natural theology*, Paley, *Evidences of Christianity*, and Thomas Newton, *Dissertations on the prophecies* (sections I-XIII and XVIII-XXI); and thirdly, the Socinian controversy the texts being John Pearson, *An exposition of the Creed*, and William Magee, *Discourses and dissertations on the scriptural doctrines of atonement & sacrifice*.[150] The class exam at the end of the third term was based on Hebrews (in Greek), Old Testament history, Mosheim's *Institutes of ecclesiastical history* (Soames' edition) volumes one, three and four; Wheatly on Common Prayer, Potter on church government, Burnet on the Thirty-Nine Articles, Taylor's *Dissuasive from Popery*, and a subject for English composition.[151]

The exams consisted of questions on the Old Testament, New Testament, church history, liturgy, and the articles of religion.[152] A conspectus of the questions on the examinations hosted by the regius professor of divinity in 1834, after the reforms had been implemented, reveals that on the whole the content stressed facts, identities, history, dating of events, with doctrine and interpretation secondary.[153] In addition to these the regius professor

148. DUC report (E), 1852–53, 18.

149. DUC report (E), 1852–53, 17–18.

150. O'Brien, *Introductory Lecture*, 77. The exceptions in Magee were sections 53, 59, and the postscript to 69.

151. Ibid., 19. Following the exam, those who passed were divided into three classes depending on the quality of their answering.

152. DUC report (E), 1852–53, 19.

153. DUC (1835) lxxxv–cxii; see also questions on the articles and the liturgy in the "extracts" from the examination papers for the years, 1830–42 in W. Bates, *College*

continued to hold a voluntary exam for special prizes over two days in November.[154]

Bishops' Requirement

Irish and English bishops now preferred the testimonium as the qualification for ordinands. While C. R. Elrington was initially skeptical about the prospects for success of the reforms without the concurrence and support of the bishops, nevertheless the testimonium came to be preferred by the bishops as the qualification for ordinands.[155] In contrast to the initiative of the 1790s, henceforth as a result of the reform of 1833, the testimonium would only be awarded on completion of the full two-year program. However, the 1790 resolution of the bishops to the effect that they would not ordain anyone who could not produce a testimonium certifying that he had attended at least one complete course of lectures in divinity, was discontinued in the early 1840s and the bishops were subsequently not bound by such a commitment. But generally the practice in England and Ireland was to require it.[156] The lack of any development of separate theological colleges in Ireland as in the Church of England is a reflection of this close partnership.

These developments at Dublin invite comparison with the situation obtaining at Oxford and Cambridge. At the outset of the nineteenth century, theological education at Oxford and Cambridge, as at Dublin, was confined to what was obtainable as part of the Batchelor of Arts degree. But by mid-century much had changed, specifically nine new centres for Anglican theological training had been founded in England and Wales, and at Oxford and Cambridge some modest reforms had taken place. From 1824 Cambridge required undergraduate students in their fifth term to take a test based on one of the gospels or Acts in Greek, Paley's *Evidences*, and a prescribed text from a Greek or Latin author; from 1842 Old Testament history was added, and knowledge of church history, New Testament, and

---

Lectures on Christian Antiquities and the Ritual of the English Church; with Selections from Ancient Canons and the Cambridge, Dublin, and Durham University Examination Papers, London, 1845, 451–72.

154. *First Praelection*, 9, 31–35; DUC report (E), 1852–53, 18–19; O'Brien, *Introductory Lecture*, 78–79. Though open to all, it was typically taken by those in their senior year.

155. C. R. Elrington to Primate, 26 Nov. [1831] (RCB Ms 853). There are cases in the 1840s where the board gave leave for the testimoniums to be granted in advance in order for ordinations to take place, but they had to be returned subsequently: MUN V/5/8/112, 113, 117, and 266.

156. DUC report (E), 1852–53, 25–26.

Change and Transformation

Paley's *Moral Philosophy*.[157] Oxford had similar requirements by 1850. At Oxford and Cambridge while new chairs of pastoral theology and church history were inaugurated and while they came to be occupied by persons of ability, the residual issues of attendance, examinations and student quality remained.[158]

In general, attendance requirements were not rigorous, with bishops requiring Cambridge ordinands to attend only half the lectures given by the Norrisian professors, while those at Oxford were only required to attend a short series of lectures given by the regius professor of divinity. Only in 1842 did Cambridge introduce a voluntary (soon made mandatory) examination taken by ordinands because bishops required it, while Oxford had by this date a similar course of study (though not compulsory). However, because bishops did not require attandance at such exams, their usefulness was compromised. Until the 1840s there was no consensus among bishops in England as to what should be expected of candidates for orders of deacon and priest and, as in Ireland, they were content to leave the content of the curriculum to the universities.[159] Added to these deficiencies was a frank admission on the part of the tutors at Oxford in 1848 that the theological instruction of undergraduates who were potenatial ordinands, was deficient.[160] In consequence, those Oxford graduates who discerned a genuine call to ministry increasingly had recourse to theological training at some of the newly established colleges like King's College, London, St. David's, Lampeter, and St. John's Highbury, and the new diocesan colleges. Whereas deficiencies in divinity education in England and Wales emanated in the foundation of new theological colleges, this was not the case in Ireland. There, no such institutions arose and Trinity remained the seminary of choice. The focus of reform derived from within the institution itself rather than in the establishment of new foundations without.

While differences in size meant that Oxford and Cambridge had a greater complement of divinity instructors than Trinity, nevertheless Trinity was to the fore of its English counterparts in terms of governance, curriculum revision, student requirements, and additional courses offered. Lectures at the English universities were typically optional, and those that

---

157. Unless otherwise stated, the following section draws on Dowland, *Anglican Theological Training*, 182–87.

158. Park, "Theological," i, 77.

159. Park, "Theological," i, 76. In the early 1830s there was a controversy at Oxford over charges that testimonials of fitness for ministry were given to unsuitable candidates, while they were denied to others including those of evangelical conviction; ibid., i, 80–83.

160. Ibid., i, 96.

were required (as with the Norrisian professor at Cambridge) were original. At Trinity the reforms of 1833 made attendance of two years and annual examinations a requirement, whereas Oxford and Cambridge had neither feature. Trinity's requirement was reinforced by episcopal preference for the testimonium as a condition of ordination. Additionally, the combination of lecture and catechetical, professorial and tutorial systems distinguished Trinity from the virtually professorial systems of others.[161] Indicative of the strength and maturity of the Dublin curriculum was the fact that in 1848, the English bishops requested details of it from the regius professor.[162]

Universities like Oxford and Cambridge in the early nineteenth century were not primarily concerned with teaching or research (including in theology), and hence the published, scholarly output of their faculty was negligible and unexceptional.[163] Holders of chairs were typically sinecurists and pluralists, and hence often absentees from their academic posts.[164] Fellows displayed a similar disparagement of teaching and research, a reflection of the non-residence stipulation attached to their appointment, their delegation of teaching responsibilities to tutors, and their concern as clergymen to advance in the church more than in the academy. It was not until the 1870s that fellowships at Oxford and Cambridge were liberated from religious conditions including the celibacy stipulation.[165] As early as the reform year of 1833 one writer attributed Trinity's reputation in divinity education not to church officials or university administrators, but rather to "the publications of first rate men."[166] For Dublin one can cite a number of works of note indicative of faculty productivity, including William Magee, *Discourse on the Scriptural Doctrines of Atonement and Sacrifice* (1801), James T. O'Brien, *An Attempt to Explain the Doctrine of Justification by Faith Only in Ten Sermons* (1833), and William Lee *The Inspiration of Holy Scripture: its Nature and Proof* (1854). In 1835 the regius professor, Elrington, began editing the complete works of James Ussher, projected to reach sixteen volumes.[167]

161. DUC report (E), 1852–53, 27.
162. TCD MUN V/5/9/42.
163. Dowland, *Anglican Theological Training*, 185.
164. Ibid.
165. Ibid., 192.
166. *The Christian Examiner and Church of Ireland Magazine*, 2 (1833), 174.
167. *The Dublin Penny Journal*, 4, no.171 (Oct. 10, 1835), 116. He did not live to complete the task, but several volumes were published after his death (1850): B. H. Blacker, 'Elrington, Charles Richard (1787–1850),' rev. David Huddleston, *Oxford Dictionary of National Biography*, Oxford University Press, 2004; online ed., Oct 2009. The output continued with George Salmon *A historical introduction to the study of the books*

Change and Transformation

The Anglican monopoly over theological education was to remain longer in Dublin than at Oxford or Cambridge given the influx of dissenters to the latter and the arrival on the scene of the independent theological colleges. The reforms of 1833 represented a modernization of theological instruction to meet the needs of the age. Henceforth, aspirants to a career in the church had to commit to a program of studies in the arts (in which there was a strong biblical and catechetical content), two years in divinity, compulsory attendance, and a yearly examination. The academic standard was raised and the program of study proved to be more rigorous than what preceded it. One student, William Reeves, a future bishop of Down, recalled of his student days under the new arrangement: "The rules of attendance and answering which were prescribed were very strict, and the consequence was that out of a very large Divinity class, numbering at the start above 100, only twenty-six got clean through without a check."[168] Nevertheless those who succeeded were well prepared for their mission, not least their education was deemed to give clergy the advantage in public debates with their Catholic counterparts.[169]

IMPLEMENTATION: 1833–1850

In the decades after 1833 the reforms in divinity education had an impact on the undergraduate program, saw the addition of new and cognate subject areas and pastoral initiatives, witnessed chapel attendance linked to award of the testimonium, saw controversy over the archbishop of Dublin's proposal in divinity education, and saw the resolution of the celibacy issue.

The reforms impacted the undergraduate program. While catechetical lectures had been offered for both freshman years, the requirement in this area for sophisters was less stringent. Henceforth, entrants after 1831 were prohibited from attaining the status of sophister unless they had maintained four catechetical terms.[170] In 1837 a new rule required future students to receive credit either through attendance or exams in their freshman (undergraduate) years in two out of three catechetical subjects.[171] These examina-

---

of the New Testament (1885), and *The Infallibility of the Church* (London, 1888), a fifth edition of which appeared in 1952.

168. Mary Catharine Ferguson, Lady, *Life of the Right Rev. William Reeves, D.D.*, Dublin and London, 1893, 6 quoted in Oulton, "The Study of Divinity in Trinity College, Dublin," 17.

169. O'Brien, *Introductory Lecture*, 57.

170. *Dublin University Calendar*, 1835, 23. If a non-resident, four catechetical examinations.

171. TCD Board Minutes, 1830–1840 (MUN V/5/7/135).

tions tested candidates on various books of the Bible (notably Luke, Acts, Genesis, Exodus 1–20, Joshua, Judges, Ruth, I & II Samuel, I & II Kings), the prophets (though with the proviso of "omitting such chapters as do not contain direct prophecies of the Messiah"), along with the catechism and the creed.[172]

New Academic Disciplines and Pastoral Initiatives

It had been part of Provost Lloyd's original reform agenda to divide up the divinity school into a number of departments to encompass ecclesiastical history, biblical criticism, issues of controversy, and apologetics with a capable individual to head up each one.[173] However, his plan did not materialize and he died in 1837. Nevertheless, indicative of the new academic initiative unleashed by Lloyd's reforms was the creation of new subject teaching areas that were to enhance the curricular offerings associated with the school of divinity.

In 1837 a new professorship of moral philosophy was inaugurated, the appointee delivering twelve lectures during the academic year.[174] The deficiency whereby students in divinity were not obliged to attend the lectures of the regius professor of Greek was rectified with the creation in 1838 of a separate lecturership (in 1843 a professorship) in biblical Greek, though it was not initially an appointment within the divinity school.[175] In 1840 a chair in Irish was inaugurated (operative in 1843) to prepare clergy for ministry in Gaelic-speaking areas.[176] Course content included Irish grammar, translations from Greek and English into Irish and from Irish into English, and written and oral competence.[177] The incumbent at mid-century,

---

172. *Dublin University Calendar*, 1835, 23.

173. Provost to Primate, 21 Feb 1833 (TCD Ms 2770/94).

174. The following is drawn from DUC report (E), 1852–53, 94–96. As with other professorships, the incumbent held a benefice: Ibid., 95.

175. TCD Board minutes, 1830–1840 (MUN V/5/7/152); DUC report (E) 1852–53, 96–99. The duties consisted of giving 46 lectures; student attendance was voluntary and by 1848 was in excess of 100, though there were no examinations; and the subject matter included New Testament Greek, the Septuagint, critiques (e.g. Griesbach), and Romans, Hebrews, and the gospel of Matthew. Examinations ranged from Numbers, 1 Corinthians, Daniel, 1 & 2 Thessalonians, Deuteronomy, 1 & 2 Timothy, Titus, to Joshua, John, and Galatians: DUC report (E), 1852–53, 98.

176. TCD Board minutes, 1830–1840 (MUN V/5/7/144,160–161); DUC Report (E), 1852–53, 85, 87n. The first incumbent of the chair was Rev. Thomas Devere Coneys appointed for an initial two-year term in 1840 and re-appointed in 1842: TCD MUN V/5/8/23, 32, 122.

177. DUC report (E), 1852–53, 86.

Change and Transformation

Dr. Daniel Foley, was keen to advance the teaching of Irish among divinity students especially.[178] In 1850 the chair in ecclesiastical history was begun and funded by Primate Beresford, after whom it was named.[179] In a two-year cycle the incumbent sought to cover the full panorama of church history from the beginnings of the church to the present.[180] Biblical Greek apart, in none of these new additions to the academic offerings was the initiative taken by the board.

As a result of these additions, by mid-century students in divinity, in addition to the classes provided by the regius professor and the Archbishop King's lecturer, could study biblical Greek, Irish, and church history, though there was no requirement of attendance. This was a lacuna deriving from the fact that neither of the faculty members who taught these subjects were integrated into the divinity school, leading to the recommendation in a government report of the 1853 that certificates of attendance at the lectures of at least one of these professor's classes be required as a condition of attaining the testimonium.[181]

In terms of the practical application of academic theology, the importance of which had been emphasized by Bishop Jebb, initiatives were slow in coming. Although many in the school recognized the need for the academic emphasis of the school to be complemented by a practical application—even the bishop of Meath, Joseph H. Singer, recommended a professorship of pastoral theology as early as 1852—this did not transpire until 1888 when a chair in pastoral theology was founded.[182] By mid-century such a

---

178. DUC report (R), 1852–53, 50. In 1842, however, it had been stipulated that upon completion of two years of divinity studies, they were to be given credit for their attendance at lectures of the professor of Irish: TCD MUN V/5/8/85.

179. DUC report (E), 1852–53, 87. The position was tenable for a five-year period, Beresford was given the right of first appointment, and it was normally held with other college positions, usually divinity-related. The holder was required to lecture twice a week during two of the three terms each year, he could give a certificate of attendance at his lectures, was empowered to hold a prize examination each year for those students who had "diligently attended" his lectures, and he examined in his subject at the annual professor of divinity exams: Ibid., 88.

180. DUC report (E), 1852–53, 89. In its first year of operation, 1850–51, his lectures recorded over 190 students in attendance over two terms. His income was the same as that of the professor of Irish, £100 (made up of £40 interest from the endowment of Archbishop Beresford, and the remainder from college funds): Ibid., 90.

181. DUC report (R), 1852–53, 20.

182. DUC report (R), 1852–53, 20; McDowell and Webb, *Trinity College Dublin*, 164. The incumbent of a Dublin parish was viewed as the ideal candidate for such a position. The bishop also recommended a professorship in "polemical theology," presumably for the purpose of countering the Roman Catholic position: DUC report (R), 1852–53, 20.

chair already existed at Oxford and one was recommended for Cambridge.[183] Already, however, the divinity students in Dublin had taken some informal initiatives themselves in this area of practical ministry by involvement in Sunday school teaching in neighboring parishes. In Provost Lloyd's time students were given permission to absent themselves from chapel service in order to assist at Sunday school and with catechizing in local parishes, and Lloyd saw no difficulty in extending the practice as long as those concerned had completed their initial divinity courses.[184] The practice continued later as students participated as readers in a "Parochial Visitors' Society," and through the formation in college of a group for self-instruction.[185] However, the reason why the pastoral proposal did not proceed at this time was likely due to the opposition of the primate, Archbishop Beresford, who was also vice-chancellor and had endowed the chair in church history. While Beresford allowed for the role of divinity students as teachers and visitors, his reservations centered on the fact that having students in parish placements would take them away from their studies, their attendance in a particular parish would stretch its resources, and they would form a transient group and displace the natural pool of local parishioners from which such assistants would usually be drawn. Instead the primate was in favor of their placement in rural areas where proper supervision would be forthcoming and opportunities for service in Christian education would be present in an unencumbered way.[186]

Chapel

The issue of an association between chapel attendance and receipt of the testimonium arose as part of the reform initiatives of the 1830s. Trinity was, like the colleges of Oxford and Cambridge, a religious foundation and thoroughly Anglican in its ethos. The Protestant character of the institution is evidenced in the fact that provosts were expected to take part in teaching divinity and well into the nineteenth century were required to disavow

---

183. DUC report (R), 1852–53, 20. Dowland, *Anglican Theological Training*, 183. For the generally irreverent and unimpressive nature of chapel worship and preaching at Oxford which students were compelled to attend, see Park, "Theological," i, 86–90.

184. B. Lloyd to [Whately], 6 Jan. 1834 (RCB Ms 707 Whately correspondence).

185. DUC report (R), 1852–53, 20. The Parochial Visitors' Society was founded by Richard Whately, archbishop of Dublin, after his proposal for a Divinity Hall for students upon graduation: Ibid., 21.

186. DUC report (R), 1852–53, 20–21.

Change and Transformation

the doctrine of transubstantiation upon assuming office.[187] Students were required to attend chapel services regularly. The enforcement of attendance was somewhat justified in the case of students in residence and those living within a defined radius of the college, with the ultimate sanction for habitual non-attendance being denial of their rooms.[188] Yet punishment of non-attendance through fines implied discipline rather than duty and hence was generally viewed as ineffective and undesirable.

As part of the reforms under Lloyd, there was a proposal that weekly attendance at chapel be reduced from twenty per week to one per day and two on Sundays.[189] In 1839 some divinity students petitioned the board requesting that they be allowed to receive their testimoniums despite the fact that they had not attended chapel during their second year in the program.[190] The board concurred to the request on condition that the students attend chapel at least during one of their two years of study, that they be required to do so at least three times each year, and that the Archbishop King's lecturer maintain a record of such attendance.[191] Yet compulsory chapel attendance was never a satisfactory means of supporting the devotional lives of students, and for that reason was widely criticized.[192]

Whately's Scheme

Two issues of controversy were to dominate the late 1830s: the archbishop of Dublin's plans for a divinity hall, and the celibacy stipulation.

The newly appointed archbishop of Dublin, Richard Whately, who had been exposed to the separate theological colleges developing in England, came to his new office in 1831 with many reformist ideas, one of which was in the area of divinity education. As we have seen, despite the curricular

---

187. TCD Board minutes, 1810–1830 (MUN V/5/6/20).

188. Students living with the area encompassed by the North Circular Road (north of the River Liffey), and the South Circular Road (south of the River Liffey) were obliged to attend Sunday morning and three chapels during the week; those residents in the college, Sunday morning and one chapel every day during the week. During the week chapel service was available three times per day in the 1820s: *Discipline of Dublin University*, 9.

189. Edward Stopford to Primate, 18 Aug. 1831 (TCD Ms 2770/32).

190. TCD Board minutes, 1830–1840 (MUN V/5/7/223); for a description of attendance, see *DUM* 35 (1850), 585.

191. TCD Board minutes, 1830–1840 (MUN V/5/7/223). The irregularity of enforcement continued and in 1840 the board mandated that all students who had attended chapel at least once in the year be allowed to take their exam: TCD MUN V/5/8/4.

192. Dowland, *Anglican Theological Training*, 189.

reforms of 1833, the divinity course still ran parallel with the program in arts. This meant that a divinity student upon graduation often found himself with two years or more to wait until he reached the canonical age of twenty-three for ordination. This left a few years between graduation and ordination which could be spent either in preparation for November exams, tutoring, or residing in their home location.[193] To address this lacuna Whately proposed to establish a divinity hall in association with Trinity College where the graduates might engage in additional studies while they bided their time until they reached the canonical age.

Provost Lloyd, noting the reforms of the divinity school that had been initiated, protested Whately's proposal as "highly injurious to this university and indeed obstructive of its protestant character."[194] There was predictable negative comment in the conservative press to the proposal, one writer likening Whately's proposed college as one in which graduates would experience "theological quarantine of two years, until they get rid of the infection of the Scriptural principles with which their minds have been imbued."[195] Given the opposition that this scheme evoked and the fears of divinity school staff that the education of ordinands would be wrested from their control, Whately proposed the establishment of a divinity hall without the participation of Trinity College, financed by him, and under his management. In June 1839 the board declared that "the present divinity school of the university renders such additional hall unnecessary."[196] The board secured the intervention of the primate, Archbishop Beresford, through whose influence the government ultimately dropped the scheme.[197] As a result, Trinity was not

---

193. *DUM* 4 (Nov., 1834) advertisement for tutoring.

194. Lloyd to [Whately], 30 Dec. 1833 (TCD Ms 2770/103). The history of Whately's proposal can be followed in the Beresford correspondence (TCD Ms 2770 passim especially 107, 112, 113, 117–31) and in the Whately correspondence (RCB Ms 707).

195. *DUM* 3 (June, 1834), 703. Elrington who was professor of divinity and chaplain to Whately, was nominated to be principal of the proposed college: Ibid., 699–700.

196. TCD Board minutes, 1830–1840 (MUN V/5/7/202).

197. Ibid. MUN V/5/7/192, 204–10, 213–18. The board's position on the issue took a lengthy period to formulate. Initially at its meeting of April 13, 1839, a proposal that a letter be written to Whately seeking clarification as to whether he had forwarded or intended to forward a charter for the new school for royal approval, and if so to request a copy of the same, was defeated on a vote. However, by June 1, the board had gained more resolve to the extent that it requested the registrar to communicate with the primate, Beresford, and the university's members of parliament, requesting their intervention with the government to prevent the great seal from being attached to the charter for the new hall: ibid./202. See also, D. H. Akenson, *A Protestant in Purgatory: Richard Whately, Archbishop of Dublin*, Hamden, Conn., 1981, 104–10; McDowell and Webb, *Trinity College Dublin*, 165–68.

to experience the challenge of the new theological foundations as Oxford and Cambridge were in the nineteenth century.

Celibacy and Livings

In this period also the long-standing issue of clerical celibacy was resolved. The archbishop of Dublin, Richard Whately, favored repeal, as did the lord chancellor, who in 1831 drew up arguments advocating its abolition.[198] The fellows petitioned for repeal in 1835.[199] The board, however, was divided on the issue particularly as to whether repeal of the statute should involve an addition to the number of fellows, and if so in what number.[200] In 1839, following the operation of the revised statute for twenty-seven years, the board applied to the government for its repeal and this came a year later.[201]

An associated issue concerned church livings. Fellows were able to avail of the twenty-one livings in Ireland that were in the gift of the college.[202] These livings facilitated the career aspirations of the fellows the majority of whom were celibate, sons of clergy, ordained, and awaiting advancement in the church. The livings were attractive to the fellows because of the celibacy rule and because they exceeded junior fellowships in value. By the 1830s the twenty-one livings had a gross value of £16,275.[203] It was normal for the regius professor to be appointed to a college living, though his salary was £1,200. Graves, Elrington and Singer were so appointed, Singer in addition

198. Charles W. Wall to Primate, 27 Jan. 1832 (TCD Ms 2770/49); TCD Ms 2770/41. Primate Beresford and the Duke of Cumberland, and a minority of fellows favored its retention: TCD Ms 2770/137-8, 140, 192.

199. TCD Ms 2770/136, 196.

200. TCD Board minutes, 1830–1840 (MUN V/5/7/259).

201. TCD Board minutes, 1830–1840 MUN V/5/7/144,160–92, 270–71, 1840–1850 (MUN V/5/8/1); Ebrington to Primate, Jan. 27, 1840 (TCD Ms 2771/215, see also 216). As part of the repeal of the celibacy statute, ten new fellows were to be added to the body, one each year for the ensuing decade, and of the ten only four seniors were to be appointed tutors: TCD Board minutes, 1830–1840 (MUN V/5/7/272). After 1849 when the quota of ten had been reached, there was to be an annual examination for one new person to be elected to fellowship. Although, as it happened, in 1840 the examination for fellowship was not held because the repeal of the celibacy statute was seen to be in conflict with the charter of 1637; ibid., 275–76.

202. In 1610 seventeen livings were made over to the college from lands forfeited to the crown, and by an act of 1763 the college purchased a further four at a cost £16,500 from college funds: DUC report (E), 1852–53, 253. A later government investigation into the college concluded that such expenditure was "injudicious" given the need for funding for additional fellowships, professorships, and student scholarships and awards: DUC report (R), 1852–53, 22.

203. DUC report (E), 1852–53, 252–53.

being archdeacon of Raphoe.[204] When the incumbent of a living died, the vacant benefice was offered to those fellows in orders on a seniority basis, and upon acceptance by one of them, he resigned his fellowship.[205] With board approval, livings could be exchanged by mutual consent.[206]

A significant addition to the complement of livings available to the college occurred in 1833, as a result of the realignment of sees imposed by the government in that year under the Church Temporalities Act. Thus the archbishops of Armagh and Dublin were given the right to present fellows or ex-fellows of the college to ten livings each in their gift.[207] As a result the college had access to additional livings in which to place its fellows.[208]

With the repeal of the celibacy statute in 1840, henceforth, livings in the gift of the college and of the archbishops were declined by the fellows because there was less need for them to seek them (and at any rate they were less appealing because of their declining value); in consequence though the practice of giving the livings to fellows continued to mid-century and beyond, they were increasingly given to clergymen who were not fellows.[209]

---

204. Ibid., 15–16, 21.

205. TCD Board minutes, 1784–1810 (MUN V/5/5/189). A profile of the college livings in 1835 indicates that some incumbents could hold multiple benefices, that some occupied them for thirty or forty years, and that many holders had the DD degree: *Dublin University Calendar*, 1835, 59–60. In cases where such a candidate was drawn from among the senior fellows, the vacancy among their ranks was filled by one of the junior fellows selected by the provost and the remaining senior fellows; while if it was from among the junior fellows, his place was filled by a graduate of the university elected after a public examination of three days and a fourth in private. Candidates for public examination were tested in logic and metaphysics, mathematics, natural philosophy, morality, history, chronology, Hebrew, Greek, and Latin; while the private examination consisted of Latin and English composition. If there was a tie between two candidates, the provost had the casting vote, with the unsuccessful candidate being compensated in the amount of £200: *Dublin Penny Journal* 4, no.171 (Oct. 10, 1835), 116.

206. TCD Board minutes, 1810–1830 (MUN V/5/6/39).

207. TCD Board minutes, 1830–1840 (MUN V/5/7/74); Ms 2770/98–99; DUC report (E), 1852–53, 254. They were not to be worth more than £1,000 each annually.

208. The annual income varied from £207 to £898, but was typically in the £500 range: TCD MUN V/5/8/50. It was later suggested that it would be beneficial to the church and the school, if the archbishops had the power to select incumbents from among the better divinity students: DUC report (E), 1852–53, 254.

209. DUC report (E), 1852–53, 253; ibid. (R), 23; TCD MUN V/5/8/96, 104–5; V/5/9/66, 73–4, 75.

CONCLUSION

In 1846 one observer offered the following assessment of the caliber of the clergyman ministering in the Church of Ireland and the quality of education they had received:

> "The superior professional qualifications of the Irish clergy, their personal character, their parochial activity and usefulness [are notable] ... Their increased attainments in professional learning has been equally observable, and is to be traced to the efficiency of the divinity school of our university, and the care and labour there bestowed on the candidates for the ministry by the respective lecturers and especially the learned and excellent Regius Professor [Elrington], who has long presided over that school."[210]

The tenor of the comment is in marked contrast to the dire analysis of Archdeacon Forsayeth in the 1780s, the negative assessment of Rev. Henry Irwin as to the deficiency of his education in the 1790s, and Bishop Jebb's comments in 1823. More than at Cambridge or Oxford, by mid-century intentional reforms to theological education had been successfully implemented at Dublin. The impulse for reform had gathered momentum from the 1790s onward and was to achieve particular focus and direction in 1833, influenced by external threats to the church and by an internal momentum. The gains were tangible: a two-year course in theological education followed by an examination and granting of a certificate; permanent status for those appointed to the King lecturership; new faculty appointments in ecclesiastical history, biblical Greek, Irish, and moral philosophy, all of which enhanced the course of study in divinity; and the repeal of the statutory requirement of celibacy (though the appeal of church livings lingered into the 1880s). In these various ways a formal school of divinity in the university came to be instituted.

From the remarks of the commentator in 1846, it is clear that the academically rigorous nature of the program impacted the church significantly and in the 1840s an annual average of over one-hundred received the testimonium.[211] Dublin graduates not only had an impact on the Church of Ireland itself, but their influence extended beyond Ireland's shores. The number of Trinity graduates in deacons orders in the English and Welsh

---

210. *DUM* 27 (1846), 374.

211. Calculated from information in HC Accounts and Papers: *Return of Number of Students of Each College in Universities of Oxford, Cambridge, and Dublin* 1850 (7), 5; TCD MUN V 5/9, 7 Sept. 1849.

church, for instance, more than doubled from 219 in the period 1834–43 to 537 in the period 1844–53.[212] The annual number was thirty-three in 1841 (out of a total of 606), and in the 1850s it ranged from twenty-one to thirty-two.[213] Further afield, in the mid-nineteenth century about one-quarter of the clergy in the Diocese of Toronto, Canada and one-third of those in active ministry there, had been educated in Dublin.[214] Based on a rigorous theological training, Trinity graduates, therefore, had an impact on the church locally and internationally, out of proportion to the size of the Church of Ireland.

---

212. Park, "Theological," i, 2. This was out of a total number of deacons for the respective periods of 5,350 and 6,656, with Dublin graduates representing 4% and 8%.

213. Bullock, *History of Training*, 74–75. It rose to a range of 29–41 annually in the 1860s: ibid., 100. It has been estimated that between 1873 and 1914, over 1,000 Trinity graduates were ordained for English dioceses: R. B. McDowell, *The Church of Ireland 1869–1969*, London, 1975, 85.

214. W. Westfall, "'Some Practical Acquaintance with parochial duties:' Learning and practice in the Diocese of Toronto in the nineteenth century" in *Learning to Practise: Professional Education in Historical and Contemporary Perspective*, eds. R. Heap, W. Millar, and E. Smyth, Ottawa, 2005, 45, 63. I am grateful to Prof. Westfall for providing me with a copy of this essay.

7

The Waning of Protestantism in the Anglican Historical Imagination, 1874–1916

NATHAN D. WOLFE

IN THE LAST HALF of the nineteenth century, writers from the High Church tradition were motivated by the Tractarian movement to turn to the study of general English history. A number of these writers then went on to figure prominently in the various efforts advanced to modernize and professionalize the study of history, so that England would have an historiographical discipline to rival that of the Germans. These writers from the High Church tradition were active in developing academic history departments at the universities, were at the intellectual forefront in writing about historiographical theory and, perhaps most importantly, were a success in the marketplace where their books struck a chord with popular reading audiences. While these High Church historians were partially motivated by the goal of achieving a greater degree of historiographical excellence, they were also keenly motivated by a desire to prove the catholicity of the Church of England. Their main historiographical project was to articulate a robust defense of the continuity of the Church of England that minimized ecclesiological and doctrinal changes from the foundation of the Church of England up to their own present.

This essay argues, firstly, that the meta-narrative of continuity not only had the lasting effect of prioritizing the catholicity of the Church of England, but was also described in such a way as to reject any categorical "Protestant" doctrinal, ritual or ecclesiastical changes at the Reformation as outside the pale of the true constitutional development of the Church of England. Secondly, it argues that the historians who attempted to counter this High Church meta-narrative—a mix of historians whose backgrounds were Evangelical Anglican, Roman Catholic, and agnostic—were much smaller in number and generally did not have the level of academic attainment of the High Church historians influenced by the Tractarians. Because of these two factors, they were ultimately unable to monopolize the popular publishing market of the day with their own narratives that emphasized an English Reformation centered upon a Protestant religion and a rejection of the old Roman Catholic religion.

While the dates that bookend this essay are arbitrary, they do stake out significant points that are worth considering as a sort of beginning and closing, even though the process described here spanned a much greater space of time. While the publication and success of William Stubbs' *Constitutional History of England* in 1874 represented a vindication of the Tractarian view of English history, it is more important to note that at the time it amounted to the beginning of a major shift in historical thinking about the Church of England. It was from these three large volumes that the events leading to the Tractarian portrayal of the English constitution becoming the English portrayal of the English constitution, unfolded. It is from the solid foundation of the *Constitutional History of England* that the next several generations of High Church historians built the imposing meta-narrative of the continuity of the Church of England and refashioned the medieval Church of England as the Church of England in the nineteenth century. Similarly, the *Report of the Archbishops' Committee on Church and State* issued in 1916, stemming from a committee commissioned by the Representative Church Council to consider the desirability of greater spiritual independence for the Church of England, marked a significant move away from the High Church continuity theory even as it proposed a meta-narrative of the history of the Church of England that relied heavily on the work of Stubbs.

Change and Transformation

PROFESSIONALIZATION AND THE HIGH CHURCH HISTORIANS

It is well known that the Tractarians set in motion the wheels that led to a radical reorientation of the Church of England with regard to worship, ecclesiology, and theology.[1] The extent to which disciples of the Tractarian movement cultivated a professional historiography for English universities, and recast the historiography of the Church of England and the English nation, has received little detailed attention.[2] While the early leadership of the Tractarian movement, particularly John Henry Newman, encouraged young students to research and publish on the lives of the medieval English and Irish saints this same leadership had little interest in the process of professionalizing historical research.[3] Primarily from the 1850s, however, a substantial number of admirers and disciples of the Tractarians became enthusiastic about the professionalization of historiographical writing and research that German writers had cultivated and sought to replicate this new model for the elucidation of England's ancient and medieval past. Some of these figures, first and foremost being William Stubbs, E.A. Freeman, and Mandell Creighton, were considered then and now to be pioneers and were quickly enshrined in the Anglo-American historiographical canon.[4] A substantial host of High Church writers, such as William Bright, R.W. Church, Walter Hook, G.G. Perry, and J.S. Brewer, just to name a handful, may not have stood the test of time but were considered to be acclaimed historians by their peers inside and outside of High Church circles.[5]

The extent to which these writers saw their mission as one of encouraging greater historiographical professionalization and excellence varied. For instance, probably the main reason why historians like Stubbs,

---

1. For the most up to date overviews of the Tractarians see Peter Nockles, *The Oxford Movement in Context: Anglican High Churchmanship, 1760–1857*, Cambridge, 1994; Frank M. Turner, *John Henry Newman: The Challenge to Evangelical Religion*, New Haven, 2002.

2. For a detailed overview of the High Church impact on the development of professional historiography see Nathan D. Wolfe, "Mobilizing Historiography: The English High Church Historians, 1888–1906," PhD diss., University of St. Michael's College, 2010.

3. Mark Pattison, *Memoirs*, London, 1885, 90–93; Herbert Paul, *The Life of Froude*, London, 1905, 32–35.

4. For general assessments of these three historians see James Covert, *A Victorian Marriage: Mandell and Louise Creighton*, London, 2000; J. W. Burrow, *A Liberal Descent: Victorian Historians and the English Past*, Cambridge, 1981; James Campbell, *Stubbs and the English State*, Reading, Berkshire, 1989.

5. Wolfe, "Mobilizing Historiography," 16–21.

Nathan D. Wolfe *Waning of Protestantism in the Anglican Imagination*

Freeman, and Creighton have been described as pioneers of historiography, while dogged historians like Brewer and Hook are at best footnotes in the history of historiogaphy, is precisely because they worked to cultivate a historiographical profession that would nurture students and the publication of books of history for generations. Going through the citations and authorities listed in these histories it is clear that those less professional High Church historians—often men and women without the benefit of university educations—were keenly wedded to those historians like Stubbs who could provide the shelter of the authority of international renown within the European and North American historiograpical communities.[6]

What is clear is that High Church writers were key figures in the early creation of a professional and rigorous historical-critical tradition for English historiography. The key figure on the professorial side at Oxford with regard to the creation of the School of Modern History was the High Church writer Montagu Burrows.[7] While he did not work alone, Mandell Creighton was clearly the leading figure in pushing the tutors association to develop inter-collegial co-operation so that students from the various colleges could attend lectures at colleges of which they were not students.[8] The net result was a functional and self-replicating history department for Oxford with a board that was dominated by High Church writers.[9] Creighton then went on to Cambridge as the first Dixie Professor of Ecclesiastical History, a move that was crucial for cementing the future existence of the history department there and, at least for a time, enshrining the study of ecclesiastical history within the history department rather than the theology department.[10]

High Church writers were no less decisive within the realm of publishing books on history. Stubbs' *Constitutional History of England* and

---

6. For examples of histories relying on the name of Stubbs to confer historiographical proficiency see C. Arthur Lane, *Illustrated Notes on English Church History*, 2 vols., London, 1886; E. L. Cutts, *Turning Points of English Church History*, London, 1874.

7. Peter R.H. Slee, *Learning and a Liberal Education: The Study of Modern History in the Universities of Oxford, Cambridge and Manchester, 1800–1914*, Manchester, 1986, 86–88; Montagu Burrows, *Autobiography of Montagu Burrows*, London, 1908, 208–11.

8. Louise Creighton, *Life and Letters of Mandell Creighton, sometime Bishop of London*, 2 vols., London, 1904, i, 60–61; "Mandell Creighton," *Quarterly Review* 193:386 (1901) 588.

9. Wolfe "Mobilizing Historiogaphy," 29–30.

10. Slee, *Learning and a Liberal Education*, 36, 56–58, 77; H.M. Gwatkin to Mandell Creighton, May 18, 1884, Gwatkin Papers, Emmanuel College, Cambridge; Mandell Creighton to H. M. Gwatkin, July 16, 1884, Gwatkin Papers, Emmanuel College, Cambridge; Mandell Creighton to Oscar Browning, Dec. 9, 1887, OB MSS, King's College Record Office, King's College, Cambridge.

Freeman's *Norman Conquest* were the center pieces of the reading component for students of history at Oxford.[11] Creighton continued to be transformational with his publishing success the *History of the Papacy*.[12] Both he and his wife Louise Creighton edited several renowned series' for Longmans, the *Epochs of English History, Epochs of Church History* and *Highways of History*. Mandell Creighton was also the first editor of the *English Historical Review*. As the Macmillan family entered upon its quest to become the finest publisher of world history, English history, and of the history of the Church of England, E.A. Freeman pulled together a group of his daughters' friends to write histories distilling the science of historiography for children.[13] When Macmillan tapped the High Church historian W.R.W. Stephens to edit their general history of the Church of England, the *History of the English Church*, Stephens chose an eclectic group of High Church writers to complete the work.[14] Perhaps most importantly, the main writer of Readers Reports on religion for Macmillan was the High Church writer Frederic Relton. While Relton was not biased against writers who wrote from a categorically Protestant perspective, he did ensure that religious histories of England published by Macmillan were of the High Church mold.[15]

Following in the wake of the first generation of High Church historians a substantial host of students eagerly picked up on the meta-narrative of continuity proposed by writers like Stubbs and Freeman.[16] Two former tutors at Keble College, D. J. Medley and H. O. Wakeman followed Stubbs in providing Oxford graduates with standard texts on the constitutional history of England that were decidedly High Church, at least with regards to the portions of these volumes dealing with the history of the Church of England.[17] When Archbishop Benson moved to organize the Lambeth-

---

11 One Oxford tutor, A. L. Smith, taught a course called "Steps to Stubbs" to students preparing for the honors degree in Modern History: Slee, *Learning and a Liberal Education*, 102–6.

12. Mandell Creighton, *A History of the Papacy from the Great Schism to the Sack of Rome*, 6 vols., London, 1882–94.

13. Leslie Howsam, "Academic Discipline or Literary Genre?': The Establishment of Boundaries in Historical Writing," *Victorian Literature and Culture* 32 (2004) 534–42.

14. These were William Hunt, W. R. W. Stephens, W. W. Capes, James Gairdner, W. H. Frere, W. H. Hutton, J. H. Overton and F. W. Cornish.

15. For examples see Frederic Relton to Macmillan, July 21, 1899, "Report on the Divine Protestantism," Macmillan Archive, British Library, MCCIV, 55989, 86–87; Relton to Macmillan, Feb. 28, 1902 "Report on Neil and Wight's Protestant Dictionary," Macmillan Archive, MCCIV, 126–128.

16. For a relatively complete list of these historians active in the last half of the nineteenth-century see appendix in Wolfe, "Mobilizing Historiography," 228–36.

17. H. O. Wakeman and Arthur Hassall, eds., *Essays Introductory to the Study of*

sanctioned Church Historical Society (CHS), the various writers employed all worked within the High Church tradition and the first two presidents of the CHS were Mandell Creighton and William Stubbs.[18] In the realm of 'Church Defence' and adult education the Church Defence Institute (CDI) rested heavily on Stubbs in its historiographical skirmishes with organizations like the Liberation Society and the Catholic Truth Society (CTS).[19] Two writers from the Church Defence Institute, C. Arthur Land and G.F.E. Nye, were particularly effective with Lane's Magic Lantern slide lectures drawing upwards of one million attendees and Nye selling over 450,000 copies of his various pamphlets and shorter books priced for a popular market.[20]

While their motivations for writing history and their levels of historiographical sophistication varied wildly, all of these High Church writers shared a common concern to present a Catholic articulation of the history of the English nation and the Church of England. High Church historians used history to settle long disputed points regarding the theology and ecclesiology of the Church of England. For instance, the doctrinal basis of baptismal regeneration was reinforced through historiographical analysis.[21] While there was still much dispute amongst the High Church historians regarding the nature of the eucharist, all agreed that memorialist theories were to be rejected in favor of some form of the real presence.[22]

High Church historians were not only accomplished in cultivating a body of professional students of history, they also had substantial success engaging popular audiences. A search of newspapers and journals marketed to Church of England audiences shows that High Church historians clearly

---

English Constitutional History, London: Longmans, 1887; D. J. Medley, *A Student's Manual of English Constitutional History*, Oxford, 1894.

18. Wolfe, "Mobilizing Historiography," 69–74.

19. "The Bishop of Oxford on the Publications of the Church Defence Institution—C.D.I. No. 164," published in Church Defence Institution, *The Church Defence Handy Volume, Containing the Leaflets of the Institution. Together with Papers, Speeches and Statistics by Bishops, Eminent Statesmen, Members of Parliament and Others*, 12th ed., London, 1895.

20. For statistics on the sales of Nye's books see *Church Times*, vol. 39, March 11, 1898, 277; the frontispiece of G. H. F. Nye, *The Church and Her Story*, London, 1894; for Lane's lecture tour see C. Arthur Lane to Edward Benson, Sept. 22, 1894, Benson Papers, Lambeth Palace Library, 129ff., 47–48.

21. H. O. Wakeman, *An Introduction to the History of the Church of England from the Earliest Times to the Present*, London, 1896, 353–54, 382–83, 442, 480–81; W. H. Hutton, *A Short History of the Church in Great Britain*, London, 1900, 218–19, 251, 274–75.

22. Disagreement on the issue became heated for a time when Wakeman concluded that transubstantiation was the medieval definition of the doctrine in England: Wakeman, *Introduction*, 254, 282–84.

fired-up the imagination of the Church of England. For example, the *Church Family Newspaper*, which was the second largest circulating Church paper behind the High Church *Church Times*, clearly supported the High Church historians even as it warned against the threat of advanced High Church ritualism.[23] The *Church Family Newspaper* billed itself as a moderate centrist paper friendly to all parties, although it is clear that the editors did not want to market the paper to the most extreme High Church, liberal, and Evangelical Anglicans.[24] Similarly, the *National Church*, a paper created to defend the established position of the Church of England, used the High Church continuity theory as the bedrock for debate against the Liberation Society.[25] High Church papers like the *Church Times* and *Guardian* went even further reviewing virtually every volume of history produced by the High Church historians and using the books for detailed editorials and articles.[26]

REVIVAL OF THE CONTINUITY THEORY

The main narrative move of the High Church historians was to revive and refine the old continuity theory proliferated by historians and theologians employed by the governments of Henry VIII, Edward VI, and Elizabeth.[27] The continuity theory was resurrected in the seventeenth and eighteenth centuries, primarily by Peter Heylin and Jeremy Collier, but had mainly become neglected by the beginning of the nineteenth century, largely retaining the legal-institutional aspect of continuity for historians of the Church

---

23. See in particular the series titled "Continuity of the English Church," "Continuity of the English Church—No. 1," *Church Family Newspaper*, vol. I, Sept. 28, 1894, 532; "Continuity of the English Church—No. 2," *Church Family Newspaper*, vol. I, Oct. 5, 1894, 548; "Continuity of the English Church—No. 3," *Church Family Newspaper*, vol. I, Oct. 12, 1894, 564.

24. "To Moderate Churchmen, both Clergy and Laity," *Church Family Newspaper*, vol. VI, Oct. 6, 1899, 561.

25. *The National Church*, vol. XXXV, March 15, 1906, 78; *The National Church*, vol. XXXV, July 16, 1906, 183.

26. See, for example, the series of articles in *Church Times* to commemorate the Augustine mission in 1897: "The Coming of St. Augustine," *Church Times*, vol. 37, May 7, 1897, 549–50; "The Coming of St. Augustine," *Church Times*, vol. 37, May 14, 1897, 581–82; "The Coming of St. Augustine," *Church Times*, vol. 37, May 21, 1897, 613–14; "The Coming of St. Augustine," *Church Times*, vol. 37, May 28, 1897, 642–43.

27. For Protestant efforts to create a type of continuity of identity during the Reformation see Felicity Heal, "Appropriating History: Catholic and Protestant Polemics and the National Past" in Paulina Kewes, ed., *The Uses of History in Early Modern England*, San Marino, CA, 2006.

of England.[28] The version of the continuity theory adapted by High Church historians in the later half of the nineteenth century had three main new features. Firstly, the new version was largely uniform and cohesive with little differentiation. Secondly, it radically minimized the changes at the Reformation and thus provided a medieval Church of England that was remarkably similar to the Victorian Church of England. Thirdly, it was preoccupied with proving the independent government of the Church of England from the Church of Rome while at the same time readily admitting that the Church of Rome had given a great gift to the English people through the mission of St. Augustine.

The new proponents of the continuity theory influenced by William Stubbs held that the Church of England stretched back into the heptarchic era of Anglo-Saxon history and retained not only an institutional continuity but also a continuity of identity:

> So long as the heptarchic kingdoms lasted, each having its witenagemot, there was no attempt at general organization even for cases of the greatest emergency, except the ecclesiastical. The provincial or family tie was as strong as ever, and although the gens Anglorum had learned to recognize itself under one collective name as early as the time of Augustine, it was only on the ancient lines that any power of organization was developed until the Church was strong enough to form a national union.[29]

They argued that the ancient Church of England was not only the same institution as the one in their own day, but was also the same organic body, developing over time much as an animal body or plant life might develop, up to the present in which the historian wrote his or her narrative.[30] C. Arthur Lane summed up the High Church position concisely: "England was a Church before England was a kingdom."[31] Before the Tractarian-influenced High Church historians arrived on the scene there was much disagreement amongst English writers regarding the *terminus a quo* of the Church of England. Some looked back to the foggy period of Romano-British Christianity for the beginning of the Church of England by appealing to stories of the

---

28. Andrew Starkie, "Contested Histories of the English Church: Gilbert Burnet and Jeremy Collier," in Kewes, ed., *The Uses of History*.

29. William Stubbs, *Constitutional History of England in its Origin and Development*, 3 vols., Oxford, 1874, i, 121.

30. For a discussion of these metaphors in Stubbs' *Constitutional History* see Campbell, *Stubbs and the English State*, 6; Burrow, *A Liberal Descent*, 145.

31. C. Arthur Lane, *Syllabus of Six Illustrated Lectures on English Church History*, London, 1888, 28.

Change and Transformation

missionary activity of Joseph of Arimathea and other figures from New Testament or Roman history.[32] However, following Stubbs, the High Church historians simplified all of this by applying an annihilationist theory of British Christianity in which the Romano-British Church was extinguished by pillaging Anglo-Saxons.[33] The defeated British peoples retreated to the margins leaving the Anglo-Saxons to their paganism. The actual beginning of the Church of England, then, was to be traced to the mission of St. Augustine of Canterbury.[34] From this starting point it was necessary to trace an unbroken line up to the present.

There were a number of narrative challenges where continuity appeared threatened or potentially broken (the English Reformation and the Interregnum were two areas that the High Church historians handled tenderly) but the overall effect was to portray a continuous Church of England that underwent very little change over its long life. When significant change was admitted, the High Church historians appealed to the proper change stemming from constitutional development.[35] This historiographical focus on the constitutional position of the Church of England was a major innovation of the High Church historians following in the wake of Stubbs' masterpiece. While High Church writers were not inexpert in the usage of theology and biblical exegesis for the articulation of their ecclesiological preoccupations, their preoccupation with the constitutional position of the Church of England gave them an advantage over their Evangelical and Roman Catholic opponents who, by the middle of the nineteenth century, were not as expert in this area of study. By demonstrating that the Church of England was in fact the originator of the English constitution and English liberty and that it had, in the anarchic age of the heptarchic kingdoms, even pre-dated the existence of the English people and English nation, High Church historians were able to identify the pre-Reformation medieval Church of England with the narrative of constitutional progress and maturation. The Church of England provided the first point of unity around which the English people and nation were born.

---

32. But pre-Tractarian High Church thought was also capable of applying the annihilationist theory and attributing the birth of the Church of England to Augustine's mission, see Robert Southey, *The Book of the Church*, 3 vols., 2nd ed., London, 1824, ii, 12–28.

33. Stubbs, *Constitutional History of England*, i, 66.

34. Ibid., 163.

35. Outside of Stubbs' *Constitutional History*, H. O. Wakeman's narration of the Church of England's backing of the reforms of Henry VIII is the fullest example of this motif: Wakeman, *Introduction*, 208–20.

Nathan D. Wolfe *Waning of Protestantism in the Anglican Imagination*

Admitting radical change to the organism of the Church of England was problematic since such an admission could imply the birth of a new church, as some Roman Catholic and Protestant Dissenters suggested happened at the Reformation with the birth of English Protestantism.[36] For the High Church historians the Church of England before the Reformation was remarkably similar to the Church of England after the Reformation and the Church of England stemming from the mission of St. Augustine was remarkably similar to the Church of England in the nineteenth century. This historiographical anachronism was difficult to challenge when dressed in the language of the sacred constitution of the English people. The clearest problem was the English Reformation and the ensuing language of "Establishment," which implied that an old church had been dissolved and a new church erected in its stead.[37] It was crucial to strike the right balance here between change and continuity and many High Church historians preferred the idea of a long and slow Reformation starting as early as the reign of Henry VII and ending with the Restoration, thus relegating Henry VIII's role to but a part of a much larger development.[38] Nevertheless, some High Church historians, confident in notions of the constitution and the royal supremacy, ascribed the Reformation to either Henry or Elizabeth. As James Gairdner wrote to S.L. Ollard:

> And yet what was done at that date was only the assertion of the Royal Supremacy (very brutally enforced, I admit, in subsequent years); and if Royal Supremacy, when it repudiated Papal jurisdiction under Henry VIII., created a breach of continuity in the Church, how could that breach be healed when Royal Supremacy restored Papal jurisdiction under Mary? Moreover, if Royal Supremacy, insisted on once more, to the exclusion of Papal jurisdiction, under Elizabeth, was in itself a fatal blow to

---

36. High Church historians referred to this argument as the "Act of Parliament theory." For the most forceful High Church retort to this theory see E.A. Freeman, *Disestablishment and Disendowment, What Are They?*, London, 1874.

37. It was important that the High Church historian, W.E. Collins, wrote the entry for the word "Establishment" in the *Encyclopædia Britannica*, see *Encyclopædia Britannica*, 10th ed., s.v. "Establishment."

38. Wakeman, *Introduction*, 258, 309-16, 377-78; W. E. Collins, *The English Reformation and its Consequences*, London, 1898, 22-23, 27-28; Hutton, *A Short History of the Church in Great Britain*, 121-141, 217-19; W. H. Hutton, *The English Reformation: A Lecture with Preface and Notes*, London, 1899, 4-5, 17-18; H. O. Wakeman, *The Reformation in Great Britain*, London, 1900, 17-21, 126-28; Malcolm MacColl, *The Reformation Settlement Examined in the Light of History and Law*, London, 1899, 120, 125-29.

the continuity of the Church, where is the remedy possible even now?[39]

To deal with this potential problem of the establishment implying the creation of a new church, the High Church historians fixated on the original constitutional independence of the Church of England from the Church of Rome because of the submission of all bodies to the person of the monarch.[40] They argued that Rome deserved thanks for sending the original mission of St. Augustine to convert the English. They also argued that the Church of England had in fact seen itself as a portion of the universal church. However, they argued that just as the eastern churches maintained national Church governments independent of Rome, so also did the English.[41] The main result of the Reformation, therefore, was the final and irrevocable assertion of the ancient right of government of the Church of England, in submission to and under the protection of the monarchy, against the claims of the Church in Rome.

REFORMATION AS THE PURGING OF THE POPES

For High Church historians the most momentous change at the Reformation was the final disavowal of any papal right of governance over the Church of England. High Church historians would generally produce a list of doctrinal changes and changes of practice stemming from the Reformation, such as a repudiation of transubstantiation in the eucharist, and substantial changes in the life of the Church of England, such as the closing of the monasteries and appropriation of monastic properties. However, these changes were nearly always minimized as not being essential or described as really beneficial and constitutional.[42]

The three-way battle between monarchs, Popes and the independently governed Church of England was *the* historical pre-occupation for High Church historians. In High Church general histories it was shown that the

39. James Gairdner to S. L. Ollard, 6 Jan., 1906, Ollard Papers, Pusey House, Oxford; Ollard requested Gairdner's permission to print this letter which can be found in "Continuity of the Church in England," *Church Times*, vol. LV, Jan. 12, 1906, 56.

40. J. S. Brewer, "The Royal Supremacy and the History of its Introduction," in J.S. Brewer, *English Studies; or, Essays in English History and Literature*, London, 1881, 299, 322–23; Walter Farquhar Hook, *Lives of the Archbishops of* Canterbury, 12 vols., London, 1861–76, v, 99–100; H. O. Wakeman, *The Royal Supremacy in England*, London, 1897.

41. E.A. Freeman, *History of the Norman Conquest, Its Causes and Results*, 6 vols., 3rd ed. rev., Oxford, 1877, i, 32; ii, 285.

42. Collins, *The English Reformation and Its Consequences*, 51–53.

faithful Church of England cultivated the proper constitutional development of English liberties by resisting the pull of power hungry monarchs and popes and thus preserving constitutional order.[43] It was made clear that the Church of England did not seek power and simply sought to protect order by working in its own sphere.[44] The Church of England was divine in origin and responsible to Christ, but as a body in England it was right and constitutional that it also submitted to the monarch. High Church historians were eager to show co-operation between the Church of England and the crown, but as the conflict with King John showed, they could portray the Church of England as capable of combining with other forces to maintain the English constitution and order over anarchy or tyranny.[45]

Not surprisingly, for High Church historians the ultimate combined effort of crown and church came in the reign of Henry VIII when it was argued that he reasserted the truly constitutional principle of the submission of the Church of England to the crown through the royal supremacy.[46] High Church historians luxuriated in the rights of the Royal Supremacy over parliament and popes. This might seem strange given the erastian implications of submission to the head of the state. However, the emphasis on the royal supremacy served an important function. From a theological perspective the royal supremacy acted as a kind of protection for the Church of England from accusations of schism at the Reformation.[47]

High Church historians were generally antagonistic towards the word "protestant" and rarely used it in their many volumes. When the word was used at all it generally pointed towards the events taking place on the Continent, largely in Germany and Switzerland. When they used the word within the context of the English Reformation they referred either to what they perceived as unconstitutional imports from Continental reformers or to the

---

43. Lane, *Illustrated Notes on English Church History*, i, 209–11; Wakeman, *Introduction*, 129–32; Wakeman and Hassall, eds., *Essays Introductory to the Study of English Constitutional History*, 297–309; W. R. W. Stephens, *The English Church from the Norman Conquest to the Accession of Edward I., 1066–1272*, London, 1901, 219–25, 331; Mandell Creighton, *The Church and the Nation: Charges and Addresses*, London, 1901, 184–85.

44. G.H.F. Nye, *A Popular Story of the Church of England*, London, 1891, 6; Creighton, *The Church and the Nation*, 9–12.

45. Wakeman, *Introduction*, 128–30.

46. A. H. Hore, *Eighteen Centuries of the Church of England*, London, 1881, 286–88; Collins, *The English Reformation and its Consequences*, 28–29, 40–41; G. F. Browne, "What Is the Catholic Church in England?," in W. E. Collins et al, *Lectures. Third Series*, London, 1898, 178–80.

47. Hore, *Eighteen Centuries of the Church of England*, 272–73.

rejection of the papal jurisdiction and Roman canon law.[48] In his history of the English Reformation, W.H. Hutton stated that the use of the word "protestant" should not be "forbidden" but he then went on to state that the word should only be understood as complementary to the word "Catholic" and that it was the latter category that was really important: "It is that Catholic history which English theologians have ever delighted to study."[49] High Church historians generally argued that the word "protestant" merely described the shedding of unconstitutional practices or religious doctrines and practices that were not apostolic.[50] They described the word as merely negative in connotation. The word 'Catholic,' however, provided a positive attribution of the doctrines and practices of the Church of England held before and retained throughout the Reformation.

ECLIPSE OF THE THEORY OF THE SUFFERING REMNANT

In the decades preceding the rise of the Tractarians, proponents of the older continuity theory generally presented a narrative in which the Church of England largely retained an *institutional* continuity across the two sides of the Reformation divide and, therefore, were willing to admit to great amounts of change regarding doctrine and practice. Even pre-Tractarian High Church writers like S.R. Maitland and Robert Southey, who held a continuity theory that was nearly as robust as the one popularized by Stubbs, and who were charitable toward the Roman Catholic Church, had reservations about Rome's influence on the medieval Church of England.[51] But most members of the Church of England working outside of High Church circles were not enthusiastic about the pre-Reformation Church of England's relationship with Rome.[52] For Evangelicals, in particular, when discussing

48. Arthur Charles Jennings, *Ecclesia Anglicana: A History of the Church of Christ in England from the Earliest Times to the Present*, London, 1882, 214–15; H. O. Wakeman, *The Church and the Puritans, 1570–1660*, London, 1887, 2–3.

49. Hutton, *The English Reformation: A Lecture with Preface and Notes*, x.

50. Hore, *Eighteen Centuries of the Church of England*, 271, 458; Jennings, *Ecclesia Anglicana*, 140–41

51. Maitland was far more charitable than Southey, see Southey, *The Book of the Church*, i, 102–3, 125, 147, 509; S.R. Maitland, *The Dark Ages; A Series of Essays Intended to Illustrate the State of Religion and Literature in the Ninth, Tenth, Eleventh and Twelfth Centuries*, London, 1844, 7–9.

52. Even some High Church contemporaries of the Tractarians had strong anti-Roman viewpoints, see Christopher Wordsworth, *Union with Rome: 'Is Not the Church of Rome the Babylon of the Apocalypse?': An Essay*, 10th ed., London, 1838. For general

the pre-Reformation Church of England the narrative focus continued to follow the old pattern of John Foxe's *Acts and Monuments* in tracing the line of descent of the suffering remnant who remained true to the faith in pre-Reformation England.[53] There were notable exceptions like Joseph Milner.[54] But it was believed by most members of the Church of England in the first third of the nineteenth century that the pre-Reformation Church England was of such a piece with the Church of Rome that it was, overall, corrupted by Rome and was, therefore, tainted by a false religion. While some proponents of this pre-Tractarian narrative followed Foxe in agreeing that the mission of St. Augustine was critical for cementing the conversion of the English, most favored some earlier and less Roman Catholic point for the origins of the Church of England.[55] Even when pre-Tractarian historians could admit that the mission of St. Augustine was important for the conversion of the Anglo-Saxons and the erection of the Church of England, it was argued that the religion brought by Augustine was either idolatrous or eventually became corrupted over time.[56] More often than not, the origins of English Christianity were sought out in the mythical apostolic missions of the Romano-British past and the history of the suffering remnant was traced from that period. This served the two-fold purpose of putting distance between England and Rome while also scouting for origins that were nearer to the age of the Apostles.

RESPONSE OF EVANGELICAL ANGLICANS, ROMAN CATHOLICS AND MAITLAND

The overall response to the new High Church continuity narrative was robust but scattered. Those who worked together to challenge the High Church front generally worked separately across theological and methodological lines. Opponents of the High Church narrative were generally historians or non-experts from the Roman Catholic Church and from the evangelical wing of

---

discussions of anti-Catholicism in England in the nineteenth century see E.R. Norman, *Anti-Catholicism in Victorian England*, London, 1968; John Wolffe, *The Protestant Crusade in Great Britain, 1829–1860*, Oxford, 1991.

53. For Foxe's conception of English continuity see Heal, "Appropriating History: Catholic and Protestant Polemics and the National Past," 114–24.

54. Joseph Milner, *The History of the Church of Christ*, 5 vols., Boston, 1809, iii, 77–91.

55. George Townsend, *Accusations of History Against the Church of Rome*, London, 1825, 25–28.

56. Milner, *The History of the Church of Christ*, iii, 197–99, 288–94; Southey, *The Book of the Church*, i, 292; 2:22.

Change and Transformation

the Church of England. On the other hand, the legal and constitutional historian F. W. Maitland, who was an agnostic, presented a formidable critique of the continuity narrative through his research into Roman canon law. Maitland's research was eagerly welcomed by Roman Catholic and Evangelical opponents of the High Church position. All of these writers attacked the High Church continuity narrative out of quite distinct and, indeed, opposite motives. Evangelicals writing from within the Church of England feared a High Church turn toward Roman Catholicism, Roman Catholics prayed for a restoration of the ancient Roman Catholic faith in England, and Maitland sought to make the intricacies of constitutional law known through historiographical methodology. However, all agreed that at the Reformation one continuity was broken and another created because of the entrenchment of a new Protestant religion within the institution of the Church of England.

The main Evangelical writers in England who proposed alternative models to the continuity theory were J. Horace Round, J.T. Tomlinson, C. R. L. Fletcher, and Charles Hole. In Canada, Dyson Hague and J.P. Sheraton, both of Wycliffe College, Toronto, worked in the same direction, but neither claimed historical expertise and Sheraton's work never went to print, only getting to the stage of lecture notes.[57] A particular point of interest is that some Evangelical historians who certainly had the training to present a cogent historiographical refutation of the High Church continuity theory, primarily Henry Wace and Charles Oman, wrote on the medieval and reformation Church of England but largely worked in the background during the continuity debate.

The most indefatigable Evangelical opponents of the High Church historians were Round and Tomlinson. Tomlinson was not a professional historian and given that his books do not mention his having taken any degrees he most likely did not have any university education. Moreover, the majority of his work was of a strictly polemical nature as a member of the Church Association. For present purposes, the main significance of Tomlinson is that he was a tireless and prolific antagonist writing against Stubbs and other High Church historians in dozens of book reviews, pamphlets and even a large book, and yet the High Church historians took no notice of his work and never saw any reason to reply to his polemics.[58] Furthermore,

---

57. For Sheraton's unpublished papers regarding the continuity theory see: Wycliffe College, Toronto: Sheraton Papers, Box 3, series 2, 3–13 Historical Works, "The True Anglican Position."

58. J. T. Tomlinson, *The 'Legal History' of Canon Stubbs being the Basis of the New Scheme of Ecclesiastical Courts Proposed by the Royal Commissioners of 1881–1883*, London, 1884; *Collected Tracts on Ritual Edited or Written by J. T. Tomlinson*, 2 vols., London, n.d.

he was a solitary voice working for a Church Association that did not utilize historical argument to any great extent. The CDI alone employed more writers to publish in the area of history than the Church Association.[59]

Round, on the other hand, was an Oxford trained historian from Balliol College who had studied under Stubbs. The popular literary magazines of the day, as well as the strictly scholarly publications in the discipline of professional history, were wide open to his pen. Round kept a strict demarcation between his professional historical research (which was mainly in the areas of early feudalism, genealogy, and local history) and his polemical works in the political arena or on the Church of England. In the realm of polemics Round was ill-tempered and did not know how to let an argument drop and this proved to be the case as he endeavored to crush the continuity theory.

Round entered the debate regarding the continuity theory in 1898. Ostensibly, he was responding to High Church book reviews of Gilbert Child's *Church and State Under the Tudors* in 1890.[60] That he waited so long to reply after the publication of Child's book suggests that he had other reasons for entering the field. It is clear from his first essay in the debate that he was upset about recent complaints in parliament about High Church histories written by Nye and Wakeman that were used in the public schools.[61] Round had a much better grasp of the scope of the High Church historiography than Child did and he knew individual High Church historians well or by reputation.[62] Given the complaints in parliament and Round's familiarity with the writers involved it is not surprising, then, that Round chose Nye and Wakeman as his initial targets. Round was concerned that historiography was being manipulated to defend theological positions. Like the aforementioned parliamentarians, Round believed that a falsification of history was becoming institutionalized in England as "our schools are flooded, through the agency of the clergy, under the guise of faithful history, with treatises in which notorious facts are either ignored or explained away."[63] He argued that books such as those written by Nye and Wakeman had two main purposes. The first was to use history to defend the established posi-

---

59. The main historians employed by the CDI were C. Arthur Lane, E. L. Cutts, and G. H. F. Nye.

60. Gilbert Child, *Church and State under the Tudors*, London, 1890; "Review of Church and State under the Tudors," *Guardian*, vol. XLV, Sept. 17, 1890, 1448; Gilbert Child, "The Present Position of the High Church Party," *Contemporary Review* 62 (1892) 737–41.

61. *Parliamentary Debates*, 4th series, vol. 68 (1898), col. 111.

62. J. Horace Round, "Popular Church History," *Contemporary Review* 74 (1898) 343, 346–50.

63. Ibid., 335.

tion of the Church of England from groups like the Liberationists, an object that Round sympathized with as he was also a member of the Church of England who supported the establishment. The second was to misrepresent the constitutional position of the royal supremacy so as to nullify parliament's role in legislating for the Church of England in the present:

> Two issues, entirely distinct, have been willfully and systematically confused, with a definite object in view. It is obvious that the claim that the Church of England is a branch of the 'Holy Catholic Church,' coeval with Christianity itself, would be in no way affected if the former were 'disestablished and disendowed,' by the action of the State, to-morrow. It is no less certain that her position as the state or National Church, with all the endowments she possesses in right of that position, are hers only so long as she remains within the four corners of Acts of Parliament.[64]

Round spent most of his space in the essay driving home the theme that continuity was broken at the time of the Reformation and that the only position of continuity that could be maintained was the continuity of the Church of England since the reign of Elizabeth. This was contrary to Nye's and Wakeman's books that offered representative High Church outlines detailing the founding of the state by the Church of England, the co-equal position of church and state without mingling of spheres until the unconstitutional interference of the popes following the Norman Conquest and the antiquity of the royal supremacy prior to the Reformation.[65] Round argued that the true historical relation of the Church of England to the state was one in which the Church of England had to respect the wishes of parliament and that trying to subvert the authority of parliament in the present, through the continuity argument, would in fact increase the chances of disestablishment: "Everything, in fact, is sacrificed to the great 'continuity' juggle, the confusion between the legal and institutional, and the doctrinal continuity of the Church."[66] By the end of the essay, however, Round showed that his interest in combating the continuity argument was just as theological as Nye's and Wakeman's efforts to defend it. Round noted Wakeman's statement that the true historical interpretation of the High Church revival of the nineteenth century was "the restoration of the Church of England to the position which

---

64. Ibid., 336.

65. Nye, *The Church and Her Story*, 5, 53, 67, 82–83, 100, 107, 215; Nye, *Popular Story of the Church of England*, 6; Wakeman, *Introduction*, 34–35, 84–86, 92–97, 107–8, 119–38, 307–11, 315–24.

66. Round, "Popular Church History," 341.

it held when Edward VI came to the throne."[67] Round went on to repeat William Harcourt's hyperbolic statement from a recently written series of articles in the *Times* that the Church of England would, if it acceded to the wishes of High Churchmen, "have everything here except the Pope."[68] He also paraphrased F.W. Farrar's argument from an earlier essay printed in the *Contemporary Review* in a debate with the High Church writer W.J. Knox-Little that ritualists wanted "the overthrow of the Reformation."[69] Round seems to have been gripped by the same notions of continuity and polarity as the High Church historians, but his understanding of continuity started in the sixteenth century and was one in which members of the Church of England could only be described as Protestant.[70]

High Churchmen were quite enthusiastic about the opportunity provided by Round's article. The *Church Times* was confident that when either Wakeman or Nye answered Round in the *Contemporary Review* they would trounce him and would be more polite in the bargain.[71] Only Nye replied and he was to prove a disappointment to the editor of *Church Times*.[72] As a member of the CDI, Nye was trained specifically to engage in polemical discourse, but the general patriotic populist narrative that had proven so successful in his books and pamphlets proved unsuccessful when debating a professional historian like Round. Much of Nye's limited space was taken up with petty details meant to make Round look mean and foolish. Nye's key argument was that the position of continuity maintained in his books must be an accurate historical fact because the books themselves had sold well, the bishops liked them and, most importantly, Lightfoot and Stubbs as professional historians had praised the books.[73] Aside from this, Nye simply restated his position, but in a condensed form, that the Church of England was older than the state, was Catholic but that the popes unconstitutionally

---

67. Wakeman, *Introduction*, 483. Round cited pages 492–93 from the 5th edition in 1898.

68. Harcourt attacked ritualism in a series of letters to *The Times* titled "The Crisis in the Church," which were subsequently collected and published: William Vernon Harcourt, *Lawlessness in the National Church*, London, 1899.

69. Round, "Popular Church History," 352. See also, F. W. Farrar, "Undoing the Work of the Reformation," *Contemporary Review* 64 (1893) 60–73.

70. Round, "Popular Church History," 344.

71. *Church Times*, vol. 39, Sept. 9, 1898, 256.

72. Wakeman did not reply as he had only recently been married and was suffering from the chronic health problems to which he unexpectedly succumbed in the following year: H. O. Wakeman to W. R. Anson, June 28, 1898, Anson Papers, All Souls College, Oxford.

73. G. H. F. Nye, "Church History for the People. A Reply," *Contemporary Review* 74 (1898) 521 and 526–27.

infringed upon the rights of the Church, and that the Church of England was the same church before and after the Reformation.[74] The *Church Times* was unhappy with Nye's reply to Round.[75]

Round's rejoinder to Nye, entitled "Church Defense," reiterated his belief that the defense of the establishment could only be served by accurate historical research, and then went on to criticize Nye for arguing that continuity must be a historical fact because the bishops had supported his books: "If his statement is historically false, all the bishops of Christendom cannot make it true."[76] Round singled out Stubbs and Creighton for the severest criticism, although he did treat his former teacher Stubbs with some care. Of Stubbs, Round simply stated that Maitland's recently published *Roman Canon Law in the Church of England* had overthrown all of Stubbs' conclusions as to the minimal reception of the canon law by the medieval Church of England.

Round's criticism of Creighton was more biting as he showed that Creighton had quoted a document once that he knew to be a forgery, and implied therefore that Creighton was not qualified to handle historical documents. Curiously, Round then went on to argue that lawyers were the professionals best suited to interpret historical material.[77] In addition to dismissing the abilities of the bishops Stubbs and Creighton as historians, Round peppered both essays with accusations against the whole bench of bishops, particularly Archbishop Edward Benson, of dishonesty, fraud and dereliction of duty in handling the question of legal ritual.[78] Round looked back nostalgically to a time when the Church of England was told what to teach by the state and noncompliant bishops were simply removed from their posts:

> The historian replies that at the Reformation there was not set up 'a new Church,' but there was established, in the language of the day, a new 'Religion' which our fathers believed to be scriptural and Apostolic, and which the old Church was compelled by the State to adopt and to teach. And those bishops who would not adopt and who declined to teach that new 'Religion' were bundled out neck and crop.[79]

Round showed a good knowledge of the High Church historiography on the relationship of the Church of England to the state and on the Reformation.

74. Ibid., 522–24.
75. *Church Times*, vol. 39, Oct. 7, 1898, 376.
76. J. Horace Round, "Church Defense," *Contemporary Review* 74 (1898) 703.
77. Ibid., 704–5.
78. Round, "Popular Church History," 353; Round, "Church Defense," 703–5 and footnote on 711.
79. Round, "Church Defense," 710.

Round also provided a solid alternative position; however, High Church writers were clearly unfazed by his articles, as there is little evidence that they even took notice of the debate. The *Church Times* simply stated: "Mr. Horace Round vigorously 'goes for' Mr. Nye in a rejoinder which seems to require to be met and answered by a more skilful controversial pen than Mr. Nye's."[80] They did not consider that Round had provided evidence to overthrow the theory of continuity. W.H. Hutton of St. John's College, Oxford, had a hand in the production of Wakeman's book, but when asked by his student, S.L. Ollard, about the debate he seemed interested in the matter, but not overly concerned with Round's attacks as he did not even bother to keep up with the debate: "No, I haven't read anything of the controversy except Round's first article. I must buy them all."[81] There is no indication from the correspondence, however, that he did buy them all. Round was approached by one publisher to collect his essays for a book to reassert the Protestant view of the Reformation. He approached F.W. Maitland and T.F. Tout to contribute to the volume, but neither was interested in the undertaking and the proposal was dropped.[82]

With the exception of Round, evangelical historians had great difficulty in even getting the attention of High Church historians. Dyson Hague wrote a comprehensive volume attacking the continuity narrative criticizing Stubbs, G.G. Perry, and a number of other writers. But his book received the same treatment of silence that Tomlinson's efforts had.[83] Henry Wace gathered Tomlinson and others to publish a collection of essays purporting to give the true meaning of the Reformation but they, likewise, were not answered.[84] Charles Hole proposed a volume of general history on the Church of England to Macmillan at some point between 1899 and 1902 but the reader report was written by the High Church historian W.R.W. Stephens who urged Macmillan not to publish it because Stubbs and R.W. Church would not have found Hole's research serious enough had they been able

---

80. *Church Times*, vol. 39, Nov. 11, 1898, 560.

81. W. H. Hutton to S. L. Ollard, (n.d), Ollard Papers: Letters of a Lifetime: W. H. Hutton to S. L. Ollard, 1893–1906, Pusey House, Oxford.

82. The proposed volume would have been entitled "The True Theory of the Reformation and its Antecedents," see J. Horace Round, *Family Origins and Other Studies*, edited with a memoir and bibliography by William Page, London, 1930, xxxii–xxxiii.

83. Dyson Hague, *The Church of England before the Reformation*, London, 1897; *The Protestantism of the Prayer Book*, London, 1893; *Wycliffe: An Historical Study*, Toronto, n.d.

84. Henry Wace, *Church and Faith: Being Essays on the Teaching of the Church of England*, Edinburgh and London, 1900; *Principles of the Reformation: Practical and Historical*, New York, 1911.

to read the manuscript.[85] The book was eventually published by Longmans, but not until 1910.[86] This was a period when Longmans was hoping to publish a general history of the Church of England to compete with Wakeman's, but Hole's volume only sold 1,500 copies of a 3,000 print run.[87]

Charles Oman and C.R.L. Fletcher were uniquely placed as Oxford academics to publish professional counter-narratives to the High Church continuity theory, but neither of the two men seemed to take any interest in the debate. Fletcher expressed reservations privately in his common place books articulating that a clear break occurred at the Reformation.[88] Fletcher's volumes are difficult to assess. His *History of England* was co-written with Rudyard Kipling and the book is lavishly illustrated. The book was marketed to children and was a great success, in spite of being banned in parts of the empire because of racist language.[89] The language is clearly tailored to children but without the historiographical sophistication Freeman sought for his series published by Macmillan. Oman's main general histories hinted at some dissatisfaction with Stubbs' meta-narrative and he characterized the Tractarians as providing a novel view of Anglican history and yet he did, ultimately, admit that the Tractarians probably worked to benefit the Church of England through their influence, even if their understanding of English church history was inaccurate.[90]

The one contemporary English Roman Catholic historian who was consistently addressed by High Church historians was Aidan Gasquet. While the High Church historians tended to ignore their Evangelical counterparts, with the exception of Round, and do not appear to have taken Evangelical histories very seriously, they did very much appreciate the work

---

85. This reader's report is clearly signed by Stephens, and it is not dated, but it has been placed into Relton's reports for 1899–1902: W. R. W. Stephens to Macmillan, (n.d.), Macmillan Archive, British Library, MCCIV, 559891, 1.

86. Charles Hole, *A Manual of English Church History*, London, 1910.

87. Longman Group Statement books, "Charles Hole's *Manual of English Church History,*" f1, Longman Group, Archive of British Publishing and Printing, University of Reading.

88. C. R. Fletcher Papers, Bodleian Library, Oxford, MS. Eng. Misc. d. 339, 17 "Some Aspects of the Early Life of England"; C. R. Fletcher Papers, Magdalen College Oxford: MC: F31/MS2—Notebooks Containing Notes on Academic Subjects, "Interleaved note Book, containing notes on Stubbs" Constitutional History: also some notes at Lectures on Edw iv—Edw vi., Vol. I, 217.

89. C. R. L. Fletcher, *School History of England*, New York, 1911; *An Introductory History of England from the Earliest Times to the Present*, 3 vols., London, 1905–9.

90. Charles Oman, *A History of England*, 3 vols., London, n.d., iii, 678–80; see also Charles Oman, *England before the Norman Conquest, being a History of the Celtic, Roman and Anglo-Saxon Periods down to the Year AD 1066*, London, 1919.

of Gasquet. In the latter half of the nineteenth century there were many histories of England published by Roman Catholic writers, but most were polemical and written by non-professional historians. One important vehicle for laying out the Roman Catholic view of English history was the CTS, and like their Evangelical Anglican counter-parts, writers for the CTS highlighted a radical break in continuity at the Reformation.[91] To counter these writers High Church writers organized under the banner of the CHS and, indeed, it can be said that the majority of CHS publications were tailored to target Roman Catholic writers who wrote of such a radical break.[92] Gasquet's books, on the other hand, were accorded a great deal of respect. For starters, Gasquet tended to avoid the polemical fireworks of a disputant such as Round. More importantly, his books highlighted the spirituality and everyday life of English Catholics just prior to and throughout the Reformation.[93] Since the High Church historians were eager to prove the real spirituality and vibrant Christianity of medieval England, Gasquet was a welcome voice. At the same time, Gasquet did highlight that the English Reformation was forced upon the people through the violence and legal manipulation of Henry VIII and his servants, but many also emphasized Henry's violence so there was common ground there as well.[94] Naturally, he did not approve of the results stemming from the Elizabethan Settlement. The result was that Gasquet's histories were written toward the purpose of a Roman Catholic revival in England in his own time. Nevertheless, the High Church historians still cited Gasquet zealously, as they tended to simply ignore the parts of Gasquet's books that implied that it was an historical normality for the government of the Church of England to submit to the government of the Church of Rome.[95]

Unlike his Roman Catholic and Evangelical counterparts, Maitland provided a critique that was essentially free of any theological, or in his case anti-theological, presuppositions. While historians have since tended to argue that Maitland and Stubbs both worked from incomplete pictures and were off the mark in many respects, at the time Maitland's *Roman*

91. Luke Rivington, *Dependence, or, the Insecurity of the Anglican Position*, London, 1889; John Morris, ed., *Historical Papers*, 5 vols., London, 1892–98.

92. See any of the essays in Collins et al, *Lectures. Third Series*; W. E. Collins et al, *Authority in Matters of Faith*, London, 1901.

93. Aidan Gasquet, *English Monastic Life*, London, 1905; *Parish Life in Medieval England*, London, 1906.

94. Aidan Gasquet, *Henry VIII and the English Monastaries: An Attempt to Illustrate the History of their Suppression*, London, 1889.

95. See James Gairdner, *Lollardy and the Reformation in England*, 4 vols., London, 1908–13, ii, 33, 59, 93, 105–6.

Change and Transformation

Canon Law had a phenomenal impact.[96] Even here, though, the majority of High Church historians seem to have not only been nonplussed by the implications of the book but even accepted much of Maitland's argument as supportive of their own position, even as Maitland stated that they were incorrect.[97] It is unclear whether they misunderstood Maitland's position or recognized Maitland's challenge and simply skipped over the commentary that undercut their theory.

Maitland's *Roman Canon Law in the Church of England* was first published in 1898, although most of the other essays had appeared elsewhere before. At the time the volume was difficult for non-specialists to obtain and was marketed to law students through a type of borrowing plan. Maitland's critique had the potential to be much more devastating to the High Church position than the polemics of historians like Round, but the High Church historians reacted much better to his criticism. Round's statement that the consensus of historians had shifted towards Maitland's interpretation of the authority of Roman canon law in English ecclesiastical courts was overdone, since Stubbs' interpretation still had adherents, although Maitland's interpretation did gain acceptance quickly.[98] Much of this seems to have been attributed at the time to his self-ascribed impartiality that was reinforced by his public disavowal of all religion, which he claimed as evidence of his lack of prejudice.[99] Maitland did not deliver polemical arguments like Child or Round; rather he conformed to the standards of historiographical discourse espoused at Cambridge and Oxford or in the *English Historical Review* while eschewing the grand narratives and teleological assumptions of historians like Stubbs and Freeman, which added to his aura of impartiality.[100] A central element of his book on Roman canon law was to show

---

96. J. W. Gray "Canon Law in England: Some Reflections on the Stubbs-Maitland Controversy" in *Studies in Church History* 3 (1966) 60.

97. W. C. E. Newbolt and Darwell Stone, *The Church of England: An Appeal to Facts and Principles*, London, 1903, 12–13; D. J. Medley, *A Student's Manual of English Constitutional History*, 3rd ed., Oxford, 1902, vi, viii–ix, xi; Walter Frere, *The English Church in the Reigns of Elizabeth and James I, 1558–1625*, London, 1904, 13–16.

98. Norman Cantor, ed., *William Stubbs on the English Constitution*, New York, 1966, 10–12.

99. In one case, the Catholic historian F. A. Gasquet argued that the unbelieving historian could act as a sort of umpire for deciding historiographical issues that protestants and catholics tended to see through their respective theological perspectives: F. A. Gasquet, *The Eve of the Reformation: Studies in the Religious Thought and Life of the English People in the Period Preceding the Rejection of the Roman Jurisdiction by Henry VIII*, New York, 1900, 446; F. W. Maitland, *Roman Canon Law in the Church of England: Six Essays*, London, 1898, vi.

100. Maitland thought that published works of constitutional history generally just emphasized conflict and were "showy." He never published this type of work, although

that Stubbs' historical appendixes written as a member of the Ecclesiastical Courts Commission were not an accurate portrayal of the reception of the canon law in England before the Reformation:

> There seems to me to be a tendency towards the confusion of two propositions. The first is this: that in England the state did not suffer the church to appropriate certain considerable portions of that wide field of jurisdiction which the canonists claimed as the heritage of ecclesiastical law. The second is this: that the English courts Christian held themselves free to accept or reject, and did in some cases reject, 'the canon law of Rome.' The truth of the first proposition no one doubts: the truth of the second seems to me exceedingly dubious.[101]

Maitland argued that the clergy of the Church of England before the Reformation accepted Roman canon law, but that the state rejected it when it was convenient: "We must not attribute to the church what is done by the state."[102] In the first essay in his book, on William Lyndwood, Maitland summed up his own position with an imaginary monologue provided by Lyndwood in which Maitland used the Lyndwood character to call the Ecclesiastical Courts commissioners heretics for denying the spiritual supremacy of the popes:

> However, I very much fear that this is not your meaning, that what you call the canon law of Rome is what I call the *jus commune* of the church, and that you are hinting that I am not bound by statutes that the popes have decreed for all the faithful. If that be so, I must tell you that your hint is not only erroneous but heretical.[103]

Maitland portrayed the Church of England not as an independent national church during the Middle Ages, but as a national church fully integrated into the larger western Catholic Church and subordinate to the center of that larger Church, which was Rome.

With regard to the state, the Church of England, like any other church, would lose out to the state in any protracted contest: " . . . and if we find,

---

a posthumous collection of his lectures, which he did not wish published, were given the title *The Constitutional History of England*. See F. W. Maitland, *The Collected Papers of Frederic William Maitland*, edited by H. A. L. Fisher, 3 vols., Cambridge, 1911, ii, 7; F. W. Maitland, *The Constitutional History of England, a Course of Lectures Delivered*, Cambridge, 1919, v–vi.

101. Maitland, *Roman Canon Law*, 51.
102. Ibid., 52.
103. Ibid., v, 1–11, 44–46.

as we easily may, that the English bishops are not persistently protesting against this usurpation, we must neither at once accuse them of neglect of duty nor at once credit them with an Anglican canon law which differs from the Roman."[104] A key evidence of this was the Statute of Provisors (1351), which High Church historians often pointed to as evidence that the state backed up the Church of England's position as an independent national church before the Reformation finally settled the issue. Maitland instead described this legislation as "anti-ecclesiastical legislation" and noted that the English bishops took no part in the enactment.[105] Like Round, Maitland believed that the Reformation broke a previous line of continuity; however, unlike Round, Maitland did not argue that a new line of continuity had been instituted. Instead he argued that the canon law had simply been surpassed by the study of civil law and the elevation of civilians to the practice of law:

> But the great breach of continuity has yet to be noted. The academic study of the canon law was prohibited. No step that Henry took was more momentous. He cut the very life thread of the old learning ... And as if this were not enough, Henry encouraged and endowed the study of 'the civil law,' and the unhallowed civilian usurped the place of the canonist on the bench.[106]

There was an *appearance* of a new type of continuity in the wake of the English Reformation, at least up through the eighteenth century, as apologists for the English state and the Church of England competing with the papacy and Catholic nations created a myth of the ancient co-equal relationship of the English state and Church: "The national ranks were to present an unbroken front to the enemy; church and state were to stand, and were always to have stood, shoulder to shoulder."[107] Maitland did not explicitly place Stubbs' work with the Ecclesiastical Courts Commission within this apologetic tradition, but it is clear that Maitland assumed that Stubbs' historical appendixes laid out the same general theory of the relationship of the Church of England to the state through the continuity theory.

---

104. Ibid., 56–57.
105. Ibid., 69.
106. Ibid., 92.
107. Ibid., 85.

Nathan D. Wolfe *Waning of Protestantism in the Anglican Imagination*

HIGH CHURCH HISTORIANS AND THE ENGLISH READING MARKET

The primary reason High Church success in monopolizing the popular reading market and overturning the old Protestant-centered Reformation narrative in favor of the continuity theory was the skill-set and luster of historiographical professionalization. In the field of public debate there were always a number of High Church historians with academic attainment who were trained to take on any topic and who could target any educational level of audience. At the pinnacle of historical study were the writers like Stubbs, Freeman, and Creighton who were internationally renowned and admired by their peers. If books written by Stubbs or Creighton were too complicated for less educated audiences, such as working-class readers or school-children, then writers like Wakeman, Lane, and Louise Creighton were able to enter the field and distill the more detailed analysis into something marketable to the less educated.

In an age infused with the spirit of nationalism the High Church continuity theory provided a robust defense of the national heritage. While other groups could claim that their parties or churches were the true bearers of Englishness or of constitutional liberty or of providential history, the High Church historians developed a seamless narrative that combined all of these elements.[108] Similarly, they were free to positively assess any of the old heroes and saints from England's rich Christian past. They received particular support here because their arguments were crucial for "church defense." Whereas the narrative of the suffering remnant and the Act of Parliament theory both seemed in many ways to play into the hands of the Dissenters, by suggesting that the Church of England was in fact established at the Reformation and therefore founded at a particular point of a bloody age from the theft of Roman Catholic property, the High Church continuity narrative described a Church of England that seemed to transcend time and to grow as a body with the English people. Finally, while High Church historians were capable of a great admiration for the office of the papacy, they nevertheless held impeccable credentials as English patriots dedicated to an independent Church of England. Attributions by their opponents of clandestine "Romanism" tended to fall flat because the High Church historians really were devoted to the Church of England.

---

108. Robert Colls has argued that from 1880 to 1920 liberal historians "misconceived the Middle Ages" and turned historical characters such as Simon de Montfort into "honorary liberals" in order to show the "continuity" of English liberalism, Robert Colls and Philip Dodd, "Englishness and the Political Culture," in Robert Colls and Philip Dodd, eds., *Englishness: Politics and Culture, 1880–1920*, London, 1986, 36–38.

Change and Transformation

While the High Church continuity theory provided a robust defense of the national heritage the various Protestant and Roman Catholic narratives provided an uncongenial dissection of the national past. The continuity theory brought all of the periods of English history into a more or less harmonious narrative of constant constitutional development. Protestants and Roman Catholics were forced to paint large swathes of English history as constitutionally improper or as aberrations from some greater providential plan. While their narratives might have made great claims regarding the genius of Englishness they, nevertheless, were forced to admit that much of England's history was inglorious. This was a tough sell to an English reading public that was enthusiastic about England's past.

A major problem seems to have been that few proponents of the old Reformation narrative really understood the ramifications of the new continuity theory or of the professional heights to which High Church historians had ascended in the world of historical writing. Although Maitland was probably aware of these dynamics we can only say for sure that Round understood the situation.

CONCLUSION

The momentum that the High Church historians built up following the publication of Stubbs' *Constitutional History* carried them well into the first two decades of the twentieth century. Of all the High Church histories, none was to have staying power with the Church of England reading market as did H.O. Wakeman's *Introduction*. First published in 1896 it went through three reprints and editions in that year alone and a total of five by the end of 1897. The volume continued to be regularly reprinted and updated by S.L. Ollard well into the twentieth century until it was surpassed by J.R.H. Moorman's standard general history *A History of the Church of England* in 1953.[109] Although intended for schools, it is clear that the book was a success for Wakeman with the popular reading market.[110]

While all seemed well an unforeseen challenge was presented with the *Report of the Archbishops' Committee on Church and State* issued in 1916. Stemming from a committee commissioned by the Representative Church Council the *Report* was intended to express the findings of the commission with regard to the question of the desirability of greater spiritual

---

109. J. R. H. Moorman, *A History of the Church of England*, London, 1953.

110. H. O. Wakeman to W. R. Anson, 10 March, 1893, Anson Papers, All Souls College, Oxford; Septimus Rivington, *The Publishing Family of Rivington*, London, 1919, 171–72.

independence for the Church of England. The *Report* upheld Stubbs' continuity theory in most respects.[111] However, it also marked a significant move away from one important feature of the continuity theory by concluding that, as a matter of constitutional history, parliament was the ultimate legislator for the Church. But the *Report* then went on to state that parliament was no longer fitted for this role as it was a body too busy to consider most matters of the Church of England, and the report thus concluded: "We recommend, therefore, the formation of a Church Council which shall have power to legislate on ecclesiastical affairs, subject to constitutional safeguards."[112] The state would have the right of veto and the Church of England could then choose to assert its independent rights by opting for disestablishment. Laying out that the state would always theoretically be in control did not run against the High Church historiography, but this unequivocal assertion of parliament's constitutional role to legislate for the Church of England with no mention of the mediation of the royal supremacy was rarely if ever noted as the true constitutional position by High Church historians. More importantly, for our purposes, this conclusion was a statement that machinery would be laid out with the potential to result in the Church of England and the nation embarking upon separate paths in the future. This was anathema to the High Church conception of the continuity theory laid out in the last quarter of the nineteenth century, but it does not appear to have been noticed by historians at the time and the High Church emphasis on the Church of England began to give way in the 1920s to an emphasis on Anglicanism.

Meanwhile, a separate development was taking place in the universities and the publishing world. As High Church writers turned toward the Anglican view of history a further wedge was driven between this and the mainstream view of history as Anglican Evangelicals, non-Anglican Protestants, Roman Catholics, and writers without any explicit religious affiliation began to enter the profession in ever greater numbers and began publishing on national history and the history of the Church of England. While historians writing from within the High Church tradition, like Moorman, would continue to graduate from the universities they would no longer enjoy the central place in the discipline they had worked so successfully to cultivate.

---

111. *Report of the Archbishops' Committee on Church and State*, London, 1916, 7–8, 11–12, 31, 209.

112. Ibid., 40 and 49.

8

Reforming Ecclesiastical Self-Government Within the Establishment
The Enabling Act, 1919

GARY W. GRABER

THE CHURCH OF ENGLAND had, since the mid-sixteenth century, been governed by Acts of Uniformity. The relationship between church and state was set upon a legal system that had last been revised in 1662. One of the provisions of the establishment was the supremacy of parliament as its guardian. The Church could not unilaterally modify the terms of this establishment, effectively meaning that the Church could not change its doctrine, worship, or the way in which it operated under the law without parliament enacting such changes.[1] This mechanism was modified

---

1. "The Prayer Book and the Articles being recognized by statute, the consent of Parliament is necessary to any change in the statements of doctrine or form of worship of the Church of England. The same is true as to every part of the legal, constitutional and administrative fabric of the Church which is at present time regulated by statute law. The Convocations do not depend on any statute for their constitution, but on custom. To alter the custom it would appear necessary to have the assent of Parliament as well as of the Convocations ... The church courts administer the ecclesiastical law, which is recognized as part of the law of the land ... [A]ny litigant who complains of lack of justice in the archbishop's court may appeal to the King, that is, to the Judicial

when the Enabling Act was passed by parliament in 1919. It represented the most significant and most far-reaching revision in how the Church of England was governed since the seventeenth century.

What conditions made such a development possible? We may describe two of the most influential developments that provided the foundation for what became the Enabling Act. These are, the Royal Commission on Ecclesiastical Discipline whose *Report* was published in 1906, and the Archbishops' Committee on Church and State, whose *Report* was issued ten years later, in 1916. Each of these gave recommendations for solving specific problems that were facing the Church of England. They provide the historical context for the reforming legislation that was passed in 1919.

ROYAL COMMISSION ON ECCLESIASTICAL DISCIPLINE, 1904-1906

Toward the end of the nineteenth century, the legislative mechanism of the Church of England had become increasingly strained. The most prominent issue was the ritualistic controversy that enveloped the Church in the late nineteenth century.[2] Anglo-Catholic ceremonial innovations—which stretched or ignored statutory rubrics—were notoriously difficult to regulate, and this made ecclesiastical discipline difficult to enforce. The Public Worship Regulation Act was passed in 1874 to deal with this problem but it was, practically speaking, a failure. The courts had ruled on what the limits of liturgical law were, but these were ignored by those who did not accept the jurisdiction of state courts in spiritual matters. Seventeenth-century rubrics did not, to the "lawless" section of high church Anglican ministers, reflect the fullness of pre-Reformation "Catholic" practice, so they could, for the sake of spiritual principle, be ignored or modified by individual priests. A stalemate over how the complex issue might be resolved ensued, and this state lasted for decades.

Committee of Privy Council. The church courts are controlled in their procedure and practice by numerous Acts of Parliament." *Report of the Archbishops' Committee on Church & State*, London, 1916, 27. See also Chapter III of the *Report*, titled "Working of the Present System of Church Government," which is an excellent overview on the relationship of the Church and the State during the period. See also P. T. Marsh, *The Victorian Church in Decline: Archbishop Tait and the Church of England, 1868-1882*, London, 1969, 120.

2. See James Bentley, *Ritualism and Politics in Victorian Britain: The Attempt to Legislate for Belief*, Oxford, 1978; Gary Graber, *Ritual Legislation in the Victorian Church of England: Antecedents and Passage of the Public Worship Regulation Act, 1874*, Lewiston, NY, 1993; Nigel Yates, *Anglican Ritualism in Victorian Britain, 1830-1910*, Oxford, 1999.

Change and Transformation

While ritualistic practices had been on the rise since the 1860s, even at the turn of the century they were still confined to a minority of parishes. Nevertheless, this minority of parishes was still numerous enough, and growing quickly enough, to create grave concern among the Protestant majority.[3] Entering the twentieth century, current law and ecclesiastical courts were unable to deal effectively with these liturgical innovators. Bishops, with the memory of failed ritual prosecutions of the recent past, were loath to take on the issue again, and routinely vetoed any ceremonial suit that was lodged, and were reduced to issuing godly admonitions to obey the law which, more often than not, went unheeded.[4] Anti-ritualists therefore made application to parliament again and again to enact new laws to get around the episcopal veto, but the legislature was reluctant to step into that controversial arena.[5]

Early in the twentieth century, there was increased agitation against the lack of clerical discipline, and momentum for parliamentary action grew. In 1904, MPs were feeling political pressure to act. The prime minister, Arthur Balfour, warned Randall Davidson, the new archbishop of Canterbury, that unless something were done, and quickly, the house would be powerless to resist some sort of action.[6] The premier believed that appointing a parliamentary select committee to investigate ecclesiastical discipline was the way forward. However, such an investigation, under the jurisdiction of parliament, would almost certainly be rejected by the very body of clergy that would be the subject of its inquiry and findings. Additionally, no one relished the thought of bishops being cross-examined by members of

---

3. Statistics from 1902 saw eucharistic vestments used in 11%, altar lights in 27%, the mixed chalice in 26%, incense in 2%, the eastward position in 40%, and daily Holy Communion in 3% of the approximately 14,000 Anglican churches in England and Wales. *Tourist's Church Guide*, London: English Church Union, 1902.

4. The episcopal veto was a provision of the Public Worship Regulation Act (1874). In spite of Disraeli's claim at the time, the act had been singularly ineffective in "putting down ritualism." For details about this act, and the unfortunate trials that followed in its wake, see Bentley, *Ritualism and Politics in Victorian Britain*, Chapters V and VI.

5. Nine bills relating to the control of ritualism were introduced into parliament from 1881 to 1899; nine more were introduced in the Commons from 1900 to the formation of the Royal Commission on Ecclesiastical Discipline in 1904; a further nine were brought forward in that same house from 1905 to 1913. Gary Graber, "Worship, Ecclesiastical Discipline, and the Establishment in the Church of England, 1904–1929," ThD thesis, University of Toronto, 2007, 360–62.

6. G. K. A. Bell, *Randall Davidson: Archbishop of Canterbury*, 2 vols., London, 1935, i, 456–57. This growing feeling was summarized the previous year with the observation that the "feeling in the House in favour of drastic measures for putting down extreme Ritualism was thus shown to be substantial." *Annual Register*, London, 1903, 57.

a committee, possibly in a hostile manner, and possibly by non-Anglicans. Such a spectacle would be intolerable. Without definite action, however, there was every reason to believe that the Commons might produce legislation that further regulated worship or ecclesiastical discipline. Such secular action would undoubtedly be met with hostility from the high church wing, and might increase calls for disestablishment. To avoid these difficulties, a compromise solution of a non-partisan Royal Commission, containing an ecclesiastical element among its members, was put forward by Davidson, and agreed to by Balfour.[7]

In April 1904, the government announced the formation of the Royal Commission on Ecclesiastical Discipline. The advantage of a Royal Commission was that it could do its work without a political bias, and with a membership drawn from qualified lay people, clergy, judges, lawyers, and academics. In the event, the chair of the commission was Sir Michael Hicks Beach, former Chancellor of the Exchequer, and among its fourteen members were the Archbishop of Canterbury, the bishop of Oxford, and the Lord Chief Justice. The Commission's work would be to determine how the law was being neglected or broken, and what should be done about it. Its terms of reference make this purpose clear. It was:

> To inquire into the alleged prevalence of breaches or neglect of the law relating to the conduct of Divine Service in the Church of England and to the ornaments and fittings of Churches; and to consider the existing powers and procedures applicable to such irregularities and to make such recommendations as may be deemed requisite for dealing with the aforesaid matters.[8]

After 118 sittings spread over two years, which included the examination of 164 witnesses, and reports in rich detail of well over 500 churches noted for ceremonial breaches of the law, the Royal Commission's unanimous *Report* was published in 1906.[9] The commissioners affirmed that

---

7. Bell, *Davidson*, i, 460–61. The *Liverpool Post* opined that "few people believe that [the Royal Commission] will lead to legislation ... The great merit of the Commission is that it will tide the Government over the present difficulty." *Church Intelligencer*, 21 (April 1904) 49–50.

8. *Report of the Royal Commission on Ecclesiastical Discipline*, London, 1906, v; Bell, *Davidson*, i, 462.

9. *Report of the Royal Commission on Ecclesiastical Discipline*, 1. The evidence gathered— and the examination of expert witnesses (including 22 Bishops) on a wide variety of topics surrounding the rubrics, the law, and the practice of the English Church—was published in the three volume set called *Minutes of Evidence taken before the Royal Commission on Ecclesiastical Discipline*, 3 vols, London, 1906. As far as the number of ritualistic parishes goes, it may be noted that the commissioners recognized that their number was but a small percentage of the 14,242 churches in England and

the worship and doctrine of the established Church of England rested on the law of the land, being governed by the Acts of Uniformity. At the same time, they fundamentally found that part of the system that regulated how the Church was run, particularly with regards to its worship, was broken. With the presenting issues being the conduct of worship, ritualism, and frustration over clergy discipline, the *Report* drew two main conclusions. First, "the law of public worship is too narrow for the religious life of the present generation." Without the "power of self-adjustment" such as was possessed by the established Church of Scotland, no reform of the system had been made for over two centuries. The result was rubrics fit for seventeenth century worship were not so well suited for services in the twentieth century:

> With an adequate power of self-adjustment, we might reasonably expect that revision of the strict letter of the law would be undertaken with such due regard for the living mind of the Church as would secure the obedience of many, now dissatisfied, who desire to be loyal, and would justify the Church as a whole, in insisting on the obedience of all.[10]

Their second conclusion was that "the machinery for discipline has broken down." Although attempts had been made to deal with ritual irregularity in the recent past, the means of enforcing the law in the ecclesiastical courts were defective and unsuitable. The *Report* then stated what should be done:

> It is important that the law should be reformed, that it should admit of reasonable elasticity, and that the means of enforcing it should be improved; but above all, it is necessary that it should be obeyed. That a section of clergymen should, with however good intentions, conspicuously disobey the law, and continue to do so with impunity, is not only an offence against public order, but also a scandal to religion and a cause of weakness to the Church of England.[11]

Wales; there was no doubt "in the large majority of parishes the work of the Church is being quietly and diligently performed by clergy who are entirely loyal to the principles of the English Reformation as expressed in the Book of Common Prayer." *Report of the Royal Commission on Ecclesiastical Discipline*, 76. After producing the draft of the *Report* in 1906, Sir Lewis Dibdin, an authority on ecclesiastical law, remarked, "They'll knock this about a good deal, I'm afraid," to which the bishop of Oxford responded, "If you've ever tried to skin a hare you'll find it is uncommonly difficult to get the backbone out of it." Bell, *Davidson*, i, 469.

10. *Report of the Royal Commission on Ecclesiastical Discipline*, 75–76.

11. Ibid., 76.

The *Report* contained ten recommendations. The one that became almost the exclusive focus for the next twenty years was the second, which said that the convocations ought to prepare revisions of the rubrics of the prayer book (particularly the ornaments rubric), with a view to enactment by parliament, so as may tend to secure "the greater elasticity which a reasonable recognition of the comprehensiveness of the Church of England and of its present needs seems to demand."[12] Significantly, the third recommendation sought to amend the law so as to give "wider scope for the exercise of a regulative authority" of the Church, particularly the bishops.[13] Most of the other recommendations were anti-ritualist in nature.[14] Although the commissioners wrote that their recommendations existed as a complete scheme, and must be considered mutually dependent, in practice, the second recommendation was viewed as being logically prior to the others. That is, no serious work would be done on the other recommendations until prayer book revision was undertaken.[15] The Church was thus presented with a challenge

---

12. Ibid., 77.

13. The commission denied that the law recognized any inherent liturgical authority of a bishop (*jus liturgicum*), which, through discretion, could set aside the authority of statute law. The third recommendation sought a limited amount of such authority, though careful to say that it would have to be authorized by parliament. *Report of the Royal Commission on Ecclesiastical Discipline*, 77. See also *Minutes of Evidence taken before the Royal Commission on Ecclesiastical Discipline*, para. 14375–80, 20929, and 23462.

14. For instance, the first recommendation said that the specific Anglo-Catholic practices listed in the *Report* as being "repugnant to the doctrine of the Church of England, and certainly illegal" should be promptly made to cease (e.g. Reservation, prayers or devotions to saints, service of benediction, interpolation of prayers and ceremonies belonging to the canon of the Mass, and several others); the fourth, which said that bishops should have the authority to refuse to admit anyone who has not satisfied the bishop of his willingness to obey the law; the sixth, which said that wilful disobedience to a church court should be punished with summary removal from a benefice (thus replacing the contempt of church court penalty of prison, which currently existed);the seventh, which said that the episcopal veto (used to prevent suits from going forth) should be abolished, along with the repeal of the Publish Worship Regulation Act; and numbers eight and nine, which provided for regular inspections of churches, giving the bishop the authority to remove any ornaments or fittings placed without a faculty. Finally, the fifth recommendation dealt with reform of the ecclesiastical courts along the lines detailed by the 1883 Ecclesiastical Courts Commission, and the tenth dealt with providing machinery for creation of new dioceses. *Report of the Royal Commission on Ecclesiastical Discipline*, 76–79.

15. The years after 1906 bear this out. Most of the energy toward reform was directed toward the second recommendation. Any time a plea went out to reform the ecclesiastical courts, or to enforce the rubrics, the response was, "Yes, but we must revise the prayer book first." See Graber, "Worship, Ecclesiastical Discipline, and the Establishment in the Church of England," Chapters 2 and 3.

to rectify a deficiency. But how could this be accomplished under the present legal mechanisms?[16] This was no small problem.

GREATER CHURCH AUTONOMY

Alongside the weaknesses exposed through the ritual controversy, there was a growing recognition that the Church ought generally to have more authority to govern its own affairs. This was partly an outgrowth from the debates about the pros and cons of disestablishment, and partly arose from practical observations that the Church ought to be able to run its own spiritual affairs more effectively through increased self-government.

The movement toward greater autonomy for the national Church actually began before the Royal Commission on Ecclesiastical Discipline was established. In 1904, tentative steps towards a more church-wide, comprehensive body were taken through the formation of a Representative Church Council. The laity did not traditionally have a voice in ecclesiastical bodies, as convocation had an entirely clerical membership. To address this, the two houses of convocation began to sit jointly with a lay house to form the Representative Church Council. This council did not, however, possess any legal authority. Its significance was entirely moral, but it did provide elected lay delegates a voice. The new body consisted of approximately 700 representatives spread among three houses, bishops, clergy, and laity. Though the resolutions of the council were non-binding, it provided a vehicle for debate, and was an advance from the old method that excluded lay people entirely.[17]

Though this was a positive step for increased representation of the laity, there were other areas of dissatisfaction about how the Church was governed. In July 1913, during a debate on disestablishment in the Representative Church Council, a resolution was passed to have a committee

---

16. The high church section of the church would chafe at laws governing worship crafted by parliament, but, apart from disestablishment, which the Commission did not recommend, the church was powerless to legislate for itself.

17. For background on the Representative Church Council, see *Report of the Archbishops' Committee on Church and State*, 40 ff. "But since 1885 there has been associated with Convocation a 'House of Laymen' in each Province chosen by the Diocesan conferences. At the beginning of the 20th cent., the practice of joint sittings of the two Convocations was also initiated, and in 1904 a Representative Council consisting of the members of both the Convocations together with the two Houses of Laymen, sitting conjointly, was begun." F. L. Cross, ed., *The Oxford Dictionary of the Christian Church*, London, 1957, 339. See also "The Proposals for the Self-Government of the Church," *Churchman*, vol. 31 (1917), 87–97.

established to "investigate the possibility of a system of legislative devolution" for the Church.[18] The resolution said:

> There is in principle no inconsistency between a national recognition of religion and the spiritual independence of the Church, and this Council requests the Archbishops of Canterbury and York to consider the advisability of appointing a Committee to inquire what changes are advisable in order to secure in the relations of Church and State a fuller expression of the spiritual independence of the Church as well as of the national recognition of religion.[19]

To address this concern, the two Archbishops appointed a special committee to research and report on the relationship between church and state, particularly with how the Church was governed. Such a committee was appointed in 1914, and its finished report appeared in mid-1916. The Archbishops' Committee on Church and State was chaired by Lord Selborne, and originally consisted of 26 members,[20] including ten clergy (among them two diocesan and one retired bishop) and a half dozen individuals trained in law. Its terms of reference coincided with the words of the council's resolution quoted above. Among its membership were former prime minister Balfour, Bishop Charles Gore, leading ecclesiastical lawyer Sir Lewis Dibdin, liturgical scholar the Rev. W. H. Frere, and the Rev. William Temple.[21] The group's findings were contained in the *Report of the Archbishops' Committee on Church and State*, and its language concerning constitutional issues reflected that of the Royal Commission on Ecclesiastical Discipline ten years earlier. It offered suggestions to solve the governance problems facing the Church.[22]

18. David Thompson, "The Politics of the Enabling Act (1919)," *Church Society and Politics*, edited by Derek Baker, Oxford, 1975, 384.

19. Bell, *Davidson*, ii, 957.

20. Because of war duty and death, its membership dropped to 23 by the time its findings were published in 1916: *Report of the Archbishops' Committee on Church and State*, 1-2.

21. "I am strongly in favour of the principle of spiritual independence ... I wish something similar [as in the Church of Scotland] could be done for the Church of England; but I confess to being anxious on the subject ... What makes the case of the Church of England more difficult ... is the fact that so many of its differences centre on ritual; and where ritual is concerned, mankind seem more than usually incapable of retaining any sense of proportion." Balfour to Davidson, January 9, 1914, cited in Bell, *Davidson*, ii, 958.

22. For two contemporary overviews of the committee, see Lord Wolmer, "The Rights of Citizens and the Rights of the Church," *Contemporary Review* 110 (1916) 574-83; and J. R. Cohu, "Church and State: The Archbishops' Committee Report,"

Change and Transformation

The 1916 *Report* was built upon the assumption that the continued constitutional connection between Church and State should continue. Disestablishment was mentioned very briefly, "more by way of giving completeness to our survey than because we conceive it as coming within the terms of our reference."[23] The royal supremacy was therefore presumed, and not argued.[24] Furthermore, the authority of parliament in relation to the Church was described and accepted, and it was asserted that the *Book of Common Prayer* and the Thirty-Nine Articles "being recognized by statute, the consent of Parliament is necessary to any change in the doctrine or form of worship on the Church of England."[25] No modification of the existing constitutional arrangement between church and state was proposed.

While the committee accepted the current establishment, it recommended some changes to its mechanisms. Such modifications were not, according to the *Report*, detrimental to the establishment, but were beneficial to both Church and State:

> The Church of England is paralysed in some directions because it has not power to adjust the organisation and the rules and manuals of worship which it inherits from past centuries to the deeply changed conditions of the present day. The wheels of the ecclesiastical machine creak and groan and sometimes refuse to move. Corporate discipline is ineffective because our rules and procedure are in many directions quite antiquated.[26]

One of its main concerns revolved around the legislative procedure the Church labored against. It was argued that the current paralysis in the Church was on account of the difficulty of obtaining necessary relief from parliament. "Parliament," the *Report* stated, "especially the Parliament of the present day—which is in no sense a church assembly—is not the right body to undertake the task of adjustment; and it could not, even if it would, find time for the work."[27] To illustrate the problem, of the 217 ecclesiastical bills affecting the national Church introduced in the House of Commons in the

---

Contemporary Review 112 (1917) 312–19.

23. *Report of the Archbishops' Committee on Church and State*, 39. Though "some members" of the committee (no names were noted) thought that disestablishment was the best way for the Church to achieve spiritual independence, most did not, and the *Report* was framed by trying to solve the problem while preserving the "historic connexion" of the civil and ecclesiastical.

24. Ibid., 202.

25. Ibid., 203.

26. Ibid., 2. Compare with Wolmer, "Archbishops' Committee," *Contemporary Review* 110 (1916) 576.

27. *Report of the Archbishops' Committee on Church and State*, 3.

period 1880–1913, thirty-three were passed into law, one was rejected, and 183 dropped, and of those dropped, 162 were never discussed at all. The measures that were passed into law "probably owed their passage to assistance of some sort from the Government":[28]

> The Church is therefore confronted with two broad facts; first, that Parliament has confined it in every department of its constitutional existence with statutory bars which Parliament alone can break or reshape; and, secondly, that Parliament is no longer fitted to legislate for the Church. The changes which began in the sixteenth century have gone on ever since unregulated and unchecked, and we submit that the time has come to arrange the relations of Church and State on a more elastic and rational basis.[29]

The establishment was not broken, but its legislative mechanisms were. Noting the findings of the 1906 Royal Commission, the *Report* advocated greater elasticity should be given to the Church, which should be able to "regulate its own affairs" without the balance between church and state being put at risk, and without challenging the existing legal position of parliament. In the end, after twenty-three meetings, they published their unanimous findings in July 1916.[30]

The *Report* contained several specific recommendations, which helped frame the debate on the subject that was to come later in the decade. Of the recommendations, foremost was the one calling for the creation of a National Church Council. This new body was to be built along the lines of the existing Representative Church Council, but with full constitutional authority. The new council would have three equal houses—one made up of bishops, one of clergy, and one with lay membership—with the provision that a measure would pass only when accepted by each house separately. After the passage of a measure by all three houses of the council, the measure would be given to both houses of parliament, accompanied by an advisory report provided by an ecclesiastical committee drawn from the council. This report would detail the effect that the measure would have on other laws, and if there were any objections from the state's viewpoint. If the report was favorable, the measure would automatically be presented for royal assent

---

28. Ibid., 29.

29. Ibid., 29–30.

30. Of the twenty-three signatories, three (Sir Lewis Dibdin, Douglas Eyre, and Lord Parmoor) signed with minor reservations, included in the *Report* as a memorandum. *Report of the Archbishops' Committee on Church and State*, 68–74. See also G. I. T. Machin, *Politics and the Churches of Great Britain, 1869–1921*, Oxford, 1987, 318.

after forty days, unless either house of parliament resolved otherwise. If the report was unfavorable, the measure would not be presented for royal assent unless both houses resolved otherwise. Such a measure, passed by the council, approved by parliament, and receiving the royal assent would have the force of an Act of Parliament. In May, 1917, the bishops announced their "general consent" for the principles and proposals of this plan.[31]

Two months later, Life and Liberty passed a resolution deploring the conditions of the spiritual freedom of the Church. This movement, under the leadership of William Temple, had been formed during the Great War, and was dedicated to increased self-government of the national Church, even if the cost was disestablishment. Life and Liberty were anxious for the sort of reform suggested by the *Report*, and they asked the archbishops "whether and what terms Parliament is prepared to give freedom to the Church in the sense of full power to manage its own life."[32] Such self-determination was enjoyed by the established Church of Scotland; why could not the same idea be applied to the Church of England? While Archbishop Davidson was sympathetic to the ideas presented in the *Report*, he consistently said that nothing could be done until the war ended. He was determined that any proposed reform go forward "reasonably, progressively, constitutionally."[33] Definite parliamentary action along these lines was therefore precluded, for the time being. But the move for increased self-government in the Church of England, encompassing a lay component and modifying existing legislative mechanisms, was in play.[34]

---

31. *Report of the Archbishops' Committee on Church and State*, 40; Bell, *Davidson*, ii, 959–60.

32. Bell, *Davidson*, ii, 961–62; David Thompson, "The Politics of the Enabling Act," 384. For Life and Liberty's contribution to the Enabling Act, see Kenneth Thompson, *Bureaucracy and Church Reform*, Oxford, 1970, chapter 6. See also John Kent, *William Temple: Church, State, and Society in Britain, 1880–1950*, Cambridge, 1992, 61ff.

33. Bell, *Davidson*, ii, 962–63, 966.

34. "The Great War affected the process of revision very potently, for not only did it discredit every kind of authority in Church and State and create a new and vehement passion for 'self-expression,' but it stirred in serious minds a great hunger for religious agreement, and a corresponding dislike of ecclesiastical partisanship." Hensley Henson, *The Book and the Vote*, London, 1928, 47–48. For the mood of the Church after World War I, see Roger Lloyd, *The Church of England, 1900–1965*, London, 1966, chapter 11; Alan Wilkinson, *The Church of England and the First World War*, London, 1978, chapter 12.

FORGING THE ENABLING ACT, 1919: THE LORDS

With the end of the Great War in November, 1918, it was not long before action was taken on the recommendations by the Archbishops' Committee. At a meeting of the Representative Church Council in February, 1919, a resolution passed by a large majority calling for an Enabling Bill along the lines of the 1916 *Report*'s suggestions.[35] Archbishop Davidson favored the idea. He said that in the last twenty-five years, when he approached parliamentarians with church issues that needed attention, the answer he received was always something like this:

> 'Probably you are quite right; but with the present pressure upon the time of Parliament ... and the present attitude of the House of Commons towards the varied work ... we never could ask the House to give up the days or the weeks that would be necessary.' They did not say, 'We are opposed to it' ... but rather, 'You are asking a machine to do it, which is already so clogged with work, and work of a different kind, that what you are asking is an impossibility.'[36]

Events moved quickly. On May 10, the archbishop presented The National Assembly of the Church of England (Powers) Bill, commonly called the Enabling Bill, to the House of Lords. It largely followed the recommendations of the *Report* of the Archbishops' Committee, and used the Representative Church Council as the basis for its provisions.

The introduction of the Enabling bill was not uneventful. When it first appeared in the House of Lords, some members were against the bill as they saw its provisions as an attack on the constitutional rights of citizens. The *Times* went on record against it.[37] Bishop Hensley Henson was one of the most vociferous opponents of the bill, and argued that it would fundamentally transform the Church of England from a national church into a denominational one. The Enabling bill, wrote Henson, "is carefully designed to express a conception of Church and State which is quite inconsistent both with the history and with the law of the Church of England."[38]

It would be accurate to say that the success of a bill would depend upon how it was presented in parliament. If it was promoted as a way to

---

35. For details on the background to the Enabling bill, see David Thompson, "Politics of the Enabling Act," 384; J. H. B. Masterman, "Liberal Churchmen and the Enabling Bill," *Contemporary Review*, vol. 116 (1919), 286–90; *Annual Register*, 1919, 72 ff.

36. Bell, ii, *Davidson*, 968–69.

37. *Times*, June 18, 1919, 13.

38. *Times*, June 5, 1919, 10. This was primarily because "electors" of the Assembly would have to qualify as Anglican to vote.

grant the church increased spiritual independence from the state, it would be met with opposition. If, however, its advocates demonstrated that the bill was designed merely to allow the church to be run more efficiently, there was more promise.[39]

The National Assembly of the Church of England (Powers)[40] bill would essentially create a new body, called the National Assembly, which would function much as the current Representative Church Council, except that it would have the authority to craft ecclesiastical legislation for the church, which would be placed before parliament. Three houses—those made up of bishops, clergy, and laity, comprising a total membership of approximately 700 individuals—would make up the new body.[41] Lay representatives would be chosen by qualified electors in parishes across the country; electors would be male or female communicants of the Church of England and not members of any religious body not in communion with the national church. For a measure to pass the Assembly, it would have to secure passage separately in each of the three houses.[42] An Ecclesiastical Committee, made up of members of the Ecclesiastical Committee of the Privy Council, would then determine if the measure provided any difficulty for the constitution or the state's interests. If this committee determined that the measure should be enacted, it would be laid before both houses of parliament, and would be sent for royal assent in forty days unless either house passed a resolution to the contrary.[43] Significantly, parliament was prohibited from amending any

39. "It is not too much too say that a championship of the Enabling Bill based on the theoretical idea of spiritual independence ... would have tumbled to ruin." Bell, *Davidson*, ii, 975.

40. This was later changed to the Church of England Assembly (Powers) bill, but was commonly referred to as the Enabling bill.

41. Membership in the house of bishops would be comprised of all the members of the upper houses of Canterbury and York convocations, and that of the house of clergy of all members of the lower houses of Canterbury and York convocations.

42. Compare *Report of the Archbishops' Committee on Church and State*, 41–42. Individual parochial church councils would elect their own parish representatives, who would then elect ruri-decanal conference representatives, who would then elect diocesan conference representatives, who would then elect representatives to the lay house of the Church Assembly. The nearest census data (1921) shows that out of a total population of over 35 million people in England, approximately 62% were baptized members of the Church of England, 30% were confirmed members, and 14% were on the Church's Electoral Rolls. David Butler and Anne Sloman, eds., *British Political Facts, 1900–1975*, 4th ed., London, 1975, 404.

43. Alternatively, if the ecclesiastical committee came to the conclusion that the measure should not become law, the measure would be laid before both houses of parliament, and would be abandoned in forty days unless both Houses passed resolutions that it should receive Royal Assent.

measure; votes had to be on the measure as laid before them. Ideally, the church could create the legislation it wanted, and constitutional safeguards would be protected through what would be, in effect, parliamentary veto power.

Davidson moved the bill's second reading in the Lords on June 3. His opening words were: "I ask your Lordships to give a Second Reading to a Bill to enable the Church of England to do its work properly."[44] His tactic was to promote the legislation simply as that which would give the Church of England the ability to do its work well. He reminded the members that the current machinery of church government originated centuries ago. Though the number of parishes and dioceses in England had remained relatively stable, the growth in population had been astonishing in the past two centuries.[45] The government of the church, which ran smoothly in earlier times, was not as suitable for modern times. As the various Reform Acts widened the franchise in Britain, more non-churchmen were elected to parliament, and it became "far more difficult to get a hearing for Church matters" than before. Noting his experience of over four decades working "behind the scenes" with the activity of church and state, he said:

> Therefore I speak with real inside knowledge when I say that the difficulties to which I have referred have been steadily increasing and multiplying on our hands. Just as our attempted activities have multiplied, so the old hampering conditions have been constantly increasing. It is literally true that in our system of administration, which now-a-days is very varied and very far-reaching, and which grows more wide and more exacting every year, I am brought up not every week but every day against the difficulties which hamper our power to serve the nation as thoroughly as we would. That is why I come to your Lordships to-day.[46]

Davidson then provided a concrete example of the kind of practical difficulties he was talking about: reform of the ecclesiastical courts. He noted that in 1881, a Royal Commission on Ecclesiastical Courts was appointed, under the chairmanship of Archbishop Tait. This commission presented

---

44. Hansard, 5th series, vol. XXXIV, 974.

45. England and Wales had a population of five million in 1700, which had grown to nine million a century later, doubled to eighteen million by 1850, and doubled again to thirty-six million people during the period under analysis here. Hansard, 5th series, vol. XXXIV, 976.

46. Hansard, 5th series, vol. XXXIV, 980.

its report in 1883, but no legislation was ever passed with regard to its recommendations:

> ... we were told on all sides, "It is impossible; you cannot get it done. It would be a most contentious matter, and the time for it is not to be got." Those attempts did not go forward. After twenty years there was another Royal Commission. This was a Royal Commission on Ecclesiastical Discipline. I was myself a member of it. Lord St. Alwyn was our chairman. Lord Alverstone, the Lord Chief Justice, was a member, and Sir Edward Clarke was a very prominent member. Other members were Sir. L. Dibdin and the then Bishop of Oxford and the present Bishop of Gloucester. There were other members of that Commission. It modified but it renewed the recommendations of the Commission of 1883, and the desire was repeated that we should attempt to get legislative aid for carrying out the recommendations. I need not ask your Lordships whether it would be worth while attempting now to get a Bill dealing with the Ecclesiastical Courts readily through the House of Commons. That is one large matter which needs attention for the right doing of our work.[47]

In the current arrangement, the church really was helpless to do much. As long as it was part of the establishment under current law, legislation affecting the church had to pass through the constituted authority of parliament, and this was terribly difficult to accomplish, especially for controversial legislation. It was not that the church was unwilling to legislate for itself, but that it was prevented from doing so. If the law prevented the church from operating smoothly, why should not the church, Davidson asked rhetorically, just ignore obsolete rules and simply do what needed to be done? The archbishop would not have anything to do with this kind of thinking:

> [P]eople say, 'Why don't you do those things without caring about the exact law; no one is going to stop you; you had better do it, though the law does not allow it.' That is the most dangerous piece of counsel to give to those who are bearing charge and responsibility. It is bad in itself. It recoils upon those who have to exercise discipline in other ways if the retort can be made to them, 'Are you obeying the law when you ask me to obey it?' and it is a baneful example for other fields than those of the Church's

---

47. Hansard, 5th series, vol. XXXIV, 981–82. The archbishop also marshaled evidence about patronage and tenure of benefices, ecclesiastical discipline for moral offences, church dilapidations, and licensing colonial clergy to illustrate his point about the pressing need for reform.

life that we should take the law of the land and encourage people by our example to feel that it does not matter, and that, provided nobody is going to object, we can act without regard to law.[48]

He acknowledged that the *Report* of the Archbishops' Committee on Church and State "formed the basis of the action which we are now taking." While the bill addressed the problems of church legislation, he stressed that it did not take away from the legislature's final authority; parliamentary power "remains exactly what it was."[49] The goal of this legislation was, he argued, to allow the machinery of the church to work properly, and legally.

Viscount Haldane, a Presbyterian, former Lord Chancellor, and no friend of episcopacy, rose to oppose the motion, largely on constitutional grounds. He said he was not against the principle of giving the church the power of "regulating its own affairs," but he thought the bill did more than that. It would, he claimed, "narrow the basis on which the National Church of to-day rests" by taking away "the restraint which Parliament has for centuries imposed" on the bishops. The constitutional balance between church and state would be put in jeopardy if the supremacy of parliament were diminished and replaced by a mechanism where episcopal authority grew at the expense of the legislature:[50]

> With control in the hands of an assembly that believes in the superiority of the prelatical government of the Church to the government by the people at large, the result of the Bill will be to render that Church no longer the Church of the entire English nation but the Church of a denomination of earnest-minded believers in their own creed, to whom are to be handed over the titles and authority of the Church as to-day established by law.[51]

While technically parliament would retain a veto over submitted measures, this was more illusion than fact, he argued. Any measure that came to the Commons (or the Lords) and was not debated within forty days would be sent for royal assent, which would produce an intolerable quandary for the leadership of the House.

---

48. Hansard, 5th series, vol. XXXIV, 984. Compare this statement with the position adopted less than ten years later by the house of bishops in September, 1928. *Times*, September 29, 1928, 10.

49. Hansard, 5th series, vol. XXXIV, 985, 987.

50. See Bell, *Davidson*, ii, 976.

51. Hansard, 5th Series, vol. XXXIV, 995–97. This reflects Henson's line of thought as well. Additionally, he thought that some high church clergy supported the bill "to assert what they call 'spiritual independence' of the Church," which he claimed would be the "first installment" toward full disestablishment. *Times*, June 5, 1919, 10.

> The Government would feel a pistol was being put to their head—"your time or your life." If they cannot give the time, then the Bill goes unchallenged. If they do give the time, the whole of their business gets into confusion. This precious Ecclesiastical Committee which the Bill proposes to set up gets indirectly control over the whole time of Parliament, and the situation is that it will be almost intolerable for the Government of the day to try and carry out its business . . .[52]

The archbishops' committee which formulated the scheme was flawed, Haldane argued, in that it presumed the rights of the bishops mattered most, and its findings flowed from this presumption. But, in fact, the church and its powers since the Reformation have been under the authority of the state. This situation would practically change should the bill become law. Haldane thereupon moved a hostile amendment, which said that the House was unwilling "to assent to legislation which would exclude the greater part of the people of England from effective influence in the affairs of the National Church as established by the Constitution, and which is so framed as to enable members of that Church to pass laws that may wholly change its character without adequate supervision by Parliament."[53] The debate was soon adjourned for the day and did not resume for several weeks. In the meantime, the full impact of Haldane's comments hit, and opposition to the bill intensified. Dibdin wrote to Davidson on June 8 saying a compromise was needed as the government could not support the bill after Haldane's speech. To this the archbishop agreed.[54]

David Lloyd George's government continued to take a neutral stance toward the bill. Many in the cabinet had lukewarm feelings about it, with more than one against supporting it in the Commons if it were to pass the Lords. Herbert Fisher, chairman of the home affairs committee in the cabinet, said the bill was "very controversial, destroying as it did the Elizabethan and Caroline settlements. It would confer on the Church of England all the advantages of disestablishment without any of its disadvantages." At their June 30 cabinet meeting, the prime minister thought the government should remain uncommitted and allow a free vote, perhaps because he did not think the bill would ultimately be passed.[55]

In addition, there was a fresh rash of correspondence in the intervening weeks in the *Times*. The newspaper came out against the bill since the

---

52. Hansard, 5th series, vol. XXXIV, 1012.
53. Ibid., 1015.
54. Thompson, "Politics of the Enabling Act," 388.
55. Cabinet notes cited in ibid., 386–87.

proposed church assembly would "almost certainly be pressed to adopt measures which would tend to narrow the basis of the Church of England," giving it a denominational instead of a national character.[56] A major component of the bill would purportedly give the church more freedom. But the paper said that "one of the most constant complaints against the Church is that it suffers from the indiscipline of excessive liberty. Whether this is true or not, it is difficult to imagine how the clergy can be less restricted in the discharge of their ministry than are the parish priests of this country."[57] The dean of Canterbury reportedly thought that the new franchise rules contained in the bill would "unchurch half the people in the country who now have the right to call themselves Churchmen."[58] Several bishops, evenly split for and against, made their opinions known through the *Times*.[59] Supporters of the measure included William Temple and F. A. Iremonger of Life and Liberty, who stressed that "corporate freedom" was the aim of the bill, and such a goal was a necessary one for the Church to go about its calling in an effective manner, echoing the line developed by Archbishop Davidson in the Lords.[60] Hensley Henson, who was by this time Bishop of Hereford, fiercely opposed the bill. He thought that its support was chiefly among "Tractarian spiritualists and secular democrats" who were allied in their intense dislike of the existing establishment.[61] Just days before the resumption of the debate, the *Times* thought it unlikely that the bill would make it out of the Lords, it being more likely that a select committee or a royal commission "considering afresh the whole question of the relations between Church and State" would be appointed, even if this meant starting the reform process on self-government all over again.[62] Complicating the issue was the fact that there seemed to be two sorts of supporters for the bill, those who saw it primarily involving "administrative reform," and those seeking "revolutionary change" leading to disestablishment, since to them self-government was incompatible with the established position of the church, which would eventually have to go.[63]

56. *Times*, June 18, 1919, 13.

57. Ibid.

58. Ibid., June 23, 1919, 10.

59. Including the bishops of Hereford, Carlisle, Bristol, and Newcastle. *Times*, June 4, 1919, 8, June 5, 10, and June 24, 1919, 8.

60. Ibid., June 14, 1919, 8; ibid., June 21, 1919, 8.

61. Herbert Hensley Henson, *Disestablishment: The Charge Delivered at the Second Quadrennial Visitation of His Diocese, together with an Introduction*, London, 1929, 7.

62. *Times*, June 27, 1919, 13.

63. Ibid., June 24, 1919, 8.

Change and Transformation

By the time the debate was resumed in the Lords on July 1, the bill's supporters were willing to explore amendments. The Marquess of Crewe, who was the leader of the opposition in the House, advanced upon Haldane's position against the bill by pointing out that the possibility of "omnibus measures"—where several measures were combined into a single large measure which parliament would have to accept or reject as a whole—was an unfortunate possibility as it now stood. He also suggested a more practical criticism, involving the "grave suspicion" of Roman Catholics by evangelicals and broad churchmen in the country:

> And, my Lords, it is because the fear exists, rightly or wrongly, in many quarters that the section, if that is the word, of the Anglican Church which can be described as sacerdotal, should somehow succeed in engrossing all the machinery and so directing the operations of the Church as a whole, that even the modified proposals of this Bill are regarded with fear by not a few. Those sentiments are largely reflected in Parliament, to some extent I have no doubt in this House, and probably to a far greater extent in another place.[64]

He appealed to supporters of modifying the bill to make it acceptable to this sentiment.

To summarize, opposition to the bill may be identified as belonging to two broad lines of thought. First, there was the view that the qualifications provided for electors of the proposed national assembly narrowed the base of the national church, specifically by insisting that individuals belonging to bodies not in communion with the Church of England were disqualified. This, of course, struck at non-conformists. This argument had been one of Bishop Henson's most potent against the bill, and was taken up in the Lord's debate by several, including Bishop E. A. Knox of Manchester, who commented:

> When you practically put, as the one disqualification for the franchise in the Church of England, membership of some other religious body you at once cause other religious bodies to feel that their status is affected and they cannot fail to challenge you as to the basis of which you have framed your new relations between Church and State.[65]

---

64. Hansard, 5th series, vol. XXXV, 14.

65. Ibid., 26. Quoting from the current *British Weekly*, Knox read, "No elector is disqualified by reason of his character. He may be a thief, or an adulterer, or a notorious evil-liver; he may be the parish drunkard or the parish rake; but he must not be a Methodist class leader or a Baptist deacon."

The second line of criticism, and perhaps the more important one, was the fear that the bill upset the delicate and traditional balance between church and state. The constitutional issue of the royal supremacy, earlier characterized by the critique of Viscount Haldane, was now advanced by the bishop of Manchester and others in the debate. Knox's criticism of the bill was conditional, and he declared if amendments were included to address this issue, his opposition would vanish. He was, however, anxious to state that "the effect of the bill is to alter the existing relations of Church and State in England." This was in opposition to Davidson's claim that the bill simply facilitated ecclesiastical legislation. Knox pleaded:

> One thing only I ask—namely, that those who are promoting this measure should not put it before us merely as some easy way of facilitating church legislation, but should honestly confess that they have given up the old theory of the Establishment and are proceeding upon a new theory, and then should justify what they are doing.[66]

In this view, the changes brought by an Enabling bill affected the authority of parliament, and went far beyond that of simply providing a mechanism for easier ecclesiastical legislation. Whether it was fear of increasing the power of the bishops, or the fear that the proposed national assembly might fall under the control of one ecclesiastical party or another, the underlying issue was whether the new bill upset the balance between church and state by skirting the supremacy of parliament.

This argument apparently struck a nerve with the bill's supporters, as several speakers provided assurances that the authority of parliament was not affected by the bill, and its supremacy was not touched.[67] They were unwilling to acknowledge that anything was being constitutionally affected, other than the provision of a limited degree of self-government for the Church by means of a more effective way to implement ecclesiastical legislation. The archbishop of York asserted:

66. Ibid., 24.

67. "The Bill does not ask Parliament to surrender or in any degree to qualify the absolute right of Parliament to initiate and to carry through independently of the Church any legislation it likes about the Church. That is the first point. The second point is this. The Bill does not ask Parliament to surrender or in any degree to qualify the absolute right of Parliament to reject any measure which comes before it from the Church expressing the desire of the Church. Now, if the absolute right to initiate legislation of its own and the absolute right to reject any legislation proposed by the Church itself together do not constitute effective influence, I am quite at a loss to know what effective influence can be." Bishop of Ely (F. H. Chase), speaking from an evangelical perspective. Ibid., 47. See also the speeches of Lord Emmott, Lord Phillimore, Lord Stuart of Wortley, and the archbishop of York during this debate. Ibid., 38 ff.

> There is nothing in this Bill which affects the position of Parliament as the ultimate source of the sanction which must be given to any changes affecting the Church of England in regard to its constitution, or its relation with the Statute Law of the country ... This Bill recognizes and desires to uphold the ultimate control of His Majesty and of the two Houses of Parliament.[68]

Was the constitutional arrangement between church and state fundamentally changed by the bill, or was it not? This was the key issue confronting the Lords; they decisively answered in the negative.[69]

These assurances were enough. Opposition largely evaporated. After two days of debate, Haldane's amendment was defeated on July 2 by a vote of 130 to 33, with all seventeen bishops present voting with the majority. With the amendment taken care of, the bill was read a second time, and went to committee.[70] Committee work on the Enabling Bill began on July 10. In addition to several small, verbal amendments, Viscount Finlay moved what was to be the most far-reaching amendment considered. He thought that instead of an assembly measure being sent for royal assent unless either House formally objected (as the bill currently read), it should be changed so that both Houses would have to approve a measure formally before it was sent to His Majesty for assent. This, Finlay reasoned, would be a way to ensure that complete control of any measure belonged to both houses of parliament. With this safeguard, he believed that the bill would transform itself into a "generally acceptable" measure.[71] Davidson somewhat reluctantly agreed, and accepted the amendment.[72] The Lord Chancellor, who at a cabinet meeting a month earlier had characterized the measure as "a thoroughly bad one" which "compromised the whole position of the

---

68. The archbishop (Cosmo Gordon Lang), speaking from a perspective somewhat sympathetic to the high church position. Ibid., 136.

69. Compare with Archbishop Davidson's assertion during the June debate: "We are not taking away from Parliament any power which it at present possesses. By all means let Parliament use that power if it will and if it can." Hansard, 5th Series, vol. XXXIV, 987. The archbishop also expressed the opinion that it would be necessary to obtain the permission of parliament before any alteration to the prayer book was done. Hansard, 5th Series, vol. XXXV, 463–64; Bell, *Davidson*, ii, 977–78.

70. Hansard, 5th Series, vol. XXXV, 150.

71. Ibid., 471.

72. Davidson noted that he was careful not to get into an "attitude of opposition, still less of angry opposition" towards Haldane and his group, which, after all, "only objected to the procedure, and their objections were largely met by my conceding that Parliament must vote in favour of passing a measure when it has been passed through the Privy Council, not merely must abstain from a resolution against it." Davidson memo of July 13, 1919, cited in Thompson, "Politics of the Enabling Act," 389.

National Church,"[73] was particularly pleased with this development and the archbishop's acceptance of it. He said that the primate "has gone a long way to satisfy those who are most deeply concerned to see that the supremacy of Parliament in these matters was maintained."[74] The amendment was passed without division. The bill was now generally acceptable to most members in the house. Furthermore, very minor alterations were made, and the bill came out of committee and received its third reading on July 21.[75]

FORGING THE ENABLING ACT, 1919: THE COMMONS

After passage by the Lords, the bill still had to be navigated through the House of Commons. It was unclear what its reception would be. In early November, three months after the Lords' action, the government of Lloyd George agreed to allow debate on the Enabling bill's second reading. By this time there were over 175 MPs enlisted as supporters, and work went on among non-conformists to enlist their support. The bill was scheduled to be read for the second time on November 7, 1919.[76]

Sir Edward Beauchamp moved the bill's second reading using much the same argument as Davidson had done in the Lords, namely, the pragmatic view that the bill would help the church do its job more efficiently by giving it the authority to create legislation. He traced the history of the Representative Church Council and the *Report* of the Archbishops' Committee on Church and State, and the bill's passage in the Lords. Without acknowledging the irony, he appealed to the members to pass this legislation since "it is impossible to get a Church Bill through Parliament," adding: "In order to enable the Church to perform her duties satisfactorily she seeks the aid of Parliament, she asks for the removal of some of the barriers which confine her efforts and render it impossible for her to take full opportunity for the exercise of her religious functions."[77]

There was some opposition expressed toward the bill. After Beauchamp's speech, Thomas Broad said that since it was proper for the Church

---

73. Ibid., 387.

74. For Davidson's and the Lord Chancellor's brief remarks, see Hansard, 5th Series, vol. XXXV, 471–72.

75. Ibid., 150. When congratulated the next day on the Lords vote, Davidson said he had lived many years on the notion that half a loaf was better than none. Bell, *Davidson*, ii, 979.

76. Thompson, "Politics of the Enabling Act," 389; Bell, *Davidson*, ii, 979; Hansard, 5th Series, vol. 120, 1817ff.

77. Hansard, 5th Series, vol. 120, 1822.

of England to have freedom of self-government, the best way to fulfill this was to disestablish it. "If this Bill passes through Parliament," Broad said, "Then Parliamentary supervision over the Anglican Church practically passes away, and it is made independent of Parliament." The unfair part of the bargain would be that the church would keep "its status and its vast wealth." The argument was that the Church of England should be given its freedom not just partially but fully.[78] Sir John Randles, a non-conformist, effectively countered this notion, noting that disestablishment was an entirely different issue than allowing the church more liberty, and when you took away the object of disestablishment, "practically no argument" had been given against the bill. Randles repeated the argument that parliamentary supremacy was not the issue here, more effective church government was:

> The question on this Bill is, Is it a good Bill, and do the members of the Church of England earnestly desire it? I believe it is a good Bill, and I believe the members of the Church of England earnestly desire it. So far as I can collect any evidence on this subject, they do not object to the effective control of Parliament; but what they object to is the effective neglect of Parliament.[79]

In addition, Sir William Joynson-Hicks sounded the voice of evangelical apprehension.[80] He announced he would support the bill, but with misgivings and anxiety. His main reservation surrounded the issue of prayer book reform, and how the new provisions would affect that. Speaking on behalf "of a very large number of Evangelical Protestant churchmen," he said they were "not prepared to have great alterations made in the Book of Common Prayer." He noted the suggestions for revision that had been proposed in recent years in the convocations, and said:

> Other proposals are coming forward to provide for the establishment of vestments, for the reservation of the Sacrament, and while I do not want to go into too much detail yet I say in detail they go a very long way towards that high section and that ritualist section, and are bitterly opposed, and will and must be if

---

78. Hansard, 5th Series, vol. 120, 1823–29. Major Barnes, speaking in favor of disestablishment, added that the church is older than parliament, and should be free: "If there had existed in the sixth century a House of Commons such as exists to-day it would have passed an Aliens Bill and prevented St. Augustine landing in Kent." Ibid., 1832.

79. Ibid., 1840.

80. See "The Enabling Bill," *Churchman* 33 (1919) 637. As home secretary eight years later, Joynson-Hicks would be a key figure in the parliamentary defeat of the Prayer Book Measure of 1927.

they are to live in the Church of England at all, by the Evangelical section of the Church whose opinions I share.[81]

If the bill only dealt with non-doctrinal issues, he would be happy to see it passed without modification. But its scope for legislation touched every area of church life, including even the theoretical repeal of the Acts of Uniformity. This was too much power to grant. Give the church power over administrative affairs, yes, but doctrinal issues should be left outside its scope. He ended by claiming that excluding Non-conformists as electors would hurt the idea of a truly national Church, and his fear was that the move for disestablishment might gain momentum. For the sake of a truly national Church, he argued, such exclusivity was not justified.[82]

Lord Robert Cecil summed up the defense of the Enabling bill by reiterating that its purpose was simply to facilitate creation of ecclesiastical legislation, and once again emphasized that after passage, it would legally leave "Parliament in exactly the position it always has been."[83] Bonar Law, leader of the house but not speaking on behalf of the government, described the bill as not perfect, but a useful change to help the Church of England do its work. His approach was quite pragmatic. "You have either got to agree to some scheme of this kind," he said, "Or to say that none of these abuses can be removed except by having a special Act of Parliament. That is quite impossible." His defense of limiting electors was also effective:

> We say also that just as in Scotland anyone would regard it as absolutely ludicrous that those who are not members of the Church of Scotland should decide its fate, so in practice there is nothing out of the way in saying that questions of this kind should be decided by men who are members of the Church of England.[84]

In the event, the vote for the second reading was an overwhelming 304 in favor, and 16 against.[85] On December 5, a significant amendment in commit-

---

81. Hansard, 5th Series, vol. 120, 1852. Compare the later speech of Sir Courtney Warner, which also expressed concerned about potential high church revisions. Ibid., 1885–86.

82. Ibid., 1854. Shortly thereafter, Welshman Hugh Edwards said he thought it strange that a non-conformist could not be an elector, but could (as in the case of Lloyd George) make episcopal appointments. Ibid., 1866. Compare with Machin, *Politics and the Churches*, 318 ff.

83. Hansard, 5th Series, vol. 120, 1869.

84. Ibid., 1879–80.

85. Ibid., 1891–96. For background to these votes, see also Thompson, "Politics of the Enabling Act," 384 ff.

tee transferred membership of the Ecclesiastical Committee from the Privy Council to 15 members from the Lords nominated by the Lord Chancellor, and 15 from the Commons nominated by the Speaker, and the bill was read the third time without a division later that same day.[86] The bill was sent to the Lords, who accepted the amended measure on December 15. Royal assent was received on December 23.[87]

While contemporary ecclesiastical legislation was notoriously difficult to pass, "to everybody's amazement," to use Davidson's words, the Enabling Act was speedily passed into law. The archbishop claimed that the inherent reasonableness of the measure, combined with the promoters' sensitive and practical handling of objections and amendments, had proved to be the difference.[88]

The act was significant not only for establishing a brand new statutory mechanism for creating ecclesiastical law in general, but for removing the biggest hurdle facing prayer book revision. Instead of sending any revision to parliament, as past law had required, and being subject to debates, political considerations, and committee work, the new National Assembly would be able to author it, work out its provisions, and simply submit its completed work to both houses of parliament for approval. While the legislature retained its constitutional authority over ecclesiastical legislation with its power to accept or reject measures, it could not modify what it received. Thus, the potential for doctrinal conflict and wrangling over line-by-line scrutiny of liturgical points was avoided. Instead, all those discussions would take place within church structures, conducted by its own representatives. This seemed the perfect solution, since it allowed the church to express a new level of self-government, while preserving the traditional final authority entrusted to the state.[89] With the new system, the church had full authority to regulate itself and its worship more confidently and effectively.

---

86. Hansard, 5th Series, vol. 122, 838–66.

87. Church of England Assembly (Powers) Act, 1919 [9–10 Geo. V, c. 76]. *Journals of the House of Lords*, 1919, 573–74.

88. Thompson, "Politics of the Enabling Act," 391. "Thus a very notable change in the constitution of the Church of England was accomplished, and with a speed that is startling to those who look back. Its achievement was due to Randall Davidson more than to any other single person." Bell, *Davidson*, ii, 979–80.

89. "The most effective cry raised against reasonable Revision has been that any touching of the Prayer Book involves laying all our Rubrics before the House of Commons for amendment, and that Jews and secularists may be drafting the suggested changes." Davidson to Robert Reade, January 3, 1911, Davidson Papers, cited in Robert F. Schmidt, "Prayer Book Revision in the Church of England, 1906–1929: Liturgy, Doctrine, and Ecclesiastical Discipline," PhD diss., Miami University, 1984, 105.

It was a remarkable reform. Two years later, Davidson commented on the nature of the act's passage:

> I doubt whether any event in the constitutional history of Church and State has ever been wrought out with so little friction, and on so smooth a current as this great change ... I think it is indisputable that if we had failed in December 1919 to get through Parliament what is popularly known as the Enabling Bill, we might have waited for it for many a year with increasing and most harmful loss of enthusiasm, and growth of irritation among the progressive groups.[90]

The wording of the Enabling Act was carefully chosen to guard the church-state equilibrium. Technically, the National Assembly was not "created" by the act; it was a representative body created by the church, which received its constitutional authority through the act.[91] This headed off the argument that the Assembly was "a creation of the State" and therefore an illegitimate body (to Anglo-Catholic thinking) to be deciding ecclesiastical policy. Furthermore, it would be customary for the convocations to pass any measure before it was submitted to parliament, thus providing proper "spiritual jurisdiction."[92] On the other hand, since any measure only became law after having been passed by parliament, the objection that the church was independent of state authority was dealt with. The Enabling Act was therefore uniquely placed to speak for the church, with the authority of the state, and, under the final authority of parliament, the balance between the spiritual independence of the church and the royal supremacy was preserved.

There was, however, a lurking danger associated with the new act. The old question of who possessed "practical" supremacy—the church or the state—and to what extent, had not gone away. In spite of the clear language of the act, and the context of its passage, the fact was, the Church's self-governance was greatly enhanced, and this left the impression that somehow the Church of England was now more "free" from state authority than

---

90. Memo from Archbishop Davidson, February 6, 1921, cited in Thompson, "Politics of the Enabling Act," 383.

91. See various editions of *The Official Year-Book of the National Assembly of the Church of England*, London, in the 1920s, for foundational documents relating to the National Assembly.

92. Each convocation had an "Upper House" made up of provincial bishops, and a "Lower House" made up of clergy. This differed slightly from the National Assembly, which had a single house of bishops, and a single house of clergy, in addition to the house of laity. Given the same membership, it would be difficult to imagine a measure being passed by convocation, and then not being passed by the house of bishops and clergy in the National Assembly.

it was prior to 1919. With this in mind, would parliament end up deferring to "the mind of the Church" on measures arriving from the National Assembly, and become more or less a rubber stamp? Or would it reserve to itself the right to reject that with which it disagreed? The act was clear that both houses of parliament had to pass a measure for it to become law, and each had the full right to exercise rejection. But would, or should, parliament feel the weight of the "moral" need to go along with whatever the National Assembly had decided? For those who had for years been advocating the spiritual independence of the Church of England, it was reasonable to interpret the act's passage as moving further along the road toward full spiritual independence.

Nevertheless, the passage of the Enabling Act was a monumental event in the history of how the Church of England was governed. The church and the bishops had achieved what they wanted. If Davidson's strategic view was correct, the chance of successfully implementing successful prayer book revision was increased immensely. From this point forward, the assembly would dictate what ecclesiastical legislation would look like. While the Enabling Act did not preclude parliament from authoring ecclesiastical bills on its own, if there had been reluctance toward parliamentary action previously, after 1919 it was unthinkable.[93]

PRACTICAL PROCEDURES AND USES

The National Assembly of the Church of England acquired constitutional authority under the provisions of the Enabling Act.[94] The assembly would normally meet to conduct its business three times per year, about five days per session. Constitutionally armed with the ability to author legislation, the assembly started to go about its business beginning in 1920, passing a single measure that first year, and three in the following, each of which were passed by both houses of parliament, thus becoming law. The assembly dealt with all sorts of reforms and issues, many of which may be described as mundane, non-controversial measures, though several were substantive. The work of the assembly proved to be productive and it operated smoothly.

---

93. For parliament to have initiated ecclesiastical legislation after authorizing the National Assembly of the Church of England would have been taken as an unacceptable intrusion on the freedom of the Church to formulate its own affairs, as defined by the Enabling Act.

94. The National Assembly was also known as the Church Assembly. A piece of legislation from the assembly was termed a "measure," as opposed to a "bill," which originated in parliament.

Procedurally, the church assembly would first receive and then consider proposals. These proposals would be examined by a joint committee of the three assembly houses. They would prepare reports on these proposals, which would then be presented to the assembly to receive "general approval."[95] This step may roughly be likened to the second reading of a bill in parliament. Upon receiving general approval from each of the three houses, voting separately, each house could propose amendments to the measure. Afterwards, the house of bishops would take all the amendments and fashion a final measure that would have to be accepted by each house. Even at this stage, however, any of the houses could "send back" the measure for change if they were not happy with the final product. Once each house had passed the final measure, it would be sent to parliament, and under the terms of the Enabling Act, would first be studied by the Ecclesiastical Committee for its recommendation. Afterwards, the Lords and the Commons could either accept or reject the measure by an up or down vote, without the possibility of amendment. If both of these houses gave their approval, the measure would be given to the King to receive royal assent. If a measure was rejected by either house of parliament, it would be returned to the assembly, where it could be amended and resubmitted later, if so desired. According to the Enabling Act, there was no constitutional way for a National Assembly measure to receive legal status apart from this method.[96]

During the initial years following the Enabling Act's passage, many measures were brought forward, debated, and not a few were passed into law. The spiritual forum was shown capable of doing the job for which it was created. The initial activity of the National Assembly is impressive. An examination of the 1920s shows that, on average, three or four measures per year received the royal assent. Many of these were on routine subjects, such as transferring parishes from one jurisdiction to another, establishing or modifying clergy pension schemes, and amending procedural rules in the National Assembly. Others addressed significant issues; five measures that became law dealt with creating new dioceses, and one dissolved the link

---

95. All votes in the National Assembly were by simple majority of those voting. It may be noted that "general approval" did not necessarily mean the house so voting approved of the specifics of the measure in question, but accepted it to the extent of allowing it to go forward.

96. The authorities were careful not to step on the toes of convocation; it was agreed that any measure affecting the church's liturgy passed by the National Assembly and sent to parliament would also receive Convocation's approval separately, to ensure that their rights were respected. Technically, there were now a total of nine houses that would have to accept such a measure before it became law (e.g. the three houses of the National Assembly, four in the convocations, and two in parliament).

between the Church of England and the Church of England in India.[97] But not all of the measures received approval from both houses of parliament. Two—the Bishopric of Shrewsbury Measure, and the Union of Benefices and Disposal of Churches (Metropolitan) Measure—were voted down in 1926, the former by a 61–60 vote in the Lords, and the latter by a 124–17 vote in the Commons. Significantly, these rejections did not engender much controversy, and did establish a precedent that served notice parliament would not automatically pass anything put forward by the National Assembly.[98] Two others—the Prayer Book Measure 1927 and the Prayer Book Measure 1928—were to provoke a constitutional crisis that was to last decades.

PRAYER BOOK REVISION UNDER THE ENABLING ACT

After 1919, all the prayer book revision work that had been done by the convocations of necessity had to be revisited by the National Assembly, since the terms of the Enabling Act were now in place. The scope of the revision had steadily grown over the years.[99] Originally recommended by the Royal Commission to be a revision of the rubrics of the prayer book to allow greater elasticity in the conduct of services, the work more and more

---

97. Interestingly, the beginning of the Oxford Movement is reckoned to be 1833, after the plan in parliament to suppress ten Irish bishoprics occasioned Keble's sermon at the university church.

98. The 30 Measures that became law between 1920 and 1928 were: Convocations of the Clergy (1920); Ecclesiastical Commissioners, Parochial Church Councils (Powers), Union of Benefices (1921); Representation of the Laity (Amendment), Pluralities Act 1838 Amendment, Revised Table of Lessons (1922); Bishopric of Blackburn, Diocese of Southwell (Division), Union of Benefices, Ecclesiastical Dilapidations, Benefices Act 1898 (Amendment), Diocese of Winchester (Division) (1924); Interpretation, Bishopric of Leicester, Diocesan Boards of Finance (1924–25); Brislington Parishes (Transfer), Rural Deaneries of Pontefract and Hemsworth (Transfer), Parish of Manchester Division Act 1850 (Amendment), First Fruits and Tenths, Ecclesiastical Commissioners, Clergy Pensions, Episcopal Pensions, Benefices (Ecclesiastical Duties) (1926); Indian Church, Clergy Pensions (Amendment), New Dioceses (Transitional Provisions) (1927); Ecclesiastical Commissioners (Provision for Unbeneficed Clergy), Tithe (Administration of Trusts), Clergy Pensions (Amendment) (1928). See *Journals of the House of Commons, 1920–1928*; *Journals of the House of Lords, 1920–1928*; *Official Year-Book of the National Assembly of the Church of England*, 1930. Of these 30 measures, 21 were passed without debate nor division in either house of parliament, and of the nine that were debated before being passed, only two required a division in either house. Graber, "Worship Ecclesiastical Discipline, and the Establishment," 375–77.

99. "Originally, the main topic of debate had been the alteration of the Ornaments Rubric." John Maiden, *National Religion and the Prayer Book Controversy, 1927–1928*, Woodbridge, 2009, 30.

took on the tone of an Anglo-Catholic revision, which handed that section of the church many things that they had been wanting, by permitting that which was currently illegal under the 1662 prayer book.[100] The more that this perception was seen to be true, the more Protestant opposition bristled. But there were typically not enough evangelical votes in the assembly to outweigh the moderates, who tended to be sympathetic to increased comprehensiveness, thus siding with leniency toward provisions advocated by Anglo-Catholics.[101] After several years of committee work, debate, revision, and more revision, the Prayer Book Measure was finally passed by convocation and the National Assembly in 1927, and sent to parliament for approval.[102]

In spite of the support of large majorities in convocation and the National Assembly, and relatively easy passage in the Lords, the Prayer Book Measure of 1927 went down to defeat in the House of Commons in December 1927, largely due to opposition from anti-ritualist MPs and non-Anglican MPs.[103] The National Assembly hastily softened some of the provisions that most troubled evangelicals, but the revised Prayer Book Measure that was passed by convocation and the assembly in 1928 was, once again, and by a slightly increased majority, rejected by the Commons, for largely the same reasons as the year before.[104]

---

100. The bishop of London, who was sympathetic to the revision, urged support for it and said: "To Anglo-Catholics I say, 'You make the mistake of your lives if you reject it, thus rejecting the substance for the shadow. The new Book embraces all for which you have fought during the past 40 years.'" *Times*, March 23, 1927, 19.

101. See Graber, "Worship, Ecclesiastical Discipline, and the Establishment," chapters 3 and 4.

102. *Canterbury Convocation*: Upper House: 21–4 in favour; Lower House: 168–22 in favor. *York Convocation*: Upper House: 11–0 in favour; Lower House: 68–10 in favour. *National Assembly*: House of Bishops: 34–4 in favour; House of Clergy: 253–37 in favor; House of Laity: 230–92 in favor. *Times*, March 31, 1927, 19; *Times*, July 7, 1927, 11.

103. The Measure passed the Lords by a 241–88 vote. Jasper, *Development of the Anglican Liturgy, 1662–1980*, London, 1989, 122. While it is true that the measure was also attacked from the more extreme Anglo-Catholic wing for not "going far enough" to satisfy their views, the bulk of the opposition came from those who felt that the revised prayer book "went too far" towards Rome, was a repudiation of the findings of the Royal Commission of 1906, and was therefore unacceptable. Provisions of the revised prayer book that came under the most heightened criticism were the rubrics that permitted reservation, the new, alternative canon, and rubrics that legalised a variety of Anglo-Catholic ceremonial practices. See Maiden, *National Religion and the Prayer Book Controversy*, 144–47; Graber, "Worship, Ecclesiastical Discipline, and the Establishment," 262–82; and Gavin White, "That Hectic Night," *Theology* 77 (1974) 639 ff.

104. The Prayer Book Measure (1927) was defeated 240–207, and the Prayer Book Measure (1928) was defeated 268–222, both in the Commons. Maiden, *National*

Change and Transformation

The bishops now had three main options to consider. They could revise the Book yet again to take into account parliament's opposition, and resubmit a new measure; they could withdraw from revision completely; or, if these options impinged too strongly on their spiritual rights, they could press for disestablishment in order to authorize the prayer book of their own choosing. The bishops, however, chose an unlikely path. They opted to ignore the will of parliament, and crafted a policy that recognized services conducted according to the 1662 or the 1928 book, even though the latter stood outside the law. After a late September meeting at Lambeth the bishops issued a policy statement:

> During the present emergency, and until further order be taken, the Bishops, having in view the approval given by the Houses of Convocation and the Church Assembly to the proposals for deviations from and additions to the Book of 1662 set forth in the Book of 1928, cannot regard as inconsistent with loyalty to the principles of the Church of England the use of such additions or derivations as fall within the limits of these proposals ... Accordingly the Bishops, in the exercise of their legal or administrative discretion, will be guided by the proposals approved in 1928 by the Houses of Convocation and by the Church Assembly, and will endeavor to secure that practices which are consistent neither with the Book of 1662 nor with the Book of 1928 shall cease.[105]

Significantly, the appeal for this policy was to the houses of convocation and the National Assembly, a position they claimed was not "inconsistent with loyalty to the principles of the Church of England." There was no rationale provided as to how this position was congruent with the establishment and the constitution. There was no appeal to the law nor a call for disestablishment. The bishops simply offered a stunning reversal of policy which, until the Prayer Book Measures encountered difficulty, had not been advocated by anyone.[106] Following the lead of the two archbishops, this "provisional"

Religion and the Prayer Book Controversy, 157. See also Graber, "Worship, Ecclesiastical Discipline, and the Establishment," 308–21.

105. *Times*, September 29, 1928, 10; *Church Times*, October 5, 1928, 378. The bishops' policy was passed by the convocations in the following July: *Canterbury Convocation*: Upper House: 23–4 in favor, Lower House: 96–54 in favor; *York Convocation*: Upper House: 11–0 in favor (with one abstention), Lower House: unanimously in favor. *Church Times*, July 12, 1929, 38; *Church Times*, July 19, 1929, 90, 92.

106. If the underlying policy was based on a new, expanded understanding of the bishops' *jus liturgicum*, the *Churchman* commented that such a claim "has never been made in this bold fashion before. The Royal Commission of 1906 was quite emphatic that such a claim was inconsistent with the constitutional realities of Church and State

policy was adopted because of "the acknowledged inadequacy of the existing law," and would last, presumably, only until the law was changed to meet the bishops' demands.[107]

What quickly emerged after the publication of the bishops' policy statement was that there could now be over forty ways in which the liturgical expression of the church might be administered, as there were over forty diocesan bishops.[108] There was hope that "some strong and capable committee of statesmen and churchmen may be appointed to weigh afresh the provisions of existing law in order to see whether any readjustment" would be required.[109] As it turned out, the interim policy governing the "present emergency" lasted for decades.[110]

While opinion was split between those who found the new policy imperfect but necessary, and those who found it abhorrent, there was much comment about how the bishops' policy was not based on law, and should be rethought.[111] One of the most outspoken commentators against it was Sir

---

in England." *Churchman* 43 (January 1929) 3. Dom Gregory Dix called this action by the bishops "a very bold claim indeed," and wondered what part of English law allowed them to "set aside the force of parliamentary statute 'in his own diocese' or anywhere else. Nothing had been heard of it by the Royal Commission of 1906 or by anyone else before 1929." Dom Gregory Dix, *The Shape of the Liturgy*, 2nd ed., Westminster, 1945, 709.

107. *Times*, September 29, 1928, 10.

108. For example, a bishop might use his discretion to insist upon obedience to a 1662 rubric (or a 1928 rubric) for a particular liturgical or ceremonial point, or, using that same discretion, might turn a blind eye toward a use that technically went beyond both. Given that there were any number of liturgical or ceremonial points, expecting uniformity of "discretion" among the bishops was not to be expected. For examples of different initial policy statements from different bishops, see *Church Times*, August 9, 1929, 163; September 6, 1929, 251; October 11, 1929, 405; October 18, 1929, 449.

109. Davidson, writing in the *Church Times*, July 6, 1928, 5. A commission on the relations between church and state was eventually appointed by the Cosmo Gordon Lang, the successor to Davidson at Canterbury, in November 1930. After six years of work, they published a report, which recommended removing parliament's veto power over liturgical measures, as well as recommending that the Archbishops summon a round table conference between representatives from different wings of the church to find workable solutions to controversial issues. Such a conference was duly called, and "gathered at Lambeth in 1938 to evolve a liturgy which the bishops could enforce. After wasting some months without providing itself with any very definite agenda, it was anaesthetised by [World War II]." Dix, *Shape of the Liturgy*, 713.

110. Writing in the late 1950s, Stephen Neill noted that the, strictly, illegal use of the 1928 prayer book had become a normal way of life for many within the Church of England, and called this "an impossible, intolerable, and humiliating situation. But it has lasted for thirty years, and seems likely to last for many years yet." Stephen Neill, *Anglicanism*, Harmondsworth, 1958, 398.

111. Dr. Carnegie Simpson, moderator of the Presbyterian Church of England,

Change and Transformation

Lewis Dibdin, leading ecclesiastical lawyer, friend of Davidson, member of both the Royal Commission of 1906 and archbishops' committee of 1916, and member of the National Assembly. Dibdin penned a pair of lengthy articles for the *Times* that traced the history of the present crisis, along with observations about what should be done to resolve it.[112] He offered a stinging rebuke of the bishops' policy:

> It is perhaps unnecessary to point out that the issue before us is not whether the Deposited Book [i.e. the 1928 Prayer Book] should be approved by Parliament, but whether the condition contained in the Enabling Act that no Measure should pass without the assent of the two Houses of Parliament should be disregarded by the Bishops. I regret as strongly as anyone the two decisions of the House of Commons. I have voted throughout for the new Prayer-book in the Church Assembly ... But they are bad advisors who invite the Bishops, notwithstanding the House of Commons, to allow the Deposited Book by abstaining from prosecuting, and by using their veto to prevent others from prosecuting offenders against the existing law. It has been said that letting it be known that no prosecutions will be allowed for use of the Deposited Book is not a breach of the Enabling Act. But such a general use of the Episcopal veto, intended to be employed with reference to the particular facts of each case, would be wholly illegitimate, and the common sense of the country would be right in rejecting such an evasion ... The conscience of the country is shocked by thin and futile arguments of this sort, and not less so by an open flouting of the conditions of the Enabling Act, to which the Bishops along with other Churchmen joyfully agreed.[113]

---

wrote: "To bring in a Measure under [the terms of the Enabling Act] and then, when this proves an obstacle, to invoke the principle of spiritual freedom to escape from it will not do. It is 'not cricket.'" *Times*, June 11, 1928, 15. Hensley Henson argued that "Disestablishment is to be preferred to the confusions and humiliations which we now endure." Ibid., January 11, 1929, 14. Charles Mallett said that "To claim the privileges of an Established Church and to evade its obligations is an impossible policy for honourable men." "The Bishops and the Law," *Contemporary Review*, vol. 134 (1928), 707. F.A. Iremonger observed that "one of the few remaining canons of middle-class morality had been broken, and that the way out of the impasse taken by the bishops was 'not quite straight.'" F.A. Iremonger, *William Temple, Archbishop of Canterbury, His Life and Letters*, London, 1948, 356. Writing years later, R. C. D. Jasper called this policy "inconsistent with the principles accepted in the Enabling Act ... and it was this inconsistency which helped earn for the Bishops the reputation of being rather shifty." Jasper, *Development of the Anglican Liturgy*, 149.

112. *Times*, January 7, 1929, 15–16; January 8, 1929, 13–14.
113. *Times*, January 8, 1929, 14.

But the bishops had set their course, and would not be swayed from it. The Enabling Act remained in the statute book, unchanged, and continued operating. The National Assembly kept meeting and crafting measures, which continued to be passed by Parliament. The "present emergency" in worship dragged on for years. Prayer book revision was put off indefinitely. Church life carried on.

CONCLUSION

In spite of the contentious results of the two rejected Prayer Book Measures, the Enabling Act may be seen as a successful, ground breaking advance in self-government for the Church of England. Not only was the role of the laity enshrined in the National Assembly, but the church could now craft legislation for itself. The fact that so many ecclesiastical measures were passed into law, and the fact that the provisions of the act proved to be workable and uncontroversial, give testimony to this.

What about the act in relation to the revision of the liturgy? If there was a flaw present in the act, it was, perhaps, the not unreasonable assumption that both parties—church and state—would respect the legal standing of the other, abide by the act's provisions, and would, in short, "follow the rules." The idea that the bishops would ignore a measure's rejection by Parliament, and on Church authority alone recognize the provisions of a new prayer book was quite novel. Such an option—except when linked with disestablishment—was not one contemplated before the twin rejections of 1927 and 1928. If succumbing to the legislature in liturgical matters was too humiliating to countenance, the rule of law could have been preserved if the bishops had pressed to dissolve the link that existed between the national church and the state. This would have been a completely legitimate option, but was not taken. Instead, the bishops opted for liturgical no man's land. But the Enabling Act's mechanisms endured.

The Enabling Act of 1919 granted to the church a much needed increase in its self-governing ability, while at the same time it preserved the delicate balance between church and state authority. Forged from the same historical context that produced the Royal Commission on Ecclesiastical Discipline and the Archbishops' Committee on Church and State, it continued to provide the church with the governing ability it needed. As such, the Enabling Act may be viewed as one of the most important pieces of ecclesiastical legislation passed in the twentieth century. It fundamentally changed the way in which the Church of England operated and took church government out of the seventeenth century and into the twentieth.

9

Anglicanism and the Search for Christian Concord

EPHRAIM RADNER

THE TOPIC OF CONCILIARITY has reemerged as an important focus of discussion in contemporary Anglicanism. "Conciliarity" itself refers to a form of ecclesial life ordered by church "councils." The category drew renewed ecclesiological interest within Roman Catholicism both before and after Vatican II, with all of the period's challenges and changes caught up in the debate over hierarchy and collegial decision-making. At the time, the discussion was informed by, but also encouraged further, scholarly investigation into the historical phenomenon of "conciliarism," the late medieval movement that sought to reengage the Western Church's polity to a conciliar model.[1] Similarly, the current conflicts within Anglicanism over teachings about sexuality and biblical authority have stirred up interest in ecclesial decision-making as well. Once again, debates have taken

---

1. The distinction between "conciliarity" and "conciliarism" is not always made. Paul Valliere, for instance, in his recent book prefers to stick with the single category of "conciliarism" to describe the life of continuous life of conciliar decision-making in the Church from her origins: Paul Valliere, *Conciliarism: A History of Decision-Making in the Church*, Cambridge, 2012. For another overview, see Francis Oakley, *The Conciliarist Tradition: Constitutionalism in the Catholic Church, 1300–1870*, Oxford, 2003.

up the findings of ongoing scholarship on conciliarity and conciliarism both. By default and by design together, Anglicans have ended up acting out a debate over whether our Christian lives as churches *together* are to be governed by "common consent" within a council, or by some other, more local, individual, or informal means, or finally by some contrasting and more centralized system of authority. What *does* it mean to be governed by "conciliar" methods? What ought to be the role of the Lambeth Conference, or of local synods versus Communion-wide gatherings, or of some new structure by which Anglican Churches order their decision-making in some kind of connection with other Anglican Churches?

WHEELS WITHIN WHEELS

Although the discussion here is not theologically oriented in its purpose, it does in fact presuppose a certain theological way of understanding how the Church's conciliar life *ought* to work, at least ideally.[2] In summary, we can try to understand the meaning of conciliar life, or of taking "counsel" within the Church, in terms of the prophetic phrase "wheels within wheels." The phrase, from Ezekiel's vision (Ezek 1:15–21), is one borrowed mostly from Gregory the Great's reflection on the work of God in time, as it is accomplished through the power of Scripture's comprehensive testamental reach in and through the Church.[3] The Church, according to Gregory, engages the various meanings of Scripture's broad scope in both testaments in an effort, over time, to apprehend their "concordance." The effort itself shapes the Church into her proper form, such that the practice of discerning *concordantia* within Scripture's multiple texts and meanings itself proves an ascetic discipline. Applying this notion to the conciliar life, and with Gregory's specific definitions in mind, the phrase "wheels within wheels" provides an accurate sense of the way the Church's many councils are to work in time, engaged by and with the Scriptures, to move together and lead the Church within God's transformative purpose. The theological character of council, I believe, derives from this kind of vision: council is the punctuated means by which one-mindedness and one-spiritedness—*concordia*

---

2. For further elaboration, see Ephraim Radner, *A Brutal Unity: The Spiritual Politics of the Christian Church*, Waco, TX, 2012.

3. Pope Gregory, *The Homilies of St. Gregory the Great On the Book of the Prophet Ezekiel*, trans. Theodosia Gray, Etna, CA, 1990. See also Angela Russell Christman, "The Spirit and the Wheels: Gregory the Great on Reading Scripture," in Paul M. Blowers et al, eds., *In Dominico Eloquio: In Lordly Eloquence. Essays on Patristic Exegesis in Honor of Robert Louis Wilken*, Grand Rapids, 2002, 395–407.

or *concordantia* in conciliar language[4]—take shape, through being called together, through their gathering, through their Scriptural deliberation, and finally through a transformation of the heart on the part of participants; and this one-mindedness is an ongoing and elaborating practice that draws one council into relation to another.

Conciliarism, in the fourteenth and fifteenth centuries especially, was an ecclesial-political movement seeking to bring unity to a Western Church divided by rival popes and regional factions. The movement itself was informed by a range of theological visions of what unity actually embodied. In our day, probably only the names of Nicholas of Cusa and Jean Gerson are still remembered from among the many theologians who contributed to the rich ferment of ecclesiological reflection associated with the larger conciliarist movement.[5] The Gregorian idea of *concordantia*, then, represents at best only a kind of synthetic typologizing of some of the main approaches at work in this era. As Anglican fragmentation and the various challenges to communion have gained force over the past decade, the interest in conciliarity and its historical models has grown, in particular around discussions over the proposed Anglican Covenant. But is there really any valid connection between even this larger synthetic picture of conciliarism and the Anglican experience over the past few centuries? Does a conciliarist vision "fit" or does it not fit our life as Anglicans both locally and more broadly, and should we wish it to even if it did? It is both the question of "fit" and of "will" that we need to assess.

The Church of England theologian Paul Avis is one of the most recent crop of scholars to have revisited the history of conciliarism with a view to its relevance for contemporary ecclesiology. His book *Beyond the Reformation?*, while ordered especially to the larger ecumenical scene, offers a

---

4. One of the densest conciliar uses of the term is that of Nicholas of Cusa. See his *The Catholic Concordance*, ed. and trans., Paul E. Sigmund, Cambridge, 1991. On Nicholas of Cusa see Gerald Christianson and Thomas M. Izbicki, eds., *Nicholas of Cusa on Christ and the Church: Essays in Memory of Chandler McCuskey Brooks for the American Cusanus Society*, Leiden, 1996.

5. In addition to Valliere, *Conciliarism* and Oakley, *Conciliarist Tradition*, see also John Neville Figgis, *Studies of Political Through from Gerson to Grotius, 1414-1625*, Cambridge, 1907; Brian Tierney, *Foundations of the Conciliar Theory: The Contribution of the Medieval Canonists from Gratian to the Great Schism*, Cambridge, 1955; Francis Oakley, *Natural Law, Conciliarism and Consent in the Late Middle Ages*, London, 1984; A. J. Black, *Monarchy and Community: Political Ideas in the Later Conciliar Controversy, 1430-1450*, Cambridge, 1970; A. J. Black, *Council and Commune: The Conciliar Movement and the Fifteenth Century Heritage*, London, 1979; J. H. Burns and Thomas M. Izbicki, eds. and trans., *Conciliarism and Papalism*, Cambridge, 1997. For an interesting claim about the role of conciliarism in forging a "European" identity, see Denys Hay, *Europe: The Emergence of an Idea*, 2nd ed., Edinburgh, 1968.

number of pertinent challenges to Anglicanism in particular. Avis, a long-time student of ecumenical theology and ecclesiology, has been the head of the Church of England's Council for Christian Unity. He introduces his book with a comment on Anglicanism's unique "conciliar principles and structures," and writes that Anglicans have been "pioneers" of episcopal government in synod. But he then raises the question that has haunted conciliarism from the beginning: is it up to the job? Noting our present circumstances, Avis describes the 2003 consecration of the partnered gay bishop Gene Robinson as a "brutal and unavoidable new fact in the Anglican ecclesiastical landscape." He proceeds to say:

> It is because that consecration or ordination was, like all ordinations, a sacramental act, an ecclesial sign with universal intention, of what is true of the Church and of the values that the Church stands for and of the message that it proclaims, that at the time of writing it has placed a question mark over the viability of Anglican polity and the cohesion of the Anglican Communion. In that sense, it was parallel to the event that sparked the greatest trauma ever to afflict the Western Church before the Reformation itself: the election, in 1378 of two popes (subsequently enlarged to three) who reigned simultaneously, each claiming the allegiance of Christendom and roundly anathematizing the other(s). The sets of responses that have been offered to these two events (so widely separated in time that it seems to be a painful effort for some otherwise educated Christians to discern any connection or analogy between them ...) bear an uncanny resemblance to each other.[6]

Indeed: and does the Council of Constance's rapid loss of focus, after seeming to be the high point of conciliar integrity, and the Church's quick movement back from council to pope, and finally into Reformation division, presage some new and analogous disintegration in our midst today? But the analogy would bear scrutiny only if Anglicanism could claim for itself some original and ongoing conciliar ordering. Can it?

CONCILIARISM: ORIGINS AND CHALLENGES

It is true that representatives of the English Church were not themselves very active at the actual gatherings of Constance and Basle, nor had they offered much to the debate itself, but they were not without interest in

---

6. Paul Avis, *Beyond the Reformation? Authority, Primacy and Unity in the Conciliar Tradition*, London, 2006, xv.

these councils. By Henry VIII's reign, there were many in England who had imbibed the conciliar teaching of the continent. As the struggle between monarch and papacy unfolded in the 1530s, entangled as it was already with growing calls for ecclesial and theological reform, Henry and his counselors drew on conciliar arguments to appeal his case to a larger gathering, that is, to a "General Council." Various churchmen, earlier and later, were active in this attempt and in the wider discussions of council that it engendered—Edward Fox, Cuthbert Tunstall, Thomas Starkey, and even Stephen Gardiner and Thomas More.[7] These figures were all "catholics" in certain key respects, and some of them even later suffered for their refusal to embrace fully the reforms of Henry or of Edward and Elizabeth. But their willingness to engage the question of the papacy's limited powers, to different extents, and of the council's relation to it and to the secular monarch, makes them all "conciliarist" in a fundamental way. Each was able to raise the question and sympathetically analyze the arguments on constraining the pope's authority, and ordering the Church by more general realities of "consent" according, in this case, to the national identity and its representatives (including the monarch, of course, as responsible for the imposition of divine and natural law). In particular, earlier fifteenth-century debates over "national" representation at general church councils had already framed ecclesial self-understanding in a way that Henry's own commitments would happily embrace. In a kind of theoretical fashion, these discussions laid a seed for later constitutional concerns. Behind many of their ideas lay Jean Gerson's writing, and its dissemination through various theological routes.[8]

In point of fact, however, this broad conciliarism in Henry's court was quickly diluted by the larger needs and demands for decision-making within this era, and the theological substance of the debate—broad enough to engage anonymous writing and publishing—was soon set aside. We know that Cranmer, both early but also at the very end of his life, sought the authority of a general council to bring order to the increasingly anarchic situation of ecclesial and political life in England and Europe, but this desire was hardly at the center of his more consistent vision.[9]

7. Paul O'Grady, *Henry VIII and the Conforming Catholics*, Collegeville, MN, 1990; D. A. Sawada, "Two Anonymous Tudor Treatises on the General Council," *Journal of Ecclesiastical History* 12 (1961) 197–214; for a more general discussion see G. R. Evans, *Problems of Authority in the Reformation Debates*, Cambridge, 1992.

8. John J. Ryan, *The Apostolic Conciliarism of Jean Gerson*, Atlanta, 1998; Mark S. Burrows, *Jean Gerson and De consolatione theologiae (1418): The Consolation of a Biblical and Reforming Theology for a Disordered Age*, Tübingen, 1991.

9. The fundamental work was done by John T. McNeill in 1930: *Unitive Protestantism: The Ecumenical Spirit and its Persistent Expression*, rev. ed., Richmond, 1964. See also Valliere, *Conciliarism*, 163.

The famous Reformed English statements on councils, e.g. in Article XXI of the Articles of Religion (which date in the Latin version from 1563), seem to relegate their status. First, they make the convening of councils a matter of the "prince's will"; second, they affirm councils' potential for "error," even in essential matters pertaining to the faith; finally, they subject councils stringently to the higher and ultimate authority of Scripture. But rather than marginalize councils, this constraining of their authority proved, at least in the minds of many Anglican reformers, rather to indicate the shape of their necessary application. Thus, Cranmer's own appeal to a council, as already noted, was viewed as central to the way the "Church Militant" needed to order its life. It was, furthermore, a view shared with others in the next generation, as we see in Jewel's published desire that "God grant that we may once see that day that a General Council may be called, wherein Christ may sit president, and all these matters that are now in question may have indifferent hearing, and may be decided by the word of God."[10]

The point here is that councils do their work only as Scripture remains their key, and gatherings are oriented primarily to the vocation of scriptural engagement. This marks English reformed conciliarism as at least broadly in line with the Gregorian ideal of *concordantia*. Hence, William Whitaker, the great—indeed, normative—Elizabethan expositor of Protestant Anglican scriptural hermeneutics, insisted that "we allow that it is a highly convenient way of finding the true sense of Scripture for devout and learned men to assemble, examine the cause diligently, and investigate the truth; yet with this proviso, that they govern their decision wholly by the Scriptures ... such a proceeding we, for our parts, have long wished for."[11]

Richard Hooker and Conciliarism

By the late sixteenth century, conciliar ideas returned to the English theological and political arena, as controversy with Roman Catholics and then with more radical Protestants demanded more acute and subtle historical argument—the writings of people like John Ponet and Matthew Sutcliffe fall within this genre of interest. In addition, popular works like Foxe's *Actes and Monuments* (1563) presented the conciliar period, especially Constance, Basle, and Pisa, as the dawn of the Reformation itself, and the period and its characters took on a new luster. Scholars like Patterson and Avis consider Richard Hooker, within this new stream of interest in councils, to be among

---

10. Cited in Avis, *Beyond the Reformation?*, 139.
11. Ibid.

the most robust and rich Anglican explicator of conciliar ideals.[12] But that is not because Hooker devotes much explicit space to councils, let alone to their peculiar place within the Church of England. He does not. But in the *Laws* he focuses so forcefully upon notions of law and consent—and Hooker was well versed in the constitutional concerns of late sixteenth-century England—that the essential character of conciliar action inevitably hovers behind much of what he argues with respect to the Church's proper self-ordering. Law and consent, as Hooker presents these two categories, are things got at relationally, or socially, via corporate discernment and ordered decision-making, within the proper outworking of the law of nature and of social bodies, and according to the particular directives of God's supernaturally revealed will. It is not surprising, then, that when Hooker does mention church councils, he has both a very high view of their need and authority, but also a realistic one of their relative historical place within the scope of God's purposes.

Most famously, Hooker compares the general council, and church councils more broadly, to the natural—that is divinely originated—emergence of laws among the Christian nations. "Communion," literally, is his theme, and it derives from the reality that "there is one Lord, one faith, and one baptism." In this context, councils are "a thing whereof God's own blessed Spirit was the author; a thing practiced by the holy Apostles themselves; a thing always afterward kept and observed throughout the world; a thing never otherwise than most highly esteemed of, till pride, ambition and tyranny began by fractious and vile endeavors to abuse that divine intention unto the furtherance of wicked purposes." But *abusus non tollit usum*—wrong use does not preclude proper use—and Hooker insists that councils, and the laws by which they order the Church, must be revived and continue.[13]

So, for instance, he continues to describe the Church's "general council" as "the best, the safest, the most sincere and reasonable way" of deciding controverted matters authoritatively—well nigh equal to "apostolic" injunctions in their weight, if rendered as a "verdict" taken from an "orderly" ecclesial gathering.[14] But the context of these kinds of remarks

---

12. W. B. Patterson, "Hooker on Ecumenical Relations: Conciliarism in the English Reformation," in A. S. McGrade, ed., *Richard Hooker and the Construction of Christian Community*, Tempe, AZ, 1997, 283–303; Avis, *Beyond the Reformation?*, 141–49.

13. Richard Hooker, *The Works of the Learned and Judicious Divine, Mr. Richard Hooker, with an Account of His Life and Death by Isaac Walton*, edited by John Keble, Oxford, 1836, hereafter cited as *Laws* and cited by book number, chapter, and section, I.10.14.

14. Ibid., IV.13.

by Hooker is invariably that of ecclesial turmoil—such as that engendered by the Puritans—and the "peace" of the Church becomes an overriding goal that imbues a legitimate council with its power over and beyond the actual content of its decisions. Councils may indeed "err," as the Anglican Articles of Religion had insisted. That is not in dispute. But their authority is near apostolical, not because of this content—that may be erroneous—but because of its goal, the peace of the Church and society, and its "sincere" commitment to engage the truth of God's will. It is this engagement that must, if pursued over time, finally provide the Church with the correctives its decisions may require. Personal or minority resistance to the decisions of lawful church councils, even if in fact these decisions prove erroneous, is not a faithful response, precisely because it rejects the Christian calling to conciliar engagement and the promise of divine ordering to which it is fundamentally subject. Thus, in his Preface to the *Laws*, Hooker lays out this rather extreme claim as a basic commitment when he writes, as against Puritan calls to ecclesial resistance because of purported ecclesial error: "howbeit, better it was in the eye of [God's] understanding that sometimes an erroneous sentence definitive should prevail, till the same authority perceiving such oversight, might afterwards correct or reverse it, than that strifes should have respite to grow, and not come speedily unto some end."[15]

Hooker extends this claim, not just to "general councils" but to all politically legitimate representative bodies charged with making "judicial" and "final" decisions, even to secular "commissions" granted authority in these matters. These must stand over and against all individual judgment that leads to the overturning of corporate peace. Hooker—out-puritaning the Puritans in this case—cites Deuteronomy 17:12 on this score: "And the man that will do presumptuously, and will not hearken unto the priest that standeth to minister there before the LORD thy God, or unto the judge, even that man shall die: and thou shalt put away the evil from Israel." And all this is because the character of all "law" functions, as a gift from and reflection of God, via a network of communal relations of discernment and judgment for the sake of truth and peace together over time. "Conciliar life," we could say, derives from the very nature of created human communities of all and any kind; and church councils from the nature of God's ordering of the Christian community as it is engaged in discerning God's will, most centrally within the Scriptures. Within this process—that is, within this history of God's creative ordering—the Church, bit by bit, follows her pilgrimage through a common settlement of purpose that consistently reflects the "weightier" matters of the law—mercy and justice—as Hooker quotes

15. Ibid., preface, 6.

Matthew 23:23, and as the Body of Christ orders herself in peace as she seeks the understanding of the Kingdom.[16]

Hooker's remarks are brief, yet within the context of his own concerns and even the immediate focus of his writings, they are significant in their re-grasping, politically, of *concordantia* as outlined above. After all, what Hooker is ostensibly analyzing is the nature of scriptural authority within a community that must make decisions in the face of various and varying demands that affect, in various ways, the range of members within that community. It is understanding the character of Law—divine, natural, communal, supernatural, and so on, and their relationship to one another—that allows one (so Hooker argues) to navigate these decisions. This is precisely a matter of discernment, not of simple calculus according to some set of formulae. God is indeed ordering the world through time, according to the larger order of His purpose; and churches must exist in "history," insists Hooker, which means they must find their own order within this purpose. Scripture has a unique place in this ordering, because it both reveals aspects of it specifically, but also because Scripture acts as a kind of shadow to the more fundamental order of God's purpose as it is being played out in the whole network of divine law within human society. Hence, Scripture does *not*, as Hooker claims versus the Puritans, explicitly tell us everything that is true. But it *does* "reflect" everything that is true, even the shifts of historical experience and understanding. This takes place, as much of Hooker's own discussions demonstrate, through the interplay of the testaments themselves, as they are bound to the shape of human communities—Jewish, Christian, and even pagan.

If this issue is to be resolved—and we must, as Hooker himself recognized in writing his book in the first place, in response to the turmoil of the Church in England—it can only be done through the careful and common discernment of scriptural law as it takes its living form within the community. This is exactly why "council" is both natural and necessary from Hooker's standpoint, even when that council presents itself in the simple forms of political arrangements. In a sense, Hooker's own work is a part of this "conciliar" process that must include open debate, but also careful and extended study, analysis, and communal evaluation. Actual church councils, formed through the coming together of representatives acting according to specific forms of discussion and decision, are but the particular sign of this larger conciliar action in which public theology, oriented towards scriptural reading and interpretation in its comprehensive scope and social context, is a key element.

16. Ibid., VIII.6.

CONCILIARISM: IDEALS

All this may seem more than a little idealistic. But it is an ideal that has attracted the attention of many. In 1998 the Anglican-Roman Catholic International Commission published their report on *The Gift of Authority*, which sought to lay out an agreed statement on how the Church's exercise of authority flows from the acceptance of the truth of God's commitments in Christ Jesus, the "Amen" to all God's promises (2 Cor 1:20).[17] The way the Church does this is through its common faithfulness and subjection to the teaching tradition of her apostolic life. And one long section of the Report (s. 34-40) is devoted specifically to the reality of "synodality." This constitutes "the walking together" or "common way" that is given, first in the Eucharist, and that then extends through joint representative counsel, especially within the office of the bishops and, where necessary, reaching to broader and larger councils, which are received by the faithful. Anglicans and Roman Catholics together are committed to this, the Report insists. The entire section is an important one to read, in order to get a grasp of a major contemporary perspective on living conciliarism. But the paragraph (s. 39) on Anglican conciliarism is worth quoting in full:

> In the Church of England at the time of the English Reformation the tradition of synodality was expressed through the use both of synods (of bishops and clergy) and of Parliament (including bishops and lay people) for the settlement of liturgy, doctrine and church order. The authority of General Councils was also recognised. In the Anglican Communion, new forms of synods came into being during the nineteenth century and the role of the laity in decision making has increased since that time. Although bishops, clergy, and lay persons consult with each other and legislate together, the responsibility of the bishops remains distinct and crucial. In every part of the Anglican Communion, the bishops bear a unique responsibility of oversight. For example, a diocesan synod can be called only by the bishop, and its decisions can stand only with the bishop's consent. At provincial or national levels, Houses of Bishops exercise a distinctive and unique ministry in relation to matters of doctrine, worship and moral life. Further, though Anglican synods largely use parliamentary procedures, their nature is eucharistic. This is why the bishop as president of the Eucharist appropriately presides at the diocesan synod, which assembles to bring God's redemptive work into the present through the life and activity of the local

---

17. Anglican-Roman Catholic International Commission (ARCIC), *The Gift of Authority: Authority in the Church III. An Agreed Statement*, Toronto, 1999.

church. Furthermore, each bishop has not only the episcope of the local church but participates in the care of all the churches. This is exercised within each province of the Anglican Communion with the help of organs such as Houses of Bishops and the Provincial and General Synods. In the Anglican Communion as a whole the Primates' Meeting, the Anglican Consultative Council, the Lambeth Conference and the Archbishop of Canterbury serve as instruments of synodality.

This really *is* an ideal. Not only is the jump from the Reformation to the present Anglican Communion one that masks some rather odd conciliar witness over the intervening years, but we all know too well that the present moment is not one in which this calm paean to Anglican life-in-council reflects the spirit of actual dialogue. How, in fact, did and does the conciliar ideal find its form in Anglicanism?

Conciliar Ideal in Anglicanism

At the outset, the debated question of heavy-handed rule, from Canterbury and court, under Archbishop Laud and Charles I and the strange contortions of parliament over several decades during and after this period, must be set aside. It is arguable that "conciliar life" was embodied during these times; and even if so, hardly in a way that could be judged as furthering *concordantia*, unless we accept that such a reality includes intra-Christian violence. But even after the Restoration, indeed already by 1700, the tenor of debate and relationship between the lower and upper houses of Canterbury's convocation were so strained that meetings were being held only sporadically. By 1717 this tension had become so bitter, and the proceedings so scandalous to the larger populace that convocation was prorogued indefinitely. Apart from certain minor matters convocation never met again until 1856. This was possible, constitutionally, because of certain complex laws linking crown and archbishop; but it hardly represented the Church's "conciliar" functioning through consensual means on behalf of the people. Obviously, church life went on, and in some areas, blossomed spectacularly from the grass-roots up, e.g. the religious societies, Methodism, diocesan renewal, and so on. Still, "council" more or less disappeared from the Church of England, and the character of Christian life within England suffered deeply as a result.

Ironically, it was in *America*, and in the United States specifically, that the conciliar character of Anglicanism found new and vital form. This happened with the calling of the General Convention in 1785 and 1789, made up finally of a house of bishops and house of deputies including lay representatives, and meeting at regular and constitutionally guaranteed moments. It is probably fair to say that the Episcopal Church's General Convention—of which it was self-consciously proud and for which it offered numerous apologies based on broad readings of the early church—exercised more influence than anything else upon the revival and re-invention of conciliarist or synodical life within Anglicanism over the next two centuries.[18] It is, of course, "ironic" that this is so, given the American Episcopal Church's recent role in disrupting this development up to the present so thoroughly.

But perhaps it is not so ironic. For it is also significant that the model for revived conciliarity within the Anglican community came out of a frankly and unabashedly political context—the American Revolution—where the questions of representation and consent were paramount, and the theological concerns regarding the Body of Christ and the discernment of the Scriptures were at best secondary, if that. It has only been with difficulty that Anglicans have clawed back, as it were, to the presenting issues of conciliarist commitment, which involve the *salus populi Dei in Verbo suo*—the salvation of God's people through His Word.

Certainly, the synodical form of government by which churches are ordered through the council of their bishops and other leaders has now become normative within Anglicanism around the world. This has transpired, often with an explicit sense that the character of the Gospel itself impels us to this form. There was a kind of Anglo-Saxon chauvinism, not too pretty at times, that originally lay behind the floating of a general Anglican council in the 1850s (from the American side), as a means of extending the triumphant Anglo-Saxon Christian culture to new corners of the earth. But the real impetus for a larger Anglican council, as we know, came from a concrete worry over the Anglican fracture within South Africa, and the ripples of tension it was causing among mutually-recognizing Anglican bodies. When the first Lambeth Conference was in fact convened in 1867, at the urging of Canadian bishops, it was responding, in part, to a new sense both that the Anglican Church (as opposed to a Church of England with some subsidiaries) was a reality, however ill-defined, and that this reality demanded a certain way of life if it was to maintain its Christian integrity.[19] Obviously, even more than the American General Convention, this conference marked

---

18. For first-hand accounts of the discussions surrounding the formation of this synodical ordering, see Francis L. Hawks and William Stevens Perry, eds., *Journals of the General Conventions of the Protestant Episcopal Church in the United States of America from A.D. 1785 to A.D. 1853 Inclusive*, Philadelphia, 1860, vol. 1.

19. See Randall T. Davidson, ed., *Origin and History of the Lambeth Conferences of 1867 and 1878: With the Official Reports and Resolutions*, London, 1888.

the first full step towards a larger conciliar *self-understanding*. Preceding, as it did, the First Vatican Council, its significance for the wider Church cannot be overestimated. Even if Scripture itself was only very indirectly involved—its interpretation and authority lay, after all, behind the divisions in South Africa that Lambeth would try to sort out—the dynamic of *gathering* because of the Scriptures was now officially, as it were, reinstated.

Lambeth Conferences

The first Lambeth Conference, furthermore, acted as a synod, despite the clear statements beforehand that sought to limit the gathering's scope of authority: the conference deliberately tried to bring order into Natal (cf. res. 6 and 7);[20] it claimed the right to judge the character of various provincial Books of Common Prayer, through a declaration regarding the right of synods to revise the Prayer Books of member provinces (res. 8); and it sought the organization of a "doctrinal tribunal" for "appeal"—although the Conference carefully called it a "voluntary spiritual tribunal"—whose work, nonetheless, was aimed at the heart of the disputative character of the churches (res. 9). And nothing could be more synodically "definitive" than the issuance, at the 1888 Conference (res. 11) of the so-called Chicago-Lambeth Quadrilateral that, although couched only in terms of an "opinion" of the conference, has quickly become a touchstone for Anglican self-understanding not only across the globe, but within the eyes of most other churches.

It is true that there was a steadfast rejection of formal "synodality" by the conference, and the 1930 Conference (res. 33) was adamant that it had not "been summoned as a synod to issue any statement professing to define doctrine." Furthermore, the conference (res. 49) insisted that the churches of the Communion "are bound together not by a central legislative and executive authority, but by mutual loyalty sustained through the common counsel of the bishops in conference." On this basis, the conference also rejected the recommendation of the first Lambeth gathering that an "appellate tribunal" be set up as something "inconsistent with the spirit of the Anglican Communion" (res. 51). These limiting statements were made, however, even as the conference began to argue that "unity in faith and discipline" depended on the "subordination" of lesser synods to greater ones (1867, res. 4) and that interdependence demanded that larger bodies within

---

20. The resolutions of all the Lambeth conferences can be found at the Anglican Communion Office website: http://www.lambethconference.org/resolutions. Subsequent references to resolutions are to this archive.

the Communion should take responsibility for common concerns (cf. 1968, res. 44 and 1988, res.14).[21] Furthermore, one might justly ask: what exactly is "common counsel of bishops in conference," if not a synod?

It was almost as if the Lambeth conferences were deliberately kicking against the pricks. "No, we are *not* a council," they have said insistently. But for all that, Lambeth's stature, at least in the public and ecumenical perception, grew during all this time. One reason for this positive perception was the general renewal of awareness of conciliar ideals as the World Council of Churches took its form in 1948, after the moral and ecclesial debacle of World War II, and the failure of previous "conciliar" practice had risen to the level of blatant ethical scandal. People were looking to Lambeth not simply as a living example of some alternative, but as a place where that alternative, if not yet truly visible, could in fact be tested and given flesh.

But it was probably the *ressourcement* associated with the ecumenical Liturgical Movement that did more to reorient this set of political concerns, as they converged towards renewing council, in a specific direction: that is, towards the reality of not only re-appropriating Scripture as a central facet of taking council, but actually making that scriptural focus the very purpose of council altogether. This took place in the wake of a growing interest, from the 1920s on, but especially in the 1950s, in restoring patristic understandings and experiences of a common baptism and eucharist, for instance. As this interest came together with a new ecumenical focus upon biblical theology, which drew various traditions together (including newly directed Roman Catholic scriptural studies), the new orientation blossomed. The result offered an unexpected common ground in the appreciation of synodical (and especially episcopally synodical) council. In this context, for instance, the Chicago-Lambeth Quadrilateral gained a new profile and standing: Scripture before Creed, upheld by sacrament and episcopacy, and granted historical shaping in the context of local life. Conciliar life, even if the phrase was not used, had at least a living conceptual model.

With the emergence at the same time, in the 1950s and 1960s, of newly independent younger churches, in Africa and Asia, Anglicanism was poised to present itself in a new form, as a restored conciliar body, a communion of churches bound by deep scriptural roots of Reformation and Catholic concern, and representing, more perhaps than any other church, the shape of the primitive ecclesial ideal of local and regional churches gathering, taking counsel, and deciding together. This new profile was not simply pretence, although it was historically a kind of novelty: there was a sense

---

21. This amounts to the so-called "Lund Principle," as it was later named after the version articulated at the 1952 Faith and Order Conference of the World Council of Churches held in Lund, Sweden.

Change and Transformation

that this is what Anglicanism had been leading towards, in all of its fits and starts, from the beginning. So much did this seem to be the case that other churches accepted the new image readily and genuinely, as is evident in the recent ARCIC statement. The ideal had become a living hope, because it was being imbued with the breath of life through its enactment. The younger churches, many engaged in what appeared (and not only romantically) to be a reconnection with the thrill of the primitive church's evangelical ardor, both scripturally and evangelistically, were bringing to the staid structures of the Communion's gatherings a sense of divine vitality and raw power. Once again, taking place in tandem with a large Roman Catholic council, Vatican II, that now turned to the Scriptures as its own foundation of ordering truth, the conciliar vision seemed about to bloom.[22] The old conciliarist adage that *Salus populi lex suprema esto*—the health (or salvation) of God's people is the supreme touchstone for all law—would indeed now take the form of an Anglican, and perhaps even ecumenical, commitment to let the Scriptures form the people of God freely yet consistently.[23] Decision-making would be on this basis and would actually embody its reality.

CONTEMPORARY CONTEXT

If this narrative thus far sounds a bit wistful, there is an obvious reason for this: the promise was never much more than a hope, and is in any case—and almost from the moment of its birth—under threat in a great way. It was not a vain promise, to be sure. Despite accusations about the horrendous ordering of Lambeth 1998, there were aspects of its form that marked a serious progress within this conciliar promise, and that is primarily the attempt at and exercise of extended Bible studies among the bishops, so that discussion and finally decision could indeed be made "according to the Scriptures."[24] Bishops who were present at that conference have, almost uniformly, spoken of the remarkable grace of this single and simple commitment to pursue *concordantia* in the way defined here within the Christian tradition. But Lambeth 1998 also exposed the weakness of *actual* conciliar practice within the Communion. The Bible studies proved a kind of passing technique, brief

22. See some of the influential early essays of Hans Küng, *The Council, Reform and Reunion*, trans. Cecily Hastings, Garden City, NY, 1965.

23. The phrase is from Cicero, *De Legibus* III.1.8. See the English edition, Marcus Tullius Cicero, *On the Commonwealth; and, On the Laws*, trans. and ed. James E. Zetzel, Cambridge, 1999, 159.

24. A useful account is given in Miranda K. Hassett, *Anglican Communion in Crisis: How Episcopal Dissidents and Their African Allies Are Reshaping Anglicanism*, Princeton, 2007.

and faltering, and unrelated to many of the actual issues under discussion for action, that collapsed under the weight of a long-brewing conflict that had never found an extended context for its confrontation, engagement, and definitive resolution. It is well-documented that the 1998 Lambeth Conference was plagued with bluster, sudden shifts of parliamentary maneuver, and finally recriminating debate over the "one-mindedness" of its actual decisions. Certainly, once adjourned, the conference sent back into the world, not a group of renewed and re-focused bishops, but a group of seemingly angered and hostile parties, chained to the politics of local image and personal gain, and set upon a global battle over sexual discipline. So that, just as some tentative steps were being taken, it seemed, to embrace the conciliar call, its infant weakness proved incapable to sustaining the burden of an adult conflict laid upon it.

What shall we make of the fact that the next robust attempt at conciliar commitment by the Communion, engineered mainly through the leadership of the Archbishop of Canterbury—the proposed Anglican Covenant—has now become hostage (and fatally so perhaps) to the refusals to exercise discipline on organizing council (on the part of Canterbury), self-discipline, by the American Episcopal Church as being essentially a part of a council, or *self*-giving for the sake of council (on the part of the Global South Primates)? It is, arguably, but a sign of the still-incomplete acceptance of the conciliar vision by Anglicans world-wide. There have been several recent statements by the various global churches that the Lambeth Conference is basically dead, and that such gatherings are now something of the past; or that the global "focus of unity" that the Archbishop of Canterbury once represented is now finished; or the repeated insistence by more liberal groups within the Communion that, in any case, Lambeth Conference was *never* a "synod" in any sense—all this, and more, represents a general exhaustion, but also weakness in the face of a true spiritual challenge. Anglican conciliarity seems just too hard to accomplish as an ongoing practice.

For if council is to make sense, it must be given time, it must be given the means to progress, to engage the sharing of the Word, to reach outwards, to be judged by the power of its holiness, and finally to result in the change that the Word's encounter, in its comprehensive grasp, must accomplish. It is not as if there is ignorance about or rejection of this vision of council. The Windsor Report, arguably, provides a concrete (if not always clear and admittedly sometimes lurching) articulation of it in its essential linkage of interdependent communion and the life of scriptural engagement through the collegial and episcopally-led discernment of the synods of the Church.[25] Archbishop Rowan Williams, for all the invective aimed at him, consistently pressed for a church and Communion where the Scriptures are read "eucharistically," that is, explicitly through and within the gathered community's subjection to the Holy Spirit's listening gifts and transformative power to empty us into Christ's own self-emptying grace.[26]

One can, however, easily list the failures in taking hold of this vision over the past few years: "inter-Anglican" commissions that meet, and in their haste and accepted "distance discussion" come up with nothing but vacuous statements acknowledging "difference," as if their job was to be sociologists of diversity, not seekers of concord; diocesan, episcopal, and provincial synods that are littered with menu items, resolutions, advocacy agenda, unwieldy participations, and compressed political posturing at microphones, such that prayerful study and discernment are not only impossible but actually unwelcome and sometimes even ruled illegitimate; Primates' Meetings that, although coming out with relatively clear directives, are so driven by constrained scheduling and the pressures of the media, as well as personal grand-standing and political maneuver, that the ability to read the Scripture together, to study it, to dwell with it, to work with it and be worked over by it, has never even been broached. The failures are legion, and they center mainly around the reading of Scripture together, progressively, pneumatically, and submissively.

What we have seen, over the past few years, even as the promise of conciliarity was made with alluring hope is, in expressed response, a great *fear* of council, which evidences a fear of God's own power and judgment. What, after all, are we to make of claims by Lambeth to lack of money to meet or to have the primates meet, or claims by other primates and bishops to their inability to sit in the same room as their heretic fellow primates, to being manipulated by external powers (Anglican Communion office, Primates and their followers)? How are we to assess refusals to grant representative status to bishops, the most venerable representatives of the people the church has ever had? It is as if, having revived the conciliar ideal at last, Anglicanism has beaten a retreat into its most craven political understandings, so as to avoid God's own presence. It would be difficult to criticize too strongly those on the right and left for this cowardice, from Lambeth to

---

25. The text of the Report can be found at http://www.anglicancommunion.org/windsor2004.

26. Rowan Williams, "The Bible: Reading and Hearing," Larkin-Stuart Lecture, Toronto, April 16, 2007 http://www.trinity.utoronto.ca/News_Events/News/archbishop.htm.

Lagos to New York to Sydney to Cardiff. Hooker's lament over the decline of council, because of "pride, ambition and tyranny" linked to "fractious and vile endeavours" rings ever loudly in our midst. If we will not take the time and spend the money and adopt the expectant attitude to come together before the living Word of God, who are we, really?

THERAPEUTIC SURVEY

There are a number of aspects of conciliar life that must be rediscovered and reasserted if the present devolution of its promise within Anglicanism is to be halted.

First, we must reaffirm the conciliar imperative itself, and put aside the ever-reiterated fears of stating the synodal character of our gatherings within the Communion. Rather than continually limiting the meaning of every gathering and its work, we should rather embrace the actual conciliar movement that has welled up within the history of Anglicanism itself: Lambeth, for instance, *is* a "synod," a council; so is the meeting of the Primates; so is the Anglican Consultative Council; so too are our diocesan synods and the gatherings of clergy or laity who come together to pray and study and form a common mind. The attempt to hedge the import of these meetings is proving, more and more, a Jonah-like flight from the vocation to be gripped by the proffered authority of God's Word. Christians are *called* to a synodal existence, and we must embrace it at every point. If Anglicanism does not wish to order her life according to synods or councils, in the simple but fundamental sense outlined here, that is a stark judgment on her potential participants and, frankly, a marked rejection of the *salus populi Dei* in this troubling time.

Secondly, of course, that Word must also be acknowledged as being at the heart of council itself. The conciliar life's central purpose of engaging and being engaged by the Scriptures of God in their fullness must reemerge. There are specific pragmatic realities that the councils of Anglicanism must deal with, and must do so straightforwardly. But these realities—what to do with churches that do not accept consultative consensus in their decision-making, or with boundary-crossers or with those congregations fearing destructive oversight from their bishops and so on—have so overwhelmed the possibility of God's confrontation through His Word of the Church of Christ in time that the latter has been rendered irrelevant to the proceedings of gathering altogether. Even in the face of the most concrete problems of common life that need resolution, these must be grappled with only from within the larger scope of the Scriptures' ordering of our lives. If that takes more time or money than we desire then it is our desires that must be curtailed, not the power of God's Word.

If this were to be pursued, the new (to Anglicanism, that is, although not to the Church, alas) penchant to threaten or enact boycotts and premature departures and the staying out of rooms because of bad smells, however metaphorized, must also come to an end. Where there is conflict, Paul and Peter must face each other (Gal 2:11), and say their worst, their most, their deepest convictions; and they must each endure it. Not for a moment only, through the publishing of declarations or the giving of speeches, and the hiding behind press releases and blog sites, but through the hard reiteration of difference in daily prayer, study, and listening, not to human words, but to the Word of God within which human words are to be judged.

Thirdly, this assumes, however, a new kind of open-endedness to council, something that Anglicanism has perhaps (unwittingly) permitted through its constant punting of decisions to a later meeting, but that, in truth, has never truly been allowed for through the strict scheduling of agenda according to dates and times. Councils, quite frankly, should have no scheduled ending-times—much as ecumenical dialogues do not. This could only happen were they to be held in places where such freedom could be granted, both in terms of domicile and resources (e.g. schools, monasteries, large churches—not hotels), but so they should. Three days, five days, ten days, it is hardly possible, any longer, that such limited deadlines can contain the work that God would do with those who gather in the Word. Who can say? The councils of the past were what they were in this regard, sometimes better, sometimes worse. But this we can learn from them: the time they are given, no matter its extension, is never to be feared. We have become cowards in the face of time.

Fourthly, to be sure, such open-endedness requires smaller groupings. Here, quite frankly, the fear of representation, particularly ecclesial representation in the form of bishops or other comparable figures, must also be overcome. Concern over representation has been, of course, a central conciliar topic. But unless it is a topic subordinated to a trust in the powerful and ordering character of the Word of God, that gathers and founds the work of representation, the concern is frankly irrelevant. When it is so subordinated, it is capable of a very flexible resolution. The character of consent over time that the conciliar life demands is not given, in the first place, by the immediate direct engagement of individuals, as if the larger numbers involved in any given gathering is correlated to the achievement of or at least approach to godly concord. Rather, it is the extension and even multiplication of council that does this across the years—the wheels within wheels. The only genuine reason that some have for rejecting the proposed Covenant's granting of liminal authority to the Primates' Meeting, or to some other representative group, as much for *ad hoc* reasons as for deeply theological and pastoral, is because there is little sense left—or not yet established—that Anglicanism does indeed function through a *network of councils* among which the Primates' Meeting, or some other gathering, truly is only one among many in its deliberations, and simply cannot *in fact* exist apart from the others. Many do not believe this because they are not willing to allow the wheels to spin in their correlated fashions across history.

Finally, there is no need to dwell on the fact that the last two elements of Gregory's vision of *concordantia*—its missionary outcome and sanctifying power and result—are at best shriveled fruit without the foundation of these earlier elements of council. So it appears in Anglicanism today—although it must be emphasized that it is not possible simply to overleap conciliar demands *for the sake of* mission and holiness, as some are arguing, whose impatience has proven the bread of bitterness. Council, if it is done in and for and through the Scriptures, is a part of mission and not its prolegomenon.

CONCLUSION

All these are just the elements of *concordantia* that seem to be eluding the Anglican Communion in the present. It is unlikely that they shall simply be apprehended in a moment. Do we "fit" any longer, if ever at all, into the conciliar *typos*? It is doubtful. But whatever the case, it is irrefutable that the promises of conciliar life are probably still some ways off from fulfillment, and perhaps further off than only a few years ago. Brokenness of council among us, including the proposed Covenant that may well go down in flames before ever having risen—a kind of reverse Phoenix—is not only a looming threat, but in fact seems to be a logical outcome of our present turmoil. This may not mean, necessarily, the end of the promise altogether. We should not want it to be; nor finally, even, should it be our fate. Anglicanism has a providential conciliar calling on behalf of a larger church whose own "abuse" of council's promise has been the more spectacularly demonstrated. But the intractable and renewed brokenness of the grander goal may imply that we are being driven by God to concentrate on only some of the smaller wheels, as it were, and on their interrelations at the most basic levels—within sub-diocesan units, for instance, and within dioceses, though no more than this. It is certainly to be wondered if the great scriptural embrace of time that Gregory the Great imagined can ever grip the Church's consciousness and self-motivation without it first touching the daily life of congregations and related groups of Christians, a life that has for some time been so diluted over such great extent. There have, at any rate, long been voices calling us to this level of conciliar regard as the necessary preamble to any grander hopes. Perhaps our larger brokenness is now simply the establishment of the truth of this call, part of the press of the conciliar life's inner dynamic as it has run its course from the beginning.

In which case, Anglicanism's vocation within the larger Church will seem much less lofty than its admirers of the last century may have imagined. We shall face the choice of eliding her pieces or allowing them to be so elided into the primal ecclesial soup of the Reformation's rich, but ill-formed and ongoing confusion; or she, and we, may choose to be among the first Christian churches to truly heed the call, that remains at best partially received on Protestant and Catholic sides both: "Physician, heal thyself" (Luke 4:23). Is this a limited and self-oriented calling? Hardly, for such a heeding is also a gift to the world, when it is pursued under the grace of God's Word gathering.

Index

Abbot, George, 44
Abelard, Peter, 3
Act for the Advancement of True Religion, 32
acts of uniformity, 212, 216, 235
adiaphorism, 44–45
Alcock, John, 16
allegory
    Edward Chandler and, 105, 107–9
    Anthony Collins and, 99–101, 105, 109
    Herbert Crofts and, 103
    Latitudinarianism and, 87–91
    Arthur Ashley Sykes and, 102
    William Whiston and, 91–93, 95
American General Convention, 256–57
Ames, William, 81
Anabaptists, 57
Andrewes, Launcelot, 49, 53, 56n, 57n, 61n, 72n, 73, 82, 83
Anglicanism, 26, 33, 47, 50–51, 84, 211
    conflict over biblical authority, 246–47, 260, 263–64
    conflict over sexuality, 246
    divisions, 190, 197–205, 230
    English Bible and, 25–26, 33–34, 40, 42, 47
    liturgy, 26–27, 30, 34–35. *See also* Anglican Covenant; Anglican-Roman Catholic International Commission; conciliarism
Anglican Covenant, 248, 261

Anglican-Roman Catholic International Commission (ARCIC), 62, 255–56, 260. *See also* conciliarism
Anglo-Catholic movement, 213, 237, 241
Anglo-Saxon historiography, 191–92, 197
Aquinas, Thomas. *See* Thomas Aquinas
Archbishops' Committee on Church and State, 185, 210, 213, 218n, 219, 220n, 221n, 227, 233, 245
Arundel, Thomas, archbishop of Canterbury, 25
Atkinson, Benjamin Andrewes, 110
Augustine of Canterbury, 190n, 191–94, 197, 234n
Augustine of Hippo, 53, 68, 73, 88n
authorial intention, 86–87, 99, 104–9, 112
Avis, Paul, 248–49, 251

Balfour, Arthur James, 214–15, 219
Bancroft, Richard, 38–39, 44
baptism, 4, 8, 17, 54, 66, 189, 252, 259. *See also* Trimmer, Sarah
Barbauld, Anna, 126
Barlow, William, bishop of Lincoln, 54
Barlow, William, dean of Chester, 37, 38n
Barnes, Major, 234n
Barrow, Isaac, 88, 90, 92
Baxter, Richard, 58, 66n, 81

Index

Bayly, Lewis, 52, 57
Beach, Michael Hicks, 215
Beauchamp, Edward, 233
Bell, George, dean of Canterbury, 229
Bellarmine, Robert, 53
Benson, Edward White, archbishop of Canterbury, 188, 202
Beresford, John George, archbishop of Armagh, 161, 176–77, 179, 180n, 181
Beza, Theodore, 42, 56, 60, 68n, 70n, 72, 74, 84
Bishopric of Shrewsbury Measure, 240
Bishops Bible, 36, 39
Bois, John, 41
Bolton, Samuel, 57
Book of Common Prayer, 19n, 33–35, 41, 47, 81, 148, 167, 170, 220, 234
  collect, 25
  morning prayer, 34–35
Books of Homilies (1547, 1562), 33
Bouillon, duchesse de, 51
Bradshaw, William, 72n,
Brevint, Daniel
  assurance, 70–72
  Beza and, 56, 60, 84
  Calvinism and, 50–51, 66, 68, 70–71, 83–84
  commemorative sacrifice, 72–74
  education, 48
  eucharistic manuals, 52–53
  memorialism, 50, 59–68
  real presence, 58, 69
  signs and graces, 65–70
  self-sacrifice, 74–83
  Wesleys and, 49, 62–63, 65, 84
  See also typological exegesis
Brewer, John Sherren, 186–87
Bright, William, 186
Bristol, bishop of, 229n
Broad, Thomas, 233
Brodrick, Charles, 159
Broughton, Hugh, 40
Bucer, Martin, 84
Buckeridge, John, 49, 56–57, 83
Bullinger, Heinrich, 84

Bullock, Thomas, 101
Burnet, Gilbert, 148, 168, 170
Burrows, Montagu, 187
Butler, Joseph, 169

Calvin, John, 42, 50, 53, 57, 65n, 66, 68, 70–71, 73n, 83–84
Cambridge University, 15–16, 39, 89, 92, 141, 171–74, 177, 180, 182, 187, 206
Cambridge Platonists, 88
canon law, 2, 26, 35, 47. See also Maitland, F. W.
Capes, William Wolfe, 188n
Carlisle, bishop of, 229n
Carteret, Elizabeth, 57
Catholic emancipation, 160
Catholic Truth Society, 189, 205
Caverly, Lady, 99n
Cecil, Robert, 1st Earl of Salisbury, 44
Cecil, Robert, 1st Viscount Cecil of Chelwood, 235
Chalmers, Thomas, 170
Chandler, Edward, 86–87, 91n, 103–12. See also typological exegesis; authorial intention
Chandler, Samuel, 101
Charles I, King, 256
Chicago-Lambeth Quadrilateral, 258–59
Child, Gilbert, 199
Church Association, 198–99
church authority, laicization, 24, 27, 35, 42, 218, 224, 245
Church Defence Institute, 189, 199, 201
Church Historical Society, 189, 205
Church of England, 88, 193–94, 200, 202
  modification of, 212, 220–221, 226, 229, 231, 242
  self-government, 218, 222, 229, 231, 234, 236–37, 245
Church of Ireland, 141, 143, 150, 159–60, 182–83
Church of Scotland, 38, 45, 216, 222, 235
Church, Richard William, 186, 203

Index

Church Temporalities Act, 160, 181
Clarke, Edward, 226
Clarke, Samuel, 103, 148
Collier, Jeremy, 190
Collins, Anthony, 86, 91n, 96, 97–107, 109–12. *See also* typological exegesis
Collins, W. E., 193n
conciliarism
    Anglican Churches and, 248–51, 256–58, 265–66
    Council of Constance, 249, 251
    Council of Basle, 249, 251
    Council of Pisa, 251
    historical overview, 246–49, 251–53, 256–60, 262–66
    Hooker, Richard, 251–54
    Lambeth conferences, 258–63
    rediscovery of, 263–65
    See also concordantia
concordantia, 247–48, 251, 254, 256, 260, 265
Coneys, Thomas Devere, 175n
confession, 1–3, 5–12, 15–18, 23, 26, 31. *See also* Wyclif, John; Cranmer, Thomas
Constitutions of Oxford, 25
continuity theory in the High Church tradition, 184–85, 188, 190–194, 196–205, 208–11. *See also* English Reformation
convocations of Canterbury and York, 44, 217–18, 224n, 234, 237, 239–42, 256
Cooper, Thomas, 81n
Cornish, Francis Warre, 188n
Cosin, John, 50
Council of Christian Unity, 249
Coverdale, Miles, 36
Cranmer, Thomas, 39n, 45, 49, 53, 58, 81, 250–251
    Book of Common Prayer and, 33–34
    Erasmus and, 15–16
    indulgences and, 5, 18–23
    penance and, 1, 19–20, 23
    Reformed theology and, 18
Creighton, Louise, 188, 209

Creighton, Mandell, 186–88, 189, 202, 209
Crewe, Marquess of, 230
Crofts, Herbert, 87, 103–4, 109
Cromwell, Thomas, 28, 32
Cumberland, duke of, 156, 180n
Cutts, Edward Lewes, 199n
Cyprian, 53, 65

Davidson, Randall, 214–15, 222–23, 225–26, 228–29, 231–33, 236–38, 244
de Dominis, Marco Antonio, 45
Dibdin, Lewis, 216n, 219, 221n, 226, 228, 244
Dickens, A. G., 27–28
disestablishment, 200, 211, 215, 218, 220, 222, 227–29, 234–35, 242, 244n, 245
Disraeli, Benjamin, 214n
Dix, Dom Gregory, 51, 53, 81, 243n
Doctrine Report (1938), 62
Douai-Rheims Bible, 36
Downes, George, 151
Downes, William, bishop of Waterford and Lismore, 150
Drought, James, 147n
Duffy, Eamon, 28–29
DuPlessis-Mornay, Phillipe, 49

Ecclesiastical Committee of the Privy Council, 224, 236
Ecclesiastical Courts Commission, 207–8, 217n
ecumenism, 45, 52, 84, 248–49, 259–60, 264
education, 3, 35
    non-denominational, 160
    theological, 140–43, 171–72, 174
    See also Trimmer, Sarah; Trinity College, Dublin (Divinity)
Edward VI, King, 29, 33, 190, 201
Edwards, Hugh, 235n
Elizabeth I, Queen, 29, 33, 37, 39, 43, 44, 190, 193, 200, 250
Ellis, Humphrey, 87
Elphin, bishop of, 158

269

Index

Elrington, Charles R., 154, 155n, 160–161, 163n, 169, 171, 173, 179n, 180, 182
Elton, G.R., 27
Enabling Act (1919), 213, 219, 223–24, 231–33, 235–40, 244–45
English Reformation, 20, 26, 27–32, 34–35, 40, 53, 88, 228, 251, 255–56
  High Church continuity theory and, 185, 191, 193–98, 200–210
Enlightenment, 29, 46
Episcopal Church, the, 256–57, 261
Erasmus, Desiderius, 16–17, 96
eucharist, 8–10, 48–78, 80–84, 189, 194, 214n, 255, 259
  Calvinist consensus, 50–51, 53, 57, 65n, 66–68, 70, 84
evangelical movement, 26, 31, 185, 192
  and High Church historians, 196–205, 211, 230, 234, 241
Eyre, Douglas, 221n

Farrar, F. W., 201
Finlay, Viscount, 232
Fisher, Herbert, 228
Fisher, John, 16
Fletcher, C. R. L., 198, 204
Foley, Daniel, 176
Forsayeth, John, 142–43, 182
Fourth Lateran Council, 3, 6
Fox, Edward, 251
Foxe, John, 197, 251
Franklin, William, 87
Freeman, E. A., 186–88, 204, 206, 209
Frei, Hans, 86, 98–99, 112. *See also* authorial intention
Frere, W. H., 188n, 219
Fuller, Thomas, 37, 53

Gairdner, James, 188n, 193, 194n
Gardiner, Stephen, 53, 250
Gasquet, Aidan, 204–5, 206n
Gelasius of Cyzicus, 53, 80n
Geneva Bible, 36, 38–40, 42
Geneva, Robert of (Clement VII), 12, 28

George III, King, 114
Gerson, Jean, 248, 250
Gloucester, bishop of, 226
Gore, Charles, 219
Gratian, 2, 3
Graves, Richard, 144, 147n, 153, 154, 156, 159, 180
Gray, Robert, 148, 151
Great Bible, 28, 33–34, 36–37, 45
Green, John, 101
Gregory the Great. *See* concordantia
Griesbach, Johann Jakob, 175n
Grosseteste, Robert, 3
Grotius, Hugo, 148

Hague, Dyson, 198, 203
Haldane, Richard, 1st Viscount Haldane, 227–28, 230–232
Hall, George, 157
Hamilton, Hugh, 148
Hampton Court conference, 36–38
Harcourt, William, 201
Henry VII, King, 193
Henry VIII, King, 17, 20, 28, 39, 190, 193, 195, 205, 208, 210n, 250
Henson, Hensley, 223, 227n, 229–30, 244n
Herbert, George, 78
hermeneutics, 86, 92–93, 98–99, 106, 251
Heylin, Peter, 190
Hickes, George, 49
High Church movement, 184–211, 215, 218n, 227n, 232n, 235n. *See also* historiography
Hildesham, Arthur, 72n
historiography, 27–33, 123–24
  High Church tradition and, 184–211
  English Historical Review, 188, 206
Hole, Charles, 198, 203–4
Hook, Walter, 186–87
Hooker, Richard, 33, 169, 251–54, 263
Hugh of St. Victor, 3
Hunt, William, 188
Hutton, W. H., 188n, 196, 203

indulgences. *See* Cranmer, Thomas; Wyclif, John
Innocent III, 6, 10
Iremonger, F. A., 229
Irenaeus, 53, 80
Irwin, Henry, 145, 182

James I, King, 36–39, 42–47
Jebb, John, 145, 150, 158–59, 176, 182
Jeffery, Thomas, 101
Jewel, John, 33, 81n, 251
John Chrysostom, 17, 33, 53
John, King, 195
Jones, George, 155
Joynson-Hicks, William, 234
justification, doctrine of, 4, 17–18, 20, 67

Keble, John, 160, 240n
Keightley, Thomas, 155n
King James Version (KJV), 24, 26–27, 34–36, 38–42, 46–47
King, William, 142
Kipling, Rudyard, 204
Kirby, Joshua, 114
Knox, E. A., 230–231
Knox-Little, W.J., 201
Kyle, Samuel R., 151

Lambeth conferences, 188–89, 260–263
    Colenso controversy, 258
    conciliarism and, 247, 256–59
Lane, C. Arthur, 189, 191, 199, 209
Lang, Cosmo Gordon, Archbishop of York, 219, 231n, 232, 243n
latitudinarianism, 46, 87–93, 100, 110
Laud, William, 49, 256
Law, Bonar, 235
Le Despenser, Henry, 13
Lee, William, 173
Leslie, Charles, 167
L'Estrange, Hamon, 82–83
Liberation Society, 189–90, 200
Life and Liberty Movement, 222, 229
Lightfoot, Joseph, 201
Lima Report, 62
liturgical movement, 259

Lloyd, Bartholomew, 160–163, 175, 177–79
Lloyd George, David, 228, 233, 235n
Lobb, Theophilus, 101n
Locke, John, 46, 92n, 99–100, 148
Lombard, Peter, 2–3
London, Bishop of (Arthur Winnington-Ingram), 241
Lord Chancellor, 232, 236
Lortz, Joseph, 29–30
Lowman, Moses, 148
Lowth, Robert, 108n
Lowth, William, 148
Luther, Martin, 4, 29, 53
Luxon, Thomas, 87
Lyndwood, William, 207

MacCulloch, Diarmaid, 30–31
Macmillan publishers, 188, 203–4
Magee, William, 170, 173
Maitland, F. W., 203, 205, 210
    Roman canon law in England and, 196–98, 202, 206–8
Maitland, S. R., 196
Martyr, Justin, 96
Martyr, Peter, 84
Mary I, Queen, 29, 193
Mary, queen of Scots, 38n
Matthew Bible, 36
Matthias, Benjamin W., 150
McNeece, Thomas, 163–64, 166
Mede, Joseph, 76–77
Medley, D.J., 188
Milner, Joseph, 197
Montfort, Simon de, 209n
Mooney, Daniel, 151
Moorman, J. R. H., 210–211
More, Hannah, 122, 136
More, Henry, 89
More, Thomas, 250
Mosheim, Johann Lorenz von, 167–68, 170

National Assembly of the Church of England *See* Enabling Act (1919)

Index

National Assembly of the Church of England (Powers) Bill, 223–24, 213, 223–24, 231–40, 244–45. *See also* Prayer Book Measures
National Church Council, 221
Newcastle, bishop of, 229n
Newcome, William, archbishop of Armagh, 151, 161, 181
Newman, John Henry, 52, 169, 186
Newton, Isaac, 86, 90, 92, 93n, 96. *See also* typological exegesis
Newton, Thomas, 110–111, 148, 170
Nicholas of Cusa, 248
nonconformity, 44, 174, 193, 209, 230, 233–35
Nye, G. F. E., 189, 199–203

O'Brien, James T., 144n, 149, 163–64, 166, 168, 169n, 173
Ollard, S. L., 193, 194n, 203, 210
Oman, Charles, 198, 204
Osiander, Andreas, 17
O'Sullivan, Samuel, 151
Overton, J. H., 188n
Owen, Henry, 111
Owen, John, 67n, 81
Oxford Movement, 49, 52n, 160, 184–86, 191, 192n, 196–97, 204, 229, 240n
Oxford University, 28, 37, 39, 141, 169, 171–74, 177, 180, 182, 187–88, 199, 204, 206

Paget, Francis, 215, 216n, 226
Paley, William, 110, 129n, 167, 169, 170–72
Parmoor, Lord, 221n
Patrick, Simon, 74, 82, 88, 92, 148
Pearson, John, 167, 170
Peckham, John, 3
penance, 24–25. *See also* Cranmer, Thomas; Wyclif, John
Percy, Thomas, 148
Perkins, William, 67, 81, 82
Perry, G.G., 186, 203
Philo, 96
Phipps, Robert, 162n, 164n
Pole, Reginald, 29, 32

Ponet, John, 251
Potter, John, 167, 170
Prayer Book measures, 243–44; (1927), 234n, 240–242, 245; (1928), 240, 242, 245
predestination, 11, 17–18, 23, 50
primates' meeting, 256, 262, 265
Prior, Dr., 162n
privy council, 24, 36, 38
prophesyings, 25, 44
Public Worship Regulation Act, 213, 241n
purgatory, 3, 5, 13, 15, 18–23
Puritan, 36–38, 43–44, 50–54, 81, 84, 253–54
Pusey, E. B., 49

Rainolds, John, 37–38
Randles, John, 234
Raphoe, bishop of, 158, 181
Rattenbury, Ernest, 56, 77
Ray, John, 89
Reeves, William, 174
Reformed theology, 18, 23, 45, 49–50, 251
Relton, Frederic, 188
Representative Church Council, 185, 210, 218, 221, 223–24, 233
Ridley, Robert, 16
ritualistic controversy, 213–15, 217n, 241
Robinson, Gene, 249
Rollin, Charles, 122, 127
Roman Catholic Church, 28–29, 31, 33, 43, 55, 167, 185, 192–93, 196–98, 230, 246, 251, 259
  High Church historians and, 204–5, 209–11
Round, J. Horace, 198–206, 208, 210
Royal Commission on Ecclesiastical Courts, 225–26, 229, 240–245
Royal Commission on Ecclesiastical Discipline, 213, 215–21

royal supremacy, 22, 193, 195, 200, 211, 220, 231, 237
Russell, John, 150
Scotus, John Duns, 4

Index

Secker, Thomas, 148, 156
Second Vatican Council, 30, 33, 246, 260
Selborne, Lord, 219
Selden, John, 41
Sheraton, J. P., 198
Sherlock, Thomas, 103
Sibbes, Richard, 54n, 57
Simon, Richard, 96
simony, 10, 13
Singer, Joseph H., 144, 168, 176, 180
Smith, A. L., 188n
Smith, Erasmus, 141n
Society for Promoting Christian Knowledge (SPCK), 115
socinianism, 57, 90, 96, 167, 170
solifidianism, 20
South, Robert, 88, 90–92
Southey, Robert, 196
St. Alwyn, Lord, 226
Starkey, Thomas, 250
Statute of Provisors (1351), 208
Stephens, W. R. W., 188, 203
Stillingfleet, Edward, 88, 90–92
Stubbs, William, 185–89, 191–92, 196, 198–99, 201–11
Sunday School. *See* Trimmer, Sarah
Sutcliffe, Matthew, 251
Sykes, Arthur Ashley, 86, 101–3, 106n. *See also* typological exegesis
Sykes, Stephen, 26, 32–33, 35, 42
synodality, 255–56, 258
Synod of Dort, 45

Tait, Archibald, 225
Taylor, Jeremy, 49, 57–58, 62, 170
Taylor, John, 148
Taylor, William Cooke, 150
Temple, William, 219, 222, 229
Tenison, Thomas, 88, 92
Tertullian, 53, 96
textual criticism, 39, 96, 98
Thirty-Nine Articles, 44, 106n, 138, 148, 167, 168, 169, 170, 220, 251
Thomas Aquinas, 4, 56, 60n, 85, 88, 89, 109, 112

Tillotson, John, 88, 90, 92
Tomlinson, J.T., 198, 203
Tout, T. F., 203
treasury of merits, 5, 13–15, 23
Trimmer, James, 114
Trimmer, Sarah
  An Essay on Christian Education (overview), 113, 115–22, 136–37
  baptism and child development, 115–18, 120–121, 127–28, 134–35, 138–39
  Book of Common Prayer, 115–16, 121, 127, 135, 138
  catechism, 127–28, 138
  Christian education (general), 114, 123–27
  confirmation, 138
  early life, 114–15
  natural world, 122–24, 129
  Scripture and sacred history, 122–26, 129–34, 137
  Sunday schools, 114–15, 135
  universal history, 124–25
Trinity College, Dublin (Divinity)
  Archbishop King's lecturer, 163, 167–68
  catechetical education, 156, 168, 174
  celibacy requirements, 156–59, 180
  chapel life, 177–78
  church livings, 180–181
  Downes prize, 155
  educational inadequacy, 143–45
  educational reform, 153, 159–62, 174, 182
  examinations (general), 154–55, 169–70
  examination (ordinands), 158–59, 171–72
  faculty publications, 173
  graduates overseas, 182–83
  Hebrew prize, 151
  liberal arts education, 142, 144, 165–66
  new subject areas, 175–76
  professorship of pastoral theology, 176–77

Index

regius professorship, 153–54, 167–68
students and parish work, 177
student attendance, 164–65, 169, 173
See also Elrington, Charles R.; Whately, Richard, Archbishop of Dublin
Troeltsch, Ernst, 29–31
Tunstall, Cuthbert, 250
Turenne, Charlotte de, 51
Tyndale, William, 28, 36, 41
typological exegesis, 54–55, 74–76, 78, 86–87, 90–91, 94–95, 99, 100, 102, 103, 105, 107–8, 112, 248

Union of Benefices and Disposal of Churches (Metropolitan), 240
Ussher, James, 142, 146, 151, 173

Vulgate, 16, 36

Wace, Henry, 198, 203
Wakeman, H. O., 188, 189n, 192n, 199–201, 203–4, 209–10
Wall, Charles W., 151
Warburton, William, 97
Warner, Courtney, 235n
Waterland, Daniel, 48–49, 84, 91, 106n
Watts, Isaac, 122
Webster, Richard, 215, 226
Wesley, Charles, 49
Wesley, John, 49, 55n, 56, 62, 65, 84
Westminster Confession, 54
Weston, Frank, 83n
Whately, Richard, archbishop of Dublin, 159, 174, 177n, 178–81
Wheatly, Charles, 63, 148, 167, 170
Whiston, William, 86–87, 91–106, 109, 112. *See also* typological exegesis
Whitaker, William, 251
Whitby, Daniel, 91, 148
White, James, 30
Whitgift, John, 44
Whole Duty of Man, The, 52
Wightman, Edward, 43
Williams, Roger, 46
Williams, Rowan, 262
Windsor Report, 261
Woolston, Thomas, 89–92, 97, 101, 107n. *See also* typological exegesis
World Council of Churches, 259
Wyclif, John, 28
confession, 1–3, 5–12
indulgences, 4–6, 10, 12–15, 20–21, 23
Innocent III's decree, 10-, 12
penance, 1, 6–7, 9, 19–20, 23
Petrine commission, 5, 14
power of the keys, 5, 8, 11–13
viators, 11
Wycliffe College, Toronto, 198

Zwingli, Ulrich, 50